D1594232

LINCOLN'S FOREIGN LEGION

THE 39TH NEW YORK INFANTRY, THE GARIBALDI GUARD

by

MICHAEL BACARELLA

 White Mane Publishing Company, Inc.

This White Mane Publishing Company, Inc. publication was printed by
    Beidel Printing House, Inc.
    63 West Burd Street
    Shippensburg, PA 17257

In respect for the scholarship contained herein, the acid-free paper used in this book
meets the guidelines for permanence and durability of the Committee on Production
Guidelines for Book Longevity of the Council on Library Resources.

For a complete list of available publications please write:
    White Mane Publishing Company, Inc.
    P.O. Box 152
    Shippensburg, PA 17257

E
523.5
39th
B33
1996

Library of Congress Cataloging-in-Publication Data

Bacarella, Michael, 1948–
    Lincoln's foreign legion : the 39th New York Infantry, the
    Garibaldi Guard / by Michael Bacarella.
        p.   cm.
    Includes bibliographical references and index.
    ISBN 1-57249-016-0 (alk. paper)
    1. United States. Army. New York Infantry Regiment, 39th
(1861–1865) 2. New York (State)--History--Civil War, 1861–1865-
-Regimental histories. 3. United States--History--Civil War,
1861–1865--Regimental histories. 4. New York (State)--History-
-Civil War, 1861–1865--Registers. 5. United States--History--Civil
War, 1861–1865--Registers. 6. Soldiers--New York (State)-
-Registers. 7. New York (State)--Genealogy. I. Title.
E523.5 39th.B33 1996
973.7'447--dc20   96-33042
                                                            CIP

To my wife, Lois

Contents

Preface

This is the story of the 39th New York Volunteer Infantry Regiment, the Garibaldi Guards. Like the nation it was formed to defend, its story is at once simple and complex. Like America did at its inception, the regiment took its name from an Italian of great international renown in his day. Geographers and explorers intent upon defining a new world named it for an Italian navigator, Amerigo Vespucci; Northern and Southern recruiters intent upon raising men to fight a looming civil war attracted recruits using the name of a world-famous Italian patriot, Giuseppe Garibaldi. Accordingly, the regiment's story began long before it was actually formed, and its heritage gave it a special character, at once similar to its sister regiments and yet unique among them.

It was not uncommon for recruiters to exploit the names of famous men to recruit soldiers during the Civil War, sometimes on the flimsiest grounds. However, there was nothing flimsy about Giuseppe Garibaldi. During the middle decades of the nineteenth century, every schoolboy knew about Garibaldi's daring deeds and military exploits. His passion, charisma, and dedication to the cause of the common man were internationally renown, and his reputation and actions drew men from throughout Europe and the United States to his side during his battles for Italian unification. The phrase in their biographical sketches, "served with Garibaldi," lent stature to many officers who obtained commissions in the Union and Confederate armies. That phrase alone told recruiters searching for any sign of prior military experience that that man was a veteran of battle. President Abraham Lincoln's administration entertained the idea of commissioning Garibaldi as a major general to exploit his military presence.

Garibaldi's name subsequently helped to recruit an entire regiment of volunteers for the Union army. The regiment drew a representative complement of the untutored and the educated that populated the units of its day, but it did not draw anyone who would afterwards write its history. Others were left to describe the regiment, and they often did so in backhanded ways that reflected their own prejudices, characterizing the Garibaldians as near-barbaric "Huns" or as the Union's version of the French Foreign Legion, with a reputation to match. This book is an effort to set the regiment's record right. It is a compilation of the 39th's regimental books, muster rolls, letters, manuscripts, newspaper articles, and eyewitness accounts set in a relatively chronological order, against the backdrop of Garibaldi's legacy and the circumstances of the war, so that a reader can achieve a broader, deeper understanding of the regiment.

It is worth realizing that in 1861 the idea of an army, north or south, was a long way from what we think of as an army today. On the eve of the Civil War, the regular Army that would devolve to the Union numbered less than

17,000 officers and men, scattered to kingdom come (mostly along the western frontier). To mobilize instantly in 1861, the Federal government, frugal as ever, called for state militias for Federal service. Under the home defense laws of the time, state governors who were willing to send militias sent them—for three months only! Local folks paid to organize what was sent. The sizes of the units depended upon the abilities and the aspirations of the organizers and the recruiters, and what they could get or wheedle from their local populations. Units elected their own officers, who, like the soldiers they were supposed to lead, generally ended up learning any art of war on the job (West Point was our *only* school for army officers). The Federal government took what it got, which came in every size and sort of military organization. While the learning curve started to rise with the death of the minute man at the First Battle of Bull Run, it rose slowly; the nation slowly lengthened enlistments as war progressed, but the unit replacement system persisted and battle-tested veteran regiments were generally allowed to decline to the point of ineffectiveness, when they were often dissolved. Very few field commanders who gained lasting fame leading brigades, divisions, corps, and armies during the war had ever led anything larger than a company before the war began. Based on what they were given to do at the moment, officers were sometimes accorded ("brevetted" to) temporary ranks where they got extra prestige (but not pay); for example, George Armstrong Custer, a lieutenant colonel years later at Little Bighorn, was "General" while he commanded a cavalry division against Robert E. Lee. And unlike today, the highest rank in the U.S. Army was major general until Congress revived the rank of lieutenant general in the army, last held by George Washington, for Ulysses S. Grant when he came to Washington, D.C. in 1864 to become general in chief of all Union armies.

The master roll at the end of this book contains the names of all the men and officers of the regiment, according to their place of birth or ethnic company (encompassing fifteen American states and fifty European states), their ages at the time of enlistment, occupations, aliases or other spellings of their names, and a code of their service indicating if they were killed in action, wounded, died of disease, or met a kinder fate. The master roll is an ample genealogical research tool. Just scanning the appendices for the men's names and countries of origin provides a sense of the tremendous ethnic wealth of this regiment and cannot help but lead to a greater appreciation for the men who came from so many other places to fight to preserve our union. I only hope that I have dealt with these veterans adequately and justly, and have finally given the 39th New York Volunteer Infantry Regiment its due place in American history.

A great deal of gratitude is due to those who made this research possible. Special thanks are extended to the staff of the Newberry Library, especially David Thackery and Amy Henderson, for their assistance; to Doctor Paul Rubino and the membership of the Joliet Chapter of UNICO; and to Jack Brounas and Burt Halleman. Thanks are also in order for the American Jewish Historical Society; the National Archives; Dan Lorello of the New York State Archives; the New York Historical Society; the New York Public Library; the Park Ridge Library, Park Ridge, Illinois; Laura Linard, curator of the Special Collections of the Chicago Public Library; Valarie James of the West Addison Branch of the Chicago Public Library; the Wisconsin State Archives, Madison, Wisconsin; and the Wilmington, Delaware Historical Society. Their help was invaluable, but the greatest thanks goes to my wife and children for their patience and understanding.

Chapter One

GARIBALDI, THE PATRIOTIC EXEMPLAR

The tombs are opened,
The dead arise,
All of our martyrs have resurrected,
With swords in their fists,
And laurel on their brow,
And the fire of the name of Italy
In their hearts.

—The Garibaldi March

THE origin of the 39th New York Volunteer Infantry Regiment lay in the dreams of liberty that convulsed Europe and reverberated across Italy in the years preceding that fateful day of April 12, 1861, when P. G. T. Beauregard fired upon his old West Point artillery instructor, Major Robert Anderson, and Fort Sumter, South Carolina. The hopes for liberty and self-government that bloomed in the American Revolution and then blossomed in the French Revolution inspired Europeans to begin dreaming of forming a United States of Europe. In Paris in 1809, Carlo Botta, an Italian political activist and historian, published *Storia della guerra del'indipendenza degli Stati Uniti d'America* in four volumes. His work was the most accurate account of the American Revolution available in Europe at the time, and it was widely read. Free thinking and liberal European patriots saw an example on which to base their struggle for self-government. As democracy began to assert itself throughout Europe, nowhere was the desire for an independent republic more enthusiastically embraced than in Italy.

1

Since the fall of the Roman Empire in A.D. 476, "Italy" had been merely the name of a geographical area, a peninsula fragmented into small kingdoms, independent city states, and territories controlled by foreign monarchs. Thirteen and a half centuries later, fragmentation persisted. In the south, the foot and ankle of the Italian boot, the erstwhile Kingdom of Naples, and the island of Sicily comprised the Kingdom of the Two Sicilies, an extension of the crumbling Spanish Bourbon empire. A number of Papal States spread across central Italy. City states spread across the upper reaches and top of the Italian peninsula, all of them dominated by the powerful, repressive Austrian Empire. At the very top, front edge (northwest) of the Italian boot, a region called the Savoy, and just below it a region called the Piedmont, were allied with the island of Sardinia, directly to its south, just beyond the island of Corsica, as the Kingdom of Sardinia. Large parts of the peninsula were united briefly at the beginning of the nineteenth century by Napoleon when he invaded Italy and brought enlightened reorganization and government to the Italians, but his rule was brief and the area fragmented again upon his departure. However, in creating the Kingdom of Italy, Napoleon fanned the flames of republican dreams: he gave Italians a whiff of national independence, and for the first time a political state was called "Italy."

The fledgling independence movement began in northern Italy. Unable to fight the huge, well-equipped Austrian army and police, Italians led by Filippo Bounarroti formed the secret Carbonari Society in 1821, using the Masonic Grand Orient of Italy Lodge as a front. The Carbonaris were intent on overthrowing monarchies, establishing republics, and obtaining political freedom. They were upper class men who early on counted the already famous liberal English romantic poet George Gordon, Lord Byron as one of their own.[1] They planned and initiated revolts in Modena, Parma, and the Papal States that began in February 1831. Unfortunately, they failed to gain any footholds, as Austrian military might put down the revolts one by one, and the Carbonari fled over the Alps to England, France, Spain, and North and South America. In doing so, they joined the growing number of Poles and Hungarians who were fleeing Austrian and also Russian oppression, thus spreading their revolutionary ideas and widening their networks of sympathetic contacts across international borders.

One of leaders who fled was Giuseppe Mazzini (1805–1872). While exiled in Marseille, France, he founded Giovane Italia (Young Italy), which espoused the three inseparable principles of Independence, Unity, and Liberty. Mazzini envisioned that Il Risorgimento (the re-birth, or revival) would unify Italy, which would ignite one massive revolution throughout the rest of Europe, which would lead to a Federation of the World, which would be the final stone in the construction of One United World.[2] He explained to the young Italian patriots who joined Giovane Italia that their fight was with monarchs and rulers who caused wars and who abused their subjects for their own despotic ends. He exhorted the patriots to become citizens of the world, and to unite with patriots of foreign countries fighting for their own liberation: "The man who defends his country, or attacks other people's countries, is in the first situation a virtuous soldier, and in the second situation an unjust one; but the man who by becoming a cosmopolitan, adopts this second land as his country, and goes and offers his sword and his blood to all peoples who are struggling against tyranny, is more than a soldier; he is a hero."[3] Giovane Italia urged Il Risorgimento as a force to lead to Italian unification, and the organization took members of every class into its ranks, including the fanatical Carbonari. Much to the dismay of the Carbonari, who preferred secrecy, the youth of Giovane Italia flamboyantly sought to attract attention to themselves in order to enlist support for their movement among their fellow countrymen. Like young roosters, they crowed and promenaded as they demonstrated and lectured openly in streets and plazas; as signs of identification and open protest, they wore their hair long, grew fantastically shaped beards and moustaches, and smoked strong cigars. Like the minutemen, their American models, every member was equipped with arms, ready for action. As a precaution, however (probably on the advice of the more experienced Carbonari, who knew about eluding authorities), all the members went by false names within the organization.

In February 1834, Giuseppe Garibaldi sought out Mazzini in Marseille, to join Giovane Italia. Garibaldi had been born on July 4, 1807, in the seaport town of Nizza, which was then ruled by the House of Savoy in the Kingdom of Sardinia. His father, a captain in the Sardinian Merchant Marine, had made the lad a cabin boy at the age of twelve, and the young man had received a practical education in survival on the seas, as well as a deep respect for the diverse cultural and racial make-up of the peoples he encountered at the docks where his father's ship had dropped anchor. Mazzini's latest plans for a new insurrection began with an invasion across the Swiss border of the Piedmont by seven hundred Polish soldiers, while Genoa was attacked by the Giovane Italia. Garibaldi enlisted in the Sardinian Royal Navy in order to convince other sailors to mutiny in support of Giovane Italia. Genoese secret police uncovered the plot and notified Swiss authorities to take action. The Poles were stopped as they were about to cross Lake Geneva, and Mazzini and all of his co-conspirators fled to Switzerland, condemned to death in absentia. Garibaldi escaped to France and then went to South America, where thousands of Italians found a haven during the turbulent 1830s.

Garibaldi arrived in Rio de Janeiro, Brazil, in January 1836 and took up life in a colony of Italian political exiles. He joined a Masonic lodge and went into the shipping business with fellow revolutionaries. By the following November, he had offered to fight in the Rio Grande du Sul revolt against the government of Brazil and organized an expedition for that purpose. His first action was an attack on a merchant ship. When he discovered that the ship was a black slave transport, he emancipated the slaves immediately, setting a personal policy to free all slaves that he would follow from then on. Antonio Procopio, one of the emancipated men, volunteered to join his group. Within a year, when fifteen hundred Brazilian troops near San Antonio del Salto, Uruguay, surrounded Garibaldi and two hundred of his revolutionary followers, a well-aimed shot from Procopio severely wounded the colonel commanding the Brazilians and gave Garibaldi and his followers an opportunity to escape the trap.[4] Giovan Cuneo, a friend, began supplying newspaper accounts of Garibaldi's revolutionary activities and made him an international celebrity, reporting year after year of Garibaldi's courage and daring in constant guerrilla warfare on land and sea. In October 1839, Garibaldi met nineteen-year-old Anita da Silva, a fishmonger's wife who deserted her husband for Garibaldi and life as a revolutionary's wife, and bore their son, Menotti, a year later. By April 1843, Garibaldi led a large polyglot organization known as the Garibaldini, composed of Italians, Spaniards, Frenchmen, Portuguese, Englishmen, North Americans, freed Blacks, and Brazilians. The group lacked any sort of uniform until they confiscated a quantity of red tunics used by butchers; ever afterwards, they would be known as the Red Shirts.

Meanwhile, by April 1834, Mazzini had formed Young Europe to support the struggles of patriotic Poles and Hungarians against the Austro-Hungarian Empire. Revolutionaries united as Young France, Young Austria, and Young Switzerland all joined the Young Europe movement, and the urge for independence and constitutional government fermented throughout Europe even as despotic authorities kept a heavy lid on everything. In Geneva, a young Genoese exile by the name of Alessandro (Alexander) Repetti who wrote for a newsletter called *Typographica Elvetica* wrote a twenty-eight volume series of works called the *General Document of the War of Holy Italy*, to document the case against Austrian authority and keep the spirit of the independence movement alive in Europe during the bleak years.

On July 17, 1847, the Austrians occupied Ferrara, a northeastern Italian city southwest of Venice, and Italian hatred of Austria's constant, brutal repression hit a peak. The Austrians had reacted to wild rumors warning of an impending revolt by bracing for an attack. In fact, the leaders of Young Europe had set 1848 as the year of revolution, and Repetti and other exiles in Switzerland had secretly returned to Ferrera on a mission to spread news of the revolt. Italy was destined to be a major arena of the new thrust for independence and national unity, and Garibaldi was destined to be its standard bearer.

The first months of 1848 saw revolt erupt throughout the heart of Europe. A revolution in Paris that began on February 22 ultimately toppled King Louis Phillippe and led to the establishment of a Second Republic (the First Republic had followed the French Revolution of 1789). In Vienna, a revolt that erupted on March 13 forced the resignation of Austria's repressive foreign minister and de facto prime minister, Prince Klemens W. N. L. von Metternich, and wrung promises of reform from the emperor. A bloody popular uprising in Berlin on March 15 forced temporary concessions from King Frederick William IV before the rebels were suppressed. The British crown quickly suppressed Young Ireland's cries in March for armed uprisings. Hungarian lawyer, journalist, and parliamentarian Lajos Kossuth ignited his country's independence movement on April 10 with support from peasants and noblemen alike. A simultaneous Czechoslovakian uprising was put down on June 17, after Prague was bombarded; Austrian martial law descended on Bohemia. Radical workers rocked Paris from June 23 to 26, before their bloody insurrection was suppressed. Monarchies saw revolt everywhere.

Italy had led the way in revolt. In Palermo, Sicily on January 12, 1848, Giuseppe La Massa led an insurrection against the Bourbon King Ferdinand of Naples. It spread to the rest of the island. Early in February, Sicilian patriots chased the Bourbons from Sicily and proclaimed a republic. The revolutionary fervor spread to Naples. To reduce the chance of facing a full blown revolution, King Ferdinand granted the Sicilian and Neapolitan revolutionaries the constitution they demanded. On March 18, the "Five Days" revolt began in Milan, a far northwestern Italian city close to the Piedmont and the Kingdom of Sardinia. It ended when Austrian Marshal Josef Radetzky, eighty-two years old, withdrew his army of occupation to the east and took up a defensive posture in the Italian "Quadrilateral" fortress cities of Mantua, Verona, Peschiera, and Legnago. On March 22, the Kingdom of Sardinia declared war on Austria, and King Charles Albert of Sardinia led a coalition of Italian forces nearly twice as strong as the Austrians into the field against Radetzky.

Inspired and encouraged by the Milan revolt and the Sardinian declaration of war, Italian patriots in Venice, led by Daniele Manin, declared themselves an independent republic on March 26. Manin was made president of the new Venetian Republic of St. Mark. The revolutionaries marched to the American consulate, hailing the consul, the American flag, and the memory of George Washington: "Long live the United States. Long live our sister Republic." Manin told the American Consul, "We have much to learn from you...and though we are your elders in civilization, we are not embarrassed to acknowledge it. We have no other ambition than to live in the enjoyment of peace and liberty, to recover the heritage of our ancestors, and to contribute, in some degree, to the infinite development of the human spirit." The Venetian independence movement found popularity in the United States when the *The New York Herald* reported "that we hail with delight and satisfaction the glorious struggle which the Italian people are making to free themselves from the despotism of a foreign power....Everywhere Americans were declared to be brothers and friends....Thanks were rendered, gratitude was manifested, and every American was received with enthusiasm."[5] *The New York Evening Post* reported: "This is a most solemn moment for the Italians. May God bless their hearts and arms, and may they attain their long cherished desire—the independence and unity of their country."[6] Congressman John D. Cummins of Ohio introduced, and the House passed, a resolution expressing sympathy for the Italian cause.

Garibaldi heard about the resumption of the revolution, and on June 28 he arrived in Genoa with seventy-three of his South American Red Shirts, including Andrea Aguyar, one of the South American slaves Garibaldi had freed. The unification of Italy was more important to Garibaldi than a united Europe, and he separated himself from Mazzini's continuing republicanism and ultimate plans for a world federation. Garibaldi allied himself to the House of Savoy, declaring that he was "not republican, but rather, Italian." The press had made Garibaldi the hero of the hour, so it was a fairly simple task to enlist fifteen hundred Garibaldini recruits for the cause of Italian independence.

Radetzky used his superior military skills to resume the offensive against Charles Albert, and on July 25 just south of Verona at Custozza, the Austrians overwhelmed the Italian forces and drove Charles Albert out of Lombardy. By August 5, Milan capitulated to the Austrians. Radetzky besieged Venice with ruthless severity. Garibaldi had formed a volunteer army fighting in the Alps. On August 26 at Morazzone, near the Swiss border south of Lake Varese, he and his army were completely surrounded by five thousand Austrian troops. That night he led a counterattack, broke through the Austrian lines, and led his army to Switzerland. There was a pause; after a brief armistice the war resumed. The Garibaldini regrouped at Genoa, marched southwest to Tuscany and then north over the mountains to Bologna to continue fighting.

Austrian military might began to assert itself in every direction. Encouraged by victories over several revolts, Austria invaded Hungary on September 17, using Croatian forces. Hungarian patriots repulsed the Croatian forces and advanced on the capital of the empire itself, Vienna, in turn. On October 6, the Viennese revolted in sympathy with the Hungarians. By the end of the month, however, Austrian forces suppressed the revolt and began pushing the Hungarians back across the border and into Budapest. Budapest fell on January 5, 1849, while the Hungarian forces were driven into the mountains north of the city. Supplies and horses became desperate needs of the officers and men pouring through Budapest during the mass retreat. David Strasser, a twenty-year-old native of Tams, Hungary, was an active horse trader between Vienna and Budapest at that moment. Taking advantage of the instant, he convinced the quartermaster of the Hungarian army that he had connections to provide the army with all the horses they would need if he could receive a commission in the quartermaster's department. He was hired as a clerk, then employed in the Field Port Service. Sometime during his quartermaster service he changed his name from the Teutonic "Strasser" to the Hungarian "U'tassy" and put a "D'" before it, making it D'Utassy.[7] One day, David Strasser would emerge as Frederick George D'Utassy.

Meanwhile, as the hostilities crept closer to the Papal States, Pope Pius IX fled Rome for the safety of Gaeta, in Bourbon territory, on November 24, 1848. On January 20, 1849, Garibaldi marched across the Apennines mountains to Rieti, where he was elected a deputy to the Italian Assembly. He arrived in Rome on February 5 at the new Parliament. A Roman Republic was declared on February 9. Mazzini arrived in Rome to assume power on March 5. Fighting continued in northern Italy between the Austrians and Sardinians, and Radetzky and Charles Albert clashed in Novara, a city west of Milan, on March 23. The Italian forces got only part of their one hundred thousand men on the field and were completely defeated. Too many defeats made Charles Albert decide to abdicate in favor of his twenty-nine-year-old son, Victor Emmanuel II. In Italy troops under General Wimpffen retreated, reassembled with twenty thousand men, and won a succession of victories in taking Ferrara, Bologna, and Ancona, and then marched to reinforce the Austrians at the gates of Rome and crush the new republic.

The exiled pope's call for help from the Catholic nations of Europe met with an enthusiastic response. On April 25, the French sent an expeditionary force of seven thousand eight hundred men commanded by General Nicolas Oudinot, the Duke of Reggio and son of Napoleon's marshal, to invade the Roman frontier. Oudinot landed at Civitavecchia on April 24 and marched on Rome, where his forces joined with the Austrians to retake the city. The common French soldiers, fiercely republican in philosophy, had been told they were going to Italy to fight the Austrians.

"No foreigners in Rome!" was the battle cry. The defense of the new Roman Republic was under way. Mazzini appointed General Giuseppe Avezzana to be Minister of War and Commander in Chief of the Army of the Roman Republic.[8] The total force of volunteers and regular troops available to Avezzana amounted to twenty thousand men. Pro-republic foreign volunteers included about five hundred Poles, English, French, Swiss, and Americans. On April 27, Garibaldi traveled from Rieti to Rome with his legion of Red Shirts, ready for a fight. Two days later Avezzana gave Garibaldi the command of a brigade and ordered him to take possession of the Villa Corsini and the ridge on the heights to the west of the Janiculum gate. The siege of Rome began on April 30. Oudinot reached the western wall of the city and advanced on the Cavalleggieri gate. Defending its post, Garibaldi's artillery pounded the French; then he ordered wave after wave of troops in a bayonet charge, routed the French, and pursued them. The cost was heavy, but it was the first victory against the invaders. Garibaldi, wounded in the abdomen, urged Avezzana to pursue the French further, but Mazzini, concerned over the great losses, refused to sanction the order and instead called for an armistice. Oudinot used this time to reinforce his troops and then continued his attack.

A fresh army loyal to the pope arrived at Rome on May 1. Ferdinand II, King of the Two Sicilies, led fifteen thousand Neapolitan troops, men and artillery, to join the French and Austrian armies. One week later the Garibaldini found themselves under heavy artillery fire and surrounded by Neapolitan cavalry and infantry, reinforced with five thousand additional troops. True to form, the Garibaldini counterattacked with a bayonet charge, routing the panicked Neapolitans. On May 12, the Garibaldini re-entered Rome and learned that a Spanish army was marching on Rome from the south, even as another twenty thousand Austrians approached from the north. Oudinot was reinforced with thirty-four thousand troops of infantry, cavalry and artillery. These advances knelled the death of Mazzini's Roman Republic; attacks on Rome continued with relentless fury. Elderly Avezzana's health failed, and unable to continue, he put Roman-born General Rosselli in command of the Republican army. On May 19, Garibaldi and a small contingent of lancers met Neapolitan hussars head on. Garibaldi's lancers retreated, and as Garibaldi tried to rally his men, he was thrown to the ground. The enemy cavalry advanced, and a Neapolitan major was about to cut Garibaldi down when Andrea Aguyar pierced the officer with a lance, knocking him off his mount. A bayonet charge counter from the Garibaldini gave Garibaldi and Aguyar time to get to safety and return to the defenses.

On June 2 at about 3:00 A.M., the French attacked the Roman defenders. The surprised Bersaglieri, Lancers, and Garibaldini fought desperately to repel them, but by 6:00 A.M. the French occupied the high ground along the right bank of the Tiber River, on Roman territory. They dug in and prepared to take the city. A relentless cannonade of the city began on June 29. Garibaldi witnessed his soldiers and comrades slaughtered, including Aguyar. The Roman Republic was beaten. Garibaldi advised the Assembly to capitulate the next day. He addressed his troops: "Fortune, which today has betrayed us, will smile on us tomorrow. I am leaving Rome. Whoever wishes to continue the war against the foreigner, let him come with me. I offer neither pay nor quarters nor provisions; I offer hunger, thirst, forced marches, battles and death." The defeated Republican army, including Garibaldi's Red Shirts, retreated toward Venice, hoping to join Manin and the Italian forces besieged by Radetzky, where they meant to continue the fight. However, the combined French, Spanish, Neapolitan, Austrian, and papal armies pursued the losers with a vengeance. The retreat was one of the bravest and most tragic episodes of Il Risorgimento. Reduced in numbers through constant pursuit and fighting, the Red Shirts alone were scattered and hunted down until less than one thousand five hundred men remained. When they arrived at the independent monarchy of San Marino, Garibaldi disbanded his legion, many of whom escaped to England or the United States. Two hundred or so die-hard followers kept on towards Venice, unknowingly headed for brutal forced marches, beatings, starvation, and imprisonment at the hands of the Austrians, who bombarded and starved Venice and Manin into capitulation on August 24.

Garibaldi wandered in the marshy country of Comacchio, south of Venice. His wife Anita, pregnant, exhausted by the long retreat, lacking medical attention, died on August 4 in a peasant's house. He and his only other companion, Culico, buried her that night in an unmarked grave. In the morning they made their way to the forest near Ravenna and then southwest across the mountains toward the outskirts of Florence, onward until they reached the Tuscany coast. From there Garibaldi took a fishing boat to Chiavari, a port near Genoa. He escaped Austrian pursuit into Piedmont territory. There Italian authorities wired Genoa as to what to do with him; the answer was, "Send him to America, if he will agree....If he doesn't, arrest him." Garibaldi was allowed to travel to Nizza to visit his mother and his children, and from there he traveled to Gibraltar, then on to London. He set sail on June 12, 1850, on the *Waterloo*, bound for the city of New York from Liverpool. He undoubtedly knew by then that Venice had fallen, that Sardinia had capitulated on August 9, and that Russia had intervened to help Austria crush the Hungarian revolution on August 11. Kossuth escaped into exile in Turkey. During Garibaldi's voyage severe rheumatic attacks seized him, and crippled him to the point of helplessness.[9] Young Europe's dream of a Federation of European States had become a nightmare.

General Avezzana preceded Garibaldi to New York. At his arrival he was welcomed by Mayor Woodhull at a great banquet at the Astor Hotel, after a ceremonial parade through the streets of the city. The New York authorities planned a similar reception for the Garibaldi on July 29, 1850, when his ship arrived at Staten Island. However, Garibaldi was in intense pain, crippled with rheumatism, and had to be "lifted on shore like a piece of luggage."[10] He wanted neither parades nor a reception at the Astor. He took a ferry to Manhattan without being noticed, and moved into the home on Staten Island of inventor Antonio Meucci. During his recuperation he applied for American citizenship, joined a Masonic lodge and a volunteer fire brigade, had his photograph taken by Matthew Brady, and joined Avezzana's rifle club, the "Guarda Italiana." However, Garibaldi soon grew discontented with this life. He took to his old sailing trade as captain of a merchant ship and sailed from New York to Central America, Panama, around Cape Horn to Peru, up to San Francisco, across the Pacific to China and Australia, and back to Boston Harbor by way of Cape Horn. He was warmly received by fellow Italians in every port.

In Europe the Austrian army continued to extinguish the remnants of revolution. The best Giovane Italia had to offer was wanted and condemned by Austrian authorities. The disaster of the Roman Republic and the ensuing financial difficulties signaled the end of Repetti's *Typographica Elvetica* in March 1853; it ceased publication. Repetti escaped to the United States, where "[f]or ten years he led a refugee's life in New York, gaining only a blameless name and a qualified command of English."[11] Other revolutionaries also poured into the United States from the failed Roman Republic. Alessandro Gavazzi, a rebellious ex-priest vehemently opposed to the papacy, lectured to arouse American sentiment for financial support of renewed action toward Italian unification. He and a Felice Foresti wrote in the newspaper *Il Proscritto*, "Our chief object of attack will be the papal power, which for so many ages [has] oppressed mankind and ruined Italy." Gavazzi's lectures were not very popular with New York's large Irish Catholic population. When the former governor of Bologna, Archbishop Gaetano Bedini, came to America as a envoy of Pope Pius IX, looking for support for the papacy, he instructed Archbishop John Hughes to condemn Gavazzi from the pulpit and to encourage the rest of his congregation to do the same. Pro-papist Irishmen violently disrupted pro-unification and anti-papal meetings, with the archbishop's blessings.[12] With these acts the Irish became the pope's paladins in America, and the Italians became the most ardent anti-papists. This confrontation began a rivalry between Irish and Italians—and simultaneously kept the general public aware of the Italian preoccupation with national unification.

In January 1854, Garibaldi sailed from Boston in command of the American sailing ship *Commonwealth*, bound for London, where he would be reunited with Mazzini and his revolutionary associates.[13] On February 22, 1854, the anniversary of Washington's birthday, the U.S. Consul in London, William C. Sanders, gave a dinner party. He invited the leading European revolutionaries in London, including Kossuth and Garibaldi, to meet James Buchanan, the Minister to the Court of St. James (who would go on to precede Abraham Lincoln as president). The guests at the dinner were Garibaldi, Mazzini, Kossuth, fiery revolutionist Felice Orsini, Joshua Wolmsley, French political activist Alexandre A. Ledru-Rollin, Hungarian author Franz Pulsky, and anti-czarists Russian author Alexander Herzen and Polish patriot Count Stanislaw Wurcell. It was a historic occasion, for it would be the last gathering of all the exiled leaders of revolutionary Europe in one place at one time. The conversations led to revolutionary plots for the future of the world, among them the formation of a European Association, the Ostend Manifesto, which set forth America's claim to annex Cuba by forcible seizure or by purchase, and Orsini's plans for tyrannicide against the nobility of Europe.[14] The consul gave aid to these revolutionary figures; he went so far as to smuggle their correspondence and literature into the United States through diplomatic mail, and he offered U.S. passports to the exiles. Garibaldi himself returned to Nizza in May 1854 and purchased the island of Caprera, off the northern tip of Sardinia. His new home quickly became a hub of activity for visiting adventurers, exiled politicians, soldiers, former Garibaldini, revolutionaries of all nations, and the Kingdom of Sardinia's prime minister, Count Camillo Benso di Cavour.

The fall of 1853 brought a new struggle to Europe. Russia's Czar Nicholas I saw an opportunity to dominate Turkey and secure four-season access into the Mediterranean Sea through the Turkish Straits. A Russian army began occupying Turkey's Romanian principalities in order to gain control of the straits. France and England opposed any shift in the Near East balance of power and allied themselves with Turkey to repulse the Russians. On September 13, 1854, French, British, and Turkish forces invaded the Crimea. Early battles did not go well for the allies, whose forces happened to include many exiles from the failed Italian and Hungarian revolutions. King Victor Emmanuel II, living with Austria's oppressive shadow over the entire Italian peninsula, saw a chance to gain British and French good will by joining them in the Crimean War. This had the potential to keep old Austrian allies out of any future efforts to free and unite Italy, or even to turn past Sardinian foes into future allies! On January 26, 1855, a Sardinian army force of ten thousand Italian soldiers entered the fight.[15] Despite the allies' initial doubts about their fighting prowess, the Italians proved themselves in places like the heights above the Chernaya River, on August 16 during the Battle of Traktir Ridge. A Bostonian publication reported; "Victor Emmanuel entered into the alliance with France and England against Russian despotism, and the troops he has sent to the East have distinguished themselves by heroic bravery, and by a perfect drill and discipline, which speaks volumes in favor of the military capacity of the king...."[16] Two Italian staff officers who contributed to the Italian performance were Count Luigi Palma di Cesnola and Major Enrico Fardella. Peace was achieved at the Congress of Paris on February 25, 1856.

War weary troops returned to Italy, only to find more revolutionary ferment and Mazzini's political intrigues. In June 1857, Carlo Pisacane, a Neapolitan, led two dozen young men on the small British steamer *Cagliari* to the convict islands of San Ponza and Stefano, west of Naples. They captured the prisons and released two hundred convicts, twelve political prisoners, and one hundred old soldiers of the Italian unification war. This force got to the mainland at Sapri, on the coast of Campania (just above the instep of the Italian boot), and began to march inland to oppose the Bourbon troops sent to stop it. It ran into an outraged local population that thought of it as nothing more than a band of pirates and pitilessly massacred it. Pisacane died fighting; the others were wounded or captured.[17] Later that summer, Mazzini proposed to equip further revolutionary expeditions of his newly formed European Association by capturing the royal arsenal in Genoa. A small party of the conspirators proceeded to the arsenal and confronted the guards. A scuffle took place and a soldier was killed, the clumsily planned, ill-fated plot failed, the anarchists were rounded up and arrested, Mazzini was condemned to death, and once again he fled to refuge in England. Then in France, on January 14, 1858, Orsini tried to blow up Napoleon III, who had once fought for Italian unity with the Carbonari and repeatedly stressed the fact that he meant to "do something for Italy" to reward her for the role she played in the Crimea. The emperor and Empress Eugenie survived the assassination attempt, but Orsini lost his head. Victor Emmanuel realized instantly that his kingdom was in mortal danger, if Napoleon wanted to retaliate with French might. Under these strained circumstances, Victor Emmanuel sent an emissary to the emperor and told him in no uncertain terms that "he as the king of Sardinia, would not endure any dishonor to his people, and that he wanted to be nothing but his friend."[18] Napoleon decided to help his ally.

Only ten days after the assassination attempt on the emperor, Victor Emmanuel succeeded in gaining support from France for his plans to unify Italy. His prime minister, Count Cavour, orchestrated a secret formal treaty with Napoleon, whereby France would help the Kingdom of Sardinia drive Austria from Italy if it could be done without exposing Napoleon to a charge of aggression. Victor Emmanuel would unite all the states on the Italian peninsula, and France would get the region of Savoy (in the far northwest of Italy) and Nizza (now Nice) as a *quid pro quo*. By March 1, 1859, nearly twenty thousand volunteers from all over Italy had arrived in Piedmont, and by the end of June the number was over forty thousand; they were all incorporated into the Sardinian army. On March 2, Garibaldi met with Victor Emmanuel in Turin and started enlisting volunteers. On March 17, Garibaldi was appointed a Piedmontese major general and commander of the Cacciatori delle Alpi (Hunters of the Alps), who were actually his own Red Shirts. Former soldier patriots who did not enlist in the Sardinian army or Cacciatori delle Alpi volunteered for the French Foreign Legion in Corsica, where the Legion's First Regiment was recruiting men for its Italian expeditionary force. In May, the regiment moved to Genoa, recruited six hundred volunteers, and then joined French general Marie E. P. M. de MacMahon's corps, headed for battle in northern Italy.[19]

Austrian spies had informed their military authorities of the growing army in the north and the dissent among the populace. On April 23, Austria had given the Piedmont an ultimatum: demobilize immediately—disarm and disband the volunteers within three days, or be attacked. This gave France an excuse to intervene, and Victor Emmanuel and Cavour refused the ultimatum. France honored its military treaty in defense of the Piedmont and began to mobilize its troops the next day. On April 26, the Austrians advanced from the east on Piedmont with five army corps, numbering one hundred thousand men and four hundred cannon, but they moved forward so half-heartedly that they lost their chance to defeat the small Piedmont army of some sixty thousand soldiers before the French forces arrived on the battlefield. The Austrian forces finally reached the Ticino River, the eastern border of Piedmont, on April 29 and went to cross it. The Piedmontese obstructed the Austrians by flooding the Lomellina plain as well as the lowlands around Novarra.

Meanwhile, Garibaldi's Cacciatori delle Alpi were transported via train to Biella, north toward the Alps and on the Austrians' right flank. From there they joined forces with the Mounted Guides and the Carbinieri Genovesi and moved northeast to the town of Varese, arriving on May 25. Scouts reported that eight thousand Austrian troops of infantry, cavalry and artillery were marching on them. The Garibaldini prepared the town for defense and at 2:00 A.M. on May 26, they began the battle with repeated bayonet charges, which forced the Austrians to fall back. After a violent struggle the Austrians abandoned their positions. The next morning Garibaldi marched east toward San Fermo and Como, where thirteen thousand Austrian troops were bivouacked. The Garibaldini surprised the Austrians and drove back their Tyrolian marksmen. By 7:00 P.M. the Austrians were driven out and retreated toward the next town, Borgo Vico. The Italian troops were readying themselves for another battle when they discovered the Austrians had abandoned the town.

On May 30, the Piedmontese defeated the Austrians at Palestro, a town southwest of Novara. Then the main allied forces under the personal command of Napoleon III invaded Lombardy and began moving east. They entered Novara on June 1, crossed the Ticino River on June 4, and pushed the Austrians back in a series of running fights, entering Milan on June 8. At the same time, the Garibaldini continued winning battles on the northern flank of the retreating Austrians. On the same day that Napoleon and Victor Emmanuel entered Milan,

Garibaldi won Lecco and then marched southeast on Bergamo, where the Austrians again retreated from their position. He kept angling southeast and on June 13 he defeated the Austrians at Brescia. Garibaldi was ordered to march on Tre Ponti, where his men met the most intense fire they had yet received, but they still triumphed. Now volunteers from across Europe flooded in to join the Garibaldini. Most notably, Kossuth sent his best officer, Colonel Istavan Turr, to join the Cacciatori delle Alpi. The main allied forces pursued the Austrians as far east as the town of Solferino, which is west of Verona. The Austrians withdrew into Verona and its three sister fortified cities, Mantua, Peschiera, and Legnago, the Quadrilateral.

Austrian emperor Franz Josef I dismissed his field commander and took personal command of his forces. Then he moved out to meet the Franco-Piedmontese forces. Two weeks later the French at Solferino and the Piedmontese at San Martino, just northwest of Solferino, faced one hundred sixty thousand Austrians. The three rulers, Franz Josef, Napoleon, and Victor Emmanuel, led their armies into one of the bloodiest battles ever experienced up to that date. Skirmishing began before dawn; it was already stiflingly hot. The Piedmontese advanced upon Austrian forces under General Ludwig A. von Benedek, who was ready for their attack. He outflanked and then counterattacked them, and the Piedmontese took a terrible beating at a high cost of life. The French attack at Solferino was pounded to a standstill by well-aimed Austrian artillery and rifle fire. Assaults went on all morning and grew weaker as the dispirited soldiers crossed over the corpses of their fallen comrades. Suddenly the French cavalry charged in a final effort to rout the Austrians. Present in their ranks was Philip Kearny, an American who lost an arm in the Mexican War, serving in the cavalry of the Guard in full United States dragoon uniform. As they deployed, he had asked permission to advance with the Arab horsemen of the Chasseurs. Kearny and the yelling cavalrymen swept up the slope and drove the Austrian infantry out of their defenses. That onslaught began the end of the battle, as the Austrians retreated across the Mincio River.[20]

The fierce contest at Solferino resulted in a Franco-Piedmontese victory on June 24; it also resulted in stunning casualties of twenty-two thousand Austrians and over seventeen thousand Franco-Piedmontese. A young Swiss businessman who was traveling in Italy when the battle occurred, Jean Henri Dunant, was so shocked by the carnage he witnessed that on the spot he persuaded the people of the village to help him care for the suffering wounded of both sides. In 1862 he would publish *A Memory of Solferino*, recounting what he saw, and in 1864 he would found the International Red Cross to work on behalf of the victims of war and disaster.[21] Napoleon demanded an armistice on July 11. At the Conference of Villafranca, he and Franz Josef agreed that Austria would retain the eastern state of Venetia, protected on the west by the fortress cities of the Quadrilateral, while most of Lombardy would go to the Piedmontese (except for the two western Quadrilateral cities of Peschira and Mantua, of course). France would take Savoy and Nizza, in line with the treaty it had with Victor Emmanuel.

Victor Emmanuel himself was enraged at not having been asked to participate in the negotiations. The port town of Nizza was an annexation which did not sit well with Garibaldi, since it was his birthplace. Its name was changed to the French "Nice." The Cacciatori delle Alpi were disbanded. On March 24, 1860, the Austrians ceded Lombardy to the French, who then handed the lands to Victor Emmanuel the next day. Kearny, the man whom the American army's general in chief, Winfield Scott, once called "the bravest man I ever saw...a perfect soldier" and who would be one of the Civil War's very best Union generals, was awarded the French Legion of Honor for his action at Solferino.[22]

The Treaty of Zurich that ratified the agreements of the Conference of Villafranca enraged many Italians. They wanted Venetia under Italian control. They wanted Austria out of Italy. Piedmont stayed at the center of efforts to shake off foreign predominance and unify Italy; the entire peninsula continued in revolution. On April 4, 1860, revolts in Naples against the Kingdom of the Two Sicilies and King Francis II were severely suppressed, arousing widespread revulsion in Italy and abroad against the Bourbons. That same day brought clashes with the police in Palermo, in northwestern Sicily. The uprisings spread to Messina and Catania on the eastern side of Sicily. Bourbon troops were sent in to put down the rebellion. The fuse had been lit and three Garibaldini generals, Francesco Crispi, Giacomo Medici, and Nino Bixio, prepared an expedition of Garibaldini to go to the aid of the rebels in Sicily. On May 5, Garibaldi and a thousand Red Shirts left Quatro, near Genoa, for Sicily. The expedition was transported on two captured Genoese ships, *Lombardo* and *Piedmonte*. The men were armed with one hundred revolvers and one thousand rifles, sent to them by the American gun manufacturer Colonel Samuel Colt.

The invasion of Sicily began on Friday, May 11, when the Garibaldini, supported by two English warships, landed at Marsala, on the western end of Sicily. As Garibaldi marched inland, he was joined by nearly eight hundred Sicilians who had managed to evade the royal troops. Together on May 15 they defeated the Neapolitan forces at Calatafimi, who retreated eastward toward Milazzo and Messina, and on May 27 they marched triumphantly into Palermo. Two days later Garibaldi and the Neapolitan representative, General Letizia, met on British Rear Admiral Mundy's HMS *Hannibal* in order to sign a truce. Captain James Shedden Palmer, the American commander of the USS *Iroquois*, was on board for the occasion. Garibaldi appealed to him for ammunition. Palmer explained that there was little to spare; he had received orders to sail back to the United States (later he would serve in the Union naval blockade of the South). Other American witnesses that day were Thomas Nast, a *New York Illustrated News* artist-correspondent covering the campaign, and Captain William de Rohan, a rear admiral in Garibaldi's navy (which consisted of three transports: the *Washington*, the *Oregon*, and the *Franklin*). As the Bourbons surrendered and evacuated Palermo, more Sicilian volunteers poured in to serve with Garibaldi, joined by men from a score of countries. Great Britain contributed finances and manpower. English veterans of the Cacciatore delle Alpi like Colonel John Peard sailed for Palermo with Medici's relief group of Garibaldini. Englishmen like Colonel John Dunne, who would shortly lead a group of six hundred teenaged Palermo boys called "picciotti" to battlefield victory, sailed directly from Harwich to Palermo. Colonel Hugh Forbes, a comrade of Garibaldi in 1849 who had been with John Brown in Kansas, rejoined Garibaldi in Sicily. Other English officers, cadets, and civilians volunteered for service. Garibaldi set Milazzo, on the northeast coast of Sicily, as the next objective. The whole Bourbon force of seven thousand men fell back to defend the city, pursued by two thousand five hundred Garibaldini and Sicilian volunteers. Milazzo surrendered on July 20, after three days of battle. Dunne received the Cross of Savoy for action with his picciotti. His second in command, Major Percy Wyndham, was wounded in the battle and later knighted by Victor Emmanuel. More Englishmen and some Irishmen arrived to join Garibaldi. By August 1, Garibaldi had liberated the whole of Sicily.

By August 19, Bixio's division of Garibaldini had landed at Melito, on the very southern tip of the toe of the Italian boot. With help from the British navy, Garibaldi and the main force of his soldiers crossed the Strait of Messina from Sicily to Italy on August 22. Then all of the Garibaldini and international volunteers began a rapid advance through Calabria, across the top of the foot and up the peninsula, as they marched on Naples. Edward Charles Bowra, a volunteer Englishman who was appointed to Bixio's staff,[23] gave a good description of life on the march:

> The reveille rouses you at 3 o'clock in the morning from your bed in a dry ditch or under a vineyard wall. We are supposed to start every morning at 4 by moonlight or starlight, but we seldom get off before 5 just at the break of day. We have all to be our own grooms and servants, for the soldiers appointed to each of us as ordinance or orderly, are not mounted and are always in the rear. All the work of dressing, feeding, watering, saddling and bridling our horses falls upon ourselves with only one exception, Garibaldi's, to whose horses, which are named after two of his favorite Generals, Trecchi and Piazzi [Trecchi was at one time the Sardinian Ambassador in London], insist in attending. The horses are stabled here and there in distant cow houses; forage has often to be fetched from a great way off; saddlery is limited and often out of order and I see longing eyes cast often on my equipment which is, thanks to Merry's special care, the best in camp. After a deal of trouble and delay, we mount and set off, every one scampering after the General as he best can, for Garibaldi waits for no man. We ride for 3 or 4 hours every morning, come to a halt for an hour or two about midday in some village or wood where we have to wait for a long time for the bit of dry bread and cheese or sausage which form our rations. Then at 3 or 4 we set out again and travel on, jaded and exhausted, till

dark, when our new night quarters are beset with hardships and difficulties which drive us to our wits' ends.[24]

By August 20, there were twenty thousand Garibaldini volunteers in Sicily, versus seventeen thousand Bourbons defending the region of Calabria. The Bourbons vacated their fortresses so that by August 30, Calabria was liberated. On September 1, Bowra and the English volunteers left Rogliano at four in the afternoon and reached Cosenza, halfway up the region, at eight o'clock that evening, where they were welcomed by thousands of volunteers who wanted to take up arms for the cause. Bowra was impressed with their dash and courage. The Garibaldini pressed on towards Naples. They learned that King Francis II had fled his capital city. On September 7, Garibaldi captured and entered Naples in triumph. He immediately prepared to march on Rome and Venetia. On September 8, the English Brigade en route to Salerno skirmished with the Bourbons. Bowra recalled an incident from the conflict: "One fellow, a colonel of Swiss riflemen, behaved with the utmost bravado. Mounted on a huge black horse, he was curveting about on the esplanade in front of the fort, encouraging his men, and evidently thinking very slightingly of our marksmen. Twenty rifles must have been fired at him, but no one hit him, and getting angry at his bravado, I took up a rifle myself and was just about to have a pot at him, when whiff—a shell from one of Colonel Dowling's field pieces, burst as it struck him, and when smoke and dust had disappeared horse and rider were nowhere to be seen, though their fragments might doubtless have been collected in the neighborhood."[25] The fort was captured, and the Bourbon troops were told that they were all free to return to their homes. Many of them joined the cause.

On the very day that Garibaldi entered Naples, Count Cavour gave the Vatican an ultimatum to surrender. The unrest throughout the Papal States gave him an excuse to send the Sardinian army across the border, and troops invaded the Papal States from the north on September 10. At the same time, the call had gone out far and wide for volunteers to come to the aid of the pope. By mid-autumn hundreds of volunteers from throughout the Catholic world hastened to the pope's call to enroll under his flag. Catholic Frenchmen, Belgians, Bavarians, Austrians, Swiss, Spaniards, Irishmen, and Englishmen flocked to Italy out of religious zeal and loyalty to the Church. The advancing Sardinians and papal forces met on September 18 at Castelfidardo, a town between Spoleto and Ancona, where the Sardinians scored a decisive victory. The opposing armies displayed the great self-sacrifice and ferocity of men fighting for ideals, as the young nobles who made up the French Legitimists (the regiment of the papal Zouaves) fought especially gallantly, but their leader (and the leader of the main body of papal forces), General Christophe Lamoriciere, fled from the battlefield, and the papal forces could do nothing but surrender. General Enrico Cialdini, one of two Sardinian corps commanders at the battle, reported after the bloody confrontation, "the [papal] troops attacked with great fury, the combat was short, but sanguinary. Many wounded [Sardinians] used their daggers against the enemy who would try and take them." The victorious Sardinians marched south to meet Garibaldi in Naples.[26]

While the Sardinian forces advanced to link up with Garibaldi, the French put troops in Rome and stationed a naval fleet along the Neapolitan coast, to preclude any Italian attack against the immediate papal domains. On September 19, the Garibaldini faced Fort Sant Angelo before Capua, a city north-north-west of Naples. Bowra recorded the conditions the Garibaldini faced: "The heat and dust are tremendous, for the summer has been unusually fierce...there has been no rain for more than three months. Occasionally by way of variety we come to lordly quarters, some Palazzo or mansion in the large towns, and then travel-stained and dusty we sit down to champagne suppers or cold collations supplied with every luxury. Horses carry all we possess—a change of linen and a map to the route...being an Englishman is alone sufficient to ensure kind treatment from Garibaldi."[27] Action began on September 25, when two squads of Hungarian cavalry trotted forward, keeping concealed from the Bourbons. The Bourbon infantry moved forward in a flanking maneuver, and eight hundred of their cavalry moved in support. Turr ordered Mancini to bring up the rear guard and the English cavalry column advanced at a trot, then swept down on their flank. Turr ordered the Hungarian cavalry to form a line and charge. Fighting was furious. The Bourbons were dispersed and driven back, but had the Garibaldini cavalry in range of their artillery batteries. They commenced to fire and mowed down the cavalrymen with round shot. They reformed with the remains of their decimated ranks and retreated. By September 30, the English cavalry was reunited with one of Bixio's brigades at the outposts of Sant Angelo and Santa Maria. On October 1 and 2, the Battle of the Volturno River was fought. One attack after another gained victory over the demoralized Bourbon Neapolitan forces. Lasting ten hours, the battle cost the Garibaldini and the volunteers two thousand killed and wounded. Garibaldi wired to Naples, "Victory all along the line!"

The joy in Naples following Garibaldi's victories was ecstatic. The experience of some six hundred fifty English volunteers who arrived too late for the battle at the Volturno River and only took part in an outpost affair showed how the Neapolitans felt. For a group that had not participated in the main action, the Englishmen were astounded by the reception they got from grateful Neapolitans: "The National Guard, carrying an English flag, went out to meet them, with music playing. Ten thousand people accompanied them...the military bands, posted here and there, struck up the National Anthem while the Legion passed them..."[28] The people's enthusiasm for Garibaldi and his accomplishments had to impress all of the Americans there, too, from Colonel C. C. Hicks, on Garibaldi's staff, to the Americans who came to Italy with the English volunteers to fight for Italian unity. Interestingly, that group included several Southerners like Joseph Bufour, Bradfute Warwick, Henry Allen, Robert Gory Atkins, and six foot, four inch tall General Chatham Roberdeau Wheat, late of the Mexican army.[29] Other volunteers included Alfred Van Benthuysen of Louisiana, Lieutenant Frank Maury (aka Manes) from Nashville, Tennessee, a Mr. Baughman from Richmond, Virginia, and Captain Henry W. Spencer, Jr., son of the American Consul at Paris. Northerners included William H. Baldwin, Alexander Moore from New York, and Captain Watson.

A turning point was at hand for Italy. On October 26, Garibaldi and his forces met King Victor Emmanuel II and his army at Teano, a city northnorthwest of Capua. Garibaldi saluted the king, saying, "Saluto il Primo Re d'Italia [I salute the first King of Italy]." Italy became a nation. Bowra observed, "All the previous experiences sink into nothingness compared with those of today, for I have been a witness of a great event in history. Garibaldi and King Victor Emmanuel II have met and parted. [T]hey stood together, King and King maker face to face, he who had formed an army and conquered a Kingdom and he who was to receive the fruits...."[30] King Francis II of the Kingdom of the Two Sicilies, leading twelve thousand men, made his last stand on November 3 against the united Italian forces at the seaside city of Gaeta, where the pope had fled in 1848. The French fleet stationed offshore withdrew, which made it possible for Sardinian warships to shell the city. When General Cialdini moved up with his land forces, the Bourbons surrendered. The war finally ended. On Wednesday, November 7, Victor Emmanuel entered Naples, and the next day Garibaldi presented him with the annexation of southern Italy. The British, Hungarian, Polish, French, German and American volunteers and their units were disbanded and sent home. Garibaldi, internationally famous patriot and soldier for national unity, set sail for his home on the island of Caprera that Friday. As a *Saturday Review* writer remarked, Garibaldi was "the subject of more discussion in a day than all the parties and all the orators in America in a year."[31]

Half a world away on the day before King Victor Emmanuel II entered Naples, a new American president was elected. The fourteen hundred-year-old Republic of San Marino immediately conferred citizenship on President Abraham Lincoln and offered him its allegiance. That August, in Nova Scotia, Canada, Frederick G. D'Utassy, once a Hungarian horse trader, resigned from Dalhouse University and relocated to New York. D'Utassy became a teacher of modern languages, employed by New York society's best people. To everyone he was the Count; his father was a landowner in Hungary, of the noble family of d'Utassy. D'Utassy boasted of having a polished European education from Budapest military schools, where he had acquired his remarkable skill as a swordsman. In 1845 he was a cadet in an Austrian military academy; in 1848 he graduated from Turin University; from there he entered the Austrian army as a second lieutenant. When the revolution began, he fled to the Hungarian side, where he joined as a private and rose to the rank of major. When the revolt collapsed, he was taken prisoner and confined in a dungeon, escaping to Turkey, England, and then New York. He impressed everyone with his image as a refugee nobleman and easily moved within the highest social circles, where he was treated with the respect ostensibly due him.

There were those who reported that he was a mere adventurer, a dance master, and someone recognized him as an ostrich rider from Henri Franconi's Hippodrome circus.[32] Count Frederick George D'Utassy defended his honor and his family name, confronting his detractors. Fearing the skilled swordsman, they retracted their obviously erroneous statements and let any mysteries surrounding him go uncontested.

Chapter Two

THE CALL TO ARMS AND ASSEMBLY

Give a desperate, despised man something to fight for, his own manhood, or, better still, something beyond himself—his country or a dream of universal freedom—and you will see the soul of the cowardly criminal set free to rise like a bird, transformed into a selfless, fearless warrior for truth, for freedom.

—*Giuseppe Garibaldi, on winning battles against heavy odds*

GARIBALDI'S hopes to unite all of Italy would have to simmer for ten more years until the French ended their occupation of Rome, so for the time being there would be peace on the Italian peninsula. But as Italy became united, America severed in two when on December 20, 1860, South Carolina seceded from the Union, and the other Southern states followed in quick secession. In anticipation of the gathering storm, the militia in Louisiana was organized for the defense of New Orleans. In answer to the call, Captain Joseph Santini raised a company of men for the Cazadores Espanoles Militia: "The call to organize a Garibaldi Legion went out Saturday [January 19, 1861], and within four days there were one hundred seventy [Italian] names on the roll.... [T]he officers had seen combat in Italy.... [T]he unit would be a valuable addition to Louisiana's volunteer force...."[1] Louisiana seceded from the Union on January 26. By March, this Southern Garibaldi Legion marched in full uniform for the first time. Its uniform consisted of a dark blue felt hat, turned up on the left side, with red, blue, and green feathers and a green cord and tassels, red jacket, black belt, knapsack, and cartridge box, grey zouave breeches and

20

leather leggings. Its arm was the Minié rifle and sword bayonet. On March 17, a United Kingdom of Italy was proclaimed by an all-Italian Parliament, with King Victor Emmanuel II as its first constitutional monarch. The same day in the city of New York the annual St. Patrick's Day celebration took place. Irish veterans of the Castelfidardo campaign paraded down Broadway, proudly wearing the "tin medals" awarded to them by the pope for their military service. The *L'Eco d'Italia* responded to the occasion with an editorial condemning the Fenian brotherhood as being anti-Garibaldi and for supporting the papacy against King Victor Emmanuel II in Italy.

On April 12, Brigadier General Pierre Gustave Toutant Beauregard, who had resigned from the Union army after serving only five days as superintendent of West Point, opened the bombardment of Fort Sumter. The fort's federal garrison capitulated on April 14. The American Civil War was on. President Abraham Lincoln called for seventy-five thousand volunteers from throughout the states. His call was heard throughout Europe as well. Idle soldiers from a dozen nations, veterans of the Crimean War and the Italian campaigns, offered a reservoir of battle-ready men for service in the Union and the Confederate armies. Hundreds of officers and soldiers from the Sardinian army and the Garibaldi Red Shirts sought to volunteer for duty. "The American consulates throughout Italy received so many applications, by letter and in person, of volunteers for enlistment in the army of the United States of America, that Romanie Dillon, the American charge d'affaires, was obliged to publish a public notice dated Turin, May 17, in the *Gazzetta Ufficiale*, declaring that 'he has no knowledge official or non-official of any instructions of his government authorizing any such enlistments, out of the United States.'"[2]

There was obviously no obstacle to participation by veterans who were already in America. Italians who joined the Union army included men like Enrico Fardella, who was commissioned a colonel in the 101st and then in the 85th New York Infantry.[3] Count Luigi Cesnola became the colonel of the 4th New York Cavalry. Captain Alberto Maggi was commissioned the colonel of the 33rd Massachusetts Infantry. Garibaldini captain Carlo Lombardi would be commissioned a second lieutenant of the 39th U.S. Colored Troops. Achille di Vecchio and his fellow former Garibaldini artillery officer, Luigi Navone, met Lincoln as formal representatives of Garibaldi. Later, di Vecchio was appointed a captain of the 10th Massachusetts Light Artillery. Red Shirts from the Sicilian campaign who joined the newly forming 39th New York Infantry included Captain Ercole Salviatti, Luigi Delucchi, Luigi Roux, the son of one of Garibaldi's personal lady friends,[4] and Amborgio Scopini, who would go on to serve in the Enfants Perdus.[5] Olivero Bixio, the brother of Garibaldini General Nino Bixio, became a lieutenant in the 24th New York Cavalry. Their brother, the Reverend Joseph Bixio, a pastor at Staunton, Virginia, would be held as a spy by both the Union and Confederate armies. Count Carlo De Rudio, one of the conspirators to assassinate Napoleon III, was advised by Mazzini to join the Union cause; he joined the 79th New York Infantry as a private and later became a second lieutenant in the 2nd U.S. Colored Infantry (after the war he would make the army a career, serve under Major Reno, and be engaged in the Little Bighorn Indian campaigns of 1876). Alfred Cipriani became a captain in the 53rd New York Infantry (his brother, Leonetto Cipriani, Sardinian army officer from 1848 to 1849 and the Italian consul at San Francisco in 1850, would offer Lincoln a plan to kidnap Beauregard during the war). Antonio Arrighi, a drummer boy with Garibaldi in 1848, enlisted in the 1st Iowa Infantry (and would later write his autobiography, *The Story of Antonio the Galley Slave*). Soldiers in Louisiana's Garibaldi Legion, its European Brigade's Italian regiment, the 6th Louisiana Cavalry, the 25th Louisiana Infantry, the 1st Native Guard, and the New Orleans Fire Regiment included

Enrico Fardella
Served in the 1848 Italian war of liberation, in the Crimea, and the 1859–60 Italian war of liberation. Immigrating to New York he was commissioned a colonel of the 101st New York Volunteer Infantry.

Library of Congress

men named Brescianni, Guidi, Maggi, Reina, Venuti, La Rosa, Morino, Ventura, and Vigo.

Both the Confederate and the Union armies attracted many Americans and other foreign veterans of Garibaldi's old armies and campaigns. Northerners who fought for the Italian cause and now answered the Union call included Felix Angus, a veteran of the 3rd Zouaves, who rose in the ranks of the 5th New York Infantry and then became a major of the 165th New York Infantry. William H. Baldwin became a lieutenant colonel of the 83rd Ohio Infantry.[6] A Ferdinand Fix became a captain in the 58th Ohio Infantry. Lieutenant Bausenwein, who had been a Garibaldini aide-de-camp, became a staff officer to Major General George B. McClellan, who would lead the Union's Army of the Potomac for some time. Thomas Nast, an illustrator and war correspondent who had covered Garibaldi's liberation of Sicily, would become a leading artist for the Union during the Civil War, with drawings so strong and persuasive that Lincoln called him "our best recruiting sergeant." Garibaldi's old British Legion yielded several volunteers. Major Percy Wyndham became the colonel of the 4th New York Cavalry. George St. Leger Grenfel,

Percy Wyndham
Former Garibaldini in the English Legion, 1860. He was a captain in Cesnola's 4th New York Cavalry.

National Archives

sixty years of age, became assistant aide-de-camp to Confederate Brigadier General John Hunt Morgan and subsequently devised a plot to liberate five thousand Confederate prisoners of war from Camp Douglas, Chicago, Illinois, in August 1864 during the Democratic convention. Chatham Roberdeau Wheat organized the 1st Louisiana (Tigers), a unit of Zouaves, and Robert Gory Atkins served as a captain of Company E in Wheat's battalion. Henry Allen became a colonel in the 4th Louisiana Infantry, in Waddle's battalion. Joseph Bufour became a major of a Mississippi regiment; Bradfute Warwick became a lieutenant colonel in the 4th Texas Infantry.

Count Constantin Blandowski and Valery Sulakowski, veterans of Garibaldi's old Polish Legion, answered the call to arms. Blandowski served as the captain of Company H, 3rd Missouri Infantry, and Sulakowski, who proposed buying arms from Garibaldi's store of one million muskets, became the colonel of the 14th Louisiana Infantry Regiment. Louis Zychlinski took a personal letter of introduction and recommendation for an officer's commission from Garibaldi to Colonel Felix Confort of the Enfants Perdus, a regiment made up of Crimean War veterans, and served as a second lieutenant. Ernest Hoffman, who served under Garibaldi as an engineer, came from Prussia to become a captain with Missouri and Arkansas artillery batteries. Karl Spraul, a former infantry officer from Baden who campaigned with Garibaldi, came from Germany to join the Union and became an aide-de-camp to Brigadier General Carl Schurz. Gustave Paul Cluseret, who commanded Garibaldi's French Legion, became a colonel and aide-de-camp to McClellan, and then achieved brigadier general rank himself in October 1862.[7] Many French and Italian veterans of the Crimean War enlisted in New York's foreign regiments, such as the Enfants Perdus and the 55th New York Volunteer Infantry Regiment, "Lafayette Guards." Fellow French and Italian Crimean War veterans in the South joined the European Brigade, the Casadores Espanoles, or the Avengo Zouaves (the 13th Louisiana Infantry Regiment, "Governor's Guards"), whose major, Gustave de Coppes, served under Napoleon III in the Italian campaigns.

Istavan Turr's Hungarian Legion from the Italian days also yielded a number of volunteers. Adolphus H. Adler, who rose from the ranks to serve on Garibaldi's staff, became a colonel of army engineers in Confederate Brigadier General Henry Alexander Wise's brigade (and would be sent to Libby Prison in Richmond, suspected of Northern sympathies). Lieutenant Peter P. Dobozy became the lieutenant colonel of the 4th U.S. Colored Troops. Captain Emeric Szabad became aide-de-camp to Union Brigadier General Daniel Edgar Sickles. Philip Figyelmessy, a member of the 1st Squadron of Hungarian Hussars who fought in Sicily, at the siege of Naples, and at the Volturno, whom Garibaldi called a hero of heroes, was appointed to the staff of Union Major General John C. Fremont. Hugo Hildebrandt (also A. T. Hilterbrand or Hildabrant), would enlist as a sergeant major in the soon-to-form 39th New York Volunteer Infantry Regiment and rise to the rank of major. Anthony Weekey enlisted in a

Gustave Paul Cluseret
Former commander of Garibaldi's French Legion in 1860. During the Civil War he commanded his brigade in Fremont's mountain department to which the Garibaldi Guard was assigned.
National Archives

separate German company that would be incorporated in the soon-to-form regiment; he would enter it as a lieutenant and also rise to the rank of major in it.[8]

Frederick George D'Utassy, the refuge nobleman and teacher of modern languages employed by the best people of New York society, made plans to raise a foreign-born regiment and command it himself. In order to attract a multitude of volunteers to his organization, to be the 39th New York Volunteer Infantry, he appropriated the magic name of Garibaldi, calling his regiment "The Garibaldi Guard." Volunteers responded to the moment and to the pull of Garibaldi's name and filled the ranks of D'Utassy's companies. Though it was very possible that no one wanted a command made up of anarchists, radicals, and political refugees, who could be better suited to control them than a man who spoke five languages? D'Utassy became a military hero to his language students. Their well-to-do fathers supported his efforts by acting as supply contractors who boarded and lodged his men.[9] Students were engaged as clerks and a few of them served as his officers, like Cornelius Grinnell, whose father, Moses Grinnell, was a member of the Union Defense Committee, an organization of prominent New York citizens that raised and donated funds to recruit and equip volunteer military units. Two recruiting offices were set up in the Irving Building at 594 & 596 Broadway, and headquarters was at 55 Franklin Street. Down the road at the corner of Broadway and 22nd Street in the St. Germaine Hotel, Luigi Cesnola set up his own military academy, where for a $100 fee he instructed New Yorkers in the arts of cavalry warfare. Nearly seven hundred men took his training course.

Upon Lincoln's call for volunteers, Louis Tassillier organized a French company. An organization of British veterans of the Crimean War and the Indian Mutiny joined the Garibaldi Guard.[10] Poles who had volunteered for a new Polish legion, before the attempt to form it was abandoned, were consolidated into the Guard. The *New York Herald* announced that Hungarian volunteers under Captain Franz Takats [Takacs] would join D'Utassy's regiment: "The Garibaldi Guard has received another accession to its numbers with the Hungarian regiment, which has been organizing separately for some time past. The Garibaldi Guard promises to be an organization of great numerical strength, and may be able to constitute a brigade by itself."[11] Louis W. Tinelli, age fifty-nine, attorney and former U.S. Consul at Oporto, Portugal, incorporated members from the Guarda Italiana rifle club into his own regiment, The First Foreign Rifles.[12] Politically well-connected, Tinelli handled the commissary depot and did much of the recruiting for his regiment.[13] Soon the First Foreign Rifles included "brave and experienced riflemen, formed on the plans of the Swiss sharpshooters, from Italy, France, Switzerland, Spain and Hungary."[14]

On April 27, the Italian-American newspaper, *L'Eco d'Italia*, informed its readers that "a Legione Italiana was to be formed to defend the Union against the slave States of the South. The Legion was to be under the command of Italian officers, selected from among the members of the Legion proper. The enlistment office was located at 298 Broadway, New York...."[15] The men behind that legion were Secchi de Casali, editor in chief of *L'Eco d'Italia*, and none other than the exiled Alessandro Repetti. A more acerbic, blunt reporter from the *New York Herald* reported that the Italian Legion had attracted "all the organ grinders of the city... a hardy and enduring race, familiarized with hardship and exposure."[16] That same day Charles B. Norton, an American, brought in his Spanish and Portuguese volunteers to join the Garibaldi Guard. D'Utassy rewarded him with an appointment as quartermaster in the field and on the staff. On April 29, the Italian Legion, under Repetti's leadership, joined the Garibaldi Guard. Tinelli had raised four companies of volunteers, not enough to complete his own regiment, so he too threw in with D'Utassy, considerably strengthening the growing regiment.[17] D'Utassy appointed Repetti as the regiment's lieutenant colonel and designated Tinelli as major of the commissary depot. A second major was appointed, to be known as the Major in the Field. He was George E. Waring, Jr., an American, "a simple and inoffensive civil engineer in Central Park, completely ignorant of things military,"[18] who was pleased with his appointment. He commented "[t]hat it was a good colonel that makes a good regiment." Tinelli, on the other

Charles B. Norton
A first lieutenant and quartermaster of the 39th New York Volunteer Infantry.

hand, already had second thoughts about his decision to join the Garibaldi Guard and associate with D'Utassy, and started action to be reassigned.

Volunteers from Holland, Russia, Alsace Lorraine, Greece, Italy, Austria, Belgium, Scandinavia, and Slovakia enlisted to swell the regiment's ranks. Five of the ten companies taking shape were made up by Prussians and Germans who flocked to enlist to be among the German American Garibaldini. Frederick Spier, an Armenian, Frank Cosey, a freed Negro, and Giovandra Duar, a gypsy, enlisted. Men who chose to be known in pure legionnaire style only by pseudonyms, like Gimi Gionson and Francesco Radetzky, enlisted. Trades of every description were represented; farmers were the most frequent volunteers, followed by laborers. The regiment enlisted 132 rough and ready seamen from three continents. From South America came sailors like Jose Samaniege of Argentina, Jose Arellano of Chile, Santiago di Fernandez and Juan Hernandez of Cuba, and Miguel Penate and Joseph Fratus of Nicaragua. There was a large group of "seegar-makers" and confectioners, one of whom, Montegriffa, would become a regimental sutler. There were tailors, shoemakers, boatmen, carpenters, masons, stone cutters and smiths of all sorts, as well as several firemen, one policeman, one undertaker and one casket maker. A few doctors and lawyers were represented. Celestino Hornia of Spain was a "Photographist," Henry Cross claimed he was an artist, while Giacomo Rizri made looking glasses. There were two Hungarian musicians, Emanuel Lederer, a composer, and Charles Zerdahely, a concert pianist trained under Franz Liszt. Twenty-five veterans from foreign armies claimed "soldier" as their occupation. Only two hundred five men in the regiment were reported to be married.[19] There were one hundred sixty-three men over forty; the oldest soldier was a German, Lewis Schmidt, at fifty-four. Seven boys were sixteen. The youngest soldier, John Rohn, fourteen years old, enlisted as a band musician along with his father, Casper. The shortest man at a height of five feet was a Russian Jew named Herman Brod; the tallest was a German named John Boiner at six feet three inches.

It would be a rich man's war, but a poor man's fight. The very rough lot of common laborers, sailors, and refugees who enlisted in the regiment in its first days, the lowest of the lower classes, crowded into New York slums, undoubtedly felt disrespected by the Americans surrounding them. Perhaps some of them felt that joining the Garibaldi Guard was a way to earn public respect. The recruits were described as "a picturesque and peculiar regiment...a temperamental, untamed, capriciously officered, courageous body of men, the first three-year regiment recruited in New York...a goodly representation of most of the armies of Europe...."[20] The regiment's length of activation was remarked: "Known as the Garibaldi Guard, the Italian Legion, the Netherlands Legion, the Polish Legion, the Hungarian Legion, and the First Foreign Rifles which constituted the 39th Regiment New York State Volunteers, having been raised by the Union Defense Committee of New York City, under special authority from the War Department, organized, for a three year enlistment."[21]

Alexander Repetti
Lieutenant colonel of the 39th Regiment New York Volunteer Infantry.

Joining the Garibaldi Guard for three years set its recruits at the leading edge of the times, since many volunteer units were still being recruited for the traditional ninety days.

In keeping with the common practice of the day, company officers were elected. Most of them lacked any real sense of military training or discipline. In those early days of recruitment there was a great deal of galloping and prancing, bugling and countermarching through the streets of New York. One of the officers' haunts was their favorite restaurant, located at Eighth Street and Broadway. There D'Utassy attracted attention to himself by making thrilling speeches in five languages. He actually provoked a mini-riot in late May when he denounced the cowardice and treachery of the enemies of the Union following the "[d]astardly assassination of our brave and noble young comrade, Colonel Elmer Ellsworth," and "pledged the best efforts and the best blood of our regiment to vindicate, in his name, the justice and honor of the cause whose success his martyrdom has sealed."[22] The excitement was furious; swords leaped part way from their scabbards, and were driven back with great emphasis. The audience of drunken Garibaldians nearly tore the establishment to the ground. A terrified, cowering waiter witnessed the sword fights and fisticuffs. The father of Sergeant Richard Marschall graciously paid for all the damaged dishes.[23]

By the first week in May the regiment was fully organized and provisioned, but not yet fully uniformed or armed. It served as a regiment *chasseures-a-pied*—"light infantry"—and counted seven hundred fifty men, exclusive of field and staff and company officers. On May 10, the *New York Herald* described the Garibaldians as "veterans from the field of Novarra, Solferino and Magenta, and o[f] every beleaguered fortress of 1848." The newspaper went on to explain to its readers:

> A regiment of riflemen is in progress of formation in this city, on the plan of the Swiss sharpshooters, to be composed of Italians, Swiss and Hungarians officered by those who have served in Europe. This regiment is called the Garibaldi Guard, and will doubtless do credit to the name. Subscriptions and aid in forwarding this regiment to its destination may be sent to Charles B. Norton, 596 Broadway, who has kindly consented to attend to the matter.
> The following subscriptions have already been received:
>> Flues & Co., 40 Barclay Street $40
>> A. Hunzerbuhler, 691 Broadway $20
>> F. G. D'Utassy, Broadway $100
>> Wm. Prinzen, 26 Bond Street $15
>> J. P. Hlig, 60 Exchange Place $10
>> A Subscriber $50
> Total $245. All subscriptions thankfully acknowledged. Committee on finance, Charles B. Norton, Fred G. D'Utassy.[24]

That same day in Missouri a veteran of Garibaldi's Polish Legion, Captain Constantin Blandowski, was mortally wounded by gunfire that erupted while Union forces escorted captured Southern sympathizers through hostile crowds in St. Louis, Missouri, from nearby Camp Jackson down to the city arsenal. Blandowski was the first former Garibaldini in the Union army to die in the war.

On May 14, an official inspection of the Garibaldi Guard took place. Major Tinelli chose a Bersaglieri style and dress of uniform for the regiment. Major Waring described the uniforms everyone wore:

Their distinctive dress was inspired by the uniforms of Garibaldi's Italian revolutionaries. The uniform of the rank and file was a striking, but substantial ground work for the brilliant effect of that glorious array of the etat Major. The officers' uniforms were dark blue cloth. Single breasted, bordered, and its seams were faced, with narrow gold braid. Its deep cuffs and its standing collar were scarlet cloth. Its breast is padded and across its front are five frogs of heavy double gold cord, finished at the sides with trefoil loops, and fastened at the middle with straight gold buttons more than an inch long. The shoulder-knots are of the same cord. A flat braid faces the collar, where the single star of the Major's grade sparkles at each side of the throat. The three chevrons grade called for five of these, and they reached to his elbow. The trousers had double broad red stripes down the outer seam. The hat was of stiff black felt, round in the crown and very wide in the brim, and loaded with a massive cluster of drooping dark green cock-feathers on the left, a la Bersaglieri, after the type that Lieutenant Colonel Repetti wore in Italy, and D'Utassy continued to wear the Hungarian Hussars uniform. All and all this gave these soldiers an appearance of readiness for business which the other regiments lacked. The warm scarlet color of the shirt, reflected upon the men's faces as they stood in line, made a picture which never failed to impress the reviewing officer.

The soldiers wore a single-breasted blue jacket and trousers with collar, cuffs, lapels, and piping in a red, distinctive color, and a red flannel shirt with a broad, falling collar. Their heads were covered by dark green, soft felt hats with round crowns and cock feather plumes worn on the left, with the initials G.G. on the front. Their shirts were worn outside of their trousers, belted around the waist. Their trousers were tucked into their boots; gaiters protected their ankles and calves. The letters G.G. were on the back of each man's knapsack. Their cartouche boxes were like those used in the French and Italian armies.[25] They had not received their weapons.

The 39th New York Volunteer Infantry was one of the few units in the Civil War to have vivandieres (women sutlers) attached to the regiment. They were women clad after the most correct Figlia-del-Reggimento manner. The

Louis (Luigi) Tinelli
Major of the 39th Regiment New York Volunteer Infantry.

Colonel D'Utassy and Lieutenant Colonel Repetti when they were still talking to each other. The Hungarian and Italian flags stand in the background.

U.S. Army Military Institute

women wore blue frock gowns with gold lace and facings, black laced gaiters, red jackets, and feminine Garibaldini hats decorated with black and red feathers. The regiment had no less than ten vivandieres, and two were authorized per company.[26] They prepared food and drink, dispensed cakes, tobacco, spirits, and other comforts for the soldiers, and often cared for the sick and wounded. The *Washington Intelligencer* informed its readers that the vivandieres had husbands in the ranks and would march with the men on the regiment's right flank. *The Star* conducted an inquiry into the marital status of the vivandieres and discovered that two of them were runaway girls from Jersey City; another paper, the *New York Herald*, demanded that the girls be sent back to their homes.[27] The well-known Red Shirt was the fashion of the day in Washington. Civilian women wore a loose-fitting, long-sleeved blouse that resembled those worn by the Garibaldini. The favorite shades of red were named for two famous battles, Solferino and Magenta. Among the enthusiastic friends of the Garibaldi Guard was Frau Franciska Klein. She and her friends sewed the flags of the regiment. She presented the finished work to Colonel D'Utassy, two beautiful, great silk flags, one the Stars and Stripes, the other the Hungarian standard with red, white, and green stripes, bearing a wreathed "Vinccere Aut Moire" in letters one half foot high.

The Garibaldi Guards were reputed to be a rifle regiment of sharpshooters, so the men expected to get new rifles that D'Utassy had promised at the time of their enlistment. The captains were very displeased when they had to issue their men an inferior smoothbore musket. D'Utassy vowed that they would receive the expected weapons in Washington. Meanwhile, for $24.00 each he sold pistols that had actually been donated for their use by the Union Defense Committee to the officers.[28] On May 22, Private Emil Diverbois of the French company was wounded while handling one of the obsolete muskets. When he tried to pull his ramrod from the rusted barrel of his rifle, it stuck fast; then the rifle fired suddenly. The rod shot out of the barrel, and the front end of it entered his nostril with so much force that it passed up his nose and penetrated his skull.[29] This unfortunate accident exacerbated a mutinous attitude mounting among the officers. On May 23, the entire regiment prayed under the guidance of their chaplain, Theodore William Krueger, and swore allegiance to the Union in fourteen languages. The officers and men solemnly promised, in the name of God, to sustain the Constitution of the United States and its laws, and to protect with all their power Old Glory, the Stars and Stripes of their adopted country, at the "cost of the very blood" of their lives. Then they held a full dress parade at LaFayette Square in the city of New York. On this occasion, Mrs. Anna H. Stevens, a writer, presented the American banner. Miss Sylvia Grinnell was given the honor to present the Hungarian standard. The Italian flag Garibaldi carried through the wars of 1848 and 1849 was also presented. Garibaldi had brought the flag to America and given it to his friend, General Avezzana, who, in the name of the general, presented it to the Garibaldi Guard.[30] That flag attracted the most attention because it bore the legend "DIO E POPOLO."

The men prepared to march off to Washington at one o'clock on May 28. Leading the regiment were its standard bearers, Corporals Philip Hughes and Rudolph Schwickhardi and Privates Albert Hoffman and Anthony P. Zyla, all of whom would play important roles in the regiment's history. The men formed at Lafayette and 4th Streets. The *New York Herald* reported that "they looked robust and exceedingly well and active; probably no regiment that left New York had so much attention given to its spectacular side. At the presentation of a flag to the Swiss Company,...they found that the ceremony was post-poned in consequence of the banner not having been finished...."[31] After be-ing reviewed, the regiment was formed in marching order and proceeded for Jersey City. It marched up Fourth Street to the Bowery, through the Bowery to Bond Street to Broadway, up Broadway to Fourteenth Street, through Four-teenth Street to Fifth Avenue, to Washington Parade Ground, up Waverly Place, to Broadway, and thence to the Cortland Street Ferry dock for Jersey City, where the men embarked in two boats especially provided for the pur-pose. The march through the city took about an hour and a half, and all along the route of procession the troops were met with intense enthusiasm. Manahan's Band accompanied the regiment and dispensed some excellent music. A corps of buglers attached to the regiment attracted a good deal of attention. The soldiers marched without arms; their rifles had been packed in cases and sent with their ordinary baggage.

All along Broadway the regiment was received in the most enthusiastic manner, and as it passed down towards the ferry dock, the voices of a hun-dred thousand people bid them Godspeed. As the troops reached the park the scene was enlivened by the French Company's singing of "The Marseillaise" with fine effect, immediately followed by another company singing "The Star Spangled Banner." At Barmun's Museum the band played several patriotic airs, and the regiment's flags were dipped in honor of the occasion.[32] Waring witnessed the spectacle: "The Garibaldi Guards' march down Broadway was a most moving spectacle; the mass of emotional humanity, waving and cheer-ing and weeping, from housetop to curbstone, formed a great solemn aisle down which the Garibaldi Guard marched (a quick pace trot of the Bersaglieri backed by a fanfare of at least two score trumpets), with floating flags, flow-ing plumes, glittering gold, and flashing steel, singing the Marseillaise as they went. It was a proud thing to be of the Garibaldi Guard."[33] Some of the waving, cheering, and weeping, a few words shared and a few thoughts passed and prayers offered, should have been for Emil Diverbois, who died that day in a New York hospital from his head wound. The families of the common soldiers who marched away raised enough money so that each man was issued three one dollar gold pieces to take with them for expenses. At this time, the regiment numbered eight hundred fifty officers, non-commissioned officers, and men. It was destined to be attached to Colonel Louis Blenker's Brigade, in Colonel Dixon S. Miles' Division, in the Union army of Brigadier General Irwin McDowell's Department of Northeast Virginia, until August 1861.[34]

IN DEFENSE OF WASHINGTON

On May 28, 1861, the Garibaldi Guards arrived in Washington and marched to their assigned camp site. They witnessed a spectacle of thousands of men in colorful uniforms of every description. They marched passed brass bands, Zouaves, gala chasseurs, rumbling artillery, men from New York, Pennsylvania, Michigan, Vermont, New Jersey, and Connecticut, a fine display of Union might and majesty assembled to put an end to the rebellion. A young soldier from Connecticut, Theodore Winthrop, commented, "It seemed as if all the able-bodied men in the country were moving with all their property on their backs, to agreeable, but dusty lodgings on the Potomac." The Washington *Star* reported, "Of soldiers the country is full. Give us organizers and commanders. We have men, let us have leaders. We have confusion, let us have order...." The regiment encamped on Abington Farm, Virginia (just south of modern-day Washington National Airport), immediately adjoining Sumner Hill. D'Utassy named the site Camp Grinnell, after Moses H. Grinnell, his friend and sponsor. The Garibaldi Guard laid away its dress uniforms and put on the Red Shirt, which was suited for camp life, work, and drill. The Garibaldians spoke very little English in camp. Olive oil and garlic flavored their stews, and they enjoyed their "Garibaldi Tea," a mixture of whiskey and hot water. But they were ridiculed by American soldiers in nearby camps, who looked on them with scorn, labeling them as "Zouave Fancy Pants!" Irishmen in the sutlers' tents bullied them. They set aside every Saturday as a washing and cleaning day. They made their own washtubs out of barrels obtained from the quartermaster and commissary department, and all of the camp kettles of each company were put at the disposal of the men for heating water. They had to make ready their arms and accessories for Sunday inspection. Officers were required to wear clean, white, and starched shirts.

For about a month the men remained in camp, and grew fast in military deportment. D'Utassy lived in a splendid house several miles away and had his meals cooked in Washington, then gently transported to him by ambulance, packed carefully so that they could be placed before him warm and palatable.[35] The Washington *Star* praised D'Utassy as the "theatrical commander of the Garibaldi Guards" and ascribed his idiosyncrasies to his "mercurial foreign temperament."[36] Waring observed "that in matters of discipline D'Utassy was useless and left it all to his officers to run those matters, chiefly Repetti."[37] While D'Utassy was busy with the commissary, Repetti devoted himself faithfully to the men's instruction in the skirmish drill. The men were instructed to use their instincts and every possible means to trick an enemy in Garibaldini guerilla fashion. They were trained to use cunning to throw an enemy off guard and to take advantage of his confusion, to maneuver and conceal themselves behind solid obstacles or in trenches, to crawl and hide under brush, and to run from place to place in serpentine irregularity. Repetti wanted no repeat of the Diverbois accident, so he trained the men in the care and use of firearms. In the process, he became a harsh disciplinarian, actually using the sheath of his sword as a disciplinary device to beat those who did not comply with his drill. Chaplain Zyla reported to D'Utassy that in an incident involving a Swiss company soldier who fired his weapon unintentionally, Repetti demanded, "Who dared to fire? [Upon] seeing the smoke cringing about the body of the Swiss, he took the rifle out of the frightened soldier's hands[,] dealing him there with several blows on the back. It appears that, as far as Capt. Schwarz orderly's report goes, four Companies rushed forward with the cry, 'Shoot the Tyrant!'"[38] Repetti gained such a reputation as a sadistic tyrant that privately there was a plot to assassinate him at an opportune time.[39]

Waring asserted that it was not only D'Utassy who was useless, but "the whole army was similarly neglected—superior officers who did not themselves know they were guilty of neglects. Ours was an army of great capabilities, marching from a fool's paradise to a fool's fate—the fate of learning wisdom by hard knocks."[40] But as time passed, the regiment's evening drill parade became one of the better shows of the Union army units encamped around Washington and the occasional object of President Lincoln's admiration. On May 30, the Guard marched to the president's house and was received by him, general in chief Lieutenant General Winfield Scott, and Secretary of State William Henry Seward. Afterwards they drew up in line before the residence of the Sardinian Minister.[41] On Friday, May 31, D'Utassy received his commission as a colonel. That same day the old muskets that had been crated up in New York were re-issued to the men. Captain Takats of the Hungarian company wrote to D'Utassy and informed him, "My company will accept the muskets offered them today for the use of service in the near days, but all men expect to get the rifles for which they enlisted, and got promised as a Rifle Regiment."[42]

The Saturday afternoon concerts by the Marine Band, conducted by Bandmaster Francis Scala,[43] were offered as one of many diversions among regimental concerts, operas, stage shows, dress parades, and drills.[44] Every day, the population turned out to see the parade on Pennsylvania Avenue. Unfortunately, the drills took a toll on some of the men. Luigi De Lucchi, one of the original Red Shirts of the Thousand in the invasion of Sicily, complained that Garibaldi's approach to military life was simpler: "The General demanded discipline on the battlefield, not in the barracks!"[45] This marching around and drill was different from what De Lucchi had been used to as a Garibaldini in Italy. Then there was all the hoopla, first in New York, then in Washington. De Lucchi hoped action would be soon in coming. While he drilled and marched at Camp Grinnell, the copper rivets of his leather leggings caused a deep abrasion on his right leg. He paid no attention to this slight injury until his leg became so inflamed that he was taken to the camp hospital, where Dr. Ciro Verdi treated him. The doctor put him in the hospital, and after nearly a month the surgeon declared De Lucchi's blood had become poisoned and "scarpela" had set in. His right leg had become inflamed and ulcerated, and its discolored, swollen veins appeared about to burst. Amputation of the leg was recommended if it became gangrenous. Fortunately, De Lucchi would keep his leg—and be discharged for disability on July 17 with an injury that would plague him for the rest of his life.[46]

Frederick George D'Utassy
The first colonel of the Garibaldi Guards.

Camp life proceeded apace. On June 2, Leopold Zander and Adolphus Majer were commissioned as regimental surgeons. Sergeant Major Hugo Hildebrandt was promoted to adjutant. Sergeant Boas and Corporal Dreher of C Company transferred to F Company. Then First Lieutenant Junger of F Company transferred to D Company. The officers continued to wait for their commissions despite D'Utassy's solemn oath that when they reached Washington they would have their official commissions as officers and receive the pay owed to them from the time of their enlistment. On June 6, Repetti and Waring both received their commissions. On Friday, June 7, Corporal Louis La Croix of K Company, the French company, gained the dubious distinction of being the first man to desert the regiment. Sergeant Carl Theodore Pausch of H Company was promoted to first sergeant.

On Saturday, June 8, J. W. Quiggle, the American consul in Antwerp, Belgium, wrote to his acquaintance, Giuseppe Garibaldi. Quiggle wanted to verify the validity of certain rumors he had heard about the general. Was it true that it was Garibaldi's "intention to go to the United States, to join the Northern army in the present conflict? If you do, your fame will be greater than that [of] Lafayette's!" In addition, Quiggle declared that he would "resign his commission as United States consul in order to follow the 'Washington' of Italy."[47]

On June 11, less than two weeks after arriving in Washington and joining the grand encampment of Union volunteers assembling along the Potomac River, the regiment lost its first officer. Tinelli's quiet efforts to obtain a reassignment had begun to bear fruit, and the Garibaldians were stunned by the

Painful emotions experienced in camp at the announcement of the resignation of Major Tinelli, who had been informed from high quarters that the application made by him some few months before, for a foreign mission, would be granted in a few days. Both Major Tinelli's letter of resignation and the answer addressed to him by Colonel D'Utassy were read before all the officers of the corps, collected in the Colonel's tent. The report, and the solemnity was a very moving and painful one...tears were seen flowing on many noble and time worn cheeks when the news was spread in the camp and every company deputized their sergeants and corporals to Mr. Tinelli's tent to express their feelings of regret at such an unexpected separation from their favorite friend...[who,] by his kind, gentlemanly and soldier like deportment, enlisted the general sympathies and affection of the whole regiment, and his absence could not fail to be deeply felt by us.[48]

By August, Tinelli would become the lieutenant colonel of his own regiment, the 90th New York Volunteers.[49] D'Utassy took over Tinelli's post and paid great personal attention to the supplies. The Garibaldi Guard was well fed and clad, but beyond this he did little. It would slowly become clear that he cared less for his mob of immigrants than he did for the fortune he could gain through its exploitation. In the months to come, he meant to maneuver and manipulate his regiment to wrench every dollar he could from the Federal war chest.[50] He began to add his own heavy markup to the price paid by the Union Defense Committee for the uniforms, equipment, and lodgings for his new recruits.

As of June 14, after over two weeks in camp, the commissions for the officers had failed to come through as promised. Captains Otto Bernstein and John Siegel were compelled to write letters of protest to D'Utassy. Bernstein wrote him: "I never had, I have not now, nor shall I ever have anything against you personally. I always have been a loyal officer towards you, and I assure you, most solemnly, that I am ready to shed for you my blood, even to its last drop, if you manifest satisfaction with my readiness and good faith to serve you. Should you, however, feel inclined to dispense with those courtesies to which I believe myself entitled, by my precedent as well as by the spirit of serviceability, evinced under your command, then, I would, although much afflicted, be obliged to ask from your rectitude, the granting of my dismission according to the rules and articles for the government of the United States Army, saving me, thereby, from further mortification." Siegel simply wrote, "Having suffered so many [sic] unfriendliness in [sic] the last time, I feel myself bound to resign my commission." Captain Tassillier took a more strident approach against D'Utassy by organizing the officers to sign a letter of protest detailing their discontent with the colonel. Tassillier charged that D'Utassy lacked concern for his officers and men, was not worthy to command a regiment, asked for his resignation, and requested that the command be given over to an American, Major Waring, who by his own later testimony knew nothing of the letter sent off to the *New York Herald* for publication. The same captains who signed the public letter of protest confided in Repetti the idea of traveling as a group to Washington and personally handing their petition to Major General [Colonel] Edward S. Sanford, the supervisor of military telegrams at the War Department, who had the authority to order arrest and imprisonment [for careless administration of censorship!]. Repetti advised the captains to wait for D'Utassy to return from headquarters and to report their discontent to him. Then Repetti informed D'Utassy of the plot in a letter: "The captains of the report have presented me with a petition to the General for the dismissal of the Colonel and giving command of the regiment to the major. They want to go en mass to Washington. I was able to prevent them from acting until your return in order to report to you their griefs. I will solicit your group of eight and will speak to you later."[51] Though Repetti's warning alerted D'Utassy of an impending mutiny, it also made the colonel suspicious of him. D'Utassy included the lieutenant colonel as part of the conspiracy.

On June 17, Repetti assigned musicians George Blum of E Company and Constant Cassen of G Company to muster up fifty musicians in three days. Repetti requested passes and authorization from the colonel to go to the local Washington, D.C. police authorities to arrange for the capture of some absentees. D'Utassy gave Repetti fifty dollars to pay to Colonel Blenker for his authorization and the passes.[52] Magnus Bader and Louis Willing, two trusted men from E Company, the German company under Siegel's command, accompanied Repetti. That evening Repetti went to the corps hospital and visited several very ill Garibaldians, among them First Lieutenant Antonio dal Molin and Corporal Pietro Mancini of A Company, the Italian company, Corporal Louis Schweikt of G Company, the Hungarian company, and Corporal Jean Desouter of K Company, the French company. All of the men suffered from dysentery and jaundice, and Repetti had his personal doctor attend to them. Mancini and Desouter and Mancini would eventually be discharged for disabilities, and Schweikt died on June 23, the first Garibaldian to succumb from disease.

Off the coast of Italy on the sunny island of Caprera, Garibaldi replied to Quiggle's letter on June 27, writing, "The news given in journals that I am going to United States is not exact. I have had, and still have, a great desire to go, but many causes prevent me. I [have said that], however, in writing to your Government, and [if] they believe my service of some use, I would go to America, if I did not find myself occupied in the defense of my country. Tell me also, whether this agitation is for the emancipation of the Negroes, or not! I should be very happy to be your companion in a war in which I would take part by duty as well as sympathy. I kiss with affection the hand of your lady, And I Am, with gratitude, G. Garibaldi."[53]

Camp life continued. On Friday, June 28, the third death in the regiment occurred when Joseph Buhler of Company H drowned in the Potomac River. Assistant Surgeon Foster Swift, who was unable to revive Buhler, saw his "muster in" revoked on the same day he was enlisted. He promptly re-enlisted in the 8th New York Militia. On Sunday, June 30, Sergeant Max Lieser was transferred from Company G to B and reduced to corporal; to replace him, Corporal Desire Jacheresse of Company K was promoted to sergeant and transferred to replace him. July 1 saw several promotions in Company E: Second Lieutenant John F. Bauer and First Sergeant Charles Zimmerman were promoted to first and second lieutenant, respectively, of Company H; Sergeants Henry Lindner and Anton Schada were promoted to second lieutenant and sergeant major, respectively, and Corporal Jacob Surer was promoted to sergeant in their company. Sergeant Gustav Fost of Company E and Corporal Wilhelm Ertinger of Company B were discharged for disability. Corporal Juan Argumosa of Company D deserted. On Tuesday, July 2, the 39th New York was officially assigned to Colonel Louis Blenker's brigade, the first brigade of Colonel Dixon S. Miles' division, in Brigadier General Irwin McDowell's army, as his forces prepared to take the field against the enemy. Waring was not impressed with Miles: "He seemed to be ashamed of his uniform, and he wore as little of it as he could. His general make-up was more that of a quartermaster's clerk than that of a general officer. He habitually wore two hats—first the high, steeple-crown, regulation felt hat, with large holes cut around just above the cord, and then, on top of this, a low-crowned felt hat of which the brim formed a sort of upper piazza roof, shading the windows cut below. It may have been a cool headgear, but it had not a commanding appearance."[54]

On Caprera, Garibaldi celebrated his fifty-fourth birthday. On that day he received Quiggle's response to his letter; that "the war was not being fought to emancipate slaves, but to put down rebellion and insurrection, and restore to the Government her ancient prowess at home and throughout the world."[55] That same day at the Independence Day parade in Washington, D.C., the Garibaldi Guard, dressed in their red shirts and Garibaldi kepis, marched past President Lincoln. An observer reported, "And as the Garibaldi Guard passed by, each man tossed a spray of flowers or evergreens toward the platform, while a bouquet was thrown from the head of each company. A pretty carpet was spread before the dignitaries, and Major General Sanford who sat with the President was garlanded with blossoms. Everyone was impressed by the graceful ceremony, but the owners of the ravaged gardens in the neighborhood of the Garibaldians' encampment."[56] The impressive parade spectacles had become common—and boring to the correspondent of the *London Times*, William Russell. He reported that the Union army was "a horde of battalion companies, unofficered, clad in all kinds of different uniform, diversely equipped, perfectly ignorant of the principles of military obedience and concerted action.... They think that an army is like a round of canister which can be fired off whenever the match is applied."[57]

Two days later, on Saturday, July 6, 1861, the company commanders' patience ran out when they learned that they would not receive their commissions, their rifles, or their pay. Repetti could no longer restrain them. Led by Tassillier, the captains petitioned D'Utassy with their demands:

> We the undersigned officers and company commanders of the Garibaldi Guard, hereby would respectfully remind the Colonel on his word of honor, given unto us in the city of New York, before our leaving the same for Washington, viz:
>
> 1. That we should have rifles as soon as we would reach Washington.
> 2. That we should have our commissions as officers at the same time.
> 3. That we should have our pay just as well.
>
> To these 3 paragraphs we have to say, that we, in consequence of your having given us your word of honor, that we should have rifles, we have given the same to our soldiers, and as officers of men of honor are bound to fulfill to the very letter.
>
> Therefore, we do hereby declare, that, if the Colonel will go with us to General E. S. Sanford, and that, if we should have his signature in behalf of this 1st paragraph, we are ready, to die on the spot.

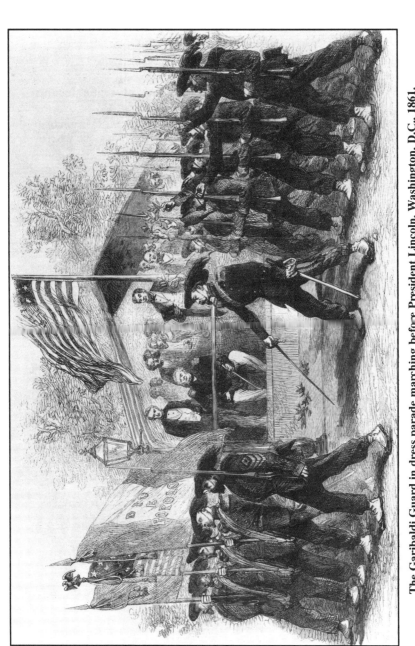

The Garibaldi Guard in dress parade marching before President Lincoln, Washington, D.C., 1861.

National Archives

Sir, Colonel

1. We have enlisted and sworn to sustain the consolidation of the U.S. and also their laws, and further have sworn, to protect with all our power the glorious stars and stripes of this our adopted country should it cost the very blood of our life, and, Sir colonel, we must do it as already said, so help us God; but our word as officers and men, given to our soldiers, must and shall be fulfilled.

2. That, if we should die on the field of battle, without our commission in hand, we die as non-commissioned officers.

3. As regards to our pay, the Government of the U.S. is security enough for us.

At last, Sir, we would respectfully ask the Colonel, that William Lugh, now the hospital nurse[,] be informed to quit the camp inside 3 days. Begging the Colonel to give his attention to the above we will give him 72 hours of reflection.

Respectfully Submitted
by your obedient servants,

[Signed by:]

Company A, the Italians, Captain Caesar Osnaghi, Second Lieutenant Allegretti,

Company B, the Swiss, First Lieutenant Giovanni Marco Colani,

Company C, the Germans, Captain Charles Schwarz, First Lieutenant Weekey, Second Lieutenant Aigner,

Company D, the Spanish and Portuguese, Captain Joseph Torrens, First Lieutenant Romero and Second Lieutenant DeLa Mesa,

Company E Captain John Siegel, First Lieutenant Robitsek and Second Lieutenant Bauer,

Company F Captain Charles Wiegand, First Lieutenant Von Schondorf and Second Lieutenant Hollinde,

Company G, the Hungarians, Slavs and Prussians, Captain Franz Takats, First Lieutenant Junger and Second Lieutenant Tenner,

Company H, Captain A. Otto Bernstein, First Lieutenant Baer, Second Lieutenant Kaufmann,

Company I, Captain. A. H. Von Unwerth, Second Lieutenant Brey,

Company K, the French and French Canadians, Captain Louis Tassillier and First Lieutenant Chandone.[58]

First Lieutenant James C. Rice of Company I said that he did not know the hospital steward and agreed to everything but the dismissal of that man. Lieutenant Molin, who remained in the hospital, Company B's Captain Joseph De Schmidt and Second Lieutenant Alfred Muller, and Second Lieutenant Anthony Dumazer of Company K did not sign the petition to D'Utassy. Acting on the information given to it by Tassillier, the *New York Herald* conducted its own investigation and claimed "[t]hat D'Utassy was not Hungarian, but an American Imposter.... He was suffering from insubordination, desertion, ill treatment and theft on the part of those through whose hands contributions passed."[59] The newspaper's informant was an unidentified Hungarian who served with D'Utassy and knew him when he was Strasser. This was the first report of D'Utassy's activities in American newspapers; his career in Nova Scotia had yet to surface.

By Sunday, July 7, D'Utassy had received an order from his higher headquarters to get his regiment in order, or it would cease to exist. He used the seventy-two hour period specified in the petition to carry out a unique strategy. Trying to separate, disorganize, and confound the defiant leaders, he redesignated the companies. This confounded their payroll records, as new muster rolls had to be made, and gave him time to sort out his allies from his enemies and devise a new strategy. Company A, led by Captain Osnaghi, now became Company C, and the original Company C, led by Captain Schwarz became Company A. Company B, the Swiss company, did not change. Company D, led by Captain Torrens, became Company I; Company I, led by Captain Unwerth, became Company D. Company G, led by Captain Takacs, became Company F, trading designations with the original Company F, led by Captain Wiegand. And the French company, Company K, became Company F and later Company G.

All the while, the common soldiers carried on. On Monday the 8th, Corporal Antonio Mazzini of the new Company C was discharged for disability; Pietro Bennet was mustered in as a corporal and Privates Ferdinando Maggi and Silvio Ronzone were promoted to corporals to fill vacant positions in the company. In Company K, Sergeant Victor Leseine was mustered in as second lieutenant and Corporal Louis Grimiaux was promoted to sergeant to fill his position. Corporal Juan Madrid of the new Company I deserted at Washington.

In a few days the regiment would take the field against the enemy in Virginia. It was rumored that the road it would take had been made unsafe by the enemy, and the men felt that with the inferior rifles they had been issued, they would be marching unarmed. On July 9, Companies C, F, I, and K marched to the Washington Arsenal (present-day Fort Lesley J. McNair) to turn in their old smooth bore muskets. Was D'Utassy actually fulfilling his promise? No; instead of being issued the new Model 1861 U.S. rifled musket, the men were issued weapons which another regiment had recently turned in. The soldiers led by Captains Osnaghi, Torrens, Takacs, and Tassillier took the weapons under compulsion, with great dissatisfaction; once again they were promised the issuance of better rifles soon. The spirit shown by men and officers was by no means reassuring. In actuality, the new rifles that had been furnished for issue to the companies had been taken away in their original crates and disappeared from view after reaching camp.[60] Suddenly, the frustrated Hungarian soldiers of I Company refused to continue without the better arms they had been promised. The few officers on hand to coerce and disperse them instead agreed to march to Washington for redress. The mutinous company marched toward the Long Bridge,[61] backed up by the other three. Army correspondent Charles Carleton Coffin, an eyewitness to the event, recalled,

> It was past sunset on the 9th of July, when, accompanied by a friend, I left Alexandria for Washington in an open carriage. Nearing the Long Bridge, an officer on horseback, in a red-flannel blouse, dashed down upon us, saying: "I am an officer of the Garibaldi Guard; my regiment has mutinied, and the men are on their way to Washington! I want you to hurry past them, give notice to the guard at the Long Bridge, and have the draw taken up." We promised to do so if possible, and soon came upon the mutineers, who were hastening towards the bridge. They were greatly excited. They were talking loud and boisterously in German. Their guns were loaded. There were seven nations represented in the regiment. Few of them could understand English. We knew that if we could get in advance of them, the two six-pounders looking down the Long Bridge, with grape and canister rammed home, would quell the mutiny. We passed those in the rear, had almost reached the head of the column, when out sprang a dozen in front of us and levelled their guns. Click, click, click went the locks.
>
> "You no goes to Vashington in ze advance!" said one.
>
> "You falls in ze rear!" said another.
>
> "What does this mean?" said my friend, who was an officer.
>
> "Where is your captain?" he asked. The captain came up. "What right have your men to stop us, sir? Who gave them authority? We have passes, sir; explain this matter."
>
> The captain, a stout, thick-set German, [more than likely Hungarian Captain Takacs] was evidently completely taken aback by these questions, but, after a moment's hesitation, replied, "No, zur, they no stops you; it was von mistake, zur. They will do zo no more." Then approaching close to the carriage, he lowered his voice, and in a confidential tone, as if we were his best friends, asked, "Please, zur, vill you be zo kind as to tell me vat is the passvord?"
>
> "It's not nine o'clock yet. The sentinels are not posted. You need none."
>
> A tall, big-whiskered soldier had been listening. He could speak English quite well, and, evidently desiring to apologize for the rudeness of this comrades, approached and said, "You see we Garibaldians are having a time of it, and...."
>
> Here the captain gave him a vigorous push, with a "Hush!" long drawn, which had a great deal of meaning in it.

"I begs you pardons for ze interruption," said the captain, extending his hand and bowing politely. Once more we moved on, but again the excited leaders, more furious than before, thrust their bayonets in our faces, again saying, "You no goes to Vashington in ze advance." One of them took deliberate aim at my breast, his eyes glaring fiercely. It would have been the height of madness to disregard their demonstration. They had reached the guard at the Virginia end of the bridge, who, at a loss to know what it meant, allowed them to pass unchallenged. They halted on the avenue, while we rode with all speed to General Mansfield's quarters [Brigadier General Joseph K. F. Mansfield was inspector general of the army's Department of Washington].

"I'll have every one of the rascals shot!" said the gray haired veteran commanding the forces in Washington. An hour later the Garibaldians found themselves surrounded by five thousand infantry. They laid down their arms when they saw it was no use to resist, were marched back to Alexandria, and put to the hard drudgery of camp life.[62]

The fact was that it was Blenker and his staff that compelled the Garibaldians to do what they did. After some discussion, Blenker promised to arm the Garibaldians with adequate rifles. After this incident *L'Eco Italia* called the unit "a band of malefactors who had dishonored Garibaldi's name!" Repetti suggested that the regiment's name be changed back to First Foreign Rifles, so as to not drag the name of Garibaldi in the mud. But the 39th New York Volunteers would remain the Garibaldi Guard to the end.

Gambling was a way for the soldiers to pass the time, and next to drinking, the Garibaldi Guard carried on gambling to its fullest excess in violation of military law. Disgruntled losers from other camps reported horse racing. The provost marshal inspected the Garibaldi Guard for the purpose of uncovering and turning in all irregular means of transportation and horses used by soldiers. No infantry soldier was allowed the use of public horses. The officers had to be reminded that horses where issued at rates of two for army wagons, two for ambulances, and four for ordnance wagons and authentic medical wagons. The men would bet on anything, so taking away their cards had been only a temporary setback; they had soon found another amusements, among them horse racing in camp, wrestling matches, and dog fights.

In camp on July 10, Company I saw a spate of promotions: Sergeant Major Carl Rulberg was promoted to second lieutenant, Sergeant Christian Enke was promoted to fill Rulberg's position, Corporal Jean Dessauer was promoted to sergeant, and Private Philipp Petri was promoted to corporal. On Friday, July 12, Lieutenant Dal Molin of the Italian company was discharged due to illness. Captain Takats had been absent without leave since the arsenal incident; on July 15, his Hungarians in Company F found out that First Lieutenant Anthony Weekey, a member of Schwarz's company (originally Company C, now Company A), had been promoted to replace him. That same day the entire regiment was ordered to Halifax Court House. The men broke camp and marched away, carrying their bread rations stuck on the bayonets of their old rifles, French style.[63] As the companies marched off to their first battlefield, they were led by captains who had still not received their commissions. Most of the captains had helped to recruit in New York during the regiment's early days. Now accused of incompetence and insubordination, one after another they resigned, disgusted with the whole affair, and promptly went on to join other Union regiments, glad to be rid of D'Utassy. Only Schwarz and Wiegand would appear to actually benefit from the situation by becoming D'Utassy's allies, for at least as long as the colonel might need them.

Chapter Three

OUT TO BULL RUN AND BACK

There you are, shoulder-straps!, but where are your companies? where are your men? ...Sneak, blow put on airs there in Willard's sumptuous parlors and bar-rooms, or anywhere, no explanation shall save you. Bull Run is your work....

—*Walt Whitman*

ON Tuesday, July 16, McDowell's army advanced on Manassas, Virginia, and the Confederate forces located there, as part of the Union plan to march west and then south to capture Richmond and defeat the Confederacy. Two and a half days later, after twenty miles of tiring marching, the army reached Centerville, a town some six miles north-north-east of Manassas. Blenker's brigade, as part of Miles' division, was part of the Union reserve. The brigade consisted of five infantry regiments: Blenker's own original regiment, the 8th New York, the 29th and the 45th New York, the inadequately armed 39th New York, and the 27th Pennsylvania. Blenker reported the positions that his brigade's regiments took up:

> Pursuant to the orders of Colonel Miles, [on Sunday] the brigade advanced from the camp and took their assigned position on the heights east of Centreville about daybreak; the Eighth Regiment...on the left of the road leading from Centerville to Fairfax Court-House; the Twenty-ninth...on the right of the same road, both fronting towards the east; The Garibaldi Guard, commanded by Colonel [D']Utassy, formed a right angle with the Twenty-ninth..., fronting to the south. The artillery attached to the brigade occupied the fol-

49

Louis Blenker
Colonel of the 8th New York Volunteer Infantry. Commander of Blenker's brigade.
The 39th New York Volunteer Infantry was attached to this brigade during Bull Run,
circa 1861.

lowing positions: The battery of Captain Tidball stood in front of the left wing of the Garibaldi Guard; three pieces left in Centerville were placed near the right wing of the Twenty-ninth...three others on the left wing of the Eighth.... The last-named six pieces were served by experienced artillerists.... The Twenty-seventh...was detached to the village of Centreville for the protection of the headquarters and hospital.

Waring recalled: "On the morning of Sunday, the 21st of July, I lay, with the left wing of the regiment, on the brow of a long slope outside of Centreville. Repetti, with the right wing,—and perhaps with the Colonel,—was a mile or more to our left on another road. Miles' whole division, lying near Centreville, constituted a substantial reserve force of about thirteen thousand fresh troops; we were its foremost line, and our position overlooked the whole field of Bull Run. I was lounging in a hay-field with [Frank] Vizetelly, the artist of the *Illustrated London News*; he was comparing the battle then going on, three miles to our front, with some aspects of battles he had watched in the Crimea. Julius Bing stopped to chat with us. He was then a correspondent, I think, for the *Tribune*. He said he was going through the lines (protected by his British passport), hoping to get to Richmond in advance of the retreating rebel army."

While the Garibaldi Guard lay in reserve with the rest of Miles' division, two other divisions of McDowell's army, led by Colonels David Hunter and Samuel B. Heintzelman, succeeded that morning in turning the enemy's left flank by maneuvering north and west beyond the Confederate positions and crossing Bull Run, a stream with steep, heavily wooded banks, at Sudley Springs, about five miles west of Centreville. The two Union divisions attacked the enemy to their south, while a third Union division under the command of Brigadier General Daniel Tyler made a secondary attack from the east at the Stone Bridge, where the Warrenton Turnpike from Centreville crossed Bull Run, and demonstrated farther downstream at Blackburn's Ford to hold the enemy right flank forces in place. The Union forces successfully pressed their attack into the afternoon. (McDowell's fourth division, led by Colonel Theodore Runyon, was stationed as a rear guard well east of Centreville and never joined the action.)

Miles was returning to Blenker's position when he received orders to post two brigades on the Warrenton Turnpike at Stone Bridge. He sent a staff officer to order his division's other brigade, under Colonel Thomas A. Davies, to move forward, but while the staff officer was conveying Miles' instructions, Davies sent word that three thousand of the enemy were advancing toward him, attempting to turn his flank. The staff officer suspended the order and immediately reported the fact to Miles. Miles then advanced Blenker's brigade to the position on the Warrenton Turnpike. Waring had been watching something, he later recalled, that appeared to be "a cloud of dust coming through a gap of the Blue Ridge, which we assumed to indicate [Union

Major General Robert] Patterson's column coming—too late—to take part in the fight. Our whole line was evidently advancing, and the fury of the battle was abating. Obviously there would be no need for the reserves, and we were to remain idle spectators. Suddenly, firing began, and soon became furious, on our extreme right. It was not Patterson's, but [Confederate, then Brigadier, General Joseph E.] Johnston's dust we had watched with so much composure."

Miles evidently had only a partial picture of the severity of the fight to his west and of the Confederates' actions. They feinted against his division from the south, which suggested staying in place to protect McDowell's line of communication with Washington, while they rushed Johnston's units from the Shenandoah Valley north to the main fight as soon as the reinforcements arrived at Manassas Junction. Miles continued reviewing the defensive dispositions of his soldiers: "I then followed Blenker; found Tidball's battery in admirable position, supported by the Garibaldi Guard, Blenker, with three remaining regiments and the Fourth Pennsylvania Battery being in advance. When I was informed that the commanding general had passed, I then returned to Centreville heights to await events, when I found all my defensive arrangements changed. Davies' and [Colonel Israel B.] Richardson's brigade, with Greene's battery, was placed about one-half mile in advance of Centreville heights, his line of battle was facing Blackburn's Ford [about three miles due south of Centreville]. Not knowing who had done this, and seeing Colonel Richardson giving different positions to my troops, I asked by what authority he was acting, when he told me he had instructions from my superior officer. I soon thereafter met the commanding general, and complained of this change. The general's arrangements were completed, and left me without further control of the division." Blenker sent four companies of the 29th New York east from Centreville toward the Union Mills road, which intersected the road from Fairfax Court House, to keep the enemy from outflanking the army's left wing. During this time he was ordered to disarm one company of the 12th New York, which Conferedates had routed at Blackburn's Ford; two companies of the 8th New York promptly executed the order.

The road from Centreville to Blackburn's Ford forked to the west about a mile south of Centreville, near the end of the Centreville heights, and the fork road paralleled the Warrenton Turnpike all the way to Bull Run, to Ball's Ford. From his report and the fact that the Guard was positioned south of Centreville, Waring was obviously positioned along the road to Ball's Ford while Repetti was positioned with Richardson on the road to Blackburn's Ford. Waring received an order at about noon "to join Repetti at Blackburn's Ford." He moved out and quickly ran into trouble: "As we were marching briskly along the road, we were met by General [*sic*] Miles and his staff. He seemed to be very drunk. He called out, 'Halt! What have you got there?' 'The left wing of the Garibaldi Guard,' Waring answered. 'Where are you going?' 'To join the colonel and the rest of the regiment,' Waring replied.

Miles stormed back, 'Bout face and march to the battlefield. Damned quick too!'" Waring thought and acted quickly, according to his recollections thirty years later:

> There were two roads to the battlefield, diverging just out-side of the village—as plainly seen from my former position. I gal-loped ahead, overtook Miles, and said:
> "General, which road shall I take?"
> "Follow your nose, G——d d——n you!" he replied. I told him that the road forked and the branches went to very different parts of the field. He could only sway in the saddle and repeat
> "Follow your nose, G——d d——n you!"
> I never saw him again. A little outside of Centreville, I was hurriedly overtaken by a very young officer, who came up on a dashing gallop, held a cocked revolver in my face, and cried:
> "Halt! Turn your men into this field and form line of battle."
> "Put up your revolver," I said. "Who are you, any way, and what is the matter?"
> "I am General Miles's aide! Our whole army is beaten and retreating! We must rally them here!"

The whole army was not beaten yet, although most of it would be as the afternoon progressed intense fighting continued, Confederate reinforcements kept coming, and inexperienced Union leaders, starting with McDowell be-came increasingly engrossed in personally leading forces on the battlefield. Miles would be heavily criticized for not reinforcing the attack with his re-serve division at the critical moment, but McDowell never ordered him for-ward, as he should have done. Senior Union officers lapsed in directing their entire commands, and unguided, barely disciplined Federals began to retreat from the battlefield in increasing disorder. The retreating soldiers ran into pic-nickers who had come out from Washington to watch a battle on a fine sum-mer Sunday and now felt that they should also be getting back, as they saw more and more soldiers straggling east along the road. A grand traffic jam of soldiers and civilians developed on the turnpike. Rumors of Confederate cav-alry attacks began to multiply, and then a Confederate cannonball burst in the middle of the congestion. Everyone's anxiety burst into self-perpetuating panic, completely snarling traffic. About 4:00 P.M., McDowell ordered Blenker's brigade to advance west from Centreville along the Warrenton Turnpike to help cover the Union retreat. Blenker's advance was executed with difficulty, since the road was jammed with battlefield fugitives. Blenker recalled, "The road was nearly choked up by the retreating baggage wagons of several divi-sions, and by the vast numbers of flying soldiers belonging to various regi-ments." Miles remembered encountering fleeing soldiers: "When these [men] were passing my headquarters I endeavored to rally them, but my efforts were in vain.... I would make a personal allusion to my condition during the day. I had lost my rest the two nights previous, was sick, had eaten nothing during the day, and had it not been for the great responsibility resting on me should have been in bed."

Moving by road itself, the normal way for Civil War infantry units, Blenker's brigade got into position. Blenker reported afterward how his brigade got onto the turnpike at Centerville and deployed in the face of the retreat: "[Due] to the coolness of the commanding officers and the good discipline of the men, the passage through the village was successfully executed and the further advance made with the utmost precision, and I was thus enabled to take a position which would prevent the advance of the enemy and protect the retreat of the Army. The Eighth Regiment took position one and a half miles south[west] of Centerville, on both sides of the road leading to Bull Run. The Twenty-ninth Regiment stood half a mile behind the Eighth, *en echiquier* [French: in squares, checkerboard pattern] by companies. The Garibaldi Guard stood as reserve in line behind the Twenty-ninth Regiment. The retreat of great numbers of flying soldiers continued till 9 o'clock in the evening, the great majority in wild confusion, but few in collected bodies." Waring remembered, "It could not have been far from three o'clock when the first of the fleeing rabble came to our line. It was after dark of the long summer day when the last had passed by, and all these hours were hours of burning disgrace. One at last became ashamed of his kind; if such men could be so transformed by terror, of what real value could it be to be a man at all?"

Blenker boasted of his command that while his "five regiments had withstood a force far larger and flushed with victory[,] they had only a brush with Stuart's Cavalry." Blenker reported that after the flow of fleeing soldiers finally died down that evening, "several squadrons of the enemy's cavalry advanced along the road and appeared before the outposts. They were challenged by 'Who comes there?' and remaining without any answer, I being just present at the outposts, called, 'Union Forever.' Whereupon the officer of the enemy's cavalry commanded, '*En Avant; en avant.* Knock him down.' Now the skirmishers fired, when the enemy turned aound, leaving several killed and wounded on the spot. About nine prisoners, who were already in their hands, were liberated by this action. Afterwards we were several times molested from various sides by the enemy's cavalry." Waring and the Guard were also ready to repel enemy cavalry, for he observed, "We held the line to which we had been removed, east of Centreville, until long after dark—and repelled the mythical charge of the 'Black Horse Cavalry,' which, so far as I know, was never made."

While the Union forces streamed back to Washington, exhaustion and confusion on the Confederate side kept the victors from initiating any effective pursuit and sealing a real victory. About midnight, McDowell ordered his rear guard to withdraw to Washington. Blenker reported that his brigade "retired in perfect order, and ready to repel any attack on the road from Centerville to Fairfax Court-House, Annandale to Washington.....arrived in Washington in good order at 6 o'clock [the next evening], after a fatiguing march of nineteen hours." The Guard trudged east after its comrades. Waring remembered, "Then we took up our rear-guard march, lasting all that night and far into the next day, all in a pouring rain, and over the rejected impedimenta of the fleeing army of terror-stricken cowards." Miles boasted, "If the Enemy command had any plans to continue on and take Washington they were shattered by the opposition of Blenker's regiments. Blenker's men were able to retain their organization, to take up a position despite the panic about them, and thus to prevent the advance of the Enemy army. Although tired out by upwards of thirty hours of marching and fighting, these units covered the retreat until about midnight, when, under General McDowell's order to march to Washington, the brigade retired in perfect order, bringing back their own six guns and two stands of Union colors left on the field by other soldiers." Blenker noted the particular contribution of his own original regiment: "...the Eighth Regiment brought in safety two Union colors left behind by soldiers on the field of battle. The officers and men did their duty admirably...."[1] The Garibaldians lost two men killed and fifty missing in action, of which fifteen were sergeants and corporals from Companies D, F, G, H, and I. Most of the men missing in action returned to camp during the following week and were demoted to private.

On the day the Federal army was beaten at Bull Run, Secretary of State Seward received the correspondence between Garibaldi and Quiggle. Seward decided to convince Lincoln to offer Garibaldi a high ranking officer's commission in the Union army. Henry S. Sanford, the American minister in Brussels, was dispatched to meet the general in Caprera and invite him in person to join the Union side.[2]

By July 27, the Garibaldians were back at camp near Washington, digging in to defend the city against enemy attack. D'Utassy received orders to send his pioneers to assist the Corps of Engineers in the building of earthworks, lunettes, and redoubts. Repetti was sent to do the task. Captain Frederick E. Prime, chief engineer in charge of the construction, was a competent, old veteran of the Italian army and the U.S. Corps of Engineers whose experience dated from 1850.[3] The construction team built fortifications in Centreville and a battery near Fairfax. Repetti sent back a request for more tents, provisions, forty men and five officers for the work.[4] The pioneers constructed a redoubt with two embrasures so as to sweep the old Braddock road, and resist any outflanking from the left by the Union Mills road or the road from Gaines Ford.[5] The construction lasted well into the next month. Repetti, now occupied with executing his task, could not interfere with the colonel's plan to rid his regiment of enemies.

Waring was at the top of D'Utassy's list of distrusted officers. But word traveled fast about D'Utassy's modus operandi: "Such officers as would not tamely endure his tyranny, and wink at his dishonest practices, were forced by one pretext or another to resign, or were dismissed by court martial on trumped up charges, their places being filled in every case with creatures of his own selection to whom the commissions were sold at the best prices he could extort." To replace officers who left, D'Utassy had a reserve of men in the ranks, men who were unaware of his blackmail.[6] Promotion was always tempting. In the Company G camp, Captain Wiegand confided in his tent to Second Lieutenant Emil Hollinde that the colonel told him it would cost $200 to be promoted to major. Hollinde advised him not to take the offer, but Wiegand feared that if he did not pay now he would pass up his opportunity for the position. They were still talking over the offer when D'Utassy entered. He wanted to talk privately with Wiegand, so Hollinde left, but remained within hearing distance, and overheard D'Utassy ask for the money. Wiegand left his tent and went to a sutler named John May to make a loan, but all he could get was $180; he returned with it, and gave it to the colonel in the tent.[7]

Camp life for the Garibaldi Guard resumed its human flux. On Sunday, July 28, First Sergeants Annibal Ferrari and Germain Sayve, of Companies C and K respectively, were discharged for disability. Before the ink was dry on his discharge papers, Ferrari reenlisted in the 51st New York Infantry (and later became a first lieutenant of the 120th U.S. Colored Troops). Sergeant Louis Riege was promoted to first sergeant, and Corporal Carl Franz and Private John Wagner were each promoted to sergeant, in Company C. Corporal William Formansky of Company K disappeared from camp. On Tuesday, July 30, First Lieutenant James C. Rice of Company B was transferred to G and then to Company H. Sergeant Alphonse Pasquet from Company B was promoted to first lieutenant in Company G, and Second Lieutenant Alfred Muller was transferred to Company G. First Lieutenant Conrad Von Schondorf of Company G was transferred to Company B to replace Rice. Since Captain de Schmidt of Company B, the Swiss Company, had remained absent, his muster was revoked, and First Lieutenant John B. Junger of Company F was promoted to captain to replace him. In the French company, Company K, Second Lieutenant Anthony Dumazer resigned; Corporal Emile David deserted, and Corporal Leo Doerndinger was transferred in to replace him. Sergeant Joseph Wachter returned to camp, had his stripes taken away and was reduced in rank to private, and then transferred from Company F to Company E.

August began with thirty-eight resignations, eighteen dismissals, and another scramble of officers under arrest or in search of transfers to other regiments. The men's esprit de corps crumbled. On Thursday, August 1, Tassillier was arrested for organizing and leading the officers' mutiny against D'Utassy. First Lieutenant Victor Chandone, an Hungarian, was promoted to captain the French company. Chief Surgeon Adolphus Majer argued with D'Utassy for unwarrantably discharging so many men for medical disability. Majer resigned and easily found service in the 4th New York Cavalry, Colonel Cesnola's regiment. Since the incident involving the petition, D'Utassy

Charles Wiegand
Major of the 39th Regiment New York Volunteer Infantry who replaced
Major Waring.

U.S. Army Military Institute

viewed Waring only as an enemy. On August 2, Wiegand received his new promotion to major. Waring later wrote, "It was no longer a proud thing to be major of the Garibaldi Guard, and I rejoiced when, with my mare Vix, I was transferred to Fremont at St. Louis, and commissioned to raise a cavalry regiment."[8] Waring would serve with Fremont as a major, then as colonel of the 4th Missouri Cavalry, where Fremont's Hussars earned him a reputation as a good cavalry officer. As the *creme de la creme* of officers left, D'Utassy's actions rekindled the fear that the regiment's honor was at stake and that Garibaldi's name was being dragged through the mud.

Second Lieutenant Ciro P. Verdi was one of the officers who left the Guard rather than stay with D'Utassy. He transferred to Colonel Enrico Fardella's regiment, the 101st New York Infantry, where he regained his previous rank. The brother of Dr. Tullio Suzzara Verdi, the personal physician to Union Secretary of State William Henry Seward, Ciro had arrived in America together with his brother in 1850 as political exiles.[9] Lieutenant Cornelius Grinnell was eased out; his muster-in as adjutant was revoked despite the fact that his father, Moses, sponsored D'Utassy's civilian business endeavors. The overburdened quartermaster, Charles Norton, left for the 50th Engineers; by May 1862 he would be in the division as a captain on the 3rd Brigade quartermaster's staff. Schondorf was transferred from Company B back to Company K. Once again the gaps left in the officers' ranks were filled by enlisted men. Sergeant Major George Bennett was promoted to second lieutenant to replace Louis Tenner. Corporal Sebastian Dreher was promoted to first sergeant of Company F. Hollinde was promoted to first lieutenant in Company K. First Sergeant Francisco Lugue was promoted to second lieutenant in Company I, while Corporal Heinrich Scheideman of Company D was discharged for disability.

In response to the appointment of Chandone to captain the French company, a number of French, Spanish, Hungarian, and Italian Garibaldians deserted throughout the month; most of them followed Ferrari's example and reenlisted in Union regiments of other states. Sergeant Jose Maria Moreno of Company I, the Spanish company, deserted and returned to California (on January 20, 1864, he would reenlist in Company D of the 1st Battalion of Native Cavalry). On Monday, August 9, Sergeant Franz Haug of Company A was discharged for disability, and Sergeant Ricardo Dominguos of Company I deserted. The next day, Doerdinger was promoted to sergeant. Private Augustine Montegrifa of Company C was discharged for disabilities, but would return to become the regiment's new sutler. That same evening brought more desertions; Privates Thomas Mack, Thomas Manning, James Dempsey, and John Tomson from the Spanish company all deserted together and were never apprehended. While the turmoil in the Guard continued, Louis Blenker had been named brigadier general on Sunday, August 4. He retained command of his 1st Brigade, 5th Division, in the army of the Department of Northeastern Virginia. His brigade, where the Guard would remain until October, now consisted of the 8th, 29th, and 39th New York and 27th Pennsylvania Infantries.

Major Wiegand and Colonel D'Utassy in dress uniforms in the style of Hungarian Hussars.

August 10, 1861, was payday. Union privates were due sixteen dollars a month. The paymaster was to pay the Garibaldi Guard for the month of June. Companies A, B, C, D, and E were mustered at 10:00 A.M., and at 2:00 P.M. Companies F, G, H, I, and K were mustered. A bugler sounded "Assembly" fifteen minutes before each designated muster time. The appropriate companies formed on the parade ground, in order from right to left, and stood inspection before being paid. The men were inspected to ensure that each man had a clean uniform and a full complement of clean and serviceable military equipment, besides his weapon. Then the muster was read off and as the men answered, the first sergeants distributed their pay envelopes to them.[10] As a safety precaution, many of the men had devised secret pockets or hiding places on their persons, where they secured their money. But they never dreamed they would have to protect their valuables from their own colonel. D'Utassy concocted a plan to appropriate the three gold dollars each man had received as a gift from his family in New York. That day every man found that his pay was three dollars short. D'Utassy collected it, claiming that he represented the Union Defense Committee donors and was required to return the money to them. His explanation was that the money was only a loan, for which he was personally responsible. In all he collected about two thousand dollars from the men.[11] Shortly after this incident another twenty-five men deserted.

At Roach's Mill, Virginia, D'Utassy needed $150 for expenses and obtained that amount from the new sutler, Montegrifa.[12] Montegrifa complained to Captain Caesar Osnaghi that the colonel was cheating him. Under the circumstances Osnaghi could not help him; he was ill himself, and when he confronted D'Utassy on the matter he was simply ignored. Then twice Osnaghi sent letters to D'Utassy. On August 12, Osnaghi wrote,

> Having once presented my resignation to you, and having been accepted, but since nothing having been said about it, I take the liberty again, to address the same to you, particularly after the unpleasant conversation, that we had, viz: "that you have said to me, that yours or mine blood ought to be spilled, and that you could not be, where I was, because we do not agree, and more that it was utterly, impossible for us to agree in future." For all of this consideration, I again formally present you, my resignation, which you will grant me, for reasons of sickness, of which I have been suffering for the last week more or less and moreover I am still very sick, without hope of soon getting better, and thus being compelled many times, to keep away from duty. While your kindness will see, that the discharge from the regiment will take this course without delay, and as some time is indispensable for such a course, I must pray your kindness a second time, to do all you can so that I should have a permit of about ten days, which are to my health a real necessity....[13]

The two soldiers in the background standing to the right were privates in the Garibaldi Guard.

National Archives

Eleven of Osnaghi's men deserted within the month. Sutler Montegrifa would never get back his money, and soon found he faced new problems.

On August 11, the *New York Tribune* had jumped the gun and announced Garibaldi's appointment as a major general in the Union army. The Washington government neither denied nor confirmed the report. The reaction of the American press was mixed. The *World* was supportive; the *Herald* advised Garibaldi to stay put. The *New York Times* reacted, "We trust that the war would not go on long enough to make his participation necessary." Southern sympathizers were anxious that Garibaldi was approached to take an appointment in the Union army. He had about him a group of old comrades of many nationalities, who were utterly devoted to him and impatient for new adventures, and who would follow him at his order to do battle in America. On August 13, Minister Sanford received Seward's orders and met with Consul Quiggle in Brussels.

Then Sanford wrote to George P. Marsh, the American consul in Turin, Italy, to tell him that he was traveling there to meet with him and discuss the matter of recruiting Garibaldi. On August 15, Quiggle sent a letter to Garibaldi, offering him the "highest Army Commission which it is in the power of the President to confer."[14]

As the diplomats tried to get Garibaldi into the Union army, more Garibaldians tried to get out of the Guard. More men asked for transfers to other commands; nine men were transferred to the 13th Artillery. James Mullen of Company F was promoted to regimental quartermaster sergeant and replaced within the month by E. D. Lazelle after proving incapable of the task. On Monday, August 19, in Company B, Sergeant August Ruckersfeld was discharged for disability, and Private George Ziegler was promoted to take his place; Second Lieutenant Charles Graham Bacon was promoted to adjutant. Two days later, Corporals Paul Haedler and Baptiste Joseph Leriche of Companies F and G, respectively, returned to the ranks after being absent since the battle at Bull Run. Haedler was transferred to Company K; Leriche was discharged for disability. Captain von Unwerth, who had been absent since the petition incident six weeks earlier, was discharged.

On August 20, Sanford reached Turin and Marsh gave him his assessment of the current Italian political climate. Eleven days later, Garibaldi replied to Sanford that he should be most happy to serve "a country for which I have so much affection and of which I am an adoptive citizen... provided that the conditions upon which the American government intends to accept me are those which your messenger has verbally indicated to me." Garibaldi sought King Victor Emmanuel II's permission to accept the American proposal and sent an old comrade, Colonel Trecchi, to speak on his behalf.[15]

More demoralized Garibaldi Guard officers turned in their resignations, men kept leaving, and duties kept changing. Theodore Krueger, the regimental chaplain, and First Lieutenant Giovanni Mario Colani of the Swiss company resigned. Osnaghi left without authorization and was discharged, effective August 29.[16] Sergeant Louis Grimiaux of Company G deserted, and Corporal Lieser, Company B, was discharged for disability. The next day Second Lieutenant Ignazio Allegretti of Company C was promoted to first lieutenant, and Anthony P. Zyla was appointed the new regimental chaplain. He was already an ordained minister in the German Protestant Evangelical Church and took to the duties of his new position with unrivaled zeal and faithfulness. He proved unfailing in the consolation of the sick and in his ministry to healthy soldiers. The whole regiment listened to his powerful and soul-stirring sermons, all of which reflected his enlightened Christian deportment and patriotic Union sentiment. He would win the respect of the men and become D'Utassy's greatest adversary.[17]

On Friday, August 30, Headquarters, Army of the Potomac, issued an order: "Captain Tassillier, of the Garibaldi Guard, having left his regiment without proper authority, when under charges of a grave and disreputable

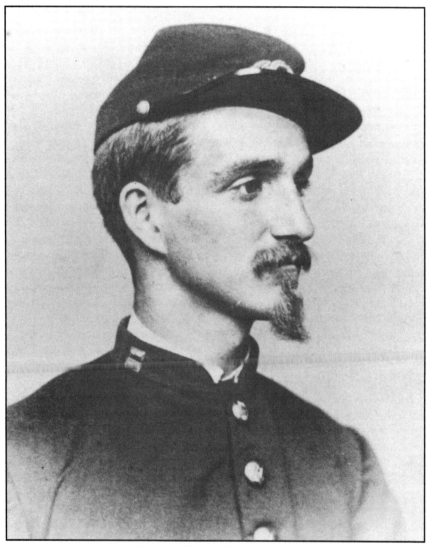

Captain Charles Graham Bacon
Company C, 39th Regiment New York Volunteer Infantry.

RG 98 S – CWP50.11
U.S. Army Military History Institute

character, is hereby dishonorably discharged from the service of the United States."[18] Sergeant Giovanni Ferralasco of Company C deserted and Corporal Luigi Roux was promoted to sergeant to replace him. Private Henry Palmer was also promoted to sergeant, and Private Giuseppe Griffa was promoted to corporal to replace Roux. Another Bull Run deserter, First Sergeant Ludwig

Seippel, returned to the ranks. On Sunday, September 1, Thomas Niedzielski, forty-one, a Polish exile who had been employed as a professor of fencing and director of the gymnasium at Georgetown College from 1856 through 1860, mustered in as captain of Company C to replace Osnaghi.[19] Anthony von D'Utassy's name appeared for the first time on the rolls as a first lieutenant in Company F, the Hungarian company. Since he had not yet arrived from Hungary to assume his position, Colonel D'Utassy drew his pay for him.

September saw no change in the turbulent situation of the Garibaldi Guard. Hospital Steward Herman Bendell was discharged (later he would serve as assistant surgeon in the 6th New York Artillery and then as surgeon of the 86th New York Heavy Artillery). Corporal Herrmann Theune of Company H returned to the ranks and then transferred out to the 73rd Pennsylvania. Sergeants Carl Sutter and Marie Olivry of Companies D and G, respectively, and Corporal Wilhelm Utzl of Company F all returned to the ranks and were reduced to private. In Company B on Thursday, September 5, Sergeant Otto Peter was discharged for disability and Corporal Leopold Sachs was promoted to take his place. The next day, Corporal Henry Bartholomie was discharged for disability; to replace him, Corporal George Glassenapp was transferred from Company B to Company G, while Corporal Charles Hahn was transferred the other way. Private Filippo Mirande, Company C, was discharged for disability (he would reenlist in Company D, 5th New Jersey on February 14, 1865). On September 12, newly minted Captain Rice, barely a month after replacing Unwerth as company commander, accepted a commission as lieutenant colonel of the 44th New York Infantry.

More wholesale personnel changes followed. First Sergeant Christian Enke of Company B was promoted to sergeant major in his company. Sergeant George Hoell was transferred from Company A to Company B. First Lieutenant Alphonse Pasquet was discharged, and to replace him Second Lieutenant C. Lindner was promoted and transferred from Company H to Company D. In turn, Sergeant Major Anton Schada was promoted and transferred from Company E to Company H to replace Lindner. Sergeant Bernhard Franz was promoted to second lieutenant and transferred from Company K to Company I. Sergeant Edward Boas, Company F, was discharged for disability. On September 13, Tassillier was dishonorably discharged; Chandone, his replacement, was discharged for disability! Chandone took a commission as a captain in the Veteran Reserve Corps and returned to New York, where he assisted the Garibaldi Guard recruiting office. Hugo Hildebrandt, who briefly served as adjutant, was promoted to captain the French company. That same day, Commissary Sergeant Alex Biscaccianti achieved the distinction of being promoted to second and then first lieutenant in Company I on the same day. On Monday, September 16, Sergeant Angelo Gori and Lieutenant Allegretti of the Italian company were discharged for disability (Allegretti recovered, soon afterwards married the sister of fellow lieutenant Andrew Fontana, and reenlisted in the 29th New York Cavalry as a first lieutenant). Eleven men re-

Captain Hugo Hildebrandt (Hilderbrant)
Company G, 39th Regiment New York Volunteer Infantry.

R6 98S – CWP26110
Roger D. Hunt Collection

quested and received transfers to the 15th Artillery. Corporal Jean Wiedemayer, Company B, was discharged for disability.

Meanwhile, on September 3, Sanford had met Colonel Trecchi in Turin, Italy, and then relayed his conversation to Seward, saying that "they saw no prospect of retaining the General in Italy; the only question to arise would be with regard to the position he was to occupy in our service, which from letters received from one of our consuls and the conversation of the messenger, he thought to be the commander-in-chief of our army."[20] On September 9, Sanford arrived on Garibaldi's island home of Caprera. He found the general crippled with a severe case of rheumatism. Garibaldi stated that he ardently "desired to accept the American offer only if he were made commander in chief of the Union Army." Sanford explained that the American president alone held that position, but that the commission offered to Garibaldi would be that of a major general and carried with it command of a large army corps. Garibaldi was a man who had twice been saved by a freed slave. Prophetically he argued that unless Lincoln would declare that he was fighting for the emancipation of the slaves, the Civil War would be fought for issues which were of interest only to the citizens of the United States, and not to the rest of the world. He also knew the practical effect of granting freedom to a slave, for to a slave freedom was worth his life, and that was worth fighting for. Garibaldi's convictions remained firm, "that had I accepted to draw my sword for the cause of the United States, it would have been for the abolition of Slavery, full, unconditional." Garibaldi and Sanford talked again on September 10, but to no avail. Disappointed with the results of the meeting, Sanford left for the mainland that afternoon.[21]

Garibaldi wrote to Quiggle, "I have seen Mr. Sanford and I am sorry to be obliged to say that I cannot at present go to the United States. I have no doubt of the triumph of the cause of the Union and that it will come quickly; but if the war should by evil chance continue in your country, I will overcome all the obstacles which hold me back, and will hasten to come to the defense of that people which is so dear to me." On September 17, Garibaldi received a letter from a group of his followers who wished to serve in the Union army:

> Your Excellency:
> The Undersigned refugee Polish officers discharged at their own request from the Southern Army of Italy, who have had the honor to serve you, beg to ask your Excellency—in the event that your Excellency accepts the rank of Commander-in-chief of the Army of the United States—to accord them the favor to follow your Excellency and to form a separate division in your Army—should your Excellency refuse this important honor, we beg you to take us under your protection and urge the Government of the United States to admit us into its military service. It will be our duty to be worthy of this great honor.
> Please accept the expressions of our deep respect and sincere devotion with which we are your Excellency's
> Very humble and devoted servants
> [17 illegible signatures][22]

Back in America, on September 26, Francesco Ornesi was mustered into Company C as a first lieutenant to replace Allegretti; Sergeant Raphael Frizone was promoted to second lieutenant and transferred from Company C to D. Two days later, on Saturday, Second Lieutenant DeLa Mesa was promoted to first lieutenant in Company I. Sergeant Jean Dessauer was transferred from Company B to G. On September 30, Corporal Gottlieb Jehele was discharged from Company D for disability. First Lieutenant George Brey was promoted to captain on October 1 and replaced the departed Rice. Captain Bernhard Baer of Company I and Second Lieutenant Richard Marshall of Schwarz' Company A were discharged. Second Lieutenant Francisco Lugue of Company I and First Lieutenant Alfred Muller of Company B resigned. Following their resignations, twenty more men deserted. Private Daniel Mathies of the Swiss Company B died in camp of heart failure.

General McDowell had been receiving reports that some Garibaldi Guard officers were "more than suspected" of selling rations to their own men and taking money from the sutlers. In fact, one Ignaz Batory paid $420 for the position of regimental sutler. He set up a shop that included a camp brothel and a saloon for the officers, and he paid D'Utassy a hefty percentage to protect his operation.[23] D'Utassy placed the names of Michael Jacky, the Company G musician from Alsace Lorraine, and George Blum, the Company E musician from Duzsenbach, Bavaria, on the regimental field and staff and band rolls for September. In October, knowing that these two men were not members of the band, D'Utassy collected $86 in their name from the paymaster. In November and December he repeated his actions. When Blum protested, D'Utassy ordered him dropped from the regimental rolls as of December 31. Jacky remained on the rolls. D'Utassy also had another racket going. He was back to his old horse trading again; this time he was selling government-owned horses. His biggest trade in government horses was in the contraband taken from the farms around Virginia. He had a chemical process that removed the U.S. brand from the horses' hides, and during this time in his personal stable he had up to thirty horses awaiting sale.[24]

Immediately after the battle of Bull Run, Major General George B. McClellan had been called to Washington and given command of all Union forces in the vicinity, to reorganize them and shape them into the Army of the Potomac. McClellan had a brilliant military reputation at the moment and was hailed as the "Young Napoleon." He had graduated second in his class at West Point, served with distinction in the Mexican War, been a military observer of European tactics during the Crimean War, and won the Union army's only victory to date by beating a small Confederate army at Rich Mountain in western Virginia. McClellan was charged to make the Union army around Washington into a real fighting force. As summer passed into fall, the Garibaldians remained in Blenker's brigade, but now they found themselves reorganized into Brigadier General Joseph Hooker's division of the Army of the Potomac, where they would stay until January 1862.

The *Boston Pioneer* called the German troops in Blenker's brigade "Attila's Huns," and the Garibaldi Guard was maligned by association. While the Nativist press scorned the "Dutch" regiments, McClellan enjoyed Blenker's foreign troops, thinking of them as elaborate showpieces in his army. On his many visits to their encampments, McClellan would see Blenker among his polyglot collection of officers awaiting him and ceremoniously shout, "Ordinaz numero

Frederick G. D'Utassy, circa 1861.

Eins!" Champagne corks would pop, exotic foods would be served, and Principal Musician Luigi Adamoli of the Garibaldians would have the band play Italian, German, and French marches for the general. McClellan's own writing about the immigrant soldiers reflected his lack of real knowledge about them, his reliance on stereotypes, and his own inherent, smug sense of American superiority:

> [Most] remarkable of all was the Garibaldi Regiment. Its Colonel, D'Utassy, was a Hungarian, and was said to have been a rider in Franconi's Circus.... His men were from all known and unknown lands, from all possible and impossible armies: Zouaves from Algiers, men of the "Foreign Legion," Zephyrs, Cossacks, Garibaldians of the deepest dye, English deserters, Sepoys, Turcos, Croats, Swiss, Beer-Drinkers from Bavaria, stout men from North Germany, and no doubt Chinese, Esquimaux, from the army of the Grand Duchess of Gerolstein. Such a mixture was probably never before seen under any flag, unless, perhaps in such bands as Holk's Jagers of the Thirty Years' War, or the Free Lances of the Middle Ages. I well remember that in returning at night from beyond the picket lines I encountered an outpost of the Garibaldians. In reply to their challenge I tried English, French, Spanish, Italian, German, Indian, a little Russian, and Turkish; all in vain, for nothing at my disposal made the slightest impression upon them and I inferred that they were perhaps Gypsies or Esquimaux or Chinese. Most of the officers thus obtained had left their own armies for the armies' good, although there were admirable and honorable exceptions, such as [Luigi] Cesnola, and some others. Few were of the slightest use to us, and I think the reason why the German regiments so seldom turned out well was that their officers were so often men without character.[25]

As 1861 wound down and everyone settled into winter quarters, the Garibaldi Guard remained in a state of turmoil. Captain Edward Venuti, a veteran of the Red Shirts, became the new captain of Company H. A hotheaded corporal in the Italian company, Giacomo Antonali, was reduced to private for threatening the life of a cook. The food must have been very bad, for Antonali was known to be a loner and kept to himself when not on duty. Official word came that Captain Francis Takats of the Hungarian company resigned. Five more men from the Spanish company deserted. Captain Joseph Torrens of the Spanish company resigned to take a position as captain in another multi-ethnic regiment, the "Enfants Perdus" New York Light Infantry. Within three months sixteen men would desert and follow their captain to his new company.[26] Gustav Wiener, a New York recruiter for the Guard, contacted Bernhard Baer, the former captain of Company I, to coax him into taking a commission to replace Torrens. Baer agreed and re-enrolled; Wiener went on a New Year's Eve spree and never returned to the recruiting office in

Frederick D'Utassy, circa 1861.

U.S. Army Military Institute

New York. Ten more men deserted in December. In late December Dr. Leopold Zander resigned his commission as surgeon, bringing the total loss of doctors since August to four. The Garibaldians ended the year at a strength of nine hundred five officers and men, fifty-five more than when they left New York.

D'Utassy was as villainous as ever. On Thursday, November 21, he ordered Montegrifa to give him $300 for regimental expenses.[27] Six days later, D'Utassy presented a bill of $3,265.40 to Lieutenant Elwood, an agent of the paymaster of the United States government, for reimbursement of expenses D'Utassy incurred in recruiting his regiment, to include the rent for the recruiting offices and subsistence of recruits. As a precaution, Elwood had D'Utassy sign a sworn affidavit before a notary public in Washington, certifying that the account was correct and that the services were rendered as stated. Elwood paid D'Utassy in full and notified his superiors.[28] Colonel Henry Steel Olcott, Special Commissioner to Investigate Military Expenditures, was assigned to watch D'Utassy's actions from now on. That same day D'Utassy ordered the regimental band members' names to be placed on the payrolls of different companies for the months of September and October 1861. Musicians Constant Casser, Francis Schreiber, Anton Unruh, Reinhold Hubner, Caspar Rohn, George Schreiber, Francis Hecker, Charles Weise, and Conrad Lang signed powers of attorney giving D'Utassy the right to collect their back pay from the time they enlisted. Then he drew their fraudulent back pay, plus the back pay of another musician, John Rohn, the sum of $26 per man, from the U.S. paymaster. The soldiers had to pay the extra money back to D'Utassy as interest, and he collected $260 for their phantom services, willfully cheating his own men.[29] The year ended with yet more colorful, outrageous rumors circulating about D'Utassy. Supposedly, he corresponded with a Confederate newspaper editor, exchanging information through certain females who visited him regularly. And he was supposedly paying off high officials in Washington for a brigadier general's commission—which hardly sounded like a rumor in D'Utassy's case.

Chapter Four

SOUTH TO NORTH ON THE SHENANDOAH

We scraped out a grave, and he dreamlessly sleeps
  On the banks of the Shenandoah River;
His home or his kindred alike are unknown,
  His reward in the hands of the Giver.
We placed a rough board at the head of his grave,
  "And we left him alone in his glory,"
But on it we marked ere we turned from the spot,
  The little we knew of his story....

—Grant P. Robinson

THE start of 1862 found the Garibaldi Guard in Brigadier General Julius Stahel's brigade of what was now Blenker's division, in the Army of the Potomac. Stahel, a Hungarian, had served with Kossuth in the 1848 revolution, fled to Berlin, London, and then New York where he established himself as a newspaperman. At the start of the war Blenker made him lieutenant colonel of his regiment, the 8th New York, and later gave him the command of the 1st Brigade in his division. D'Utassy coveted that position and held Blenker in contempt for passing him over. The resentment would fester into open conflict.[1]

Stahel's Brigade was composed entirely of regiments in which the men were foreign born, most of whom were Germans. Throughout the war the German and Prussian volunteers in the Union army exceeded two hundred eighty thousand enlisted men and officers. As mentioned earlier, six of the ten companies of the Garibaldi Guard were composed of men from the various Prussian states. The German-born editors of the foreign press reported that

72

"the Nativist Press (the *New York Tribune* and the *Pioneer*) accused those foreigners with commands in the army, such as Louis Blenker, of being a swindler" and that the men in his division were called "Hungry Junkers," "Attila's Huns," and "European Saber Rattlers" to discredit them."[2] The Germans concluded that this anti-Dutch ["Deutsch," German for "German"] sentiment of Know-Nothing party political reactionaries, who loathed immigrants, was an attempt to scapegoat the Germans for the incompetence of native generals and colonels. The French were subject to bad press as well. *New York Tribune* correspondents characterized the French "Gardes Lafayette," the 55th New York Infantry, at the battle of Fair Oaks, Virginia on Saturday, May 31, 1862, as foreign-born "cowards." The French American press was indignant at the prejudice directed at the soldiers, explaining that a major portion of them were good soldiers who had seen action in the Crimean Conflict.[3]

The year 1862 began with more personnel turbulence. On Saturday, January 4, Second Lieutenant Charles Hoffman of Company A promoted to first lieutenant and transferred to Company B; Sergeant Major Charles Galluba was promoted to second lieutenant to replace him, and Sergeant Bernhard Pollak was promoted to first sergeant of Company F. On January 8, Lieutenants Henry Lindner and Charles Zimmerman, of Companies K and E respectively, were discharged for disability. First Sergeant Louis Riege of Company K was promoted to second lieutenant and transferred to Company E. Sergeant Franz Weinberger was promoted to first sergeant; Corporal Philipp Washeim was promoted to sergeant. Eight days later, Second Lieutenant Bennett, Company F, and Private Alphonse Pasquet, Company D, were promoted to first lieutenant. On Friday, January 24, Major Wiegand was discharged; his bought promotion had lasted barely six months. First Lieutenant Charles Ruelberg of the Swiss company was also discharged. In Company D, Corporal Heinrich Dietrich was promoted to second lieutenant, Sergeant Emil Joerin was promoted to first sergeant, Corporal Jacob Cordet was promoted to sergeant, and Private Bernhard Duesberg transferred in from Company A as a sergeant. Captain Anthony Weekey was given command of Company F.

Eight days later, on February 1, Weekey was promoted to major. A Hungarian, a brother of one of Kossuth's trusted men, he had practiced law and fought in the 1848–49 Hungarian Revolution as a first lieutenant under Kossuth. In 1850 he emigrated to the United States; then he entered the Garibaldi Guard as a first lieutenant on the original muster, making himself one of the regiment's surviving original officers. On February 2, Second Lieutenant Anton Schada was transferred from Company H to D and promoted to first lieutenant. Corporal Francisco Gutienes was transferred from Company I to C to replace Corporal Verdier, who deserted at the same time as Corporals Wilhelm Utzl and Jacob Seip of Company E (Seip returned to the ranks and was demoted). Private Joseph Wachter was promoted to corporal. Sergeant Jean Beaudoir, Company G, simply disappeared from the record. On Monday, Feb-

ruary 10, D'Utassy sold another government-owned horse. The next day he
ordered his band members' names to be placed on various companies' payrolls to draw pay as soldiers as well as musicians, this time for November and
December. Caspar Rohn, the band leader, Constant Casser, Frank Leifels,
Casper and John Ellenberger, Conrad Lang, Charles Weise, Francis Hecker,
Reinold Huboner, George Schreiber, and Anton Unruh never saw a cent of
their fraudulent soldier's pay; D'Utassy collected it.

Unruh disclosed the double payroll swindle to Chaplain Zyla and asked
him for help. Zyla questioned D'Utassy about it; he became infuriated and
menaced Zyla, then challenged him to a duel. When Zyla refused, D'Utassy
had him arrested and held in close confinement.[4] On February 18, D'Utassy
himself was arrested by order of General Blenker on suspicion of being
connected either directly or indirectly with the publication of certain articles, derogatory to Blenker, which had appeared in the German papers,
similar to the anti-German comments in the nativist press. General McClellan
ordered D'Utassy to Washington and confined to quarters until March 18,
the date of his court-martial. Repetti assumed command of the regiment.

The month of March for the Garibaldi Guard began with still more personnel shifts. First Lieutenant Victor Leseine, Company G, reported to Company B, where Corporal George Bonin was promoted to sergeant. Captain
Venuti, Company H, joined Company C, where Sergeant Ferdinando Maggi
was promoted to first sergeant and Private Olivry was promoted to corporal.
Captain Niedzielski from Company C, First Lieutenant Alphonse Pasquet from
Company F, and Corporal Gottlieb Andreas from Company B all went to Company H. Second Lieutenant Juan Castillo transferred from Company K to I,
which also mustered in Red Shirt Erciole Salviatti as its captain. Second Lieutenants Giovanni Boggialli, Company G, and Charles Hoffman, Company B,
switched to Company K. Second Lieutenant Charles Galluba transferred from
Company A to E, and Second Lieutenant Bernhard Franz transferred from
Company K to F.

On Tuesday, March 18, D'Utassy went on trial in Washington. He was
accused of being the source of the disparaging remarks made to the press
regarding Blenker and his "foreign division's" alleged criminal activities.
There was a direct line from D'Utassy to the *New York Tribune* for the flow
of derogatory press. William Kent, a correspondent for the newspaper, was
employed as D'Utassy's private secretary. Kent, a newsman at the right place
at the right time, used his position to gather information around the camps
and send it to his editor. (This would catch up with him in July 1864, when
Major General Winfield Scott Hancock complained about Kent's "[f]alse
and Injurious statements of the army now in the field." Major General George
G. Meade permanently revoked Kent's passes to the Union army then operating around Richmond for abusing his privileges, stating that he published
articles "full of malicious falsehoods and should be punished for it!") Blenker
was vindicated of all charges. D'Utassy was released from arrest, never dream-

ing his own criminal activities were under investigation. By Saturday, March 22, he was in need of funds to sustain himself properly, and he appropriated $100 from the regimental sutler once again. He remained in Washington to attend a gala party put on by Hungarian officers and civilians in the city to celebrate the anniversary of the Revolution of 1848 and Garibaldi's birthday (a little premature since it was on July 4). Among other guests, D'Utassy mingled with Colonels Philip Figyelmesy, Edward Detshy, and Anselm Albert, late of Major General John C. Fremont's staff, Major Charles Zagony, and Captains Sarpy, Dsinka, and Emeric Szabad, the aide-de-camp of Brigadier General Daniel Edgar Sickles, a New York lawyer and legislator who left his seat in the U.S. House of Representatives for a star and command of New York's Excelsior Brigade.

On March 17, McClellan's army began to embark at Alexandria for Fort Monroe, Virginia, on its way to capture the Confederate capital at Richmond with an attack northwest up the Virginia Peninsula. Several units remained around Washington to protect the city, to include the Garibaldi Guard. On March 27, the Garibaldians served as advance guard for the army's movement that day, and in the evening five of the ten companies were ordered out for another twenty-four hours of picket duty. Another company reported for Headquarters duty. The remaining four companies, "having furnished the line of skirmishers during the whole march," were too tired to leave their bivouac, so Repetti ensured that he, Weekey, and Bacon made the rounds of the regiment's picket lines every two hours to make sure order prevailed. The regiment faced an obvious communication problem. Though D'Utassy could communicate in the various languages of his regiment, his officers could not. This inevitably led to trouble in things like picket duty; an officer could put a foreign-speaking soldier on picket duty and instruct him to call out the sign and receive the countersign, and the soldier would act like he understood his instructions fully, responding "Yes, yes!," but as soon as anyone approached the picket line, the soldier was as apt as not to shoot first and then shout out the sign afterwards.

The regiment's camp was located in a neighborhood of Washington, D.C. One day civilians living near the camp started a fight with several Garibaldians who were off duty in the camp at the time. Two companies turned out to join in the brawl, and it turned into a riot. In retaliation the Garibaldians looted, plundered, and undoubtedly trampled a few of the residents' gardens. The Garibaldians and Repetti were blamed for the disorder. On March 29, Major General Edwin V. Sumner, his corps commander, arrested Repetti for neglect of duty in permitting his regiment to run amok. D'Utassy, still in Washington, reported to the *New York Herald* that it was Repetti who was arrested for the riot, not himself. Upon hearing about the riot, Hancock remarked that he was not at all surprised to hear one of the Garibaldian companies had mutinied, no more than he would have been to hear it had performed heroically in some action.[5] On March 31, Repetti was taken under arrest to Headquarters for trial. Weekey, gravely ill, was hospitalized in Winchester, Virginia. D'Utassy intercepted Weekey's mail and read it in the hope of uncovering enemies within his command. With one major resigned and the other one sick, the colonel had already picked the next man in line for major, Captain Charles Schwarz of Company A, one of his allies since the mutiny at the Long Bridge.

Major General John Charles Fremont commanded the newly formed Mountain Department, which included the mountains that form the west flank of the Shenandoah Valley and the east side of West Virginia, a state carved out of Virginia by Union sympathizers who refused to secede in 1861. The Shenandoah Valley did not lead to anywhere special as far as Union advances were concerned, but for the Confederates it exposed Union railroad lines at Harpers Ferry and opened the back door to Washington defenses, and that worried President Lincoln, so Fremont was put out there to help protect things. Pathfinder, hero of the Mexican War, and 1856 presidential candidate of the new Republican Party, Fremont had been strongly supported for election by abolitionists and German-Americans in what was now the 48th Pennsylvania Infantry. He respected the German-Americans so much that throughout this war he would keep an entourage of German and Hungarian officers on his staff.[6]

Fremont originally had a plan to invade East Tennessee, but it evaporated when Confederate forces moved into the Shenandoah Valley. At the end of March, Lincoln ordered Blenker's division, which reported 8,616 men present for duty, to leave McClellan's command and join Fremont in West Virginia. As part of Stahel's brigade, the Garibaldi Guard again marched off to war. Weekey remained in the hospital, Zyla was released from arrest, and Schwarz now commanded the regiment. Blenker was totally unfamiliar with the Shenandoah Valley. The march there lasted six weeks, and the foreign soldiers became notoriously known among the people of northern Virginia as "Blenker's Bummers." Neglected by the War Department, the soldiers set off without basic military necessities, including foul weather gear, and they suffered great hardship during cold, wet April days. Supplies gave out; hunger and an epidemic of dysentery set in. They were reduced to looting and thievery for what food they could gather to feed themselves. An unsympathetic brigade commander, Brigadier General Robert Huston Milroy, commented, "The Dutch brigades are composed of the most infernal robbers, plunder[er]s and thieves, I have ever seen, our army is disgraced by them. They straggle off from their companies and regiments for miles on each side of the road as we march along and enter every house, smokehouse, milk house, chicken house, kitchen, barn, corncrib, and stable and clean out everything, frequently open drawers, trunks, bureaus, etc. for plunder, leaving women and children crying behind them, but no tears or entreaties stop or affect them, the only answer they make is, 'Nix Forstay.'"

In the Garibaldi Guard, Private Miguel Oliver of Company I lived up to the reputation of "Blenker's Bummers." He actually boasted about his ma-

Charles Schwarz
Captain in Company C, 39th New York Volunteer Infantry, circa 1861. He replaced
Major Weekey as the regiment's major in 1862. He is dressed in Garibaldi Guards
fatigues, consisting of a red shirt and scarf, and the Bersaglieri-type hat with cock
feathers and the G.G. insignia.

rauding. When he and his gang, Juan Rodriguez, Manuel Guetierrez, and Manuel Jacoma went out on a spree, they would speak French or call themselves Frenchmen. Traveling from Alexandria to Hunter's Chapel, Virginia, they met a man and a woman on the road. Oliver and one accomplice caught the woman, the other two caught the man, and they demanded their money. When the woman denied that she had any, Oliver and the other soldier insulted and menaced her, and then threw her down on the road and searched her. They left her there while her companion, still restrained by the other two, broke down and cried. Another tactic was to wait for payday and lay in wait for soldiers who spent their time drinking at the sutler's tent. Oliver would chose likely victims, and then the gang would beat up the inebriated soldiers and rob them. On another occasion Oliver and an accomplice went to a farmhouse, knocked on the door, and asked the young woman who answered for something to eat. A man who seemed to be her father was in the house with her. The man refused to give them anything. Oliver and the other soldier forced their way inside and searched the house. He denounced the woman, saying, "You refuse to give me anything to eat, now I want your money." Oliver searched her, taking the money she had. When the woman began to cry, Oliver slapped her. The man cried out for help, saying, "You have all my money. I am a poor man." Oliver struck him with the butt of his gun, knocking him down. Getting what they wanted, the two soldiers ran away. Oliver went so far as to boast about several murders he had committed, even revealing his involvement in a plot to assassinate Repetti.[7]

On April 28, Weekey died in the hospital at Winchester. Sergeant Julius Hintze of Company A and three men from Company C, Raphael Castelbecchi, Francesco Luraschi, and Giuseppe Raggio, deserted from picket duty. On Thursday, May 1, while D'Utassy remained in Washington, he promoted Captain Schwarz to be the new major, the Guard's fourth. On Wednesday, May 14, Blenker's division finally arrived at Fremont's headquarters at Franklin, (West) Virginia, with 7,885 men present for duty, 731 fewer than it had reported upon leaving camp at Washington six weeks earlier. An editorial in *L'Eco d'Italia* that appeared during Blenker's horrendous march deplored the regiment's bad reputation from plundering, "that because of a few admittedly bad apples, the reputation of the whole regiment and division was slandered." The paper reported later that "[Major] General [William S.] Rosecrans obtained food, clothes, medicine and horse fodder for the regiments of the Blenker's Division, including the Garibaldi Guard." The month ended with yet more personnel moves. On May 29, First Lieutenants Emil Hollinde, Company A, and John F. Bauer, Company E, were promoted to captain Companies D and F, respectively. Sergeant Magnus Bader was moved from Company F to I, and Corporal Franz Wilhelmi, Company H, was promoted to sergeant upon Sergeant Henry Lindner's discharge for disability. Adjutant Charles G. Bacon became a second lieutenant in Company D, which saw Second Lieutenant Bernhard Franz become a first lieutenant in Company K.

On Friday, May 30, Fremont received orders from Lincoln and Secretary of War Edwin M. Stanton to trap Major General Thomas J. "Stonewall" Jackson and his Confederate army. Jackson's victories against Union forces had taken him all the way down the Shenandoah Valley to Harpers Ferry. Lincoln ordered McDowell, who became a corps commander when McClellan replaced him as army commander, to go west instead of joining McClellan on the Virginia Peninsula. Fremont was to converge rapidly with McDowell at Strasburg, a town several miles southwest of Harpers Ferry, farther up the valley on Jackson's escape route. He could be cut off and defeated. But Jackson beat everyone to Strasburg, and McDowell and Fremont had to chase him. From June 1 through 5, the race was on. The Confederate rear guard destroyed bridges over rain-swollen streams; Fremont's soldiers built and crossed safely over pontoon bridges, retook the trail, and pushed steadily forward, pursuing the enemy. Progress was delayed by burned and blazing culverts which the Confederates had set aflame along the road, but Fremont kept getting closer. Federals passed deserted Confederate camps where cooking fires were still burning. When the Garibaldians bivouacked beyond New Market, Castelbecchi and Hintze returned to the ranks. Carl D'Utassy, the colonel's brother, arrived from Hungary and mustered in as a second lieutenant in Company C.

On Friday, June 6, Fremont regained contact with the enemy with an early, rapid march near Harrisonburg. Sharp artillery and cavalry skirmishing began again at midmorning. At about 2:00 P.M. the Union advance drove the Confederate rear guard through Harrisonburg. The Union forces encamped around the town with the intention of resuming pursuit in the morning. Later that afternoon, Fremont sent out scouts from the 1st New Jersey Cavalry with a battalion of the 4th New York Cavalry, Luigi Palma Di Cesnola's unit. Confederates surprised the cavalrymen and drove back the 4th New York with serious losses, capturing Captains Shelmire, Clark, and Haines, and the unit's colonel, Sir Percy Wyndham.[8] Wyndham was a genuine mercenary who had spent five years in the French navy and eight in the Austrian army, the same former English Garibaldini whom King Victor Emmanuel II knighted for his performance in Sicily during the battle for Milazzo. Chatham Roberdeau Wheat of the 1st Louisiana Tigers welcomed Wyndham, who was soon paroled and returned to service, into the Confederates' lines with an explanation that he too had fought alongside Garibaldi in Italy.[9]

Fremont's advance parties and Jackson's rear guard had been clashing frequently for five days now. Slightly before sundown, Brigadier General George D. Bayard entered the woods southeast of Harrisonburg, in the direction of a village called Cross Keys, with the 1st Pennsylvania Cavalry and four companies of Kanes's Rifles, the "Bucktails."[10] Almost immediately after getting into the timber, the Rifles encountered a regiment of enemy cavalry with artillery and a regiment of infantry, from which they received very damaging fire. A severe half-hour engagement followed, during which the Rifles suffered nearly forty men and officers killed, wounded, and missing. Colonel Gustave Cluseret, a former Garibaldini who commanded the French Legion during the Italian wars and was breveted for gallantry at Capua, brought his brigade, which now included the Garibaldi Guard, forward to support the Rifles. The continuing clash resulted in the death of Colonel Turner Ashby, one of the South's most promising cavalry officers. It was a serious blow to the Confederates, who retreated in disorder, leaving their camp, their wounded, and their dead in the Federals' possession. As darkness grew, the Union advance troops continued their assault, the Confederate rear guard its retreat.

By Saturday, June 7, Confederates under Major General Richard Stoddert Ewell occupied a stronghold just southeast of Cross Keys, where they commanded the roads and a bridge to nearby Port Republic. They had the advantage of knowing the area. Their main line was advantageously posted upon a ridge, protected in front by a steep downward slope, almost entirely masked by thick woods, and covered by fences. They massed their artillery near their center and on the summit of an abrupt ascent close to a marshy creek, where it exposed any attackers to crossfire and flank attacks that could drive them onto unfamiliar ground. This made any attack very risky. Although he outnumbered Ewell nearly two to one, Fremont thought that the Confederates outnumbered him and that both of their flanks overlapped his flanks. Fremont lacked reliable maps or guides, but he judged that the Confederates' right flank was the strategic side. He decided to press them from that side, with the object of seizing their line of retreat, so he weighted his brigades to his left flank. The Garibaldi Guard was one of the left flank units, so now it had a good chance of seeing battle. Fremont sent Brigadier General Robert Milroy on a reconnaissance in force southwest, directly towards Cross Keys and Port Republic, while other scouts pushed out to his flanks. One scouting party pushed east to Keezletown and McGaheysville; another pushed south on the Staunton Turnpike to the Middle River. After his scouts found that the bridges both east and south had been destroyed, Fremont concluded that Jackson had headed toward Port Republic and might be about to dispute the Union advance.

On Sunday, June 8, Fremont resumed his march, taking the road directly through the woods from Harrisonburg to Cross Keys. Cluseret's brigade, consisting of the 16th Ohio and the 8th [West] Virginia, reinforced by the Guard, formed the vanguard of the Federal advance. The brigade came upon Confederates at a point near Union Church about 9:00 A.M. and immediately engaged them. The Confederates fell back through timber and across open ground for about a mile, with Cluseret in hot pursuit. He advanced until he reached a spot where the firing became continuous, and he concluded that he faced Jackson's main force, drawn up in battle order. Cluseret's brigade kept up continuous firing against the Confederates while Fremont deployed his army from its line of march into a line of battle directly in front of Ewell's positions. The battle of Cross Keys was about to begin.

As Cluseret's brigade fixed the enemy to its front with its weapons fire, it became a natural pivot point for the deployment of Fremont's army. Stahel's brigade passed from the line of march over to Cluseret's left flank, and Blenker's division, with Bohlen's brigade in reserve, became Fremont's weighted left flank. Brigadier General Robert C. Schenck's brigade moved from its march to Cluseret's right flank and became the center of Fremont's line of battle, where it would constitute the reserve. Milroy's brigade came up on Schenck's right to anchor the Union's right flank. Schenck's cavalry guarded that flank while Colonel Christian F. Dickel's 4th New York Cavalry guarded the left flank, and Captain Conger's company guarded Fremont's headquarters itself. When the line was ready, Fremont ordered Blenker to attack. Stahel and Cluseret ordered their men forward, and the Garibaldi Guard became hotly engaged under heavy fire that lasted from noon until 4:00 P.M.

Captain Hildebrandt of Company G commanded the five skirmishing companies of the Garibaldi Guard. If any officer in the Guard had the ability and courage to lead men, it was Hilderbrandt, an officer in Hungary's 1849 war for independence and a veteran of Garibaldi's Sicilian campaigns who stayed with the general when they victoriously entered Rome. Now it was time for the Guard to prove itself. The Confederate position was most advantageously situated, and the Garibaldians had to attack through woods, across a marshy creek, over fences, and uphill. Captain Venuti led the lead company, Company C. The moment the Garibaldians were ordered to charge, they immediately rushed in like lions to the assault with shouts of "Viva Garibaldi, Vive L'Unione" and a spirited Bersaglieri style bayonet charge. Their fight began when the first line of attackers, waving the 1848 tri-color flag and led by Company C Sergeants Giovanni Ferralasco, Ferdinando Maggi, Luigi Roux, and Raphael Castelbecchi, reached the Confederate line. The Garibaldians used their bayonets freely and most effectively as the Confederate right was driven back in confusion.[11] Union canister shot tore gaps in the Confederate defenses. Cluseret's brigade, with the Garibaldi Guard, pushed the Confederates back upon themselves and firmly held a good forward position.

Venuti and Company C skirmished as far as they could go, until they occupied the woods around and behind the original Confederate position. Captain Hollinde's Company A had initially accompanied the five lead skirmish companies and supported them in driving Confederates out of the woods to their front till the heavy firing began, when the company halted to stand by as a local reserve force. At this time the firing to the left was hot and the smoke too thick to see through. Suddenly, Venuti and those around him, Corporal Antonio Godini, Giovanni Piccioni, Antonio Olivari and Jose Samaniego, fell wounded. Then Captain Junger's Swiss Company was hard hit. Karl Hockheimer was killed. First Lieutenant Albert Jordan, Sergeant Jacob Cordet, and Heinrich Krabell were all gravely wounded. In the confusion, Privates

Stephan Costa, Giovanni Guisti, Thomas Dragutinovich, and Giuseppe Gerazio (Geraci) and several other members of Company C became separated, lost sight of their company, and sought cover in a house. As intense enemy fire "got dangerously hot," Lieutenant Ornesi noticed the stragglers and went after them. Second Lieutenant Carl D'Utassy, the remaining officer of Company C and Colonel D'Utassy's brother, was nowhere to be found; momentum carried the officerless company past the house and ahead over two fences.

Sergeant Major Pollak was advancing behind Company C, when, as he testified later at the court-martial of Ornesi, he "thought he saw" Ornesi turn back and head toward the house. He reported this to Venuti, who was being carried back toward the field hospital. Venuti called out to Ornesi, "Save the honor of our company; if you, an officer behave in such a manner, what may be expected of a common soldier?" His words were lost in the surrounding roar of cannon and intense gunfire. Hildebrandt, seeing no company officer with Company C, ordered Pollak to take command and continue to advance. Pollak and Company C continued on through thick smoke and musket and cannon fire, which had become heavier than before. As Hollinde watched Venuti being carried off the field, "his uniform totally drenched with his blood," Colonel Leopold Von Gilsa of the 41st New York rode up and ordered Hollinde to take his reserve company and close up to the skirmishers. When Hollinde and Sergeant Eduardo Woodbury neared the house they saw Ornesi acting "like he was afraid of bullets." Hollinde called immediately for Ornesi to go forward to his company, telling him he "could have no control of the men at the place where he was." Ornesi yelled at the gathering stragglers, and everyone but Costa, Guisti, Dragutinovich, Gerazio, and Ornesi subsequently rejoined the company. Ornesi led the other four to the right into the woods, where they met Lieutenant Frizone of Company D with more stragglers. They halted near the field hospital. Dragutinovich found a full haversack, and they thought they were near the rest of the regiment.[12]

Stahel advanced forward on the main road and turned sharply to the right, and formed in upon Cluseret's right, becoming the right of the first line of soldiers. Stahel's men encountered a strong line of Confederate skirmishers in the first belt of woods, but the hard fighting of the 8th and 45th New York pushed them out across the open ground lying in front of the main Confederate line. There the Federals met the troops of Brigadier General Isaac R. Trimble's brigade, with its 15th and 16th Alabama, 21st North Carolina, 21st Georgia, and 16th Mississippi. The woods had diverted Stahel's best regiments, the 27th Pennsylvania and the 41st New York, to the right, and the shock of the entire battle was sustained by the 45th and the 8th, principally by the 8th, Blenker's Germans, which was attacked in front and flank by four enemy regiments. The 8th charged into the Confederate ranks and for a time held its position, but against superior numbers, it and the 45th were driven back over the open ground and through the woods upon Bohlen's brigade, which had advanced to support Stahel. Bohlen joined the action, supported by two batteries. Stahel's brigade took position in the open ground, forming the left of the first line.

The Confederates brought additional artillery up on the open ground on Fremont's extreme left, and Confederate Brigadier General Richard Taylor's reserve brigade entered the woods; the fighting continued with great severity all along the timber in front of the Federal position. The additional enemy artillery and fresh troops threatened to envelope Fremont's left. The Confederates retook the belt of woods they had lost at the beginning. Musket and artillery fire was incessant and fighting throughout the field generally severe. A bayonet charge by the 27th Pennsylvania countered a Mississippi regiment's Rebel yell charge upon one Union battery, and a counterfire of canister and grapeshot from another Union battery blasted a Louisiana regiment of Taylor's brigade that charged it, nearly destroying the regiment. Every effort of the Confederates to emerge from the cover of the woods was repulsed by artillery and infantry counterattacks, and the losses were very great. After an ineffective attempt at the Confederate batteries, Cluseret's brigade stubbornly held every foot of its advance ground, steadily repelling repeated Confederate assaults.

After further maneuvering and skirmishing, Fremont decided to re-establish his whole line in conformance with apparent enemy changes on his left, preparatory to a renewal of the battle. Accordingly, the brigades on the Union right were withdrawn for a space, and except for part of Cluseret's and the Garibaldi Guard's strong center position and for occasional artillery exchanges, the firing subsided, but not without the loss of many men. In the Garibaldi Guard's Company B, First Lieutenant Victor Leseine was killed, and Privates Valentine Gebel, Michael Hennout, and Jaques Bright were wounded and captured in action. The Confederates held their positions, and Union pickets securely occupied the points relinquished by their skirmishers.

To add to the Guard's difficulties, about 2:00 P.M., assistant surgeon Rudolph Ribbeck had been captured from the field hospital. Second Lieutenant Charles Galluba, the temporary quartermaster officer, was bringing back the ambulances with wounded from the battlefield. The wounded included men of Venuti's command and four other men, including Lieutenant Albert Jordan, who were dying from their wounds. About three-quarters of a mile from the front lines, in the woods, Galluba met Ornesi and Frizone with the stragglers. They asked him where the regiment was. The firing ahead of them was plainly audible, so he gave them no answer and drove on to the field hospital without stopping. Ornesi never did find the regiment that day and told his "lost patrol" to make camp. There were no encounters with the Confederates after night fell. The next morning, Major Waring, now with Fremont's Hussars, observed his old regiment: "As I saw it [Garibaldi Guard], as it came out of this first campaign, it was shorn of its cock feathers and of all its bravery of dress and drill. It was a rain drenched rabble of disorganized companies of many nationalities, huddled in the wet edge of a road-side wood."[13] The stragglers finally found the regiment. Major Schwarz asked Ornesi to explain himself, but he could not give a satisfactory answer. Schwarz placed him and Frizone under arrest.

Fremont noted that Stahel's brigade and the Garibaldi Guard had been in the hottest part of the battle. Union losses were approximately one hundred twenty-five dead and five hundred wounded. Many of the casualties were officers in Stahel's brigade, which lost five officers killed in action and seventeen wounded. The 8th New York buried sixty-five men alone. The Garibaldi Guard was the next hardest hit regiment. It suffered forty-four casualties: one officer and three men killed in action, one officer and five men dead of wounds received, twenty-two men wounded in action, and one officer and eleven men captured in action. In addition to the five companies originally sent forward as skirmishers, Companies E, F, and H suffered losses as well. In Company E alone, Corporal Albert Mehl was killed, two men died of wounds, three were wounded in action. The Garibaldians had to reorganize. Sergeant Adolph Lingner of Company H was promoted to first sergeant to replace Carl Menzel in Company B, who had been wounded. First Sergeant Carl Theodore Pausch of Company H was promoted to be its sergeant major. For taking over Company C, Sergeant Major Pollak, Company F, was promoted to second lieutenant in Company G. (Later Captain Niedzielski, Company H, would be transferred to Company C to replace Venuti.) For its action the Garibaldi Guard won special mention in Fremont's official report.

Early on June 9, the day after his battle at Cross Keys, Fremont resumed his march against the enemy, entering the woods in battle order. The Confederate cavalry appeared on his flanks. He found that the Confederates were in full retreat toward Port Republic, about four miles to the south. Confederate detachments were occupied in searching the grounds covered by the dead and wounded, and Fremont's advance on the enemy rear guard came on so suddenly that some Confederate officers still on the Federal side escaped with the loss of their horses. A cannonade during the forenoon apprised Fremont's forces of fighting. Across the South Fork of the Shenandoah River at Port Republic, Stonewall Jackson had attacked the two brigades of Brigadier General James Shields' division that had reached the area from the northeast, as part of the Union effort to trap Jackson. After a severe battle, Jackson drove Shields northeast down the river and pursued him. Fremont sent a cavalry detachment to open communications with Shields and in the meantime prepared to bridge the South Fork with pontoons.

On Friday, June 13, the court-martial of First Lieutenant Francesco Ornesi convened at Mount Jackson, Virginia, pursuant to Special Orders No. 60, Headquarters, Mountain Department, Blenker's Division, dated June 13, 1862. Lieutenant Colonel Cantador, 27th Pennsylvania Infantry, presided. Ornesi was charged with cowardice before the enemy and conduct unbecoming an officer. He pleaded not guilty. The court deliberated upon the evidence and found him guilty. Ornesi was sentenced to the loss of rank and honors, and was to be shot.

D'Utassy returned to the regiment just in time to intervene for the hapless Ornesi over the outcome of the case. What Ornesi might have paid D'Utassy, who sold commissions, for a revised verdict is unknown, but D'Utassy proceeded to counterfeit and forge the official record. He ordered Sergeant John Dessauer, who acted as a clerk, to make a new copy of the proceedings, including the charges, findings, sentences, and orders. The testimony of the witnesses for the prosecution conveniently covered a confused period when two lieutenants were caught away from their units, and officers who could have defended one lieutenant were either too wounded to testify or dead. Effacing the record was certainly impossible, but switching names was not. Instead of Ornesi, D'Utassy ordered Dessauer to put down Second Lieutenant Raphael Frizone as defendant and change the sentence to dishonorable discharge. Dessauer boldly protested the revisions to D'Utassy, but he was threatened enough to forge the court-martial proceedings as ordered. Then D'Utassy certified the forgery as a true and correct copy of the original proceedings. Frizone was dishonorably discharged from the service. Ten days later Ornesi and Frizone were both out of the army. The question of Lieutenant D'Utassy's whereabouts during the time in question evidently went unasked.

The Garibaldi Guard's leadership continued to change. On Sunday, June 13, Sergeant Major Emil Joerin of Company D paid $50 to the colonel to be promoted to second lieutenant in Company E. With his appointment, Joerin transferred out of the regiment to the 15th Artillery as an officer. Jordan died of his wounds from Cross Keys, and Second Lieutenant Bernhard Franz transferred from Company K to take his place. Sergeant Jacob Hafeli was promoted to first sergeant, Company D. In Company C, First Sergeant Cesare Cavrotti was reduced to sergeant, and Corporal Silvio Ronzone was promoted to take his place. On June 16, Lieutenant Galluba of Company E was promoted to first lieutenant. Three days later, a Thursday, Repetti, alone in Washington, bitter, angry, and mortified, went to answer charges of neglect of duty in the Washington, D.C. riot incident for which he had been arrested on March 29. Shocked when he heard the charges against him, he realized that it was his own name being dragged through the mud.[14] He wrote to General Sumner, "I have undergone the punishment [a long arrest] which you have thought fit to inflict upon me. My Regiment has also suffered the punishment you ordered, and this without murmuring, as is the duty of every good soldier. But if it is the soldier's duty to obey, it is also his right to protest after the punishment when he thinks he has been wrongfully dealt with...it is usage in every country to make an investigation before punishing...and this has not been done, neither against my Regiment, nor against myself. Whereas, this is the first time I have ever been put in arrest during my whole military career of over eighteen years having gained my position rank after rank in the service of the Swiss Confederacy, my country, and whereas the whole regiment is to be punished for offenses which are not to be done by him, you will not find it strange that...I beg you to accept my resignation."[15] In Special Orders No. 139 from the War Department, Item 13 states, "Lieutenant Colonel Alexander Repetti, of the 39th Regiment New York Volunteers, (Garibaldi Guard), having tendered his resignation, is discharged [from] the service, to take effect this date." Repetti returned to his home in Genoa and faded out of the picture for the time being.

D'Utassy confiscated everything of Repetti's he could get his hands on, including Repetti's writing desk, which contained valuable documents. D'Utassy broke open the desk and took the papers for himself; then he ordered Private Dan Koester, the regimental carpenter, to repair the broken desk and paint it a different color to make it unrecognizable. D'Utassy used it until the end of his service in the regiment. Major Schwarz was promoted to lieutenant colonel to replace Repetti, and Captain Hugo Hildebrandt became a major to replace Schwarz.

On Monday, June 23, the Guard camped near Romney, (West) Virginia. Now the Mountain Department provost marshal, D'Utassy received payments of $100 and $125 from a regimental sutler. He found out that a member of the band had told Chaplain Zyla about the list of counterfeit payroll reports. Therefore, he had the entire band mustered out that same day to rid himself of any potential witnesses against him. At this time Sergeant Dessauer refused orders to falsify another month of regimental payrolls. After the Ornesi incident, this second disloyal act convinced D'Utassy that Dessauer was untrustworthy. Soon afterward when he sought a lieutenant's commission, D'Utassy deprived him of the promotion by making malicious misrepresentations about him. More evidently less threatening men were promoted instead: Christian Enke was promoted from second lieutenant in Company B to first lieutenant in Company C. In Company A, Corporal Friedrich Dress was promoted to sergeant, and First Sergeant Rudolph Schwickhardi went to second lieutenant in Company B.

On Thursday, June 26, for their failure to defeat Jackson, President Lincoln ordered the independent commands of Fremont, Banks, and McDowell, which included Shields, to be consolidated into the Army of Virginia under the command of Major General John Pope. Fremont refused to serve under Pope and was relieved on June 28 by Major General Franz Sigel. Blenker saw no further action after Cross Keys and was ordered to Washington, where he was relieved of his command. The Garibaldi Guard was assigned to the 3rd Brigade, led by Colonel Julius White, of the 1st Division, I Corps, Pope's Army of Virginia, at Winchester, Virginia. Duty at Winchester would last from July to September, when they would battle Jackson again at Harpers Ferry.

The Garibaldi Guard began its second summer at war. On June 30, Captain Junger was discharged from Company D. On Tuesday, July 1,

Doctor Franklin, the acting regimental surgeon, was arrested for refusing to obey orders and resigned. Private Adolph Bauer was promoted to hospital steward, and Second Lieutenant Louis Rieger, Company E, was promoted to first lieutenant, Company B. Sergeant Leonard Doerndinger, Company F, was promoted to first sergeant, and Second Lieutenant Juan Ruize y Castillo, Company I, was promoted to first lieutenant in Company K. Still recovering from his wounds, Venuti was transferred to Company C and then to G. On July 4, a Friday, First Sergeant Carl Menzel was discharged for wounds from Company B, and Sergeant Gustav Raefle was promoted to first sergeant to replace him. Ten days later, Corporal Louis Riedel became a sergeant in Company A. Sergeant Louis Willing from Company I was captured on July 15. On Thursday, July 24, in the same company, Sergeant Woodbury was promoted to first sergeant and Corporal Aljandro Calvo was discharged for disabilities. Second Lieutenant Rogella Gerranna briefly appeared on the rolls as an unassigned officer (maybe D'Utassy wanted to collect his pay for him!). Captain Conrad Von Schondorf resigned, and First Lieutenant Charles Hoffman was promoted to captain Company K in his place. Second Lieutenant Boggialli was discharged from Company K for disabilities. While camped near Middletown, Virginia, regimental elements engaged in a small skirmish. Two Garibaldians were wounded by gunfire and four were missing in action, including Philip Winter of Company K.

Captain Victor Chandone became the Garibaldi Guard's recruiting officer in New York on Saturday, July 26. The regiment had an office at the corner of North 53rd and Franklin Streets that was open daily from 9:00 A.M. to 4:00 P.M. The regiment took out advertisements in all the foreign papers. One advertisement appearing in *L'Eco Italia* called for the enlistment of one hundred men. Charles Edward Zerdahelyi was a most notable man who answered the regiment's call. A distinguished Hungarian pianist, pupil of Franz Liszt, and acquaintance of violinist Edward Rememyi, Zerdahelyi had resided in Vienna and personally knew Kossuth, Garibaldi, Mazzini, Thomas Babington Macaulay (famed British historian noted for his *History of England*), and William Ewart Gladstone (preeminent British politician destined to be four times prime minister). When the Hungarian war of independence broke out, he had been appointed an officer. He was arrested by the Austrians and imprisoned for two years. Escaping to America, he became a popular member of Stearn's Hungarian Club in Boston.[16] On Wednesday, July 30, he enrolled as a second lieutenant in Company K, replacing the disabled Giovanni Boggialli.

That same evening, far to the south in Virginia, Miguel Oliver carefully watched an old Irish soldier of the 9th Vermont get drunk at the sutler's tent. When the soldier tried to buy more whiskey, he presented the sutler, Ramler, with a ten dollar Vermont bill. Ramler refused to take it and put the soldier's charge on account. The old fellow staggered off, back towards his camp. Oliver tailed him. Three days later Oliver tried to purchase some whiskey for himself with the very same Vermont bill. Ramler inquired where the Spaniard got the ten dollars, and when he received no answer, summoned Sergeant Major Theodore Pausch to his tent. Ramler explained to Pausch that Oliver was trying to change the old Irish soldier's bill, whereupon the Spaniard was placed under arrest and put in the guardhouse. Pausch reported the incident to Major Hildebrandt and Adjutant Bacon, who ordered him to keep the bill until given further orders. Shortly afterward, D'Utassy summoned Pausch to his headquarters and ordered him to surrender the ten dollar bill and release Oliver. D'Utassy told Pausch that he would hand over the money to the colonel of the 9th Vermont, but he was rankled by Ramler's actions regarding the ten dollars. Ramler owed D'Utassy one hundred dollars a month for the privilege of being sutler, which of course he could not pay; he could deliver only fifty dollars. D'Utassy ordered Pausch to have Ramler pack up and move out of the regimental area.

D'Utassy's paranoia grew and his search for enemies increased. He confiscated a large chest belonging to the Swiss company. He ordered Sergeant Major Pausch to break it open, claiming that there may be stolen goods hidden inside. D'Utassy removed everything the chest contained and gave Pausch a "Garibaldi" poncho that belonged to one of the Swiss soldiers. D'Utassy evidently thought twice about the matter, for soon afterward he told Pausch to return the poncho to its legal owner. Tampering with the mails was another way the colonel used to find out intimate information. Evidently suspicious of everyone and everything, he opened two private letters directed to First Lieutenant Anthony Schada, who at the time was under arrest and held in close confinement, charged with "suspicion."

August came, and on the 12th another sutler, Agostino Montegrifa, was discharged from the regiment for disability. Sergeant Julius Hintze of Company A was also discharged for disability, and Sergeant Magnus Bader of Company I became first sergeant of Company E. On August 14, Quartermaster Sergeant Subit was promoted to second lieutenant in Company I and Lieutenant Bacon, Company F, who had been acting as assistant adjutant, was appointed adjutant. First Lieutenant Ellis D. Lazelle resigned as regimental quartermaster, after serving as an officer for six months. Sergeant Leopold Sachs, Company B, was discharged for disability. Sergeant Carl Sutter, Company D, returned to ranks and was transferred to Company G. Sergeant Silvio Ronzone, Company C, was promoted to second lieutenant in Company K. At the end of August, First Sergeant Woodbury, Company I, was promoted to second lieutenant in Company A. Captain Venuti received a medical discharge for his wounds (in February 1863 he would enroll as a major in the 52nd New York Infantry). Lieutenant Colonel Schwarz was sent to the recruiting office in New York. Fifteen new recruits, mostly French, Spanish, and Italian sailors, were reported enrolled, although they remained unassigned to a company.

Some people had begun to think that things were not going as they should go, on either side of the Atlantic. In Italy, the pope still controlled

Rome, and Garibaldi was as determined as ever to liberate the city in the cause of Italian unification. While the Garibaldi Guard was chasing out Stonewall Jackson in America, Garibaldi went to Palermo, Sicily and recruited an expeditionary army of three thousand southern volunteers to chase the pope out of Rome. He traveled to Palermo, Sicily and recruited three thousand men. King Victor Emmanuel II sent General Alfonso Ferrero di la Marmora and General Enrico Cialdini with the Italian army and the Bersaglieri to stop him. On August 29, at 3:00 P.M. at Santo Stefano d'Aspromonte, at the toe of the peninsula, the two sides confronted each other, with the possibility of starting an Italian civil war hanging in the balance. Garibaldi ordered his men not to fire and went out to meet the other side in the open, when he was shot in the foot and the thigh. The two opposing forces attacked each other, resulting in forty-six casualties. Finally, Garibaldi surrendered to the King's forces and was imprisoned in Fortress Varignano at La Spezia, on Italy's northwest coast. Back across the Atlantic, success was equally elusive. On August 4, Lincoln had called on the states to enroll another three hundred thousand militia to serve nine months, with a threat to draft men if volunteers did not come forward.

In Virginia, several female friends of D'Utassy arrived at camp and were to be entertained by him in town. He called a meeting of several officers. He gathered together Chaplain Zyla, B Company's Captain Encke, First Lieutenant Hoffman, and Second Lieutenant Schwickhardi, G Company's Captain Baer and Second Lieutenant Pollak, and I Company's First Lieutenant Pasquet in a "court of honor" and informed them that they were to contribute $90 each, supposedly to be used for recruiting purposes in New York. Zyla protested. The colonel threatened to "break his neck!" and Zyla calmly replied, "In no other regiment would I have unnecessarily been imprisoned during 44 days, for the sake of my colonel; hence, before any Court composed of your officers, I shall keep silent like a brazen statue, but put me on the legal platform, that is to say before a General Court Martial and there you will hear me speak like Paul before Agrippa." D'Utassy threatened to "turn him out of the regiment." In order to rid himself of such a troublemaker, D'Utassy detailed Zyla to the post officer of the brigade, where he remained until Lieutenant Colonel Schwarz asked permission to have him sent back. This action prompted Zyla and Schwickhardi to begin piecing together evidence for charges against the colonel.[17]

Chapter Five

DEFENDING HARPERS FERRY

"I hear the distant thunder hum,
Maryland! My Maryland!
The Old Line's bugle, fife and drum,
Maryland! My Maryland!
She is not dead, not deaf, nor dumb—
Huzza! she spurns the Northern scum!
She breathes—she burns! she'll come! she'll come!
Maryland! My Maryland!"

— *J. R. Randall*

THE Union army's Maryland Campaign began on September 2, 1862.[1] The regiment marched from its camp near Winchester, Virginia to its camp at Harpers Ferry, where it became part of a force that was supposed to assure the safety of the Shenandoah Valley and protect the Baltimore & Ohio Railroad line that ran east to west through the town. Luigi Depicto and Dragutinovich, who was a defense witness at Ornesi's court-martial, went on a furlough in Baltimore and mysteriously disappeared. Miguel Oliver and his gang deserted and went into the rural area, robbing country folk they met.[2] Private Emile Steiger continued to wait anxiously for notification of his promotion to second assistant surgeon. D'Utassy held onto the papers and waited for Steiger to give him twenty-five dollars in order to receive his promotion. Unaware of the need for a bribe, Steiger would remain a private and not learn of his promotion until March of the next year.

On September 3, as General White and his brigade arrived at Harpers Ferry from Winchester, the Confederates were on the move toward western

90

Maryland. As usual, the Northern forces had very little idea of exactly where the Southerners were at the moment, but they had to be nearby (telegraph communications with Baltimore kept being interrupted), and commanders made decisions anyway. Colonel Miles, the Guard's division commander at Bull Run, now commanded the Federal garrison at Harpers Ferry. When he learned on September 4 that White's brigade had arrived, he immediately ordered White himself to Martinsburg to take command of the forces at his former position. D'Utassy, who had repaired to Baltimore days earlier because he was ailing and needed comfort (Hildebrandt led the Guard on its march to Harpers Ferry), rejoined the Guard now. He could scarcely contain himself when White appointed him acting commander of the brigade. He was closer to his dream of becoming a general than he had ever been before. At this point the brigade consisted of the 39th New York under D'Utassy, the 32nd Ohio under Colonel Thomas H. Ford, the 60th Ohio under Colonel William H. Trimble, the 9th Vermont under Colonel George Jerrison Stannard, with Rigby's and Potts' Indiana and Ohio batteries, respectively, the 1st Maryland Cavalry under Captain Charles Russell, and a Rhode Island cavalry battalion under Major Augustus Whitemore Corliss.

By September 5, Major Hildebrandt commanded six companies comprising two hundred sixty Garibaldians. He received orders late in the afternoon to prepare the regiment for a probable evacuation at night. D'Utassy had come up to the camp to find everything being made ready; even the quartermaster's goods and commissary stores were being packed. About 5:00 P.M., D'Utassy saw White and asked him, "General, you promised us a fight here; shall we have again to abandon the place?" White answered, "The first duty of a soldier is to obey, and we must leave; I have preemptory orders from the War Department." Nonetheless, the Guard and its brigade stayed at Harpers Ferry. White went to Martinsburg as ordered and assumed command of the forces there. Miles took command of the operations at Harpers Ferry. Colonel Ford took command of the forces on Maryland Heights, high bluffs at the south end of a long north-south mountain called Elk Ridge, that loomed over Harpers Ferry from across the Potomac River. Colonel Maulsby commanded the troops placed at Sandy Hook, an area along the Potomac's north shore at the southeastern foot of Maryland Heights, and at Solomon's Gap, a defile midway up Elk Ridge's eastern side, which led directly to the ridgetop road that ran straight onto the summit of Maryland Heights (later Maulsby's troops would move onto Maryland Heights' eastern slope of before evacuating those positions as well).

On September 4, Lee began crossing the Potomac near Leesburg, Virginia, down river from Harpers Ferry, and moving his army toward the town of Frederick, Maryland, destroyed the Monocacy Bridge to hinder anyone approaching his east flank. By September 7, his army of about fifty thousand infantry, artillery, and cavalrymen was completely on Northern soil, marching and singing "Maryland! My Maryland!" as it went in a futile effort to inspire

Marylanders to rise against the Union. Now Lee had Union troops on his rear flank at Martinsburg and the Garibaldi Guard and other Federal troops at Harpers Ferry behind him, almost on his lines of communication to Virginia. Lee evidently thought he could remove that threat before McClellan, who was notoriously slow and cautious, could march against him. So, Lee sent Stonewall Jackson off to drive the Federals from Martinsburg and capture Harpers Ferry, and then rejoin the main army, as the Confederates prepared to invade Pennsylvania.

On September 6, McClellan left Washington, under recently issued orders to conduct "active operations" against Lee, to drive the Confederates from Maryland. While McClellan cautiously marched northwest into Maryland, Miles made a passing effort to organize his position. On September 8, he asked D'Utassy to accompany Captain Von Sehlen onto Maryland Heights and make observations of the position. That evening D'Utassy reported to Miles:

> Headquarters First Brigade Miles Division, Camp White, Bolivar Heights, near Harper's Ferry.
>
> In obedience to your verbal orders to inspect the position of Maryland Heights and report to you accordingly, and to make such suggestions as I many deem beneficial to the interests of the service I have the honor to lay before you the annexed topographical sketch, and to state as follows: I left at 11:00 A.M., in company with Captain Von Sehlen. After having thoroughly inspected our position of present under command of Colonel Ford, I find it, in my judgement, almost impregnable, and so stated to Colonel Ford, who replied, "I know it, and certainly never will leave it." The heavy guns so happily posted as to control not only Loudoun Heights, but could very easily shell any enemy attempting to take position on Bolivar Heights, provided the trees, which are in the hollow to the right of Bolivar Heights, could be felled; for which I asked permission. I cannot but praise the general good arrangement of artillery. Would, however, suggest to have two of the four 20 pounder brass guns moved higher on the road leading to the so-called observatory, which Captain Von Sehlen tells me could be accomplished with facility. It is this section that should be properly supported by infantry, and a few additional abatis [obstacle of felled trees] be made, I feel convinced that no force whatever could possess itself of this position, which, as you so wisely suggested, is our main reliance. I deem the force at present under command of Colonel Ford amply sufficient; but am most willing to dispose of any of my regiments should you so desire, and consider it needful. Feeling proud of the confidence you have shown in me, I can assure you will find me at my post, as you found me at Bull Run, when first under your command.
>
> D'Utassy

When McClellan began his march into Maryland after Lee, he asked Major General Henry Wagner Halleck, now the Union army's general in chief, to order Miles and the Harpers Ferry garrison to join him at once. McClellan forever needed more troops than he had for his field army. Halleck told him no, apparently convinced that movement would be too difficult for Miles, who would have to defend himself until McClellan could relieve him. McClellan grandly telegraphed Miles: "Our army in motion. It is important that Harper's Ferry be held to the latest moment. The Government has the utmost confidence in you, and is ready to give you full credit for the defense it expects you to make." Miles responded, "Thanks for the confidence. Will do my best."

On September 10, D'Utassy received an order from Miles telling him to "Send a regiment to Maryland Heights immediately; ammunition, one or two day's rations, canteens quick!" On Friday, two days later, Colonel Ford asked Miles for reinforcements. Elements of the 32nd Ohio were located at various points on Maryland Heights; Ford's main force was located on the crest of the mountain near a lookout and slight breastwork of trees. Ford had requested axes and spades for his pioneers to construct solid defenses on the Heights, but all he got were twelve axes belonging to a Maryland regiment, so only the breastwork was built. Suddenly skirmishing began. Confederates drove in the forces at Solomon's Gap. Meanwhile, D'Utassy had ordered Hildebrandt to proceed to Maryland Heights early that morning to support Ford. Two companies were absent from the Guard; Hildebrandt had begged D'Utassy to lift the assignment or send him two other companies. D'Utassy gave him two companies from the 115th New York. Then D'Utassy ordered half the soldiers disarmed in order to replace their defective weapons with new ones. They turned in five hundred old guns and left without any new weapons! Together with the 126th New York and Lieutenant Colonel S. W. Downey's regiment from the Maryland Home Brigade, the Garibaldians and the two companies of the 115th New York arrived at 5:00 A.M. at Ford's headquarters. Ford had learned that there were two companies of exhausted Southerners in Solomon's Gap. He ordered Hildebrandt to reconnoiter as far as the Gap with six companies and take the Confederates prisoner, if possible.

Hildebrandt proceeded with four companies of Garibaldians and two from the 3rd Maryland Potomac Home Brigade, the latter two leading the way to the road toward the Gap. It was a very narrow road, and it was nearly impossible to ride a horse through the surrounding thicket. The cavalry pickets posted as lookouts told Hildebrandt that they had been driven in from their positions by a heavy force and had been shelled out of the gap. Hildebrandt disregarded this information because he had his orders. He sent out skirmishers immediately, but the woods were so thick that it was not possible to skirmish normally. When the Garibaldians neared the Heights, the two lead companies of skirmishers received very heavy fire. Hildebrandt drew up his column by its flank but could not advance against the large

Confederate force, so the Garibaldians withdrew and took a better position, to make a better stand if the enemy came after them. In this brush, two Marylanders and four Garibaldians were killed, and one was missing.

The Confederates remained in their position, and the Garibaldians held their position near the cavalry picket line. Soon they heard some firing on the ridge of the mountain. The Maryland pickets posted earlier on Maryland Heights to cover the Garibaldian flank were under attack. The Garibaldians went as a whole force and rescued the pickets, suffering another two killed, fifteen wounded, and one man missing. After a few hours Hildebrandt returned to camp with his command, reported his action to Colonel Ford, and stood by at Ford's headquarters. Then Hildebrandt and two companies of the Guard, with an officer and two companies of the 32nd Ohio, were ordered up to the Heights, to report to Major S. M. Hewitt, the 32nd's senior officer there. The companies were to stay the whole night under arms to protect the two batteries on the mountain, the battery of four 12-pounder guns commanded by Captain Von Sehlen and the battery of two 9-inch Columbiads and one 50-pounder rifled piece commanded by Captain Phillips. A slight earthwork was built to the right of Phillips' guns to protect the artillerymen.

Early on the morning of September 13, Hildebrandt received orders to take three companies to the Heights to support Hewitt. Leaving the batteries under their captains' command, he reported to Hewitt, who ordered the three additional companies posted on the extreme right of the line. The Confederates made an attack on the crest of the Heights at 7:00 A.M., and after a short engagement, the companies pulled back in some confusion to the breastwork, where they rallied against a second attack, which occurred about 9:00 A.M. Garibaldians ensconced behind the log breastwork met the attackers with gunfire. Colonel Eliakim Sherrill of the 126th New York had his jaw shot away. When his raw officers and men saw him carried off the field with his tongue "waggling out of [his] wound," all but two of his raw companies broke and fled in utter confusion, leaving their positions and everything behind them.

Miles was on the Heights at Phillips' battery that morning, and as the panicked 126th New York ran past, Ford, Lieutenant Samuel Barras, his adjutant, and some officers of other regiments attempted to rally them, calling out, "Boys, what are you doing here?" Some answered, "We was ordered to fall back." Miles shouted, "By whom?" "By some major!" was the answer. Miles told them,"I have given no order to fall back, and no major could get one unless he got it from me!" Whether that order was ever given was problematic, since two companies from the 126th New York did stay in the fight. Private T. Nelson from that regiment later wrote, "The 126th fought for 3 days and stood their ground as well as any Regiment in the fight, they had it in the papers that we didn't stand to the fire; it is not so. I was in the thickest of the fight all day and know that our Regiment did not give an inch till we were ordered to fall back in which we did in good order...."

Miles was furious and ordered Hildebrandt to fix bayonets and shoot everyone who tried to go through the Garibaldians' line. Efforts to rally the panic-stricken men failed; the men ran right through the Garibaldians, passing entirely behind the breastwork. It was impossible to restore order. Most of the routed regiment fled to the left rear of the Garibaldians, who remained steady and disciplined. Hildebrandt, his two companies, and Hewitt with the 32nd Ohio had to go forward of their main line to keep the Confederates at bay. Hildebrandt and his small force of Garibaldians held off the Confederates for a very long time before retreating again behind the breastwork. Then, later, Hildebrandt sent out a few companies, some one hundred eighty men, to find the fleeing Federals and spent the rest of the day looking for them. The Garibaldians were being stretched thinly along the line.

Hildebrandt received orders from Barras to go down to Von Sehlen's battery and give up two companies from his reserve to strengthen Captain Crumbecker's observation post, which was set on a large rock, from where a heavy force of advancing Confederates was visible. Hildebrandt took command of Von Sehlen's battery for its protection and remained there with two Guard companies, together with two companies from the 32nd Ohio. Sometime after 4:00 P.M. Hewitt sent instructions to his own regiment's captains to retire in good order if so compelled to do. The remaining forces at the breastwork began to fall back. Hildebrandt watched most of the forces come down, not knowing why they were retiring. The men said they had orders to withdraw themselves. After a short time he saw the 32nd Ohio companies with him fall back, too. He realized the Garibaldians were too thinly strung out, but he had no orders to leave, so the Garibaldians stood their ground until all the rest of the regiments retired. He sent adjutant Lieutenant Bacon to Ford, who was very ill at the time, and was not at his quarters; Barras ordered Hildebrandt to assemble his companies and retire to Bolivar Heights, the moderately high ground back across the river and immediately west of Harpers Ferry. The Garibaldians were also ordered to stay wide awake for the whole night, after two straight days of stressful combat activity. Hildebrandt collected his men, marched back across the Potomac River and through Harpers Ferry to Bolivar Heights, and reported to D'Utassy. The colonel asked him why they left Maryland Heights. He told D'Utassy that the Garibaldians were one of the last to leave Maryland Heights, and that he was following orders from Ford's adjutant. Upon hearing this report D'Utassy became angry at Hildebrandt. He had been upset about the evacuation all day long:

> On the day the heights were evacuated I went down to Colonel Miles and asked him, "How is it possible that those heights were evacuated?" The evening before General White was down, and we were speaking of what our facilities would be if we had to withdraw, and General White, as well as myself, suggested the plan to draw our

forces over the pontoon bridge and hold Maryland Heights. Colonel Miles said, "As a matter of course; it is the only chance we have." At that time we believed we were to be attacked in front. In consequence, I wrote this letter to General White, immediately after the evacuation of Maryland Heights:

Headquarters First Brigade,
Harper's Ferry, September 13, 1862.
Brig. Gen. Julius White:

My Dear Sir: May I ask you, semi-officially, how and why it is that the position on Maryland Heights, which in my opinion, as well as that of highly experienced officers, was almost impregnable, and which Colonel Miles himself told me was his main reliance, as it commands Bolivar and Loudoun Heights, and as a matter of course, the whole valley, has been abandoned? I am informed by commanding officers of the different regiments lately across the river, that, after a successful shelling from the battery, the enemy in Maryland had entirely disappeared. The enemy is now distinctly visible on Loudoun Heights. I suppose, at least, that the force to be seen there is the enemy. From whom am I to expect orders, as no one is here, I do not know where to find Colonel Miles! Am I authorized to act according to the dictates of my own judgement? A written reply will greatly oblige, your sincere friend,

F. G. D'Utassy Commanding First Brigade.

White endorsed D'Utassy's letter back to him, writing, "Deference to [Major] General [John Ellis] Wool has alone prevented me from taking command here. Colonel D'Utassy will use his own discretion until he gets positive orders. This post would not be surrendered without a fight!" After the day ended and all was quiet, and he felt assured of his safety, D'Utassy came out to be among the men during the night.

By Sunday, September 14, D'Utassy's brigade, which comprised the 15th Indiana Artillery, the Guard, and the 111th and 115th New York and 65th Illinois regiments, held the northern, right flank of Bolivar Heights, which butted up to the Potomac River. Trimble's brigade, which consisted of his old 9th Vermont, the 60th Ohio, and the 126th New York regiments and Captain Rigby's battery, held the southern, left flank of the Union position. Other troops occupied the area of the plateau lying next to the Shenandoah River between Bolivar Heights and the confluence of the Shenandoah and the Potomac, under the cover of ravines as much as possible. D'Utassy thought the Maryland Heights could be retaken, and he planned to prove his point.

Late that same Sabbath morning, D'Utassy sent an order to Hildebrandt to send two companies of Garibaldians under the command of Captain Hollinde to his headquarters, ready to proceed to Maryland Heights and retrieve the same four 12-pounders that D'Utassy had said in his inspection report to Miles should be moved nearer to the mountain top. The guns had been spiked the evening before and left under guard by an ensign. The companies came down about noon and met Major Wood and two companies of the 65th Illinois. Commanded by Wood, the companies recrossed the Potomac River and ascended Maryland Heights to the battery site. They brought off the pieces abandoned there, along with more than three wagonloads of officers' baggage and one wagonload of ammunition, returning without any loss. A Garibaldian got one hundred pairs of drawers from the quartermaster. Hildebrandt had the men who had been tailors sew them into ammunition bags for use with the 12-pounders.

About 2:00 P.M. Hildebrandt was ordered to take four companies out to the right extreme from Bolivar Heights, toward the west, on a reconnaissance to determine the Confederate strength. After an hour the Garibaldians met the Confederate cavalry in force, and the skirmishers were shelled when a Confederate battery opened fire from out beyond the Charles Town Turnpike, which ran southwest from the Union left flank. The shelling forced the Garibaldians out to the front of the woods they were in, forcing them to withdraw. D'Utassy went to Lieutenant Bacon, led the Garibaldians into the woods, and assigned that position as their post. The shelling continued, and four men were killed and fifteen wounded. Fresh troops relieved the companies in the woods and remained there waiting for an attack as the sun went down. Instead, Confederate Major General Ambrose Powell Hill's division began a spirited assault and advance from the south against the extreme left of the Northern line. Miles was not present. Trimble ordered the 9th Vermont to support Downey's Maryland soldiers, who were reinforced by the 32nd Ohio. Hill's attack continued until after dark; the firing was sharp and Trimble's troops held their ground. The firing ceased, but during the night the Confederates outflanked the Union line on the left and got a position upon and beyond it by marching along the Shenandoah River and using the ravines intersecting its steep banks to climb up on the plateau at Trimble's rear.

That night Colonel Benjamin F. Davis of the 8th New York Cavalry advised D'Utassy that he was going to take his regiment and cut his way out, and asked if D'Utassy and the Guard would accompany them through the enemy lines. D'Utassy declined the offer, explaining that he, himself, was obliged by General White to lead the general's brigade personally. At 9:00 P.M., D'Utassy ordered an attack against a Confederate battery with the purpose of capturing it. Simultaneously, he ordered Colonel Jesse Segoine to shift his regiment, the 111th New York, to the left and occupy part of the position that the 32nd Ohio had just vacated. It was extremely dark and the 111th New York skirmished with some Confederate cavalry in the blackness.

On Monday, September 15, the Federals found themselves out of ammunition and the Confederate batteries far enough around their flanks that they could rake fire down the length of the Federal main line. Miles and White were at Bolivar Heights, when at 8:00 A.M. the artillery officers reported their ammunition exhausted. White proposed that a meeting of officers be convened at once. Lieutenant Willmon went to get D'Utassy, who had been riding up and down his line encouraging his soldiers to be ready to attack. Willmon found D'Utassy and gave him his orders to join the meeting. D'Utassy rode back to Miles, accompanied by his two aides and three orderlies. The war council was convened while the Union forces were still under bombardment. On D'Utassy's approach, Miles hollered, "Good gracious Heaven! Get down from your horse. It will draw the enemy's fire on you." D'Utassy tried to assure Miles that there was no danger amidst the shot and shell exploding all around them. Miles continued to admonish him, "Well, if you don't care I don't want to be shot on your account; get down off your horse and send off your horses!"

Miles had effectively doomed his command by clustering his soldiers near Harpers Ferry rather than fighting to hold the dominant high ground of Maryland Heights. Once he let his soldiers get pushed off of those heights, it was just a matter of time until the Confederates trapped him by occupying the higher ground all around Harpers Ferry. As they gathered for their gloomy council of war, Miles said to D'Utassy, "Well my boy, we meet again under unpleasant circumstances." D'Utassy asked, "Why?" Miles continued, "Well, we don't know what to do." D'Utassy asked, "In what regard?" Miles told him, "Well, we must surrender." D'Utassy looked at him a moment and then said, "What surrender?" Miles said, "Yes sir, what do you want to do?" "Cut our way through!" was D'Utassy's reply. "Poh, Bosh! Nonsense. Today was too late," said Miles. D'Utassy offered, "Colonel, I offered to do the same yesterday, and I suggested it to Colonel Davis, who, as you see, did it."

Indeed a body of some one thousand three hundred Federal cavalrymen had fought its way out. The 8th and 12th Illinois Cavalries did escape without loss to a man and reached Union lines (whether D'Utassy, with his demonstrated penchant for trying to gain some kind of advantage in any situation, came up with the idea of breaking out is questionable). Miles argued, "Well, yesterday is not today; what shall we do today?" D'Utassy said, "Is [this] a council of war or is it a private conversation?" Miles replied, "Well, I have half determined what to do, but General White said to call you all together, then let the junior [Trimble]) give his advice. Under actual existing circumstances, nothing else is to be done but to surrender." White was near them, but said nothing. Miles went over to White and said, "Well, you hear what he says." White answered, "Hear Colonel D'Utassy's opinion." D'Utassy replied, "You know it; I will never surrender as long as I have a shot." Miles began to curse, asking D'Utassy, "How many shots have you?" D'Utassy sent for Phillips and Von Sehlen, who told him that they had four shots of long range ammunition between them. When D'Utassy heard that, Miles capitulated. D'Utassy said, "I can do nothing else but surrender only on honorable conditions." Miles told

White, "General, I will have to go out." D'Utassy turned to them and said, "Remember, I will surrender only on honorable conditions." White asked, "What do you mean, honorable conditions? Be sure I will do my best to save our honor." D'Utassy replied, "The very least we must have is for the officers to have the honors of war and to retain their side arms, and the men must be saved the disgrace of passing through the enemy's lines." White said, "That I expect to get, and better still." With that D'Utassy turned away and went down to his position. That impressed officers enough for some to later relate, "Whatever D'Utassy's faults were, lack of courage was not among them."

The war council ended with the conclusion to surrender and a decision to signal with a white flag to halt the fighting. The white flag was exhibited and the shelling stopped for about fifteen minutes. Miles started forward from the eastern slope of Bolivar Heights to arrange to surrender at 9:00 A.M. When he reached Captain Philips of Company D of the 126th New York he ordered him to raise the white flag. Philips refused, saying, "For God's sake Colonel, don't surrender us. Don't you hear the signal guns? Our forces are near us. Let us cut our way out and join them." Miles was scornful: "They will blow us out of this in half an hour." He then repeated his order. Philips protested, "I will do nothing of the kind. I never played the coward's act and I shall not commence it this morning." Aghast, Miles inquired, "Do you know to whom you are talking?" Philips replied, "I suppose I am talking to Colonel Miles; I know I am talking to a damned traitor." Miles returned to his horse and rode off. Then Philips ordered his gunner, "Gun number three! You see that man?"—pointing at Miles as he rode away— "That man on the horse? You fix that on that man! Miss your mark and you die in your boots!"[3] The gunner fired at Miles. Every inch of ground was torn up around him and his aide, Lieutenant Binney, when a shell struck and exploded, tearing the flesh from his left calf and part of his right one. Binney called for help, put Miles in a blanket, and found six men who dragged him off to an ambulance.

Miles lay there dying of his leg wounds. He began to mutter in his delirium, "Where is General McClellan; why don't he come forward and save me?...Major, is our artillery at work?...I have done my duty, and can die like a soldier; don't let my staff leave me...Go on! Go on." Private Nelson simply wrote of Miles, "...got killed and I am glad of it... We had to surrender."

D'Utassy was adamant about the surrender. Refusing to allow the regiment's colors to become a souvenir trophy of the enemy, he took down the colors from the two guidons which were set up behind him. He replaced them with white pocket handkerchiefs that he took from his trunk and nailed onto the staffs that had held the colors. Then he ordered the 111th and the 115th New York regiments to bring their large Union flags to his tent, where he severed the colors and the tassels from their staffs and then hid the colors in his trunks. He broke the staffs to pieces and cut up part of the tassels, distributing them to Lieutenants Bacon and Anton D'Utassy. Taking a piece himself, he instructed the lieutenants to wear the tassels around their waists in place of a scarf. Then he cut the large Union flags of the Garibaldi Guards from their staffs, broke the staffs up as he had done earlier, and hid the flags in another chest. Finally, he ordered Bacon and his assistant, Otto Rassmaessler, not to say what had become of the colors. D'Utassy gave orders to the artillery at his position to spike their guns and to unscrew the nipples of their rifles before White could make any terms with the Confederates. When the white flag was raised in his camp, he drew up the regiment in line of battle and ordered them to stack their arms, keeping his soldiers there until about 11:00 A.M., when Stonewall Jackson arrived. Bacon, the Garibaldi Guard's adjutant, later attested:

> Upon the afternoon of Monday, the 15th ultimo, I was directed to call upon Brigadier General Branch, of the Confederate army, and ascertain from him what disposition was to be made of the surrendered forces at Harpers Ferry, contained in the First brigade, Colonel D'Utassy. I immediately proceeded to his headquarters, and learned that duplicate muster rolls would be required; that our regiments and batteries were to be drawn up as for muster, the roll to be called, men to answer, &c; the form of parole then to be read to them, and the men, raising their right hands, to promise not to serve against the so-called Southern Confederacy until regularly exchanged; officers to sign individual paroles.
>
> I returned to my colonel and reported. Rolls of the regiments and batteries were prepared, and in the case of my own (the 39th Regiment) the names of the officers save those of company commanders were included. At about 6:00 P.M. word was sent to General Branch that the muster rolls of the brigade were ready, and we would feel obliged if he (General Branch) would come over and parole us, as he had said he would. He came. The Garibaldi Guard was formed in columns of companies, non-commissioned staff in front, Colonel D'Utassy, Colonel Segoine, of the 111th, and Mr. Kent, correspondent of the New York Tribune, who was at the time acting in the capacity of private secretary to Colonel D'Utassy. I also accompanied them. When we reached the head of the column, General Branch was handed the muster roll of the first company.
>
> Turning to Colonel D'Utassy, he remarked, "I suppose, colonel, you understand this parole as I do, viz, that you and your men understand you are not to go into a camp of instruction or drill until such time as you may be exchanged."
>
> Colonel D'Utassy immediately exclaimed, in an excited manner, "No, sir, I understand nothing of the kind. Such an understanding would not be correct. Suppose my Government desired to use this paroled force against the Indians of the Northwest, who are, like

you, in a state of insurrection; would you, sir, consider that as a violation of our parole?"

"Well, no," said Branch, "I do not think I would."

"Then, sir," said D'Utassy, breaking in, "in the present state of our forces here surrendered, some of whom are green troops, it might be necessary to place them in a camp of instruction. I must, therefore, sir, decline accepting a parole for my men on the condition now imposed by you, which I am positive was not intended at the time the articles of capitulation were drawn up." Colonel Segoine and Mr. Kent also gave it as their opinion that such a construction could not be placed upon the simple words contained in the articles of capitulation, such as "will not serve until regularly exchanged." Upon this decision of Colonel D'Utassy, General Branch refused to parole any of the troops until he could ascertain the understanding of the disputed point as entertained by General A. P. Hill. Branch then wrote a note to General Hill, sent it, and, after awaiting an answer until after dark, said he would go to his quarters, and we might send about 9 o'clock (P.M.) for his answer. At that hour, in company with Mr. Kent, I called upon General Branch, and he stated that General Hill concurred with him in his view of the parole. I reported this fact to Colonel D'Utassy, who said that he would rather go to Richmond than take such a parole. He then gave orders for our brigade to be ready to move at dawn next morning (the 16th of Sept.). This was done, and by 6:00 A.M. next morning we were in motion for the pontoon bridge. I handed the muster-rolls to General Hill at his headquarters, and asked a pass for the brigade. He asked if the brigade was paroled. I replied, evasively, I thought so. He then sat down and wrote a pass, upon which we immediately crossed the river, thus GIVING HIM THE SLIP.

Upon the announcement of the surrender, Colonel D'Utassy ordered the colors of all the regiments of our brigade to be conveyed to his headquarters. This was done, and two hours were spent in removing the various colors from their staffs and packing them in the colonel's private trunk.

The adjutant general of General [Maxcy] Gregg made several demands on me for the colors where I was engaged on the hill turning over the arms. I informed him that they had been sent to our brigade headquarters. He left, but shortly returned and stated that he could not find them. I said I regretted it, but could not aid him; that he must see my colonel. These flags are now in my colonel's private trunks in this city, Annapolis, Maryland. These are the simple facts, which, on my honor as a gentleman, I certify to.

Charles Graham Bacon
Lieutenant, and Acting Assistant Adjutant General.

Adjutant Bacon simply handed a muster roll to General Hill and asked for a pass, which the general gave the regiment with the statement that they were paroled. The original regimental books were lost. The Garibaldi Guard began to march away; just as it was about to cross the pontoon bridge some Confederate soldiers stole Lieutenant D'Utassy's horse out from under him and left him to carry his saddle around his neck. The Guard suffered six men killed in action and fifteen wounded in action during its actions in defense of Harpers Ferry from September 12 to September 15. Now the Garibaldians had come up short through the fault of inept officers who lacked adequate military knowledge and courage. Paroled or not, ten officers and five hundred twenty men joined the other captured Union regiments headed for Chicago, Illinois and a prisoner of war camp called Camp Douglas.

Chapter Six

CAPTURE, PAROLE, AND EXCHANGE

Not here are the goblets glowing,
  Not here is the vintage sweet;
'Tis cold as our hearts are growing,
  And dark as the doom we meet.
But stand to your glasses, steady!
  And soon shall our pulses rise:
A cup to the dead already—
  Hurrah for the next that dies!

—Anonymous

THE Garibaldians began their trek to Camp Douglas and the degradation of life as prisoners of war in their own country, where they would await a possible swap with a like number of (to-be-) captured Confederates at some indeterminate future date, with a march to Annapolis, Maryland. Six men escaped after the surrender at Harpers Ferry and were not heard of again. Giuseppe Bernabo, of Company A, with luck on his side, was left behind in the hospital at Harpers Ferry and received his discharge papers. On Tuesday, September 16, D'Utassy noted his arrival in Annapolis: "Arrived here in command of the 1st Brigade, composed of the 39th, 111th, 115th N.Y., the 65th Il., 15th Indiana Battery[,] about three thousand men in all from Harper's Ferry. Officers and men have been paroled and await orders where to go with troops. Men eager to be exchanged, 39th N.Y. and 65th Il., old troops." S. O. Hooker of the 9th Vermont wrote to his sister that "the Confederates got us surrounded at Harper's Ferry so we could not get any letters or send any out. You probably heard all

103

about the battle and our surrender so I will not try to write any of the particulars....We marched from Harper's Ferry to Annapolis, then took the boat to Baltimore, then the cars for this place [Chicago]." T. Nelson of the 126th New York added a few details to Hooker's brief remarks: "Got taken prisoner at Harper's Ferry, Va. got paroled, walked from Harper's Ferry to Annapolis 100 miles in 6 days. They charged us a dollar for a loaf of bread... Folks give us all we wanted to eat and wouldn't take a penny for it. I hope that we will be able to get another chance at them Confederates again if we get a Commander what will not sell us out." Reflecting a slightly different perception of their reception by the Maryland population, another soldier from the 126th named Ellis recorded the specifics of everyone's journey to Camp Douglas:

> I do not think a more appropriate elation could be bestowed upon this regiment than that of the "Wanderers." Since our departure from home, we have scarcely had a "local habitation," though I think we have earned a "name."
>
> From Martinsburg we made a forced march to Bolivar Heights, and then, after the battle of Harper's Ferry, and our capture by the rebels, we made a march from that place to Annapolis, Md.; thence by transport, on Friday, the 26th inst., we went to Baltimore, and from Baltimore, by rail, we made a continuous journey day and night until we reached Chicago, about noon on Monday the 29th inst. The cars furnished us were common freight cars, with no arrangements for sleeping, and with forty men in each car. We consequently suffered much, and were much exhausted on our arrival at [Camp Douglas]. It was a difficult matter to obtain any rest at all, such was the terrible jolting and "shaking up" we experienced in the springless and uncomfortable vehicles furnished for our transportation. Our rations consisted of hard bread and partially cooked pork fat, and had we not been supplied by the patriotic people on the route, many of us would have suffered from hunger.
>
> At Baltimore we took the Erie and Sunbury railroad, which we followed until its junction with the Pennsylvania railroad, over which we rode to Pittsburgh. Here we changed cars, taking Pittsburgh, Fort Wayne and Chicago railroad to the latter place. While on our march through Maryland, it was with great difficulty that the men could obtain anything to eat from the inhabitants, even by offering fabulous prices. We were therefore surprised as well as immensely gratified by the generous manner in which the good people of Altoona received and entertained us during our short stay at this place. Spontaneously, and apparently without organized effort, the people turned out with baskets filled with nice bread and

biscuits, spread with butter and preserves, as well as coffee, peaches and apples, which they liberally dispensed among the boys. Others invited the poor hungry soldiers into their houses and seated them at well spread tables. As you may well imagine this timely donation was properly appreciated by the regiment.

At Pittsburgh, at which city we arrived about half-past nine Saturday P.M., we were treated to a good supper at the City Hall. All soldiers passing through Pittsburgh are thus received.

After we left Pittsburgh, we saw no very considerable towns; but every little hamlet seemed rife with patriotism, and baskets of food greeted us on all hands; even at midnight noble men and women stood ready to greet us with good cheer. We could not help contrasting this generous treatment with the "cold shoulder" and extortion with which, save in a few isolated instances, the people of Maryland received us.

Stonewall Jackson drove the Federals out of Martinsburg and captured Harpers Ferry just in time, from the Southern point of view. He completed his mission and rejoined Lee's main army just as McClellan caught up with the Confederates at Antietam Creek, two days later. General Branch, who had figured prominently in the Guard's parole at Harpers Ferry, was killed in action in the fighting on September 17; the Garibaldians, already on their way to Chicago, missed what would be the Civil War's single bloodiest day for Ameri cans in battle. On the Guard's journey to Camp Douglas, at least twenty-seven German Garibaldians escaped while passing through Frederick, Annapolis, Baltimore, and Pittsburgh. With all the Indian trouble that had been brewing in Minnesota, a rumor began to circulate that the Garibaldians would spend the rest of the war at Fort Snelling, on the Indian frontier fighting the Sioux.

During this time D'Utassy conducted business as usual. He had been squeezing Frederick Horn, a sutler and band member in Company B[1], out of his earnings, and when Horn could no longer accommodate his demands, D'Utassy threatened him with imprisonment for selling bad liquor and poisoning a few soldiers. Then D'Utassy persuaded him to desert, which could forestall the rise of any difficult questions about D'Utassy's own activities and might also result in obtaining a more compliant sutler. Horn deserted on Thursday, September 18, but was apprehended six days later. He was court-martialed and sentenced to serve one year imprisonment to the end of his enlistment. Nearly a year had now passed since D'Utassy first put the name of Michael Jacky, the bugler in Company G, on the regimental field, staff, and band payrolls, and then collected excess pay from the paymaster in his name. Jacky began to complain to Chaplain Zyla about the colonel's treachery. Zyla told D'Utassy, who recommended that Jacky desert to Canada. When Jacky refused, D'Utassy was all the more determined to rid himself of another potential troublemaker.[2]

The Guard's fall season began with high, low, and in-between notes. On September 22, a Monday, after a slim Union victory at Antietam Creek, President Lincoln signed the Emancipation Proclamation to abolish slavery in any state or part of a state which was in rebellion, effective January 1, 1863. Upon learning of Lincoln's action, Garibaldi, who especially appreciated freedom's effect on slaves, would send Lincoln a dispatch hailing him as "the Emancipator" and congratulating him upon his action. On September 23 while the Guard was in Annapolis, Union Brigadier General Daniel Tyler filed a report hailing D'Utassy's bravado: "My impression is that Colonel D'Utassy is too good a soldier to have compromised himself at Harper's Ferry. I enclose a communication from Lieutenant Charles Graham Bacon, acting assistant adjutant, which I have no doubt is substantially correct. If Colonel D'Utassy exonerated himself in this unfortunate affair at Harper's Ferry, I hope he will be released from arrest and ordered back to duty at the earliest practicable moment." On September 27, without explanation, Captain Niedzielski, the Polish-born fencing instructor who had been mustered in only one year earlier, received orders that he was to be separated from the service in accordance with War Department Special Order No. 63. General Tyler signed his dismissal papers. Niedzielski had no idea what the charges were against him, nor was he taken through legal proceedings. He left camp for New York to exonerate himself. In twenty days, Adjutant Charles Graham Bacon would be promoted to replace him as the captain of Company C.

On Sunday, September 28, the Garibaldi Guard reached Camp Douglas. As the men marched through the camp's castle-like entrance into its broad, open yard, their esprit de corps plummeted. The camp was a "[h]ellish den of iniquity, where fiends incarnate in the shape of men had charge of the prison." The parolees were encamped in the yard or put up in temporary barracks that had been built the previous autumn and winter. Hooker wrote to his sister, "We arrived here last Sunday night about 9 o'clock. We slept on the ground that night and Monday moving marched to our quarter in the stalls which answer very well for barracks...." Ellis arrived a day later: "Monday afternoon we arrived at Chicago and were encamped in the vicinity of 'Camp Douglas' and but a short distance from the grave of the eminent statesman [Stephan Douglas], on the shore of Lake Michigan. The men were very much in need of soap and water, not having enjoyed that soldiers's luxury since we started on our journey. We were consequently marched down to the lake by companies, and as the waves were beating in heavily, many of the men enjoyed fine sport of bathing in the surf. We were supplied with 'shelter' tents for our temporary comfort—if comfort it can be called...."

Camp Douglas, the largest Northern prisoner of war camp during the Civil War, sat on one hundred sixty acres of land on the south side of Chicago, in an area known as the United States Fair Grounds. Prior to the arrival of the eight thousand Federal parolees, the camp held seven thousand newly recruited Illinois troops and seven hundred ninety-six Federal soldiers guarding eleven thousand Confederate prisoners.[3] The prisoners who occupied the barracks before the parolees arrived left them filthy; human waste saturated the grounds. Piles of refuse and worn-out clothes were everywhere. The latrines were completely filled with excrement and fouled the air. Some of the stinking pits were close to the barracks and a hospital filled with the infirm. There was hardly time to clean the barracks for the parolees, although it appeared that at some time the job had been begun—and then abandoned. It just so happened that the cleaned area was the only portion of the camp that the public could view.

In reality there had been no preparation to receive all the parolees. Recommendations had been made to burn or haul off all refuse, grade the parade grounds to prevent standing water, provide drains, repair and clean barracks, re-roof the hospital, transfer the sick to decent hospitals, and hire female cooks for the parolees.[4] But nothing had been done. Then, General Tyler had come on from Annapolis to command the camp with an iron hand and was exceedingly unpopular with the men. He found the Garibaldians disorganized and disobedient. D'Utassy had been sowing seeds of discontent among the officers and men by encouraging them in the belief that they had not been paroled properly, and that it was not right for them to be treated as prisoners and compelled to do garrison duty. The Guard and the 126th New York refused to do any duty and to obey orders. Hatred of Tyler led to open revolt; men unequipped for barracks life in the cold destroyed fences and tools, and burned down barracks to show their displeasure. D'Utassy continued to mistrust everyone and keep a watchful eye on his officers for potential enemies. He even confiscated the private letters of the late quartermaster, Lieutenant E. D. Lazelle, which the Guard continued to receive, and opened them for his scrutiny.[5] The end of the month found Chaplain Zyla leading by personal example to maintain order and military discipline among the men, and to keep a lid on an explosive situation.[6]

On September 30, D'Utassy, Bacon, and Hildebrandt were ordered to Washington to testify at a military commission convened to investigate the surrender at Harpers Ferry. By Friday, October 3, D'Utassy was in Washington, testifying at the Harpers Ferry Military Commission court of inquiry. After being sworn in, he asked permission to read a letter which Colonel Miles had written to him. With characteristic self-interest, he embellished his own character and actions at Harpers Ferry. He testified to the commission that he had been in the Austrian army in 1843 and fought in the Crimea. He testified as to Colonel Miles' character and physical condition in an insinuating manner: "There is an old Latin saying that 'of the dead never say anything but good.' The opinion I have formed may conflict with the opinion of others, and unless the court desire it, I do not think such an opinion should be given." Colonel Thomas H. Ford insisted upon the question. D'Utassy answered, "I think that, during the latter part of the time, Colonel Miles was broken down, the consequence of previous abuse [alcohol]. I knew him at Harper's Ferry, where he was the strictest model of abstinence. I have studied a litttle medicine and I thought that broke him down, as I knew him on former occasions as rather a good drinker. The sudden changing to new habits I think did him much harm. I spoke with him one day on the subject, and said to him, 'I believe you will ruin yourself.' He said, 'I took an oath never to touch a drop, and I have not done it.' I believe that sudden abstinence injured him greatly.... I did not consider him fit to command such a force."

Many Southern sympathizers in Chicago had relatives in the camp, and they brought food, medicine, blankets, and clothing to the Confederate prisoners. Not so lucky were the parolees. The men would bleat like sheep to Quartermaster Fake to complain loudly about their rations, mouldy bread, and no bread at all. Infuriated at their unfair imprisonment, the men set fire to overcrowded barracks and used the opportunity to escape.[7] Swiss and Prussian Garibaldians deserted and escaped into the highly populated German neighborhoods of Chicago. It was a simple task to "gopher" under the fence to freedom. Thirty Garibaldians would desert in October alone, and the desertions would continue until the troops would be exchanged in November.

From his home on the island of Caprera, Garibaldi wrote to the American Consul Turin, George P. Marsh, on October 5 about his interest in serving in the American army. Within three days, Marsh began communications on the matter with Garibaldi, the first of many which ultimately went nowhere. Recovering from a gunshot wound after his ill-fated attempt to liberate Rome from French control a few weeks earlier, the general remained at his home writing letters of recommendation for his followers who wanted to serve in the Union army.[8]

The same day Garibaldi sought to join the Union army, Captain William Robitsek of Company E became very ill and incapacitated with dysentery, and was discharged from the army at Camp Douglas. To fill the vacancy, First Lieutenant Anton D'Utassy was promoted to captain Company E. The colonel represented Anton as the "very hero" of Harpers Ferry. The colonel's other brother, Carl, remained on the muster and payroll as "von Utassy," "D'Utassy," and "Utassy," where he had been since September 1861. The colonel stopped at nothing to defraud the payroll department of every possible dollar, not even at his own brother's reputation. Meanwhile, recruiting officers for newly formed Illinois regiments enticed the parolees by offering large sums of money as enlistment bonuses. Some twenty more German Garibaldians deserted, escaped into Chicago, and reenlisted as Illinoisans. General Tyler encouraged the Chicago police to arrest soldiers who were intoxicated, riotous, or disorderly in Chicago. Accordingly, the police began making arrests, sweeping the streets of paroled soldiers out at night.

On October 17, D'Utassy returned from Washington and began to dismiss, discharge, reorganize, and otherwise clean out the ranks of officers whom he evidently feared might mutiny against him. Captains George Brey, Company B; and Erciole Salviatti, Company I; and First Lieutenants Andrew

Fontana, Company A; Bernhard Franz, Company D; Anton Schada, Company G; and Riatz Y Castillo and Jose Romero, both of Company I, were court-martialed and dismissed to a man. Captain Venuti of Company G was discharged; soon afterward he accepted a commission as a major in the 52nd New York Infantry. The vacated Guard positions were filled by promotions from within the ranks.

The Christian Commission's Northwestern branch sent the famous evangelist, Dwight L. Moody, to minister to the parolees. He had conducted services in the camp for the Confederate prisoners and could now attend to the Union soldiers. The Garibaldians attended his services to break up the monotony of prison life and listened to the fiery sermons he preached. The effectiveness of his efforts was hard to judge since the majority of the men did not speak a word of English, and he did not speak any foreign language. In contrast, Chaplain Zyla regularly arose before dawn and tried to help the Garibaldians in camp bear their discomforts. Day after day he made his reports concerning the sick and visited several different hospitals in the city. He did his duty without regard to the infectious diseases the men had or to the inclemency of the fall weather. Everyone suffered from a variety of ailments—mostly scurvy, colds, dysentery, and bowel disease. Twenty-four Garibaldians had smallpox.

On Monday, November 10, seven more Germans deserted and vanished in Chicago. Nine days later, the camp bustled with activity greater than it had seen for some time past. An unexpected order was read on parade. All New York regiments received orders to be exchanged. The Guard was ordered immediately to Washington, without unnecessary delay, by order of Brigadier General William H. Ludlow. The Garibaldians would be under the command of General Julius White. Everyone greeted the announcement with cheers. Their route would be via Toledo, Cleveland, Harrisburg, and Baltimore to Washington. The men were supplied for the trip, with the exception of arms, which would be supplied at their destination.[9] In the next three days before the Guard began leaving Camp Douglas, an additional eight Germans deserted and disappeared into Chicago, eight men apparently disappeared from the rolls, since there was no further record of them, and two were discharged for disability.

The Garibaldians began departing for Washington on November 22, as fast as transportation could be furnished for them. They were the last regiment to be exchanged, and four hundred of the five hundred twenty that surrendered at Harpers Ferry remained in the ranks. From that day through November 25, the Guard traveled to Washington. Many of the men hoped they would get an opportunity to visit their homes before again entering active service in the field. Some obviously had other ideas; Pedro Turra of Company C and William Kunze of Company E deserted when they reached Baltimore. The day after the Guard arrived in Washington, Captain Niedzielski arrived in

Albany, New York, to meet with the governor in order to vindicate himself. His dismissal was changed to a discharge from the service of the U.S. Army.

The Garibaldi Guard began another assignment as protectors of Washington, this time as part of the first brigade in Brigadier General Silas Casey's division, which was part of the Defenses of Washington. The Guard took up positions around Union Mills, just southeast of Centreville, where it could help to defend the capital against any enemy attacks from the west while the Army of the Potomac maneuvered some forty miles to the south against General Lee. On November 7 while the Guard was still at Camp Douglas, for failure to go after the enemy after his slim victory at Antietam, McClellan had been replaced by Major General Ambrose E. Burnside. Burnside was under huge pressure to go on the attack, and he decided to cross the Rappahannock River at Fredericksburg, Virginia, and attack south upon Richmond. This would let him attack with well-protected flanks and a secure supply line. Burnside's forces were camped around Warrenton, Virginia, southwest of Fairfax. All he had to do was to march his army southeast from Warrenton to Falmouth, the town on the north side of the river opposite Fredericksburg, cross the river, and occupy Fredericksburg before Lee could march there with his army.

On Sunday, November 30, Philip Kruger, captured in action the previous May near Franklin, Virginia, had been paroled and returned to duty. When he rejoined his comrades in Washington, it was apparent to all of them what his imprisonment had done to him. His health was ruined; he was finally discharged April of 1863 from the hospital at Centerville. Charles Le Marie, who enlisted with his two sons, Charles and Bernhard, in the French company at the original muster in May 1861, was also too ill to stay any longer with the Garibaldians. He had been sent from Camp Douglas to an army hospital in Columbus, Ohio, and he was discharged for disabilities from there. Both of the young men survived the war and were mustered out a month from one another.

But Lee got to Fredericksburg before Burnside could get across the Rappahannock. Burnside made a speedy march that surprised Lee and beat him to the river, but over the next three weeks he let rainy weather, worries about Lee's strength, and Washington supply authorities who did not get him pontoons he wanted as fast as he wanted them, slow him down. While both sides assembled their forces and settled in at Fredericksburg, on December 7, the Garibaldians enthusiastically received the new weapons for which they had been waiting for over a year. Lieutenant Colonel Schwarz had to write and issue an order to the Garibaldians "to stop all firing of their weapons which would be rigorously forbidden, and all old guard [detail members] discharging their arms after being released must do so at the target [for clearing weapons], and only between the hours of 10 [A.M.] to 12 A.M. [sic] under their respective commanding officers." The next day, D'Utassy opened another letter addressed to someone else, an official letter directed to Chief Surgeon Dr. Frederick Wolf.[10]

Burnside began crossing the Rappahannock on the night of December 10. At that moment, the commander of his reserve corps, Major General Franz Sigel, was en route to Fredericksburg, Virginia, and he was concerned about D'Utassy's ability to guard Washington from the west with just one brigade while everyone else was elsewhere. On December 11, Sigel reported to Major General Samuel Peter Heintzelman, commander of the Military District of Washington, XXII Corps, and the Department of Washington, D.C.:

> The main force of the Eleventh Corps is crossing at Wolf Run Shoals today, on their march to Dumfries. The cavalry attached to this corps will occupy Manassas Junction and Brentsville, with strong pickets at Centreville, Bull Run Bridge, and Chantilly. It is desirable, and almost necessary, that in case Centreville should be held as an advance post of Washington, one brigade of infantry should be sent there besides the brigade now under command of Colonel D'Utassy, which he will need to occupy Fairfax Court House and Fairfax Station, and the line from Bull Run Bridge by Union Mills to Wolf Run Shoals. If Centreville can be given up, which I do not decide, two regiments of infantry should be sent to Fairfax Court House, or Fairfax Station, to allow Colonel D'Utassy to keep his troops more concentrated. No news of importance has been received from our lines beyond Centreville and Chantilly. Patrols sent to Aldie and Leesburg have seen nothing of the enemy.[11]

On the same Thursday that General Sigel expressed his tactical concerns regarding D'Utassy, a Private Wilson of the 126th New York recorded his observations of D'Utassy's tactical tendencies. He wrote:

> [T]he monotony of camp life was broken by an odd exploit of Colonel D'Utassy, of the 39th New York, commanding the Brigade, who seems to have had a genius fertile in invention. Wishing to reconnoiter the railroad toward Manassas, he determined to send a railway train for the purpose, which was made up of, first a cart made of boiler iron with port holes on all sides, furnished with a piece of artillery and plenty of shell; then the engine, and then platform and box cars. Captain Aikins and Lieutenant Richardson, and forty men were detailed to accompany the expedition [all officers and men from the 126th New York]. Colonel D'Utassy, a detail from the artillery to serve the gun, some pioneers, a telegraph operator with a portable battery, and the infantry, set forth in the afternoon and proceeded to Bristoe Station, taking observations on the way, but at Bristoe found the track so encumbered with the ruins of cars and property destroyed in the raid on General Pope the August before, that they could not proceed, but returned to camp at eleven o'clock in the evening. No good was done by this singular reconnaissance, nor, as it hap-

pened, any harm; but had they met the enemy or roving bands of guerrillas, the little Hungarian Colonel, might have wished himself and his unwieldy apparatus back within our lines.[12]

D'Utassy's sally was much more successful than Burnside's venture, relatively speaking. D'Utassy returned unscathed; Burnside committed his forces against Fredericksburg in a basically haphazard and lackluster fashion, and by December 15 Lee's soldiers had once more decisively repulsed a substantially larger Union force. While Burnside's forces suffered casualties, the Guard suffered more garrison-type turmoil. On Tuesday, December 16, Sergeant Augustus Rumpf of Company A was promoted to sergeant major and First Lieutenant Charles Galluba of Company E was discharged for disability. In Company K, Second Lieutenant Silvio Ronzone was discharged and Sergeant Major Adolphus Wagner was promoted to second lieutenant to replace him. Unassigned Second Lieutenants Sylvis Burmazor and Charles Gallerbad resigned on December 17. First Lieutenant Louis Riege of Company B was reassigned from adjutant duty to Company G. Sergeant Giuseppe Cavrotti of Company C got into an argument with one of his men, Giovanni Picconi, who broke Cavrotti's arm with a piece of iron during their altercation. Picconi was court-martialed and sentenced to thirty days at hard labor, which he served with a twelve-pound ball and chain attached to his leg.

On December 18, the acting quartermaster, Second Lieutenant Caesar Nissen, reported that four horses of the Garibaldi Guard had died, when actually only one had. A Board of Survey was called to certify that four horses actually died. Assistant Quartermaster Sergeant Ferdinand Leibnitz was ordered to get some men and tools and dig up the four carcasses. D'Utassy got wind of it. While the order was being carried out, he ordered Leibnitz to report to the board that they found the carcasses of four dead horses.[13] D'Utassy pondered this situation for two days. On December 20, he had Nissen make an additional report that four more horses had died and made the requisition one for eleven horses. Three days later, as Major Waring had presaged, the Guard's cock feathers were clipped when orders were issued to insure uniformity in dress. The regulation Union army blue coat and kepi would replace the Bersaglieri uniform. The orders said, "The coats and jackets or blouses will be at all times buttoned and hooked and only the cap as prescribed worn, or citizen's hat or Zouave covering would be endured. The black [dark blue] overcoats of the Garibaldians will be exchanged and given to musicians and sergeants or to the flank companies. Enlisted men [will] not carry pistols or knifes on their belts. Officers must always carry a side arm." On Christmas day, a Thursday, First Lieutenant Alexander Charles di Biscaccianti, the adjutant, went on medical leave. Two days later, D'Utassy altered the Guard's payroll muster so that he could personally receive the pay for all the men who had deserted at Camp Douglas.[14]

As 1862 drew to a close, the Garibaldians remained in Casey's division as part of the Defenses of Washington. At 5:00 P.M. on December 28, a

George Waring, Jr.
Former major of Garibaldi Guard posed here in his uniform as major in the
Fremont's 4th Missouri Cavalry.

*Massachusetts Commandery
Military Order of the Loyal Legion
and U.S. Army Military Institute
C.S. Vol. 17, p. L733*

mounted messenger of the 1st Michigan Cavalry came in Woodyard's Ford
and notified D'Utassy that the Confederates had crossed the Occoquan River
at Snyder's Ford, intending to attack Fairfax Station and capture and destroy
the supplies there. D'Utassy heard next that the Confederates had from one
thousand five hundred to three thousand cavalry and six artillery batteries in
their force. He went into action to strengthen his picket line. He ordered Colonel Percy Wyndham to take his four hundred cavalry of the 4th New York and
take a post at Fairview, just east of the heart of present-day Fairfax.[15] He
detailed four companies and an artillery section to reinforce Wyndham. He
posted eight companies at the fork in the road leading west from Union Mills.
He covered his rear with sixty cavalrymen, some infantry detachments, and
four artillery pieces. He formed a chain of posts around Union Mills and was
in communication with Fairfax Station, about six miles southeast of Union
Mills, ready for approaches from all directions. The Guard was put in reserve,
for commitment where needed.[16] Then orders telegraphed from General
Stoughton told D'Utassy to take two regiments and a battery to Fairfax Station, and ordered Wyndham to the northeast of Chantilly, today land that is
Dulles International Airport, to check the enemy. By now it was 2:00 A.M.
and too dark to move the artillery. At dawn, D'Utassy marched to Fairfax
Station and found the telegraph wires cut and some railroad track torn up. The
Guard's pioneers went to work repairing the wires and track. Men were fa-
tigued; some were sick with measles, and a few had smallpox. The regiments
had shrunk to an average of no more than four hundred men fit for duty.[17] On
the eve of 1863, the brigade went into winter quarters where it was, where it
would stay for the next seven months, defending Washington.

Chapter Seven

RASCALITY AND RESURRECTION

Saint Peter at the gates of Heaven,
Oh ye, intrepidly shameless fellow,
March most quick, disappear from here,
Who this like you, had asked when Earth
Does not deserve to walk in Heaven's realm,
Here, take your pass for Hell, approved!

Devil to his grandmother says,
Nanna, I can's understand, God's present
Doing upon my honor,
It is an abhorrence and shame that,
He sends us this bank of thieves.
My Devils, without complaint take these dirty,
Gallows-birds by their necks and turn them out from here,
I, art but justly, such rascals are too mean for Hell.
              —*"An Invitation to the First Fancy Ball,"*
              written by Gustave Lindenmueller[1]

As 1862 turned into 1863, the Garibaldi Guard's parent brigade went from being the first to the third brigade in Casey's division. D'Utassy inaugurated the new year with a high and mighty statement to his newly renumbered command on New Year's Day, a Thursday:

> This is a season for self-examination, it should be one of promise also.

115

Over the ashes of the dead past, let us then address to our veteran Chief [Casey], with renewed energy and ardor, let us be ever mindful of the many benefits he has conferred upon us. In this wilderness to which our duty directed us, he has made a new home. Every rail road facility has been granted, telegraphic communications established. Each requirement of mine for your benefit or comfort as soldiers has been cheerfully met, a Brigade Hospital is in progress of completion, but alone all must thank him for the soldiers guide on "Casey's Tactics".

I recommend to each officer and soldier its study, and the faithful performance of the duties already and able set forth. By following this advice our beloved General though absent, is ever present.

I take this occasion to mention my approbation and pleasure for the kindness with which all my orders have been received, by my officers and for their energetic execution, by both officers and men, from this day we will hail as the 3rd Brigade of Casey's Division, let the new bond be cemented by mutual promises of good feeling and an earnest determination for the fulfillment of our labor of love to our noble country, and the preservation and restoration of its great principle of Liberty.

We must remember the reverses of the year which has passed only as an incentive to sterner action; turning our eyes upward to the Stars and Stripes; fighting onward to the goal of victory; hoping for a continuation of the pleasant relations which unite us and for an opportunity of proving our devotion to the service where present. Wishing you all the compliments of the season and a very Happy New Year.

F. G. D'Utassy Colonel

Commanding. 3rd Brigade

Casey's Division

In keeping with the custom of the time, Lieutenant Colonel Schwarz issued a corresponding message to the regiment, that was to be read in front of each company of Garibaldians:

Soldiers,

A new year has again appeared before us not withstanding all misfortune, hardships and battles this nobel [sic] regiment fought through the last year, which has been buried in the grave of eternity. I hope and desire that the rest of veterans will stand together in all emergencies the current year may bring us.

Parting with you from New York city I was the witness of your good behavior, endurance and bravery you always [have] shown and was honored on the memorable day the 8th of June 1862 at Cross Keys, Va. to be in your first battle where you exhibited yourself worthy of the nobel [*sic*] cause we defend.

Heaven may please me, to bring the small band of brave Garibaldians who are the last of a great number of men who departed with us. Gloriously and victorious to their home. Should however the country need again our life to uphold the Stars and Stripes against Rebellion I hope and am sure that Garibaldi Guard will do their duty and stand to their flag. Praying for the welfare of the Regiment. I wish you all a Happy New Year.

Chas. Schwarz Lieutenant Colonel.

Another January in wartime winter quarters stretched out before the regiment. The only promotion in the ranks was that of Sergeant Jacob Surer in Company E to first sergeant. On Saturday, January 10, Second Lieutenant Eugene Subit of Company B was dismissed, and Magnus Bader reenlisted as the first sergeant in Company E. One week later, Lieutenant Heinrich Dietrich was appointed provost marshal. Brigadier General Alexander Hays, an 1844 West Point graduate and Mexican War veteran who had recently joined the division and just taken command of the brigade containing the Garibaldians, commented on them in a letter to his sister, "We have no less than three counts, Count D'Utassy, Count Biscaccianti and another (I forget his name), all men who have seen foreign service, well educated, and are gentlemen." Robert Shriber and Carlos DeLa Mesa were the other noblemen in the Guard.[?]

Hays took an immediate liking to Charles Biscaccianti, dubbing him "Bisquit Scantio," and thought of him as a good soldier. In a letter to his wife, Hays wrote, "A few days ago 'Bisquit Scantio' got a blow from his gray horse which quite discouraged him. It was most amusing to have his account with pantomime of the action. As a consequence, the fearful brute was turned over to me for summary punishment. I rode him over the roads, as they are, to Centreville in 40 minutes, and found him to be a noble animal, and aspire to own him."[3] Eventually Hays would own the gray horse and christen him the Count after Biscaccianti.

January drew to a close with change imminent. Hays began to assert command of the brigade, while D'Utassy still appeared to be very much in charge. January 28 found him in command of two regiments of infantry, the 39th New York and the 111th New York, and a battery of six guns, posted at Centreville: "Colonel D'Utassy had his headquarters in the largest house in Centreville. General Hays left him there with part of the Brigade, but made his headquarters in tents at Union Mills, where the Orange and Alexandria Railroad crossed Bull Run...." Hays had a reputation as a maker of soldiers; his professional training as a military officer and his prior combat experience evidently served him well. He began to overhaul the regiments. With the insight of an officer who had been promoted for leadership in the Mexican war and already in this war, on January 31 he observed about the Garibaldians and their fellows, "Although the brigade has been identified with one of the most disgraceful surrenders of the war and suffers a corresponding sense of humiliation, I have full confidence that in time, 'The War Cry of Harper's Ferry' will incite them to rival the deeds of older and more fortunate soldiers."[4]

Hays began to "clean up" the Garibaldi Guard by discharging many of its "lackadaisical" noncommissioned and commissioned officers and by whipping the men into a disciplined organization. He accomplished this through a constant barrage of drill, inspections, and picket duty. When his orders were disobeyed or not carried out in a satisfactory manner, the guilty suffered cash fines or corporal punishments. Hays was tireless about discipline and on the go day and night, particularly in bad weather: "This sort of actual training quickly began to improve the command[,] the efficient ones replacing the inefficient ones in every way the general could arrange."[5] His headquarters issued strict orders regarding the prevalent indifference of company officers toward the training and care of the men in their companies. Officers would assume appropriate, serious responsibilities for the discipline, health, safety, and comfort of the men under them, and this was to be done in a military way. Officers were to be present at morning roll, tattoo, and reveille, and not remain asleep in their tents. They were to be responsible for daily inspections and to insure that their men policed the camp and kept it clean. Reveille was set at 5 A.M., an hour earlier than before. The men were ordered to not destroy army property or to break up wagons to gather wood for fires. A regimental order was issued for gathering wood in an organized way instead of an everyone-for-himself manner, and to reinforce the idea that this was a military function: "[O]n account of the detail not being supplied with axes, it is hereby ordered that each company commander shall furnish to the Sergeant Major, for the use of the wood detail, one axe in good condition. These axes shall be returned when the necessity for their use ceases. Companies failing to comply with this order will be short of their supply of wood tomorrow." New latrines were dug for the regiment's use, and if any man relieved himself anywhere except at one of those four latrines he would be apprehended and summarily punished. Company officers were to command and control their men properly or suffer the consequences. Discipline developed as quickly as could be expected.

February 1863 found the Garibaldi Guard in the 3rd brigade of Brigadier General John Joseph Abercrombie's division in XXII Corps, Department of Washington. First Lieutenant Riege, Company G, was discharged due to wounds received in battle, and Second Lieutenant C. Theodore Pausch, Company E, was promoted to replace him. Sergeant Mathias Monnet of Company D was discharged for disability. Those of his "enemies" whom Confederate bullets or disease failed to eliminate, D'Utassy went after with false information. On Saturday, February 7, Captain Niedzielski, whom Hays reinstated after investigating his earlier dismissal and concluding he was falsely accused, unhappily discovered he was again dismissed with no explanation. D'Utassy continued to encourage his officers to believe the notion that the Garibaldi Guard still had not been exchanged properly after the Harpers Ferry surrender, and thus were still on parole and not subject to duty. The tactic worked for him at Camp Douglas; why not here, too? Hays knew D'Utassy's claims were groundless; infuriated, Hays wanted this notion "knocked out of their heads." On February 10, he ordered two of his artillery pieces aimed at the Guard's camp and then fired a shot over the tents to make every man understand who was in command and who gave the orders.[6] Captain Albert Hoffman of Company K and Lieutenant Pasquet of Company I resigned.

That shot across the tents evidently gave D'Utassy a choking feeling, that the noose of military discipline was tightening around him. In a move designed to impress Hays and improve his stature, D'Utassy "invited the general, with one or more of his aid[e]s to dine with him in his big house, to elaborate meals, that were cooked in Washington, 30 miles away, and hauled out by a government ambulance with four horses attached, and relayed at a half-way point. Despite the bad roads, the food was so well packed against the cold, that it was put on the table warm. The quality and quantity of the food and drink was all that could be desired, and General Hays' aid[e]s were glad to sit down to such unusual soldier rations. The general did not tell any of his staff his opinion of Colonel D'Utassy."[7] Self-assured, D'Utassy seemed to have all the answers to all the questions and after the heavy meal, he retired to his comfortable surroundings, satisfied that he had accomplished a brilliant bit of diplomacy with his superior.

Hays' next action showed his opinion of the colonel's military qualifications better than words could express. That night, just after dark, with a heavy, wet snow falling, Hays took his aide-de-camp, Lieutenant David Shields, to ride the picket line, which was eleven miles long. Shields, speaking of himself in the third person, remembered the fateful ride:

> On this night, as we got to D'Utassy's post, the first regimental camp had not a single guard, neither had the second regiment [111th New York]; then the general and Shields got going fast to the colonel's headquarters, where all were comfortable indoors, with no guards out, and the enemy, in shape of [Major John Singleton] Mosby, close at hand. The general pulled up in front of the colonel's big house, jumped off his horse, went up the broad steps to the great door, which quickly gave way to the weight of his body pushed against it. As the door broke open, Colonel D'Utassy was seen at the head of the stairs, dressed in red flannel under-clothes. The general ordered him to come down at once, just as he was, and get out his horse and go along. When a short distance had been covered the colonel dropped back alongside of Shields, and asked him what the matter was. He was told of the grossly unsoldierly condition of his post. He then asked what the general was going to do. "Ride the picket line," came the answer.

"I cannot go as I am; I will perish. I will go back to my quarters, put my clothes on, and I will join you on the line, where the Braddock road crosses Cub Run."

Shields replied: "Do not think of such a thing. Keep close after the general." And he did.

Most of the distance was through scrub pine, with low hanging limbs, bending, often to the ground, with their load of wet snow. There was about 300 pickets stationed on this line at irregular distances, but so posted as to have accurate control of all the line, that no one could get through unknown to the picket. It was hard, trying, difficult, and dangerous duty. The snow had obliterated any sign of a path. The picket was stationary, keeping hidden and quiet, usually behind a tree, or bush, but just where was the serious puzzle, even to a friend; as he might mistake any coming upon him for enemies and shoot. This experience had happened to General Hays and Shields on two occasions of their numerous rides along the picket line at night.

The colonel had never ridden at night, and seldom in daytime along a picket line; this unpleasant and dangerous duty if he could ever think it necessary, would be put upon a subordinate, who would shirk it, with the certain result, negligent or cowardly pickets. When the picket line was reached [the extreme right], Shields was sent ahead and remained in advance through the entire night, and ride; his positive knowledge of a picket's position was the earnest, firm challenge: "Halt, who goes there?" Shields would quickly answer: "Friends with the countersign." [The p]icket would reply: "Dismount one: advance and give the countersign." Being satisfied, the picket would say: "Countersign is correct." Then the general and colonel would join Shields; so it went, there not being a picket post missed.

There was no talking, all was serious and real, even the cussing at the horses or the slap in the face by a limb of a tree. The ride was such a novelty to the colonel that he had nothing to say. When the trio got to the general's headquarters, after break of day, D'Utassy was so used up he was not able to say anything. Speech had failed him. The general dismounted and went into his tent, not saying a word to the colonel or Shields, who went to the general and asked what he had to say to the colonel, who was nearly perished, and almost speechless with fatigue and cold, which his red flannel underwear had but slightly kept out. The general said: "Tell him to go to his headquarters under arrest;" and off the colonel rode, his last ride as a soldier, and was fitting and altogether right, in disgrace and almost dead from exposure. Whether or not shame mantled his cheek could not be seen in the darkness, and when daylight came, Colonel Count D'Utassy was too cold to blush.

"Get something to eat, and a fresh horse, as we are going at once to Washington [30 miles away]," said the general and they went, but were only a short while in Washington. While going back to camp the general stated a court martial had been called at once, at his request, to take action on Colonel D'Utassy's case. The court met the next day. Evidence was presented, chiefly by General Hays, showing utter incompetency as a soldier by Colonel D'Utassy.[8]

D'Utassy, rattled to the bone, went on sick leave "having ostensibly discovered suddenly a cancer in his stomach, but in fact to escape numerous serious charges." Madame Bacon was also in Washington to support the colonel who helped her son Charles' military career along.[9] Hays related to his wife that "[s]he really takes the affair most deeply to heart, and looks as old as Methuselah's sister. Poor Shriber and `Bisquit Scantio' are involved.... After D'Utassy's departure, I suppose I will have to move quarters to Centreville."[10] D'Utassy was heard on February 14 to complain that as far as he was concerned the "Garibaldi Guard might go to the Devil." However, on sick leave he was seen everywhere, contacting friends and old acquaintances and conjuring ways to escape his troubles. On February 18, back at his command post at Centreville, D'Utassy made one last try to rid himself of key witnesses against him. He ordered Jacky detailed to General MacDougall's Livery Stables in Alexandria and had his brother Anton telegraph ahead to the provost marshal at Alexandria to arrest Jacky for deserting. Jacky disregarded D'Utassy's order and confided the story to Zyla. D'Utassy advised other witnesses, like carpenter Daniel Koester, Benoit Baise, and First Sergeant Adolph Lingner of Company H, to desert near Centreville. Lindger and Baise deserted that night,[11] making it fifteen desertions that D'Utassy had instigated since January and the disciplinary crackdown. Meanwhile, also on February 18, First Lieutenant Schwickhardi of Company A was promoted to the captaincy of Company K, and he and Zyla compiled more evidence against D'Utassy.

Hays wrote to his wife on February 23, "Colonel D'Utassy and madam [Bacon] left me ten days ago, and from appearances, intended to stay away. I wish they would. It appears as if young 'Charley' Bacon was the choice for colonel of the 39th if D'Utassy vacates. I believe he is qualified, but if he succeeds won't the 'old woman' make a spread eagle, and won't I catch——. If I do, I'll insist upon disbanding the regiment."[12] Four days later, Schwickhardi and Zyla composed and sent a letter which detailed their complaints against D'Utassy to the Office of the Special Commissioner of the War Department at New York City. Three days after that, on March 2, the two officers swore before a Mr. G. C. Thomas, a notary public in Washington D.C., to thirty-one charges and specifications against D'Utassy. Zyla preferred seventeen additional charges against D'Utassy two days later. On March 1, meanwhile, Sergeant Bader of Company E was promoted to second lieutenant in Company B, Sergeant Major Rumpf of Company A became a second lieutenant in Company

E, and Corporals Giuseppe Griffa and Henry Palmer of Company C were each promoted to sergeant.

Discipline in the Guard's winter quarters at Camp Hays, near Centreville, hit a low point on Sunday, March 8. At 2:00 A.M., the clear, dark night was very cold, so cold that Giacomo Antonali decided to wear several pairs of pants and an overcoat to retain body heat to bed. He and Giovanni Picconi lay asleep on their cots, while the third man in the tent, Miguel Oliver, a known thief from the Guard's march to Harpers Ferry, stealthily worked to cut a small hole into Antonali's clothes. Antonali kept his money sewn in a secret pocket in his pants. He felt a hand on his waistcoat. He caught the hand, but it jerked away. He jumped up from his cot and looked down, to see that his pants pocket was half cut off. He took his pignard, a double-edged knife that he kept under his knapsack, and approached Oliver, who had retreated to his cot and covered himself with his blanket. Oliver, readying himself to attack Antonali, was about to spring out of bed at him, but was knocked down and stabbed repeatedly—in the knee, on the thigh, all the way through the right forearm, across the left hand. Oliver began crying and swinging wildly to fend off Antonali's attack. Antonali had him down on his cot and thrust the knife into the right side of his chest. It penetrated between the second and third ribs and plunged through his right lung, cutting open the right branch of his pulmonary artery. Oliver grasped at his clothes, pulled his coat and shirt open, saw his mortal wound, gasped a few times and died. The cries awakened Picconi, who got out of bed in time to see Antonali lift his pignard to stab Oliver again. Oliver sat on his cot, his back against the tent wall, motionless and silent. Picconi caught Antonali before he could strike and put him to his bed. Antonali sat on his cot and told Picconi to go to bed. Picconi complied, eyeing the corpse and Antonali for a moment. Antonali looked for his pipe, found it, struck a match, and lit it.

Picconi was so afraid he got up, took his shoes, and ran barefoot out of the tent, straight to the tent of Fifth Sergeant Raphael Castelbecchi of Company C. Antonali called out after him, "Do not be afraid." Picconi told Castelbecchi that he thought Antonali had struck and killed Oliver. Within half an hour the sergeant sent for a corporal to go to the guardhouse for a guard, as he kept watch on Antonali's tent. Antonali would be arrested. Orderly Sergeant Castelbecchi went to Second Lieutenant Jacob S. Kittle and told him there had been trouble in their company. Kittle went to the tent of Second Lieutenant Magnus Bader, the regimental officer of the day, and woke him, telling him, "Come out. A man was stabbed." Kittle informed Bader of the situation, and Bader told Kittle to send a corporal and four men to arrest Antonali. Corporal Giovanni Yelitz of Company C was on duty that night. He received Kittle's orders and took four men, loaded their guns, and left the guardhouse. Drawing near Antonali's tent, the corporal ordered in Italian, "Come forth quick!" Antonali answered in Italian, "What's the matter?" Yelitz told him, "You are under arrest." Antonali asked to open the tent. Yelitz opened the flap of the tent, and Antonali threw his bedroll out. This startled the men, who ducked out of the way, but the corporal held his ground and cocked and aimed his rifle. As Kittle turned around to see what was the matter with the men, Antonali came out of the tent and took his blanket under his arm, appearing calm and collected, and smoking his pipe. It was still dark. A guard was placed over the tent.

Antonali was arrested and taken to the tent that served as the guardhouse. Bader, as officer of the day, requested to make a search of the prisoner. Antonali told the officer that there was no need to search him for weapons, for as soon as an official search was made, they would find out what there was to be found. Yelitz responded, "It would be better to search immediately for the arms." He thought he discerned the form of a knife or handle of a knife under Antonali's clothes. Since there was no light in the guardhouse, Antonali was searched outside in the corporal's presence. Two men were ordered to guard Antonali, and handcuffs were sent for. When Bader had come down to the guardhouse tent, he asked Antonali in Italian if he had stabbed Oliver. Antonali shrugged his shoulders, and Bader asked him again in English. Antonali did not understand English. When Bader put the handcuffs on him, Antonali played with them and joked, "They have given me the keys of the Treasury!" No one spoke with him, and thereafter he was entirely silent. Sergeant Major Giovanni Samsa searched him and confiscated about fifty dollars and a little pocketknife. Antonali made no objection to being searched. He had some blood on his sleeve, but other than that, there was not any blood on his clothes.

Bader gathered Dr. Emil Steiger, the Guard's assistant surgeon, and Dr. Rudolph Ribbeck, its first assistant surgeon, and led them to the tent to examine Oliver. The group went into the tent and found Oliver lying partly on his bed, with his head against the side of the tent, his leg hanging down. He was very pale; his face was covered with blood, as were his clothes. His shirt coat and jacket were unbuttoned and open, and revealed a gash, about an inch and a half long in his right breast. Steiger felt for Oliver's pulse and then put an ear to his chest to listen for a palpitation, but found none. He declared Oliver dead. Ribbeck made a re-examination. Then he ordered Kittle that nothing in and around the tent should be moved and that a guard should be placed outside the tent until a board of inquiry could examine it. The doctors left, and Bader put a guard over the tent.

At 6:00 A.M. that morning at the guardhouse, Samsa was asked to take a knife away from Antonali. Samsa had known Antonali since they enlisted together in New York in May 1861. When he arrived at the guardhouse, Samsa asked Antonali if he had a knife on his person. Antonali said that whatever he had in the line of weapons he was ready to deliver to the proper authority, a commissioned officer. At that moment Captain Schwickhardi entered the tent. Pointing to Schwickhardi, Samsa told Antonali that there was a commissioned officer present to whom a weapon could be delivered. Then Antonali took a pocketknife from his left breast pocket and presented it to Samsa. He also handed over to Samsa about fifty-four dollars from his watch pocket, telling him that it was the pocket Oliver had tried to cut through. The pocket was cut nearly all the way through.

At 11:00 A.M. a board of inquiry composed of Captains Hollinde (president), Bacon, Schwickhardi, and Baer met at the Garibaldi Guard adjutant's tent and went down to the tent where the dead man lay, together with Steiger and Ribbeck. The body was now covered with a blanket. The doctors uncovered the body and found another wound on the left knee. The pants were nearly cut off at the knee, and there were three larger cuts in the drawers at about the same place. The thickness of the drawers in the vicinity of the cuts was doubled by a sewn-in patch, which formed a pocket and appeared to be a secret compartment, not a repair. Only one of the three cuts in the drawers nicked the patch, which also appeared to have been cut only a little from a cut thrust up and across the leg. Steiger and Ribbeck also noted that Oliver's left hand was bloody and cut in different places. Then the body was removed to the hospital tent for a postmortem examination. When they moved him they found his blanket cut and bloody in several places. They also found forty-eight dollars and sixty-five cents in his pocket, along with a silver watch and a brass chain.

After Oliver's body was removed to the hospital tent, Antonali was brought in, in irons and under guard, for questioning. He appeared very calm and self-assured. Now Schwarz, Hildebrandt, Zyla, and First Lieutenant John Dessaur were present, in addition to the board of inquiry. Antonali was asked, regarding Oliver, "Do you know this man?" Antonali answered yes. He was shown the wound in the right side of Oliver's chest and asked, "Do you see that?" He replied yes. To the next question, "Did you kill him?" Antonali said, "I killed him." Then he was asked, "Why did you do it?" "Oliver tried to rob me!" he said as he made signs with his hands in an effort to have everyone understand that Oliver had tried to rob him. He was shown the knife and identified it as the knife he used to stab Oliver. He was taken back to the guardhouse, where he would remain imprisoned until his court-martial next month, in April.[13]

Before the Oliver murder, on March 3, Zyla had written a request to Schwarz: "Enclosed you will find my commission as Chaplin [*sic*] of the regiment dated August 28th, 1861 and testimonials of my good standing, as a regularly ordained minister of the United German Protestant Evangelical Church, with a recommendation for my appointment as an Army Chaplain from an authorized Ecclesiastical body, and five accredited ministers belonging to said religious denomination. Thus answering to the requirements of General Order Number 152, which like all other General Orders was purposely withheld from the conscience of this regiment by Colonel D'Utassy, formerly acting Brigadier and later Post commander, I most respectfully request you to forward this enclosure, through the proper channels to higher authorities in order to have me duly mustered into service by an officer of the regular army of the United States." Eight days later, Schwarz wrote to Lieutenant R. C. Perry, the post adjutant:

Sir: enclosed please find returned from higher headquarters, relative to a petition of Anthony P. Zyla, to be mustered into service as Chaplain of this regiment, on the grounds of certificates and a Commission, which I, hereby transmit for the purpose of having them, through Colonel MacDougall, commanding post, again forwarded to higher authorities, you will fervently obliged me, if you will draw the attention of Colonel MacDougall to the endorsement from headquarters of the Division, which says, that if the above Zyla has not discharged his duties faithfully, General Hays has a perfect right to refuse to muster him into the U. S. service.... I know, and all the officers of this regiment know that he performed and are to prove that he performed his temporary duties of a brigade postmaster with his accustomed austerity and faithfulness. Though the reason, that general orders No. 152 was not, timely, put to his knowledge, he was, at the end of January, 1863, unable to present all the testimonials, required by said order, as he never had asked one simple day of leave of absence. For the facts, transmitted testimonial enclosures marked A and B by a communication, which you will please find among the enclosures, marked as C, it was left to me, to re-nominate Chaplain Zyla for this position as soon as he produced such evidences, which would entitle him to hold a chaplaincy under the order allowed to Chaplain Zyla having on account of his efficiency, become a necessity, and hence a most desirable reception for this regiment he did measure the documents required, as soon as he received from brigade headquarters a letter, which I transmit under D ever since his return to this regiment, Chaplain Zyla is performing his pastoral duties with un-wearied eagerness, probing most efficient for the maintenance of morality among the men and obedience to the orders of their superiors. It is for this as well as for all previous reasons, that I beseech you, Sir, to interest Colonel MacDougall to have our worthy Chaplain recommended for being mustered into service, at the earliest convenience of the higher authorities.[14]

The Garibaldi Guard's personnel situation continued to ferment. On Saturday, March 16, five hospitalized men were mustered out from their beds. Captain Shriber returned from Washington. Hays investigated Niedzielski's dismissal in February and concluded that Shriber had harassed and persecuted Niedzielski and, as the adjutant, improperly wrote out his own brigade order with instructions to discharge Niedzielski from the Guard. Instead, Shriber was dismissed and his musters as lieutenant and captain revoked. Niedzielski's dismissal was revoked in turn, and he was mustered in as captain of Company

D, replacing Shriber.[15] "Shriber, when his rascality and Judas acts were fully brought to light, completely upset General Hays, who was dumfounded, so great was his confidence in the man."[16] Hays relieved Schwarz and passed command of the Garibaldians to Hildebrandt, "one of the better ones" in Hays' esteem. By Monday, Shriber's mere name was a red rag to a bull in Hays' presence. He wrote to his wife, "Colonel D'Utassy is now at Washington, in arrest, under the most infamous charges ever preferred against a man. Shriber is deeply implicated and disgraced, for complicity with D'Utassy, and for practicing deceits upon his beloved 'mein Shen-e-ral.' May the Lord forgive me, and I will never trust their kind again. The brigade is now under orders of regeneration. Yesterday I secured 5 horses belonging to the United States that D'Utassy had presented to his friends. It has given me much trouble, but you know when I sweep, I sweep clean. Every man connected in any manner with the former provincial brigade has been ordered back to duty in his regiment."[17]

On March 24, Assistant Surgeon Dr. Hoyt of the 126th, detailed to the Garibaldians, wrote, "This morning the regiment [126th] left for Centreville. Vermont troops to supply our place at Union Mills. Arrived at Centreville at 2 P.M., and immediately set to work arranging a new camp. All the stores, lumber and other camp equipage are to be brought from Union Mills. We find the 39th, 111th, and the 125th New York volunteers encamped here, our regiment being placed on the extreme right of the line. The seriously sick were left at Brigade hospital, and a new Brigade hospital is being arranged here prior to their removal hither."[18] The 10th Massachusetts Independent Artillery Battery was a neighbor of the regiment. The battery's late commander, Captain Achille De Vecchio, had served on Garibaldi's staff in the Sicilian campaign, in 1860. The end of the month saw Chaplain Zyla's promotion on March 28 to first lieutenant in Company A, under Schwickhardi. Hoyt recorded the serious and comical lessons in discipline that befell the Garibaldians and their fellows at camp in Centreville:

> The Brigade is under constant drill, and fast being educated in the school of the soldier.... Very few sick. A group of pickets [was] straggling back to camp at their leisure in an irregular and disorderly manner. As [they] strolled along they'd gamble on who could hit designated targets, branches, posts, etc., firing their weapons from the picket toward the camp. When stray bullets whizzed over the heads of officers they believed [themselves] to be under attack. They sent a detachment of soldiers scrambling to meet the skirmishers. When they found out it was their own pickets the Provost Marshall arrested the lot of them. Afterward the latest order was that pickets had to be accompanied by an officer and marched back in good order. Then there was the problem created by the great number of dogs kept by the men. Officers found themselves darting around the Great Nuisance when drilling the men. To avoid this problem, it was strictly

forbidden to allow any dog to stray round either at Guard Mount Drill or Drill Parade. The owners of those dogs would be held responsible.[19]

On April 3, Giacomo Antonali was court-martialed for the murder of Miguel Oliver. The proceedings were held in Centreville under General Order No. 38. Colonel G. S. Wilson of the 125th New York was president of the court; Captain C. A. Richardson of the 16th New York was the judge advocate. Sergeant Maggi and Chaplain Zyla were sworn in and acted as interpreters in the court-martial. It was rather sloppily conducted. Antonali pleaded not guilty to the charge of murder, but admitted that he was guilty of killing Oliver to protect his life and property. He was sentenced to imprisonment at "a penitentiary or other place as the President of the United States may direct, for life... I hereby approve of the sentence...justice demands that the sentence should be rigidly enforced." President Lincoln approved Antonali's sentence of life imprisonment at hard labor in a Federal penitentiary. Lieutenant Edward Walter West, a graduate of Columbia College, a lawyer, and aide-de-camp to Major General Casey, the division commander, said about Antonali's trial, "There are certain technical errors in the record but they do not seem to have worked injustice. Although the verdict seems unwarranted by evidence it should stand, in default of a better one. Sentence, although, in view of the verdict, extraordinary, should in view of the evidence be inflicted."[20]

Meanwhile, the day before the Antonali court-martial began in Centreville, D'Utassy's court-martial had begun in Washington, D.C. It convened at 11:00 A.M., pursuant to Special Order No. 152, in accordance with previous arrangements. D'Utassy was brought before the court, and the order convening the trial was read to him. He was asked if he had any objection to the members composing the court. He replied in the negative when each member and the judge advocate, Major Gaines, was sworn in. D'Utassy then asked the court to adjourn until the next Tuesday, in order to let him procure counsel and prepare for his defense. The court assented to his request and adjourned accordingly. In the meantime, he remained under armed guard. On April 7, he was brought back before the court. Gaines presented D'Utassy with a copy of the charges against him and then read aloud the following charges and specifications preferred against Colonel Frederick D'Utassy, of the 39th Regiment of New York Volunteer Infantry, in the service of the United States:

1. Persuading a soldier to desert [for example, Jacky, Koester, Baise; at least two dozen soldiers and members of the band].
2. Embezzling mail bags.
3. Extorting money from sutlers [for example, on six occasions from Montegrifa].

4. Obtaining money from officers under his command on the pretence that it was to be used for recruiting purposes [for example, on the occasion involving Chaplain Zyla].
5. Selling commissions in his regiment [such as the major's commission sold to Wiegand].
6. Plotting against officers under his command so as to cause them to resign:

1861 July 30, Second Lieutenant Anthony Dumazer of the French Company.

1861 August 27, Captain Louis Tassilier, dishonorably discharged.

1861 August 28, Chaplain Theodore Krueger of the Field & Staff.

1861 September 20, Captain Victor Chandone of the French Company.

1861 September 27, First Lieutenant Ignazio Allegretti of the Italian Company.

1861 October 7, First Lieutenants Francisco Lugue of the Spanish Company and Alfred Muller of the Swiss Company.

1861 December 9, Surgeon Leopold Zander of the Field & Staff.

1861 December 22, Captain Joseph Torrens of the Spanish Company.

1862 January 2, First Lieutenant Charles Ruelberg of Unwerth's German Company.

1862 January 8, First Lieutenant Charles Zimmerman of Siegel's German Company.

1862 January 16, First Lieutenant Henrich C. Lindner of Siegel's German Company.

1862 January 24, Major Charles Weigand of Weigand's German Company.

1862 June 30, Captain John B. Junger of the Hungarian, Slav, and Prussian Company.

1862 July 16, Captain Conrad Von Schondorf of Weigand's German Company.

1862 July 26, Second Lieutenant Rogella Gerranna, unassigned.

1862 September 10, Second Lieutenant Giovanni Boggialli of the Hungarian, Slav, and Prussian Company.

1862 October 5, Captain William Robitseck of Siegel's German Company.

1862 October 22, First Lieutenant Riatz Cartillo of the Spanish Company.

1862 December 17, Second Lieutenants Silvis Burmazor of the Spanish Company and Charles Gallerbad, unassigned.

1863 February 2, First Lieutenant Louis Riege of the French Company.

1863 February 10, Captain Charles Hoffman, Company K., resigned.

7. Slandering [*sic*] his subordinate officers in official letters.

8. Selling Government horses and stores and pocketing the proceeds.

9. Altering the proceedings of a Court Martial so as to cause the dismissal of an officer of his regiment who was never tried [the case of Second Lieutenant Frixione].

10. Counterfeiting the signature of [the] Hon. Charles H. Van Wyck, member of Congress from New York, on envelopes, and selling them to soldiers in his regiment for 3 cents each.

11. Forging pay rolls [using the members of the band to draw additional pay].

12. Making false musters and receiving pay for fictitious officers [the enrollments of brothers Anton, four times, and Carl, three times; D'utassy drew Carl's pay for several months before he arrived in America. Carl, first lieutenant of Company C, remained in the Guard till his muster].

13. Opening U.S. mail bags and extracting commissions therefrom [such as letters to the late Major Weekey and Dr. Steiger].

Among the witnesses called to testify against D'Utassy was Alexander Repetti, who had returned to Italy, joined the Italian army, and become a colonel and aide-de-camp to Major General Augusto Fogliardi (who subsequently wrote *La guerra di Secessione delgi State Uniti d'America nei rapporti del Col. Augusto Fogliardi 1866*, or *The War of Secession of the United States of America Reported by Colonel Augusto Fogliardi, 1866*). Repetti came back to testify. Evidence must have been irrefutable. At its single sitting, the court found D'Utassy guilty on all the charges and specifications, and immediately sentenced him to be cashiered with the loss of all back pay and allowances and disgraceful dismissal (dishonorable discharge) from the service. He was sentenced to Sing Sing Prison and one year in close confinement at hard labor. *The Washington Herald* and *The New York Times* covered the case; the latter paper reported "that by order of the Secretary of War the Court Martial in the case of Col. D'Utassy has been dissolved, he will be dismissed without the usual forms, or the expense of a trial."

The pace of life began to quicken and change for the Garibaldians at Centreville, too. On April 19, they were issued forty rounds of ammunition per individual, with one shelter tent per soldier and one wall tent per officer. They were to be prepared to take the field in two days, carrying seven days' rations and sixty additional rounds of ammunition per man in wagons. On

Tuesday, April 21, the Guard stood inspection; Dr. Hoyt recorded: "Brigade reviewed today by General Hays. Order of Brigade: Right, 125th New York Volunteers; left, 126th; right center, 111th New York Volunteers; left center, 39th; right Battery, Keystone; left, 9th Massachusetts; day pleasant affair passed off creditably."[21] At the inspection Brigadier General John Joseph Abercrombie reportedly commented about the Garibaldians that "the Regiment seems to be very uniform." General Hays answered, "You will always find them all right, and besides, they have a good record; they are the Regiment who did the fighting at Harper's Ferry." (The 126th, 125th, 111th and 39th New York regiments would now remain companions from the siege at Harpers Ferry through the end of the war.)

After Burnside's disastrous failure at Fredericksburg in December 1862, Major General Joseph Hooker was given command of the Army of the Potomac. While the Garibaldians occupied the Centreville area and defended Washington, Hooker had rebuilt a demoralized and badly run force into a well organized, trained, and disciplined army. Now he planned to fight Robert E. Lee. He would cross the Rappahannock River far upstream from Fredericksburg, well northwest of the city, and march southeast to envelop Lee's left flank. He began to move on April 27. By May 1, most of his army was just south of Chancellorsville, nine miles west of Fredericksburg and behind Lee's left flank, in position for a decisive victory. Then he lost his nerve and gave up the initiative. Once more Lee had time to concentrate his forces and defeat a Union army bit by bit. By Sunday, May 3, Lee was pushing Hooker back through Chancellorsville. The Guard and its fellow regiments thought they heard the heavy guns at their camps. By May 6, Hooker was beaten. During the entire Chancellorsville campaign, the Garibaldians had completely ready to move at a moment's notice. Instead, they spent some eight days engaged in digging rifle pits and throwing up earthworks on their front as protection against attack.[22] On May 18, Dr. Hoyt wrote: "I speak upon the authority of General Abercrombie, who has been in the service forty years, when I say it is probably the nicest camp in the whole army. I can't begin to tell you one half its beauty. Arches and all kinds of ingenious devices decorate almost every street and corner. You hardly see a tent the evergreens are so thick."[23] Abercrombie superseded Casey as the Guard's division commander.

After the promise of offensive action, the last half of May must have been anticlimactic to the Garibaldians. The name of D'Utassy became a laughingstock among the foreign-born soldiers. On the evening of May 21, at the First Fancy Ball, the "Colonel" was contemptuously caricatured. An actor impersonating D'Utassy, made up as a wrinkled-faced, bespeckled, old geezer wearing a fantastic Hussar uniform with pants full of money, was followed about by another actor impersonating Mrs. Bacon, the "Mighty protectress of Colonel D'Utassy." That same day, Captain Anton D'Utassy retreated to the hospital, listed as sick, and vanished from the record. He was evidently so humiliated by his brother's actions, the trial and conviction, the prison sentence and the ridicule that followed him afterward, that he seized that opportunity to desert before the colonel arrived at Sing Sing.

On Monday, May 25, Lieutenant Woodbury, Company E, was discharged, and Leo Doerndinger was promoted to first lieutenant in his place. Captain Bacon of Company C, Colonel D'Utassy's close friend, was dismissed (he reenlisted in the 36th Artillery Battery and by January 31, 1865, had become a lieutenant and ordnance officer in the 13th New York Artillery). Wednesday saw the start of new drills for the Garibaldians: skirmish line drills every morning from 8:00 to 10:00 A.M. and drills each afternoon from 4:00 to 5:30 P.M. as infantry of the line. On Fridays both drills would be bayonet exercise. Saturday mornings would be devoted to target practice and afternoons to cleaning weapons and policing camp in preparation for Sunday morning inspection. Officers were advised to study George McClellan's *Manual of Bayonet Exercises* and to adhere strictly to *Casey's Tactic* for all other drills. On Friday, D'Utassy arrived at Sing Sing Prison, in Albany, New York, and started his own new drills. He resented his reception. His head was shaved and stripes were put on him as he complained, "You treat me this way? I, who speak fourteen languages." The warden replied, "Well, we speak only one here, and damn little of that." D'Utassy wrangled with prison officials, requested employment in the office, and even asked for a salary. He would petition Lincoln for amnesty several times but serve the rest of the war in prison.

The week and the month ended on Sunday with the largest single day's discharge of officers and men that the Guard had ever experienced. Fifty officers and men whom Hays deemed unfit for service, who had been with the regiment since May 1861, were mustered out at Centreville with honorable discharges one year before their enlistments expired. Lieutenant Colonel Schwarz topped a long list of officers and noncommissioned officers who were sent packing. Assistant surgeon Ribbeck, who was captured during the Battle of Cross Keys, was dismissed, together with Lieutenant Pollak, who as a sergeant major took command of Company C when Venuti was wounded in the battle. Second Lieutenant Doerfer of Company A was mustered out, as were Captain Enke, First Sergeant Raefle, and Sergeants Dress and Hoell of Company B. First Lieutenant Carl D'Utassy and Sergeants Palmer, Giuseppe Cavrotti, and Giuseppe Griffa of Company C were mustered out (Cavrotti and Griffa then reenlisted in Company G, 20th Massachusetts). Captain Niedzielski, Second Lieutenant Bauer, and Sergeants Hafeli and Riedel (who had both transferred in from Company A), were mustered out from Company D. Captain Bauer, Second Lieutenant Rumpf, and First Sergeant Surer were mustered out from Company E; First Lieutenant Joerin transferred out to Company D and then to the 15th Artillery. Second Lieutenant Erben and Sergeant May of Company F were mustered out. In Company G,

Sergeant Bartis was mustered out. Sergeants Krebs and Zimmerman transferred from Company H to Company B and then were mustered out.

Once again people were shuffled around to fill newly created vacancies. First Lieutenant Dietrich, Second Lieutenant Otto Wilm, Sergeant Menzler, and Corporal Diefenbach, all from Company I, and Sergeant Bonin from Company B were all transferred to Company A. Second Lieutenant Louis Leviseur of Company B was promoted to first lieutenant, and the company's other leadership vacancies were filled by Captain Baer and Corporal Hoffman from Company E, Second Lieutenant Kittle from Company C, and Corporal Andreas from Company H. Captain DeLa Mesa, Sergeant Freitas, and Corporal F. Muller from Company I, together with First Lieutenant Pausch from Company G, filled out Company C. Captain Schwickhardi and Second Lieutenant Wagner of Company K, and Sergeant Sutter of Company G, were transferred to Company D. On June 1, from Company B, First Lieutenant Dessaur was promoted to adjutant, and First Sergeant Wilhelmi, who had just transferred from Company E, was discharged. The next day, First Lieutenant di Biscaccianti was discharged from Company I for disabilities (and took a commission as a lieutenant in the U.S. Volunteers).

On Thursday, June 4, Chaplain Zyla, who had had the courage to do the right thing and helped to rid the Union army of one of its most notorious parasites, said good-bye to Captain Schwickhardi and left the regiment.[24] Over the course of two years, the regiment had shrunk to a shadow of the eight hundred fifty officers and men in ten companies that had marched heroically away from New York to war. Now the Garibaldi Guard was down to a mere remnant of its original size. Commanded by Major Hildebrandt, it would have no colonel or lieutenant colonel for the next eight months. In a few short days, the Guard would number three hundred twenty-two officers and men present for duty, consolidated into four companies. On June 8, the City of New York presented the Garibaldians with new colors, and the remaining companies turned out at 2:00 P.M. for the reception.

The enforcement of discipline among the soldiers grew stronger. On June 11, at about 3:00 A.M., the Corporal of the Guard discovered Private Jose Arellano of Company C asleep at his post on guard duty near Centreville, at the Brigade Command Stores. Arellano was a twenty-two-year-old sailor from Santiago, Chile, who had enlisted in the Spanish company in May 1861. On this night he dozed off long enough to be caught. When he was awakened, he used profane language and argued, like soldiers eternal, that he was not sleeping, just resting hard. Nevertheless, he was arrested, tried, and sentenced to a month of guard duty and loss of a month's pay. The next night Captain DeLa Mesa and Company I did picket duty to pay for Arellano's catnap. Two days after Arellano's apprehension, on Saturday, Privates Julius Tushschmidt of Company C and John Britsch of Company B were court-martialed for disobedience to orders and conduct not becoming a soldier. Each man got two weeks' guard duty. Sergeant Wechsler and Gottlieb Andreas, both of Company B, Emil Muller of Company C, and John Frey of Company D were tried for misbehavior, disobedience, and disrespect towards Captain Schwickhardi. All four men, who were members of the original Swiss company, were sentenced to half a month's imprisonment, camp cleaning duty, and loss of a month's pay.

On June 23, the regiment was told to prepare to join the Army of the Potomac in the field. Assistant Surgeon Dr. Steiger was released from arrest and reported to Dr. Wolf for duty. Captain DeLa Mesa was instructed to detail two of the black men employed by his company for support duties to report at once to Wolf for further instructions.[25] Wolf examined a dozen Garibaldians. He found six men unfit for duty and transferred them to the Veteran Reserve Corps. Second Lieutenant Bader and First Lieutenant Doerndinger were transferred from Companies B and E, respectively, to Company D. The Garibaldians getting ready for the field watched General Hays go to corps headquarters. Rumor had it that Hays would return to his old brigade, which he had left when he took command of the division. Destined for the 3rd Brigade, 3rd Division, II Corps, Army of the Potomac, the Garibaldians were anything but happy soldiers when they learned they would remain under Hays' command.

Chapter Eight

REDEMPTION AT GETTYSBURG

WHILE he had defeated Hooker at Chancellorsville, Lee knew that continuing to win basically defensive battles would never win the war; to win the war, he needed to attack and defeat the Union forces decisively. Hooker's position across the Rappahannock River from Lee was too strong for direct attack, and two years of continuous fighting in Virginia had degraded the state and its ability to support Lee. There was plenty of food and clothing in Maryland and Pennsylvania, however, and an invasion of the North would force Hooker out of his position and into the open. Lee could resupply his army, and he was confident that he could decisively defeat Hooker in the open and perhaps end the war. Lee decided to invade the North, and in early June his army began slipping westward for an advance up the Shenandoah and Cumberland Valleys. Hooker soon figured out that Lee was moving into the Shenandoah Valley. Under strict orders from Washington to go after Lee and not to go after Richmond, Hooker began to follow Lee, keeping between Lee and Washington. By June 24, Lee was north of the Potomac, beyond Harpers Ferry. Hooker was moving toward Frederick, Maryland.

On Thursday, June 25, two days after their alert, the Garibaldians were ordered to join the Army of the Potomac on the march. The Guard marched out together with the other New York regiments that surrendered at Harpers Ferry, the 111th, the 125th, and the 126th, to join II Corps' third division as its third brigade. Major General Winfield Scott Hancock commanded the corps, Hays commanded the division, and Colonel George L. Willard of the 125th commanded the brigade. On June 28, while the Guard marched to catch up with its division, Major General George G. Meade replaced Hooker, who asked to be relieved after Washington refused his request for still more

134

reinforcements than he had already been given. On June 30, Hancock rested his men at Uniontown, Maryland, some twenty miles northeast of Frederick, where the citizens brought various foods and refreshments out to the worn-out soldiers. One day later, II Corps moved on to Two Taverns, Pennsylvania, about five miles southeast of Gettysburg, where it rested in the fields as the battle of Gettysburg began to take shape. The Guard remained on a forced march. Sergeant Carl Sutter was promoted to first sergeant of Company D, and Second Lieutenant Adolphus Wagner of Company D was transferred to Captain DeLa Mesa's company.

On the day II Corps rested at Two Taverns and the Garibaldians pushed northward, Confederate Major General Harry Heth led his division southeast toward Gettysburg, after a supply of shoes that was supposed to be there. On his way to the town, Heth ran into hasty defensive positions that some of Union Major General John Buford's cavalrymen had thrown up northwest of town. Buford's division was leading the Union advance, and on June 30, his lead riders had run into some of Heth's men, scouting toward Gettysburg. Buford examined the area, decided the town was a key spot, reported the situation to his corps commander, Major General John Fulton Reynolds, and to Meade, and prepared to defend the town. Now Buford's badly outnumbered troopers, using their breech-loading carbines against Confederate muskets, stalled Heth's advance for nearly two hours. By the time enough enemy soldiers arrived to start pushing Buford back toward Gettysburg, Reynolds had arrived and ordered more Federal forces forward into the fight. They came forward while more Confederates converged on the battle. By late afternoon, a sharpshooter had killed Reynolds, and the Confederates had pushed the Federals back through Gettysburg to defensive positions on the high ground south of town. Meade sent Hancock up to take charge, and the day ended as both sides converged on the area.

On Thursday, July 2, the Army of the Potomac had a formidable defensive position at Gettysburg. Its right flank lay on Culp's Hill, southeast of town. From there, the position ran west perhaps one-half mile to Cemetery Hill, due south of town, and then ran south for some two miles along Cemetery Ridge, ending with its left flank upon two bold hills, first a rocky knoll named Little Round Top and then neighboring, higher Round Top. Hancock's II Corps occupied the center part of Cemetery Ridge, with I Corps on its right and III Corps on its left, holding the left flank. The XI and XII Corps occupied Cemetery and Culp's Hills, respectively. The Confederates occupied a line roughly parallelling the Union line, capping it from the north and extending down the west. The Guard arrived that morning and went into the line with its brigade, on II Corps' right. Both sides had deployed skirmishers, to preoccupy the enemy and provide relative security for deploying their own main forces. General Hays soon ordered the four companies of Garibaldians forward to the skirmish line. Lieutenant R. A. Basset of the 126th New York remembered, "As soon as we arrived, 8 A.M., the 39th were deployed as skirmishers, and the rest of our Brigade... supported a couple of Batteries on the right of the line of battle."[1]

Private W. G. Lightfoote, a soldier in the 125th New York, recalled the Garibaldians' entrance in the developing Battle of Gettysburg: "A summer peace was in the air. But the calm, the lull in nature, only preceded the fiercest storm of conflict, when the air should be torn by the rough hands of strife and be hoarse with the voice of passion. At first, from our position the enemy could not be seen, covered as they were by the woods and houses. The rumor passed among the officers that the enemy had retired; but as the morning lengthened in the distance among some brush behind a fence, men were seen moving into position as skirmishers. The order was given for the Thirty-ninth to move to the front as skirmishers." Lieutenant Dietrich, Company A, described moving out: "General Willard gave the command 'Bayonets, forward march, charge!' his and our purpose aimed our attack. Yet we were not ready for action, but with the typical perception of an aged soldier we all felt that hot line and harsh work waiting, and went forward march it [sic], while making our line watertight against the bullet rain."[2] Lightfoote watched the Garibaldians march out across the front: "And now they pass down at our right; down into the field and deploy as skirmishers. Brave fellows—brave or stupid which is it?—there they stand in open field, and the crack of rifles is heard. The rebels are down behind the fence and are sheltered. 'Drop, Garibaldi!' Yes, they did drop, one after another, as the bullet did its work. Some to rise not again; and here come some of the poor fellows with shattered jaws and maimed limbs and cut faces."[3]

The regiment remained deployed on the battle line for over four hours, actively engaged with enemy skirmishers. The Garibaldians rendered efficient service and elicited admiration from generals who witnessed their movements and generally courageous bearing, although they must have been understandably skittish after being thrust out on the forward edge so soon after finishing a long, hard march. Hays reported, "Once in the forenoon my pickets [the Garibaldi Guards], who were posted near a barn half a mile from my front, were repulsed by the Rebel sharpshooters and retreated in disorder....I dashed over the plain, followed by [a] standard bearer. We rallied the runaways, [and] put them in position again, retaking the barn. This was in full view of both lines and fair range of the enemy's bullets." Company C alone lost both First Lieutenant Wagner and Second Lieutenant Pausch to severe wounds, together with twenty-eight other soldiers killed and wounded while holding the line.[4]

Without enough maneuver room or supplies on hand to get away easily, and with faith that his soldiers could defeat the Union troops piecemeal, before they all arrived and got organized, Lee chose to attack. On his right flank, the Union left flank, the Union III Corps had overextended itself and moved too far forward of the Round Tops, where it had been ordered to be. Lee decided to attack III Corps early in the day, but his orders got out

slowly. At 3:00 P.M., Confederate Lieutenant General James Longstreet be-
gan an artillery barrage in preparation to attack. Meade saw the attack coming.
He began to shift forces to shore up III Corps; meanwhile, Longstreet hit. The
Confederates rapidly smashed III Corps' left flank and started crushing the
Union line northward upon itself, pushing hard on Hancock's left flank. At
4:00 P.M., Willard's brigade was ordered to the left of Hancock's line to assist
in the desperate fight to keep the Confederates from turning the Union left.
Willard put the Guard on his left flank to protect the brigade and formed his
three other regiments to charge. Suddenly he was killed, his face and head
nearly shot away, falling from his horse dead at the moment victory appeared
attainable.[5] Colonel Eliakim Sherrill took command of the brigade. Word came
that Major Edward Venuti, the mustered-out Garibaldian who subsequently
joined the 52nd New York, had been killed in action.

Then the Garibaldi Guard was diverted for another immediate mission.
Lieutenant Dietrich of Company A remembered the instant beforehand, "When
we [rested] in our positions on the afternoon of July 2, in the open enjoying
full well our being. Then, in that position, we thought of ourselves and our
families." In the fierce fighting that engulfed III Corps and pulled the original
defenders forward in the effort to defend the III Corps salient, Union artillery
had rushed forward to bridge the resulting gap between II and III Corps and
keep the line intact until reinforcements could come up. Confederate Brigadier
General William Barksdale's brigade, the 21st Mississippi, then overran and
captured Watson's Battery I, Fifth U.S. Artillery, which was abandoned with
a great loss of men and horses.[6] Lieutenant Dietrich remembered:

> Captain John B. Fassett [of C]ompany F, 23rd Pennsylvania
> had just completed the work of reforming Humphrey's Division on
> Cemetery Ridge after it had been driven back and was returning to
> report to [Brigadier] General [David Bell] Birney, when he saw Lieu-
> tenant Samuel Peoples of Battery I, standing on a rock looking to the
> front. Thereupon Captain Fassett asked the lieutenant why he was
> not with his battery, and the lieutenant answered: "Because it has just
> been captured." Then pointing toward his battery, the lieutenant con-
> tinued: "And if those Confederates are able to serve my guns, those
> troops you have just been forming on the ridge, won't stay there a
> minute."
> Captain Fassett, instantly comprehending...that the battery
> could direct an enfilading fire on Cemetery Ridge, and recognizing
> that the ridge was the key to the Federal position...rode rapidly to
> the nearest troops—the Thirty-ninth New York Infantry—and or-
> dered Major Hildebrandt, the commanding officer, to retake the bat-
> tery.
> "By whose orders?" asked the major.

The captain replied: "By orders of General Birney."

"I am in General Hancock's Corps," responded the major.

To this the captain said: "Then I order you to take those guns, by order of General Hancock!"

At this, Major Hildebrandt moved his regiment by flank with superb alacrity, and when opposite the battery, he ordered a charge.[7]

The Garibaldians rushed forward and charged the Confederates, cheering as they went, "Without drum, beat, or trumpet blast, but with one great 'Hurrah!' that arose in the series of attacks," Dietrich remembered. He recalled: "Captain Fassett not only helped to move the regiment by the flank, but, being the only mounted officer, also assisted in the assault. The Confederates were not willing to give up the battery and position without a struggle, and the fight was a fierce one. As the Federal line reached the Confederates, one of them seized the bridle of Captain Fassett's horse while another raised his musket fair into the face of the mounted man. The captain struck up with his saber just in time to divert the musket ball so that it passed through the visor of his cap, and the next instant a member of the Thirty-ninth ran his bayonet through the man who delivered the shot, while Fassett shot down the man holding the bridle of his horse."[8] Dietrich appreciated the successful counterattack that "caused the enemy to withdraw into the woods. When the Mississippians were driven off from the guns, the Battery became ours as well as the just honor of the day."[9]

Lieutenants Peeples and Samuels of the 5th U.S. Artillery took charge of the recaptured guns and the equipment. The Garibaldians now helped the artillerymen to turn the guns on the retreating Confederates. By 6:00 P.M. the Union line held firm, from the Round Tops on the south along Cemetery Ridge to Cemetery and Culp's Hills on the north and northeast. Federal soldiers had held off the Confederates, but they were still out there. The Guard was withdrawn from the battery area and moved to II Corps' right flank to help secure Cemetery Hill. Somehow through all the moaning and shrieks of the wounded, surrounded by the dead, the Garibaldians bedded down for the night. Many years later, formal recognition of the day's deeds would come. In 1894 Congress would award Fassett the Medal of Honor for his quick thinking and courageous actions to recapture the guns and prevent a disaster. A monument to the Garibaldi Guard would be dedicated in 1895 at the spot where the action occurred. But at that day's end, the Garibaldians undoubtedly focussed on immediate priorities. Company B had suffered the most casualties, and Captain Baer was severely wounded. Corporal Olivry of Company C was also among the wounded, and Sergeant Bonin of Company A had been killed.

On Friday, July 3, II Corps was strung out like a thin blue line. The Confederates prepared to make one final, devastating attack upon the Federals. The Guard was in a strong position near Cemetery Hill, where it stayed for the duration of the most intensive, sustained bombardment that either side had ever experienced. Opening fire at 1:00 P.M., the Confederate batteries, some one hundred thirty cannons lined up nearly hub to hub, showered Cemetery Ridge in fire; Confederate Major Charles Howard ran from battery to battery, exhorting the cannoneers, "Give them canister! Pour it into them!"[10] Captain Basset of the 126th New York remembered that "Friday, the 3rd, the ball opened...with tremendous crashing...." At 3:00 P.M. or a little after, the crashing stopped and Confederates poured out of the woods across the fields. They lined up one mile wide from flank to flank, facing II Corps. At 3:00 P.M., General Hays reinforced the "Old Americans" regiments, the 5th New York, 14th Connecticut, 12th New Jersey, and 1st Delaware, with the Harpers Ferry regiments. Sherrill's brigade was posted with Colonel Thomas A. Smythe's 1st Delaware on his left and Lieutenant George A. Woodruff's Battery I, 1st U.S. Artillery, on his right. The Garibaldians and the 125th New York moved forward from their support positions to a stone wall, going in just behind the New Jersey, Delaware, and Connecticut regiments so that along the length of the battle line the men were four deep.

The II Corps faced Major General George E. Pickett's and Brigadier General J. Johnston Pettigrew's divisions, left to right, reinforced by Major General Issac R. Trimble's division. Fifteen thousand Confederates began to cross half a mile of open field in what would be the most famous assault of the war's greatest battle. With the warning, "Here they come!" the Garibaldi Guard with two hundred thirty men remaining in its ranks stood in position, "Hold your fire, boys; they are not near enough yet," Union generals told their men. The first volley of fire staggered but did not stop the advancing soldiers. The ranks came on, relentless, to the Union lines themselves: "Men fire into each other's faces, not five feet apart. There are bayonet-thrusts, saber-strokes, pistol shots; cool, deliberate movements on the part of some, hot, passionate, desperate efforts with others; hand-to-hand contests; recklessness of life; tenacity of purpose; fiery determination; oaths, yells curses, hurrahs, shoutings; men going down on their hands and knees, spinning round like tops, throwing out their arms, gulping up blood, falling; legless, armless, headless. There are ghastly heaps of dead men. Seconds are centuries; minutes, ages; but the thin line does not break!"[11]

The Confederate line's left flank advanced almost to the grove in front of Union Major General John Cleveland Robinson's division, which held the line beyond Hancock's right flank. In the desperate fighting, Hancock was severely wounded. His second division commander, Brigadier General John Gibbon, took command of II Corps. Pickett's charge punctured Gibbon's line before it was thrown back; Gibbon was severely wounded. Sherrill was shot through the bowels and borne off the field by Garibaldian stretcher-bearers. Lieutenant Colonel Clinton D. MacDougall of the 111th New York took command of the brigade and fell wounded, and its command passed to Colonel Bull of the 126th New York. Schwicardi took command of the Guard when Hilderbrandt fell severely wounded. Company H of the 11th Mississippi reached the wall in front of Company C despite deadly fire from the Garibaldians. The Mississippi color bearer, Billy O'Brien, fell dead near the wall; Joe Smith raised the fallen colors and fell wounded; William P. Marion grabbed the colors and was killed; and Lieutenant Joseph G. Marable planted the colors on the wall, only to fall stunned against it. First Sergeant Maggi captured Marable and his colors, and Corporal Francisco Navarreto captured another Mississippi flag. In the end, II Corps' second and third divisions stood like adamant and bore the brunt of Pickett and Pettigrew on the third day of battle. The invincible Army of Northern Virginia crashed and broke on Cemetery Ridge, its lines collapsed, and its remnants receded over ground thick with Confederate dead. The war had just turned in the Union's favor, although all any men knew then was that they had paid dearly for another day: "the dead were everywhere thickly strewn...there were broken wheels and splintered caissons; dead horses, shot through the neck, in the head, through the body, disemboweled.... dead men where they had fallen, wounded men creeping to the rear; cries and groans all around...."[12] Hays declared, "The Harper's Ferry boys wiped out Harper's Ferry."

During their two days of fighting at Gettysburg, of the three hundred twenty-two Garibaldians going in, fifteen men were killed and eighty men were wounded. Company B suffered the most death and casualties, followed by Company A and then Companies C and D. Over two dozen men were captured in action or deserted during the battle. An additional surgeon, Dr. Ebenezar Day, was mustered in as an assistant surgeon just to attend to the wounded, ten of whom would die. All told, the regiment lost over 50 percent of its men who began the action. On Saturday, July 4, Colonel Sherrill died of his wounds. That night a heavy downpour of torrential rain made the roads impassable, and swollen rivers aided Lee in his retreat. From July 5 through July 24, the Army of the Potomac cautiously pursued Lee. The Garibaldi Guard, as part of the pursuit, went back across the Potomac, and returned to Virginia.

By July 18, Brigadier General Joshua Owen had taken command of the 3rd brigade, where the Guard with its four companies was consolidated with the 111th, 125th, and 126th New York regiments. The Guard desperately needed recruits, officers and men. Hildebrandt remained hospitalized. Strict discipline remained the order of the day for everyone. Schwickhardi presided over a regimental court-martial. Among the cases heard were those of Sergeant William Kolbatz and his drinking partner, Private Jacob Scharfenberger, who were drunk on duty. Kolbatz was demoted to private and lost a month's pay, and Scharfenberger lost five dollars for a month and was to serve fourteen days of guard duty. Gustav Bischoff spoke in disrespectful terms of his superior officers and was sentenced to lose all of his pay for one month. First Lieutenant Caesar Nissen, the quartermaster officer and a protégé of D'Utassy, was court-martialed and convicted for stealing horses from the government on December 18, 1862. He was cashiered from the army and forfeited all pay and allowances due to him. Ferdinand Leibnitz was appointed the new quartermaster.

Six men from Company D were transferred to the Veteran Reserve Corps. And on July 18, the provost marshal escorted Giacomo Antonali to Sing Sing Prison.

On July 30, a Thursday, Major Daniel Woodall of the 1st Delaware assumed command of the Garibaldians. Woodall stated in his address to the command, "In conformity with these orders I take command of the 39th N.Y.V. Garibaldi Guard, and by promising to you, that I will endeavor to do my duty, I expect the hearty cooperation of both officers and men to assist me in this. This order will be read in front of every Company and will also be recorded upon the Company Books." He began his command by ordering all gambling to cease in the Garibaldian camp: "[A]ll men of the Garibaldi Guard who were found at, and reported for playing Cards were to be punished most severely. The officers would be held strictly responsible that this was carried out[,] assisted by their non-commission[ed] officers in suppressing the evil. After taps all lights within the camp of the Garibaldi Guard [were] to be extinguished and the utmost quiet was to prevail. Roll call would be held twice a day at Reveille and Tat[t]oo and commissioned Officers would be present." Evidently the order against gambling did not totally suppress the evil, since the men retained a way to send money home after gambling. Montegrifa had been reestablished as the Guard's sutler, and he conveyed money to Adam's Express in Washington, D.C. for any man who had money left after the gambling sprees and wanted to send it to his family.

In the weeks after Gettysburg, Meade cautiously pursued Lee back into Virginia. Hancock continued to recover from his wounds at Gettysburg, and Major General Gouverneur Kemble Warren assumed command of II Corps. The Garibaldians resumed soldiering at a pedestrian pace. Lieutenant Wilm was discharged on July 31 from Company A for disability and replaced by First Sergeant George Doell. Company B lost Lieutenant Kittle when he was transferred for duty in the 100th Infantry. On August 25, in the camp hospital near Elk Run, Virginia, Lieutenant Wagner of Company C died of the wounds he suffered at Gettysburg. The next day, First Sergeant Emanuel Lederer of Company B was promoted to first lieutenant, Company C, to replace Wagner. On Thursday, September 8, Assistant Surgeon Ebenezar Day was transferred to the 78th Infantry. By now the Garibaldians found themselves marching south, passing old haunts from their days of defending Washington; from September 13 to September 17, they advanced with II Corps from the Rappahannock to the Rapidan River. The last few days of September saw First Lieutenant Dietrich, who had risen from the rank of corporal, discharged. Captain Carlos Alvanzo DeLa Mesa was transferred from Company I to the Veteran Reserve Corps. A former sailor, Antonio Lopez, deserted (he would reenlist in the navy in October 1864, serve on the USS *Vandalia* and USS *Isonomia*, and muster out with a good record!).

October found the Army of the Potomac located around Culpeper, Virginia, facing south toward Lee, who was on the other side of the Rapidan

River. On Sunday, October 4, nine Garibaldians under arrest for various acts of insubordination were released and returned to duty. The next day, Acting Adjutant Otto Rassmaessler was promoted to first lieutenant in Company A to fill the vacancy created by Dietrich's departure. Woodall (who would ultimately become colonel of the 1st Delaware) relinquished command of the Guard, which was returned to Hildebrandt. He had recovered from his wounds at Gettysburg, much to the Garibaldians' relief. Captain Hollinde of Company A was discharged for disability, however, and his company fell to First Lieutenant Otto Rassmaessler and Second Lieutenant Doell to lead. The army's ability to organize everyone to support a unit actually engaged in battle continued to improve; on October 11, a new regimental order was issued: "Hereafter when this Regiment is about going into action, the Musicians of Bands and Drum Corps as well as all enlisted men employed as servants and on duty not requiring them to be armed will report to the Provost Marshall in the rear of the Column for such duty as they many be called upon to perform in the Hospital Department."

On September 24, Washington had detached two corps from the Army of the Potomac and sent them to rescue Union forces which had been routed at Chickamauga, Tennessee, and were dangerously trapped at Chattanooga. The departure of the two corps reduced the difference in strength between Meade's and Lee's armies, and Lee saw another chance to attack. On October 9, the Army of Northern Virginia moved out to try to turn Meade's western flank and get between him and Washington. Meade began withdrawing to the north in good order, along the line of the Orange & Alexandria Railroad, and gave Lee no chance for a successful flank maneuver. But Lee kept pursuing Meade, and on October 14, a Wednesday, after a halt to resupply, he pushed on from Warrenton toward Manassas Junction in two columns. Skirmishers from II Corps, the Union rear guard, kept Lee's forces at arm's length as both armies angled their ways northeast. As part of II Corps' third brigade, the Guard would be involved with both Confederate columns before the day was done.

The Garibaldians' first action of the day involved brief skirmishing with elements of Ewell's corps, Lee's right flank column, at Auburn, a village east of Warrenton. The second action involved heavy battle with A. P. Hill's corps, Lee's left flank column, at Bristoe Station, southwest of Manassas Junction. Hill's advance guard caught up with what it mistook to be "a small portion of the enemy" positioned behind a railroad embankment, and he ordered two brigades of his leading division "to dislodge them." The Confederates struck hard, and were struck even harder by Federals who saw them coming and beat them to the embankment, getting into position behind it from their side first. Hildebrandt later wrote in his official report:

In obedience to orders received from brigade headquarters....
On the morning of that day, after the column had been marching an hour, it met some of the enemy's cavalry, whose purpose, it seemed

to me, was to reconnoiter our strength, especially that of the Corps or Column in onward progress. The regiments of this brigade were soon got in position, some of them deploying...the Confederates who had but 3 pieces of flying artillery, soon disappeared. In the skirmishes of that morning my regiment acted but [as a supporting force]. We marched them unmolested forward. The column reached near Bristoe on the afternoon of the same day (14th). I heard some artillery practice and some small gun fire in toward the left very close. We were marched hastily covering a small run up to a plateau. There General Owen gave the command, "Battalion by the left flank, double quick march." I advanced accordingly by the left flank in line of battle with the Brigade, the 125th N.Y.V. on my right side and the 111th N.Y.V. on my left. The regiment charged forward amid a rather thick shower of bullets, reaching a hollow where a railroad track ran. I halted my regiment and kept up firing until the enemy in our front disappeared. I left my place as ordered, in the evening, when the column resumed its line of march. Officers and men behaved as soldiers.[13]

The official report by Colonel McDougall, 111th New York, after the fight indicated the stress everyone must have felt and the courage they obviously showed in the race for the embankment: "[T]he regiment reformed and advanced on the run under severe fire of musketry to secure the embankment of the railroad which the regiment reached simultaneously with the 39th N.Y."[14] Everyone's quick, disciplined reactions got the Guard and its fellow regiments to the embankment just in time to absorb the brunt of the Confederate attack: "General Hays, who was riding in front, saw the position of things, turned his horse and galloped down past the regiments, calling to each, 'By the left flank; double quick; march!' adding 'Get that cut, boys, before the enemy gets it!' Each regiment, as it got the order, rushed to the railroad cut; first the 125th, then the 39th, and then the 126th. It was now a race on both sides for this cut, the shot and shell of the enemy from a battery on the hillside whizzing and buzzing among our men as they ran, but doing little damage, while our skirmishers did their utmost to impede their advance. With shouts of exultation our men gained the position, which was a most advantageous one, the railway forming a nice breastwork. From this they poured a murderous fire into the advancing enemy...."[15] Five guns, two battle flags, and four hundred fifty prisoners were the third brigade's trophies that day.

The Union victory at Bristoe Station took the steam out of Lee's pursuit. He was running out of supplies, and Meade had entrenched himself in a very strong position at Centreville, north of Bull Run. Now it was the turn of Confederate skirmishers to preoccupy the Federals while Lee began to withdraw. October 15 found opposing forces skirmishing along Bull Run. At 5:00 P.M. a detachment of the Garibaldians relieved a detachment of the 111th New York which had been skirmishing with Confederates along the left bank of Bull Run and on the left side of Mitchell's Ford. The enemy occupied rifle pits on the southern bank of the stream and had been firing at the Federals, and they opened fire on the Garibaldians. Sergeant Castlevecchio was wounded along with seven other men in the ensuing action, when they returned the fire.[16] Surgeon Frederick Wolf set up a field hospital in a barn on the Brentsville road to tend to the wounded, and he and two of the wounded men were captured and sent to Richmond as prisoners of war.

On October 19, the Army of the Potomac began marching once more, once more pursuing Lee. The march itself was mostly a trudge southwest, hardly notable for any military achievements. On October 25, Sunday, Private Arrellano was in trouble once again—four plus months after sleeping on guard duty, he had wandered into camp drunk the night before, and he was placed under arrest. A regimental order was issued to say that "all suspicious persons and stragglers would be arrested by details of soldiers who would patrol the neighborhood of the Camp." Corporal John Simon (Semon) of Company H was promoted to sergeant. Five more men were transferred to the Veteran Reserve Corps. Louis Blenker, veteran of the 1848 war for democratic national unity in Germany and the Garibaldians' division commander in 1862 at the battle of Cross Keys, died on his farm on October 31 from injuries he had received in a fall from his horse. On November 4, brigade drill was scheduled to begin at 2:30 P.M. daily, and Hilderbrandt was detailed as division officer of the day. He reported to headquarters to assume responsibility for security, order, and supervision of the guard for twenty-four hours. Three days later, on a Saturday, the Garibaldians advanced to the Rappahannock River and prepared to cross it. Reveille had been at 5:00 A.M., pickets had been withdrawn at 6:00 A.M., and at 7:00 A.M. the Garibaldi Guard had marched. The supply and baggage wagons followed II Corps as far as Morrisville, about four miles northeast of the river, and then parked. The ambulance train followed Hays' division. First Lieutenant Louis Leviseur of Company B was discharged for disability. The Federals encountered a Confederate force guarding Kelly's Ford; after a battle in which they captured almost all of both brigades guarding the bridgehead, they crossed the river. Lee withdrew south below the Rapidan River. On November 9, the army commander received a telegram: "Major General Meade: I have seen your dispatches about operations on the Rappahannock on Saturday and wish to say 'Well done.' Abraham Lincoln"

Winter quarters were on the horizon again. On November 14, General Owen selected a permanent guard of infantry for his brigade headquarters. Major Hilderbrandt was ordered to detail one sergeant and twelve privates to report to Headquarters at 10:00 P.M. The men selected for the detail included a few recovering from wounds received at Gettysburg, to include Antonio Fortunes, a Spaniard; Christoforo Ghiloni, a cigar maker from Barza, Italy; and Juan Hernandez, a Cuban sailor. Hilderbrandt was detailed to Headquarters as a member of a general court-martial and turned over command of the regiment to Captain Baer for the day. When he returned the next morning, Hildebrandt informed the Garibaldians "that men who returned from desertion would at this time be referred to General Hays for his decisions and his order as competent authority and [that he would] restore those men to duty without Court Martial, but with such appropriate punishment as the General may deem necessary, for the good of his service. They were docked for a month's pay." That same day Major Augustus Funk of the 38th New York Volunteer Infantry applied to serve as colonel of the Garibaldi Guard. Funk had enlisted in the 38th New York as a private on May 7, 1861. He was promoted to captain of Company H on January 11, 1862, wounded in action on May 5, 1862, at Williamsburg, Virginia, during McClellan's Peninsular Campaign against Richmond, recovered, and promoted to major on October 10, 1862.

At this point the Garibaldi Guard could muster three hundred forty-eight officers and men present for war. Army regulations said an infantry regiment should have ten companies, each one with a captain, a first and a second lieutenant, and ninety-seven men. The Guard had four companies now: A, with First Lieutenant Rassmaessler, Second Lieutenant Doell, and eighty-one men; B, with Captain Baer and Second Lieutenant Samsa, and ninety-one men; C, with Captain Dessauer, First Lieutenant Bader and Second Lieutenant Lederer, plus seventy-nine men; and D, with Captain Schwickhardi, First Lieutenant Doerndinger, Second Lieutenant Sutter, and eighty-five men. Headquarters was supposed to have thirty-seven persons: a colonel, a lieutenant colonel, a major, an adjutant (a lieutenant), a quartermaster (another lieutenant), a surgeon, an assistant surgeon, and thirty various enlisted men. At this moment the headquarters contained exactly two persons: Hildebrandt and First Lieutenant Ferdinand Leibnitz, the quartermaster officer.

Together with the rest of the Army of the Potomac, the Garibaldians received orders to be ready to move at very short notice. Meade had discovered that Lee's forces were widely spread out south of the Rapidan River, and he devised a plan to march rapidly to the east, cross the Rapidan outside of Lee's cavalry screen, and speed back to the west to catch and defeat the Confederates piecemeal. Tents were not struck, all surplus baggage was packed, and every arrangement was made so as not to impede the troops' impending march. Officers were instructed to report existing deficiencies in camp and garrison equipment and in their commands' clothing. On November 19, the Garibaldians' brigade was formed on the parade ground at 11:00 A.M., less arms, but in every other respect the same as for a march with all rations. Each man carried forty rounds of ammunition in his cartridge box, and two days' sustenance—hardtack, sugar, coffee, and salt—in his knapsack and three days' rations in his haversack. Meade planned matters very carefully and issued detailed orders. The soldier's combat load of ammunition was reduced from one hundred forty to one hundred rounds per man;

ammunition wagons would carry sixty rounds per man to augment the one hundred rounds per man. Ammunition wagons were cut from five to three per one thousand men. All surplus ammunition was turned in at the depot at Brandy Station. The supply trains and regimental wagons carried ten days' rations. Field and staff officers were authorized one wagon to carry items like personal baggage, tents, forage, desks, papers, and mess chests. Line officers were authorized one wagon for the same purposes. Four days' rations were issued. All surplus baggage would be sent to Washington for storage. On Sunday, November 22, Divine Service was held at 3:00 P.M. at Headquarters; only sidearms were permitted.

The only flaw in the details of Meade's plan was some of the people involved. Federal engineers miscalculated the Rapidan's width and lost time improvising pontoons to cross it. On November 26, although the weather was bitterly cold and the roads were bad, III Corps marched too slowly. After III Corps crossed the river, it got lost down a wrong road. By the time Meade's five corps crossed Germanna and Ely's Fords and regrouped in the general area called The Wilderness, Lee's Army of Northern Virginia had concentrated in a strong north-south position behind a stream named Mine Run. Meade scouted the Confederate position and decided that its flanks offered the best chance for a successful attack. II Corps, with the Garibaldians, shifted south to see if it could turn Lee's right. The Confederate flank appeared to be unprotected by earthworks. Based upon this, Meade spent November 29 massing troops for an attack. The Garibaldians marched all night and on the next morning, upon reaching their position in the freezing rain, found that the Confederates had in fact fortified their position. General Warren did not attack and reported his discovery of the highly strengthened and reinforced position to General Meade. "Suspend the attack until further orders!" was Meade's angry reply, and he rode off to meet Warren and see firsthand his failed maneuver.

Meade agreed with Warren that now an attack would be suicidal. The Confederates appeared to be impregnable and Union supplies were getting low. On December 1, orders were received to retire across the Rapidan, back the way they came. The next day the Garibaldians were involved in a skirmish at Robertson's Tavern, present-day Locust Grove, Virginia, as they guarded the rear of their withdrawing corps. Twenty-nine Garibaldians were captured in this action. Prisoner exchange ratios randomly dictated the captured soldiers' fates (on November 28, Dr. Wolf was paroled, released, and returned to the Guard!). From Company A, Theodore Reinke and Nicholaus Schutz were captured and paroled, but Franz Messing, Bernhard Nilson, Christian Romany, Charles Schneider, and Albert Schwarzenbach were captured and sent to Andersonville, Georgia, and the prisoner of war camp there. Charles Schonbein, Company B, was captured and later paroled. Company C lost Antonio Daguano and Caspar Kehrig; Daguano was paroled but Kehrig would die of disease at Andersonville. From Company D, Second Lieutenant Sutter, Sergeant Arnold Happe, and Martin Maus, George Rich, Jacob Scharfenberger, Henry Scholl,

Julius Quade, Constantine Ottman and Ludwig Roth were captured; Ottoman and Roth would die of disease at Andersonville. Corporal Friedrich Burger was captured and paroled. Emanuel Costello, Antonio Fortunes, and Juan Barre of Company E were captured; Barre was paroled. Andre Singer of Company K was captured and would die at Andersonville.

This was the first time Garibaldians were sent to the now infamous prisoner of war camp. Andersonville was a camp that in the end would hold too many prisoners in too small a space, with not enough protection from the elements and almost no food to eat. Captured Garibaldians who were sent there, like all Union soldiers, faced a horrible situation. John McElroy was a prisoner of the camp who survived it. He later wrote an account of his experiences that described events like the time that captured members of New York's Les Enfants Perdus, nearly all French, Italians, Spaniards, or Portuguese, were so starved they caught and killed a snake, skinned it, roasted it, and devoured it. He also observed in *This was Andersonville*, "One of every three and a half men upon whom the gates of the Stockade closed never repassed them alive. Twenty-nine percent of the boys who so much as set foot in Andersonville died there....the average stay of a prisoner there was not four months." Over the last sixteen months of the war, sixty-eight Garibaldians in total would be sent to Andersonville. Forty-three of them, seventy-six percent, would be sent to the hospital and die. Five captured Garibaldians would be sent to Thunder Castle Prison Camp in Richmond, Virginia, and only one would survive that camp.

The fact that proportionally over twice as many Garibaldians as other Union soldiers imprisoned at Andersonville died there undoubtedly reflected some of the age's harsh prejudices. Foreigners were open to vicious stereotypes as subhuman beings who barely deserved weeding out. Confederate Captain Lamar Fountaine displayed that sort of barbaric arrogance in recalling the inconvenience caused by the capture of some Federals: "We were sorry that they were Americans, as it necessitated our return sooner than we anticipated, for we did not kill real American soldiers in cold blood, as we did the hirelings of foreign countries. Had they been foreigners, we would not have taken them prisoners, only shot them as we rode up. We killed [foreigners] in scores, as we could not take care of prisoners, for we frequently had as many as two to one in our front... They were only foreign hirelings, and were here to kill us merely for the greenbacks and gold they rescued....we had no scruples of conscience in disposing of them to the best, and sent as many out of our way as my physical endurance permitted."[17] The South was unable to feed or clothe any of its prisoners of war adequately, and the Garibaldians who were captured and imprisoned in Confederate camps might well have endured deliberate neglect at the hands of some of their captors.

Following its return north of the Rapidan to the area southeast and east of Culpeper, the Army of the Potomac caught its breath and recovered from its sally to Mine Run. On December 3, troops were ordered to keep three days' full rations in their haversacks and five days' supplies in wagons. Twelve deserters were released from arrest on the condition that they would make good the time they had been absent. That night division shelters were put up for the pickets. Sergeant Castelbecchi, an inpatient at the U.S. General Hospital at Annapolis, was ordered to report in person to the Medical Director, City of New York, who subsequently assigned him to duty in a government hospital. On December 8, Cornelius McLean, a second lieutenant of the 42nd Infantry, mustered into the Guard as an unassigned private and was soon promoted to sergeant. Andrew Hibbard enrolled as second lieutenant of the newly formed Company F and then declined his commission. Thursday, December 10, marked the start of several days' picket duty for the Guard. Commanding officers of neighboring camps complained that they noticed an unusual amount of noise and disorder in the Garibaldi camp, apparently the result of intoxication; they lamented that commissioned officers were expected to conduct themselves in a manner becoming their rank, in and out of quarters. It was the Guard saying farewell to the officer who had most upheld its reputation in its worst days; Hildebrandt received an honorable discharge and joined the Veteran Reserve Corps to serve until the war's end. Captain Baer again took charge of the regiment. One day later, sixteen Garibaldians were returned to duty while awaiting trial for desertion; one, Michael Schwarz, brother of the late major, had deserted in August 1862, eight had deserted later from the confines of Camp Douglas, and the remainder had just deserted during Mine Run.

Overly cautious Northern generalship and the reality of low military supplies in the South ended army maneuvers on both sides of the Rapidan. On December 12, the regiment went into winter quarters at Stevensburg, a village east of Culpeper and south of Brandy Station, in the vicinity where most of the Army of the Potomac encamped. Major Funk's application to be the colonel of the Garibaldi Guard, made four weeks earlier, had been approved. Lieutenant John William Funk, his brother, and another member of the 38th New York, Adjutant John McEwan Hyde, were mustered in as first lieutenants of newly reconstituted Companies G and E. They were to observe the conditions of discipline and assess the situation for the incoming colonel.

The period of November 1863 through February 1864 was to be a time of tremendous change in the Garibaldi Guard. While Luigi G. Garibaldi, a nephew of the general himself, enlisted, primarily Englishmen, Scotsmen, Irishmen, Canadians, and Americans began to fill the gaps left by so many casualties, discharges, and desertions. English sailors like William Reed, Edmund Osborne, and Henry Robinson enlisted, along with English soldiers like James Scarfe and William Reed, plus mechanics and men like Thomas Burns, a clerk, George Etherridge, an engineer, and William Hook, a carpenter. Fourteen Scotsmen included Ben Allen, a courier, Dan McDonald, a laborer, David Moore, a cotton spinner, and James Thompson, a farmer. The Irish included teacher Thomas Carr, ex-soldiers James Ward, John McGrain, William Montigue,

Thomas Moyland and David Smith, sailors, farmers, wheelwrights, and sixty-three laborers. Silas Spratt, a ship's captain, three seamen, and ten farmers came from Canada. Various Americans came from Pennsylvania, Ohio, Maine, New Hampshire, and New Jersey. Henry Hamilton and Henry Hitchcock came from Vermont. Alphonzo Chapell came from Rhode Island, Ezekiel Benton from Connecticut, and farmers like James Hayes from Massachusetts. New York was well represented by twenty-two farmers from Lisbon, including Alexander Hurst, Josiah Putney, Frank Randels, and Robert Thompson. Thirty men hailed from New York City, like carman Alexander Murray and teamster John Miller. Even a man apiece from the Southern states of Louisiana, Georgia, and Virginia joined the regiment!

Germans continued to enlist, but in fewer numbers. More northern Europeans joined the ranks. Danish enlistees included two sailors, a shoemaker, a merchant, blacksmith Christian Reimback, and Christian Nelson, a veteran of the European conflicts. Seven Norwegian sailors enlisted, including one John Thompson. Eight Swedes enlisted, including sailor Gustaff Algot, farmer John Neill, and carpenter Bernard Nilson. French recruits kept coming from New York, where Captain Victor Chandone kept on collecting dual salaries as a recruiting officer in the Garibaldi Guard city recruiting office and as a captain in the Veteran Reserve Corps. Chandone's policy was to ask no questions, just have the man sign on the line. Sign an alias, in fact, which made the 39th an ideal regiment for French sailors to desert if they later changed their minds. The merchant vessel *L'Ascension* docked in New York harbor, and Chandone recruited French sailor Pierre Francois as Leopold Frederick. The French vessel *Tissiaphone* docked at New York en route from New Orleans, transporting French and Italian subjects who desired to leave the South for New York. By December, Chandone recruited four deserters from the *Tissiaphone*: a Cuban, Santiago Fernandez, and three Frenchmen, Gustave Lambert, Charles S. Roue and Louis L'Hote, who enlisted as James Lee, Theophilus Huger, Charles Rosey, and Louis Lat, respectively. Not being a French citizen, Fernandez would remain in the regiment and be discharged from the service on March 25, 1864.

The large number of recruits received during December 1863 and January 1864 was enough to organize six new companies in the Garibaldi Guard. It was also enough to completely alter the Garibaldi Guard's character. The regiment regained its ten-company formation, but it lost its exotic accent.[18] New, untried recruits with different native tongues joined old veterans who had now soldiered together through hard times for almost three years. The impact of one group on the other was obviously significant. A sergeant who deserted to the Confederacy a few months later would tell the enemy "that there is much dissatisfaction among the old men, very few of whom re-enlist. One cause of discontent he states to be in many cases, like his own, is, that the 38th, Funk's old command, was discharged and the officers went to New

York and enlisted 6 new companies, which were consolidate[d] with his, the 39th, very much to their annoyance."[19]

Colonel Funk was supposed to take command in three weeks, at the end of the year. Other new officers were appointed and assigned. Major David Allen of the 47th Infantry was mustered in as captain of Company G. First Lieutenant Philip C. Rogers of the 55th Infantry was mustered in as first lieutenant of Company H; Edward Sturges, eighteen years old, was mustered in as first lieutenant of Company K. John Miller enlisted in Company H and was promoted to sergeant, and an additional thirty appointments to fill noncommissioned positions were made. On December 17, Captain Schwickhardi was granted a ten-day leave of absence (when he returned he was detailed to picket duty). On December 18, First Lieutenant Theodore Rich of the 31st Infantry mustered in as first lieutenant of Company F to fill the gap Hibbard left (Erskine Rich, Theodore's brother, enlisted later). The next day Adjutant Charles Haight, 31st Infantry, enrolled as captain of Company H. Lieutenant Sutter, captured in action in The Wilderness, was paroled on December 19. One day later, Sergeant Menzler of Company A was promoted to first sergeant. On Christmas Horace Walter and John Whitmore, two of Company F's new recruits, deserted. Manuel Amaro of the old Spanish company was discharged from duty; he would join the navy as an ordinary seaman early in 1865 and be stationed at the U.S. recruiting station in Washington, D.C.

The last week of the year was relatively quiet. On December 28, Captain Baer was detailed as division officer of the day. On December 30, the issuance of furloughs was suspended and permits were granted for the families of officers to visit the army for twenty days. Officers were authorized to use enlisted men as servants in their respective commands, and a monthly report had to be filed on all the men so employed. The Provost Marshal General tore down the picket shelters, because the pickets sheltered themselves instead of walking their posts. For New Year's eve, the officer of the day was directed to ensure that all enlisted men retired to their quarters immediately after taps and to arrest those who were found creating disturbances or violating any of the rules of the camps. Captain Baer, acting commander of the regiment, directed: "The Company Commanders are hereby made responsible for any firing of guns that may occur this night, within the limits of the Garibaldi Guard. It is strictly prohibited. Officers will also see, that no disturbance is made in Camp during this New Year night. The men are allowed to enjoy themselves but in a soldier like manner."

On the last morning of 1863, two bounty jumpers, John Foley and George Hand, who had enlisted in New York on December 28 and deserted while en route from Riker's Island, New York, to Alexandria, Virginia, were caught. They had collected the cash bounties offered to promote enlistments—Union General Order No. 49 of 1861 itself offered $100.00—and deserted at the first chance to avoid going to the front. Bounty jumpers had become a huge problem; many enlisted and deserted repeatedly, collecting huge sums of money,

Philip C. Rogers
Captain in Company H, 39th New York Volunteer Infantry, transferred in from the 55th New York Volunteer Infantry, "The Guarde Lafayette."

and veteran soldiers detested them. Foley and Hand were court-martialed and sentenced to serve the balance of their enlistments at hard labor at Dry Tortugas, Florida, a Fort Sumter-like bastion in the sea west of Key West. First Sergeant Franz Hermann of Company B transferred to Colonel Cesnola's regiment, the 4th New York Cavalry, and David Hurstwood, a new recruit, deserted at Stevensburg. D'Utassy's court-martial, Oliver's murder, the Gettysburg, Bristoe Station, and Mine Run campaigns, and the loss of so many comrades all made 1863 an extraordinary year for the Garibaldians, who marked its passing with gunfire, riotous carousing, and tears to salute the lost.

Chapter Nine

REVITALIZATION WITH COLONEL FUNK

ON Saturday, January 2, 1864, Major Ira Smith Brown of the 126th New York was detailed to take temporary command of the Garibaldians until the new colonel arrived. He had his orders from the high command to drill discipline into the regiment, swollen with new recruits. Assignments were created to keep the men busy, to do anything to control their attention. The men would be introduced to the spit and polish a regiment should have. Brown called a meeting of officers at his headquarters, where he outlined his intentions for the Guard, beginning with Lieutenants Rassmaessler, Hyde, Rogers, and Doell, who were there. All officers were advised to study *Butterfield's Camp and Outpost Duty for Infantry*. Brown himself would drill the officers all week to ensure that they knew how to instruct the men in the manual of arms. Every little detail would be used to instill discipline in the men. Each and every man of the regiment would be present for duty and would appear for inspection. Their arms and accouterments would be thoroughly cleaned and their shoes would be blacked. As an example to the men, the noncommissioned officers would be expected to be particularly clean. Every man's skin would be thoroughly clean and he would have on a clean shirt, drawers, and stockings. Experienced noncommissioned officers would be detailed to teach the recruits how to pack their knapsacks properly and to stand inspection.

Training began to incorporate the new recruits into the Guard before the inevitable spring campaigns began. An experienced French tar, Corporal Olivry, and three others were chosen to take charge of a detachment of raw recruits. Olivry began their training with this instruction:

Guard Mounting and Dress Parade are the Sacraments of the Military Religion, and every man will be made to stand immovable at

153

the Command "Parade Rest," looking square to the front. No tobacco chewing in ranks. If some men even choose to spit, it will destroy the whole effect. This is very important.

Hold your heads up and don't swing your left hand when marching to and from the Parade Grounds. Each company will dress on the center. The Adjutant will assure the right guides. The Sergeant Major the left. Each Commander of the Company will step out promptly two paces and left face before giving the Command, "Order Arms," "Parade Rest." They will not step out until the preceding company has come to a "Parade Rest."

First Sergeants will come to the front and center at a double quick carrying their pieces at a Right Shoulder Shift. The Bayonets will not be fixed unless for a sign of meritorious conduct. The Sergeants will return at a double quick.

Where the Adjutant dismisses the parade the officers will return saber and face inward, and march, taking the step from the Adjutant, who will not march till all the officers have faced inward. When the Adjutant marches in it will be in quick time with the Band playing.

At the Command, "Halt," by the Adjutant the officers all will raise their hands at the visor of the cap and will remain saluting until the commandant of the regiment returns it. They will then consider the ceremony finished, and will not look back nor motion to their commands.

Then Olivry had the new recruits try to execute some commands. Rifles were dropped, left was taken for right and vice versa, men walked into one another, and confusion reigned.

Brown displayed plans to build stockades for the brigade to the officers. For the next four days, at five o'clock every morning, Lieutenant Rassmaessler gave his company breakfast. Then at 6:00 A.M. he paraded his men before headquarters, where they received axes. Taking the first trees they found suitable, they proceeded to cut timber all day, loading the teams with the logs for the stockades. At 7:00 A.M. Lieutenant Samsa, detailed with as many men as necessary, supplied with shovels, axes and picks, filled in the camp's latrine ditches.

Other actions to improve the camp area, as long as they were going to remain there in winter quarters, continued apace. The road from Stevensburg to Brandy Station and the supply depot had a single track with turnouts. One plan was to build a bridge over Mountain Run in front of Brigadier General Alexander Stewart Webb's position (he commanded II Corps' second division, camped across the run) so that wagons going to Brandy Station would take that road, leaving the corduroy road open for wagon coming from there. A detachment of eighty-six men and two officers was assigned to work on constructing the bridge. With a disregard typical to Civil

War soldiers, Sergeant William McCarrick and his men smuggled whiskey into the woods, got drunk, and went to work drunk, swinging axes and hacking at trees. So many men reported accidents and wounds that Lieutenant Funk needed to assemble a fatigue party of twenty-five men, furnished with axes, to watch over Rassmaessler's men cutting and hauling timber. Inevitably, McCarrick lost his stripes. Five of his men were chosen for duty as buglers and reported to the chief bugler. Bugler Flores, Company C, was detailed to the Ambulance Corps. Four men were transferred to the 2nd Cavalry. Lieutenant Doerndinger was granted a leave of absence for ten days. Private Pat McGrow of Company F died suddenly in his tent, and Dr. Wolf attributed it to heart disease. Charles Ballou of Company C, 117th New York, was assigned to Company K as a second lieutenant on January 7.

The provost marshal came to camp to take a number of the French deserters into custody and escort them to the Military Governor in Washington, D.C., to be held subject to the disposition of the Minister of France. That did not stop Chandone up in New York, who continued to recruit more French deserters. On January 14, August Marie signed up as Jean Leopold Angel, and Paul Orange enlisted as Phillipe Jean. Pickard Heron enlisted as Jean Jacques, and Jean Marie as Banbeh. Two days later two Irishmen, deserters from the U.S. Navy, Michael May and Charles O. Farmer, enlisted respectively as Edward Snow, a fireman, and John Delaney. All of them were found out and soon in the custody of the provost marshal, on their way back to Washington to be dealt with by the French Consul or the Commander of the Navy Yard.

Now the Guard really began to fill out. The new major arrived on January 16. He was Charles C. Baker, late a captain of the 159th New York. John M. Gilfillan, a captain in the 53rd New York, was commissioned as the captain of Company I.[1] Lieutenant Hyde, Company E, was promoted to adjutant; Private William Hartley, a woodcarver, was ordered to report to Lieutenant Colonel Francis A. Walker at corps headquarters. On January 20, Colonel Funk was commissioned the new colonel of the Garibaldi Guard. James G. Hughes, a captain in the 82th New York, was commissioned as lieutenant colonel. James M. Trippe mustered in as captain of Company E, and Killian Von Rensselaer mustered in as first lieutenant of Company I. In Company K, Leonard Magnus was mustered in as captain, and Edward Sturges was promoted to first lieutenant. Sergeant Benjamin Allen of Company G died of illness. On Friday, January 22, First Lieutenant Erskine Rich, 31st Infantry, was mustered in as the first lieutenant of Company F. His brother, First Lieutenant Theodore Rich, Company F, was promoted to captain of the company three days later. The Guard was beginning to look like a real regiment again.

Then the Guard ended the month without its new commander. On January 26, Colonel Funk was ordered to proceed to New York to give evidence in a case to be tried by court-martial. Bugler Henry Knopf of Company D was detailed as postmaster of the Garibaldi Guard. Four men unfit for duty were

Augustus Funk
Colonel in the 39th New York Volunteer Infantry. Commissioned colonel of the
Garibaldi Guard nearly a year after D'Utassy's court-martial.
National Archives

transferred to the Veteran Reserve Corps. On January 29, the corps officer of the day, Captain R. L. Leabury, reported, "I visited the line carefully and found that the 3rd Brigade was very poorly instructed and the sentinels extremely inefficient, partly owing, I think, to their ignorance of the English Language. I do not consider the pickets of the 39th as safe against any attempts to penetrate their lines. The General Commanding directed that Regimental Commanders instruct a rigid examination of all officers subject to being detailed on Picket duty as to their knowledge of the English language, and the duties of Picket Guard." This portion of the report was directed toward Captain Rudolph Schwickhardi, "a Prussian who did not have a command of the English language." He had been arrested for dereliction of duty for being unable to communicate well with men under his command, but was acquitted of the charges when it was revealed that the Garibaldi Guard had a large number of German-speaking troops. A verbal test was devised in order to determine if officers of foreign birth could speak and understand English. A similar examination was designed for the men as well. Every commissioned officer would be expected to answer upon inspection in English questions such as, "How many men have you? How many men have you, present for duty? How many men have you list? How many men have you detached? How many guns have you? What is the price of an overcoat, a musket, a pair of pantaloons, a pair of drawers, a shovel, a cartridge box, a canteen, a woolen blanket, a gum blanket?" On January 30, nineteen-year-old Joseph Wilson was mustered in as a second lieutenant in Company F.

February saw more personnel changes. Assistant Surgeon Emil Steiger was discharged and Privates Edelmann, Company K, and A. Baker, Company I, were promoted to sergeant on Monday, February 1. Companies A, C, and D sent a recruiting detail to New York City to enlist troops. The group was made up of Lieutenants Funk and Lederer, Sergeant Joseph Schick, Corporals Leonard Weihrauch and William Kutruff, and seven German-speaking privates. Funk was along to observe Chandone's activities and recruiting methods. Back in camp, on Friday, February 5, recruits David Champion and a number of men in Company I met in secret to conspire to desert during the early morning hours. Charles Williams and Charles Niles, fellow New Yorkers, John Hamilton, an Englishman, and George Pease, a Pennsylvanian, were with Champion. The next night Sergeant Silas Spratt of Company I was on duty; at 4:00 A.M. he received orders to go to each tent and notify the men that at 7:00 A.M. they were to march. While Spratt was going tent to tent, he overheard Williams and Champion discussing their plan to desert with the others. Spratt reported the plan to the officer of the day, but the conspirators of Company I left just prior to falling into line. Minus the deserters, the Guard marched off with eighteen officers and three hundred ninety men under the command of recently appointed Lieutenant Colonel Hughes.

The Guard marched off with Hays' division to conduct a reconnaissance in force. Captains Baer and Schwickhardi were detailed to command all one hundred of the old soldiers of the regiment as skirmishers across the Rapidan River at Morton's Ford. The Guard was ordered to form a line on the south, enemy side of the river; Hughes later reported, "The regiment was to form a line on the opposite side of the river. It marched in line of battle to within gunshot of the Confederates' skirmishers." The Garibaldians forded the cold and rapid river, then waist deep. Here, the recruits received their baptism of fire. The Garibaldians drove the Confederates from their rifle pits on the opposite side and captured fifteen prisoners in the process. Honore Barry, a Frenchman, was killed in the action. Hughes continued in his report that at about noon, he "changed the Garibaldi Guard's front line and took positions on the Morton Ford road. [First] Lieutenant Doerndinger of Company D was wounded. Company D fell into some disorder and 8 of his men were captured and Sergeant Miller, Company H, wounded in action."[2] At about 3:00 P.M. the 111th New York was ordered to support the portion of the skirmish line held by the 39th on the left of their line. Hughes continued: "At 5 P.M., the Garibaldi Guard [was] ordered to form a line of battle to the right of General Hays Headquarters, under a heavy fire of the Confederates, which was done very promptly considering that the men under my Command were never under fire before and not two months in service."

The 111th New York remained in position as a reserve until 5:00 P.M., when enemy skirmishers, having been heavily reinforced, moved forward and began firing rapidly. The 111th immediately deployed and returned fire with such effect that, though the enemy outnumbered them three to one, the advance was stopped and the enemy held in check until night put an end to the conflict. At midnight, the 111th recrossed the Rapidan; at 1:00 A.M., the Garibaldi Guard followed. They were ordered to make a battlefield reconnaissance for information. Hughes reported: "My loss was 1 man killed 17 wounded and 17 captured (8 from company D. alone). Lieutenant L. Doerndinger was severely wounded in the left arm while on the skirmish line. I take pleasure in making honorable mentions of 1st lieutenant John McE. Hyde, acting adjutant of that regiment, who rendered me excellent service on the field; also Capt. Baer and Schwickhardi and Lieutenant Doerndinger for gallantry; Also chief bugler Anton Prang, for bravery on the skirmish line." The real misfortune for the captured men was that they were sent to Andersonville to starve and die of disease. General Hays wrote, "I regret to forward such a long list of casualties, but it is solely attributable to the faltering of 2 regiments of Conscripts or substitutes comprising the 14th Conn. and the 39th New York. I was supported by our whole Corps. I have not the least doubt that we would have been enabled to capture the whole force of the enemy including camps and artillery, with less loss than we have suffered."[3] General Owen wrote, "I beg to make honorable mention of the following officer [:] Lieutenant Colonel Hughes of the 39th for promptness with which they executed orders."[4] The Guard returned to Stevensburg, where it would remain in camp until April.

Ever since his fraudulent dishonorable discharge in June 1862 after the battle of Cross Keys, Rafael Frizone had worked to rehabilitate his reputation and reestablish himself in the army, building up his case on the now proven, disgraceful actions of D'Utassy. On Saturday, February 8, Dessauer was ordered brought in for further investigation, because he had counterfeited documents under D'Utassy's orders.[5] Dessauer deserted; Frizone would succeed in clearing himself and enlist in the 2nd Pennsylvania Cavalry. On February 9, Captain Baker, late of the 159th, received his promotion to major, and in New York Lieutenant Funk was promoted to captain of Company C. Major Henry L. Abbott, a snobbish Bostonian in the 20th Massachusetts, encamped near the Guard, vented his dislike of the Garibaldians: "[They were] a beastly set of

Dutch boors, Maccaronis, & Frogratecs, in short, the rag tag & bobtail of all creation, little short beastly fellows with big beards & more stupid than it is possible for an American who has never seen them to conceive. It is a rule in this Army the more foreign a regiment is, the more cowardly it is. A Dutch regiment is bad enough, but when you come to French and Italians, you get men absolutely incapable of showing any pluck at all...."[6] Ironically, former Garibaldians served in Abbott's regiment. First Lieutenant Edward Sturges of the Guard's original Company K had transferred to the 20th Massachusetts, where his brother Henry (Hank) was a second lieutenant under Abbott. Sergeants Giuseppe Cavrotti and Giuseppe Griffa had reenlisted for service in the 20th Massachusetts, as had the Guard's hospital steward, Charles Breiting, who had conducted an insane soldier of the 20th Massachusetts to the Government Insane Asylum at Washington, D.C.

Near Colchester, midway between Fairfax Court House and Manassas Junction, Corporal Ditts, 1st Michigan Cavalry, in command of a squad of men on patrol, on February 11 came upon a group of men who claimed they had been captured. They were the deserters, led by Charles Williams, and joined by Albert Boehler, a German who had been a private in Battery L of the 21st New York State Artillery before being sent to Company K to await trial. Ditts doubted the men's story and pressed them for further information. Pease admitted that they left their regiment on the morning of February 6. At that, Ditts arrested the deserters and returned them to camp.[7]

The Guard continued to gain experienced leaders while it kept losing men. Second Lieutenant Cornelius McLean of the 42nd New York had been discharged and reenlisted as a private in the Guard in December 1863, whereat he was promoted to sergeant and assigned to the recruiting office. He was mustered in as the second lieutenant of Company G on February 12, but took ill and remained in his quarters. The next day First Sergeant Thomas Hand of the 40th New York was mustered in as the first lieutenant of Company B. Robert Tremper, a private from the 139th New York, was mustered in as the second lieutenant of Company K and then promoted to first lieutenant of Company G on the same day. On Wednesday, February 17, Corporal Isaiah Marshall of Company C was caught stealing and reduced to the rank of private; then he deserted rather than face a court-martial.

Commanders kept trying to infuse discipline in the ranks. On February 22, Colonel Funk sent a circular throughout his command: "There is in this regiment a total disregard of regulations and orders requiring every man to be in his quarters after tattoo, and to extinguish all lights after taps. Hereafter any enlisted man found out of his own quarters after tattoo will be severely punished and if lights are not promptly extinguished at taps in all tents, with the exception of Commissioned officers and orderly Sergeants, the occupant of such will be arrested and punished." The men reacted in fashion. Corporal Samuel Schreiner offered a bribe of $1.00 to Dr. Wolf to have him transferred to the Invalid Corps. Jose Yamaniego, Company C, disappeared after a drinking spree with Corporal Welsh. Charles Roland of Company G used abusive language to his sergeant. All three privates received sentences of ten days' hard labor. Louis Dungstadter was tried and found guilty of willful disobedience to orders and sentenced to forfeit one month's salary (interestingly, he would reenlist seven days later, on February 24, be captured in action at Boydton Plank Road, Hatcher's Run, on October 27, 1864, and not be paroled and exchanged until after the war).

Disciplinary measures continued unabated. Colonel Funk insisted that his officers were to be properly attired in regulation uniforms, and if they did not comply they would not accompany their men in ceremonial occasions on the parade ground. Captain Gilfillan, Company I, was put under arrest for drunkenness and absence from dress parade, and confined to the limits of the regimental camp. Captain Schwickhardi, Company D, and Captain Rich, Company F, were arrested for neglect of duty and disobedience of the order regarding regulation uniforms, and confined to the limits of the regimental camp. Captain Magnus of Company K was discharged. George Blum, Company B, was released as regimental armorer. McLean failed to report for duty due to illness. Sergeants Joseph Wagner and Theodore Block, both of Company K, and Corporal John Welsh of Company I returned to camp and lost their stripes for being drunk and out of quarters after taps. Their positions were filled by Julius Goldsmith, who was promoted to first sergeant, and Henry Brandenburger and Louis Edelmann, who were both made sergeant. Private Oliva, Company C, was promoted to sergeant.

Back at the recruiting office in New York, Chandone recorded the names of seventeen men mustered out of Company C on the list of those who "reenlisted in the Veteran Reserve Corps." Soldiers who mustered out and then reenlisted were granted furloughs with pay. The "reenlistees" in this instance involved a number of sailors—Sergeant Fratus, Juan Gonzalez from Cella, Chile, Jose Melo Freitas, Joaquin Jorge, and Manuel Ignacio Pereira, three Portuguese, and three Italians, Pasquale Patalani, Christoforo Ghiloni, and Giovanni Picconi, who had seen Antonali murder Oliver a year earlier. Men released from the army customarily sought employment in their old trades, if they did not reenlist. All of the "reenlisted" sailors actually signed aboard ships bound for foreign ports and sailed away. When their phony furloughs ended and they supposedly failed to return to duty, they were charged with desertion. Meanwhile Chandone pocketed their furlough pay. Captain Funk began an investigation of his practices. Already enmeshed in the French naval deserter scandal, Chandone decided to relieve himself from duty and resigned before he faced a court-martial.

On Monday, February 29, a couple of thieves were caught in camp. Osee (Jose) Santos and Manuel Horer of Company E stole a shirt from Henry Warren of Company G while he was on dress parade in the afternoon, and then sold the shirt for $4.00 to John Nones of Company C. Santos and Homer were apprehended and tried by court-martial. They were convicted, and in sentence they were marched through the Camp of the 3rd Brigade for three consecutive days, under guard, with fife and drum, with the word "THIEF" printed on a board and hung round their necks, did hard labor in the Camp of the Garibaldi Guard for twenty days, and had to pay $6.00 to Warren for his stolen shirt and return $4.00 to Nones. One day after Santos and Homer were caught, Dessauer was apprehended and arrested. He was tried and dismissed from the service for being absent without proper authority and for failing to appear before a Military Commission to answer charges regarding his association with Colonel D'Utassy. Soon after the theft of the shirt, Santos was arrested again for drawing a weapon upon, and endangering the life of, a fellow soldier. He was court-martialed and sentenced to be confined with a ball and chain—twelve pounds of ball and six feet of chain attached to his left leg—for twenty days, to do six hours' hard labor each day, and to forfeit one month's pay to the government.

Colonel Funk had the sense of military discipline that Colonel D'Utassy lacked. There was not an officer or man in the division who did not know that leaving the picket line, except when properly relieved, was against all military rules. Every man was presumed to know the law, so a commissioned officer was presumed to know orders and regulations. Officers had to learn to act with judgment, discretion, and good sense, or to take the consequences. On March 2, twenty-three-year-old Captain James Trippe, very short on military experience, allowed a soldier on picket duty to leave his post. Funk charged Hughes and Baker for failure to discipline the officers under them. Hughes and Baker were ordered confined to the limits of the regimental camp until their court-martial. That same day, Lieutenant Bader of Company C was arrested and charged with being absent without authority. Captain Schwickhardi and Lieutenant Samsa went on medical leave and were soon discharged for disability; soon afterward, Lieutenant Doell was placed in command of Company D and George Plumb was promoted to second lieutenant. George Etheridge, an Englishman from Company K who was in the division hospital suffering from consumption and was on the list to be transferred to the Invalid Corps, worsened and died. On Thursday, March 3, Lieutenant Rassmaessler, Company A, was promoted to captain. First Lieutenant Rensselaer transferred from Company I to Company E, where Michael McGarry, late a captain of the 31st New York, mustered in as a second lieutenant. On March 5, newly mustered Lieutenant Plumb was transferred to Company B. By March 6, Charles Williams and the other deserters had been tried, convicted, and sentenced to serve out the balance of their enlistments at hard labor in the prison camp in the Dry Tortugas, Florida.[8] Albert Boehler and David Champion, both of Company G, were court-martialed at headquarters for desertion and found guilty. They were delivered to the custody of the Provost Marshal General for escort under guard to Sing Sing Penitentiary, to await execution.

On Sunday, March 13, Hughes and Baker were released from arrest and restored to duty. Trippe was tried and found guilty of neglect of duty. He was

sentenced to forfeit three months' pay and to be reprimanded in general orders by the division's commanding general. Due to his evident desire to try to
perform his duty properly, Trippe was restored to duty. Sergeant McCarron,
Company H, was promoted to first sergeant. Charles Summerfield deserted
from the regimental guardhouse, and Lieutenant McLean claimed he was under medical treatment in Washington and was reported absent from duty.[9]
James Jones, a deserter from Company E, 33rd New York; John Patnoots, a
deserter from the 27th New York; George Mowry, a deserter from the draft in
New York; and Alexander McFarland, a deserter from an unknown organization, were assigned to the Guard while awaiting trial. On March 15, the regiment lost fifty-seven men when it was requested to pick and send thirty of its
best marksmen, three per company, to brigade headquarters, and another
twenty-seven men were transferred to the Veteran Reserve Corps. All of their
surplus muskets and appendages were turned over to the ordnance officer.

Women who gathered around army camps were set up in their own
nearby establishments by officers and men, and sometimes passed as their
wives. "Quinine may be the need of the Confederate army," wrote the
Star, "but copavia is certainly the necessity of ours." Copavia was used to
treat infected mucous membranes. When units put down temporary roots
during winter quarters, the number of nearby ladies tended to increase. Funk
ordered:

> The Ladies be Dismissed from camp: In virtue of the near
> approach of the time that this Army may be expected to move in a live
> operation, the General Commanding considers that the interest to the
> Service requires that the Ladies now with the army, other than those
> here under the special authority of the War Department at these Head-
> quarters of members of the Sanitary Commission or other charitable
> associations can no longer remain with it. The Commanding General
> therefore desires that Corps Commanders cause the Officers of their
> respected Commands to be notified that it is expected they will make
> the necessary arrangements to send beyond the lines of the army
> with as little delay as possible, the Ladies at present visiting them.
>
> The authority therefore given the Provost marshall General to
> grant permits to Ladies to visit the Army, upon recommendation of
> the Corps Commanders is revoked.

That night after taps, following Funk's order, there was an unusual
amount of loud noise and confusion in the Guard's camp. The Officer of the
Guard and the troops at his command were unable to quiet the rowdy men.
General Owen sent the provost guard to the camp around 11:00 P.M., and
Sergeant Stephen Laugenbach of Company A, Corporal Thomas Kelly of
Company F, and hospital steward Charles Breiting (misspelled Brilling in
the daily record) were arrested for drunkenness and insubordination. They
were reduced to the ranks for being found drunk. Ashamed of his men's

conduct, Funk regretted in writing that "a man occupying such an important and responsible position should go so far as to forget himself and become so intoxicated." By Owen's order, the Guard was warned that "the General is very much chagrined that the insubordinate conduct of his Brigade should have merited such a rebuke from superior Headquarters and directs that care will be taken, to remedy at once the severe complaint."

On March 18, a Friday, William W. Goodwin was mustered in from the 2nd Artillery as an assistant surgeon. Francis Crowley of Company I was detailed to instruct the young men of the Garibaldi Guard Drum Corps in the art of drum rolls. Lieutenant Doell, who relieved Schwickhardi as commander of Company D, was placed under arrest for disobedience to orders. Three days after Goodwin joined the Guard, at the recruiting office in New York, Lieutenant Lederer was discharged for disabilities. On March 22, Captain Gilfillan and Second Lieutenant Tremper were discovered intoxicated as they celebrated the captain's imminent transfer from the army to the navy. Unfortunately, it was their second offense. Gilfillan told Lieutenant Colonel Hughes just what he thought of him, using insulting and disrespectful language. Both Gilfillan and Tremper were arrested and charged with drunkenness and conduct unbecoming an officer and a gentleman. They were ordered to deliver themselves to the adjutant of the Guard. When the examining board met to review applicants for transfers to the navy, it chose a captain from the 61st New York instead of Gilfillan for transfer to the navy and left him relieved from duty.

At retreat roll call on the evening of March 23, Companies F, G, and K were without officers. Hughes told the Garibaldians in no uncertain words that officers were expected to conduct themselves in exemplary fashion: "Such culpable negligence and disobedience of orders on the part of the officers of the Garibaldi Guard will no longer be tolerated. Hereafter a report will be sent to superior Headquarters of Companies when officers fail to comply with existing orders and the name of officers in Command of such companies will be read out on dress parades. The colonel in Command hopes he will [not need to resort] to such severe measures, but he cannot consciously punish the enlisted men for an [offence...committed] by senior officers." Funk then ordered that the officers put out all lights immediately after taps. If an officer wanted lights in his tent after taps for some reason he had to request permission from Funk. In spite of the warning, Captain Rich of Company F was placed under arrest for disobedience of Funk's orders.

On the day Santos and Horer had been caught stealing Warren's shirt, President Lincoln signed a bill that made Ulysses S. Grant a lieutenant general in charge of all Union armies. Grant subsequently decided to accompany the Army of the Potomac while exercising command, as it faced the strongest enemy army and communications with Washington were better than they would be from the field in the west. Meade kept command of the Army of the Potomac and consolidated his infantry into three corps, to better control in upcoming campaigns. But, it hurt morale now. Men from disbanded corps who were proud of their units resented being transferred, and the remaining corps were still absorbing new recruits. III Corps merged into II Corps, which gave Hancock four strengthened divisions. General Hays lost command of his division in the consolidation, however, and was reassigned to command a brigade under Brigadier General David Bell Birney, who had commanded III Corps at Gettysburg after its original commander was seriously wounded. When the Garibaldians got wind of a rumor that Hays would return to his old brigade, which he had left to take the division, one of the old soldiers joked, "Hell, old Hays is coming back and there won't be a man of us alive."[10] Instead, German-born Colonel Paul Frank took command of the brigade containing the Guard, the third brigade of II Corps' first division. The new, consolidated brigade was composed entirely of New York troops: the 39th under Colonel Funk, the 111th under Captain Aaron P. Seely, the 125th under Lieutenant Colonel Aaron B. Myer, and the 126th under Captain Winfield Scott.[11] In April, the brigade would add the 7th under Major G. A. Seidel, the 52nd under Major Henry M. Karples (who replaced the deceased Venuti), and the 57th under Lieutenant Colonel A. B. Chapman.

For picket duty on Sunday, March 27, the Garibaldi Guard supplied a noticeably large contingent of men, including two captains, three lieutenants, six sergeants, twenty-four corporals, and one hundred sixty-three privates. The next day Private Thomas Addi, 73rd New York, was mustered in as the first lieutenant of Company C, while veteran First Sergeant Menzler reenlisted for Company I. All were certain some major event was about to occur, especially when they received the order that "The Division will be on the ground promptly at 12 P.M. and every effort will be made to have all men armed turned out and in good condition." General Grant was coming to review the II Corps on March 29 at 2:00 P.M., near Stevensburg. It rained, Grant did not arrive, and there was no inspection. Instead, on that same day General Owen issued his farewell to his old brigade:

> Fellow Soldiers of the old 3rd Brigade, 3rd Division 2nd Corps.
>
> Under the new arrangement of the troops of the Army of the Potomac, I am assigned by the General Commanding the Corps, to a Command in which you are not included, I must therefore bid you adieu!
>
> You are endeared to me by your soldierly being and good discipline: your prompt obedience of all orders and especially by your valor in battle. You have cause to be proud of your military record. Be as good soldiers in the future as in the past and your new Commander will have equal cause to be proud of you. Remember the 2nd Corps, always conquers, even though it has to pluck victory from the very jaws of death. When the War is over and you return to

your peaceful homes your country will honor you as the brave defenders. I wish you finally success and honor.

Your old Commander.

Joshua T. Owen

On March 30, Dr. Wolf, who had also been arrested for failing to have permission for lights after taps, was released from arrest and returned to duty. He requested that Lorenzo Caroglio, Joseph Hauptmann, John Walker, and Franz Weiss be detailed for duty as nurses. Charles Schouten was mustered into Company H as a second lieutenant. The brigade, including the Guard, drilled constantly in an effort to prepare recruits and veterans alike to act cohesively on the forthcoming campaigns. Orders were published everywhere that cleanliness must and would be observed in the camps, and officers and men were warned that they would be severely punished if they did not comply with those orders. A thorough inspection of arms, accouterments, equipment, camps, and men was conducted on March 31. All staff officers were required to be present. The men had to have their hair cut short and no straw hats were allowed to be worn.

On April 1, the provost marshal arrested Second Lieutenant Michael O. McGarry of Company E for neglect of duty. McGarry, who had been a captain in the 31st New York prior to his commission in the Guard, was the officer in charge of several men on picket duty that day. That night after taps, several of McGarry's pickets built shelters and fires at their posts, which could distract them from being watchful. He had forbidden the men in his charge from having shelters or fires, but he took no measure to punish the man who disobeyed his orders, Patrick Dooley of Company I. On April 9, First Sergeant Maggi of Company C was promoted to second lieutenant in Company I, and Sergeant F. Muller was promoted to first sergeant in his place. The next day, First Lieutenant Tremper transferred from Company G to A. On April 15, McGarry was tried before a court-martial and found not guilty, despite the observation that "If an officer who has charge of only outposts, cannot prevent such a gross disobedience of orders[,] he is guilty of neglect of duty." McGarry was released from arrest and returned to duty.

The period of relative inactivity that had characterized the Army of the Potomac since the Mine Run Campaign almost five months earlier was drawing to a close. On Saturday, April 16, First Sergeant John E. Valentine was mustered in from the 15th Massachusetts as the first lieutenant of Company I, filling the void left by Rensselaer. One day later, on the south side of the Rapidan River, Confederate Lieutenant General Richard S. Ewell reported to General Lee, "A sergeant of the 39th New York came over today....His statements are that the 11th and 12th Corps have gone over to Annapolis; that the impression prevails that Grant is to maneuver us out of position without hard fighting; the 9th and 22nd Corps have come up; that the artillery has been brought forward from Stevensburg in line toward Pony Mountain. The regimental sutlers left."[12] April 17 found the Garibaldians camped near Brandy Station. George Bruce, a Union soldier camped near the Guard, noted, "As night came, the German recruits bedded down together and comforted themselves by singing. There were many voices of much sweetness and power among them, and for hours the camp resounded with this unfamiliar music. There was a pathos in the tones of these voices that fitted well with the pathos of their surroundings." Dr. Wolf accepted an appointment as assistant surgeon in the United States Volunteers. Privates Ingraham, Tipping, Wilson, Allen, Dwyer, Snow, Wallace, Delaney (a navy deserter), and Schreiner, were transferred to the navy on April 19.

April concluded with what would be final preparations for the upcoming Union offensive. On April 21, Colonel Frank ordered that the officers of the brigade who had ladies visiting them be informed that no leaves of absence would be granted after April 23. Colonel Funk presided over a board of investigation held to decide which men were fit for duty and who would be discharged or sent to the Veteran Reserve Corps. Garibaldians J. Behrens, Milton White, Peter Durand, and H. Hipp were detailed to the Ambulance Corps as drivers. L. Smith was detailed to the medical wagons; M. Martinez, John Wallace, David McDonald, David Smith, F. Lubrandt, and Paul Posser were detailed as stretcher carriers. Captain Gilfillan was released from arrest for intoxication. On Sunday, May 1, the three-year enlistments of the original Garibaldians expired. The rolls showed the Guard had a total strength of nine hundred eighty—six officers and five hundred fifty-four men present, and fourteen officers and four hundred six men absent. The one-year recruits enabled the regiment to continue as an organization, but a vastly changed one. Only two men from the original German companies, Second Lieutenant Charles Menzler of Company D and Private Charles Krehlich of Company G, reenlisted to serve to 1865.

Chapter Ten

PRESSING GENERAL LEE

WHEN General Grant joined the Army of the Potomac, he gave General Meade orders to destroy General Lee's Army of Northern Virginia: "Wherever Lee goes, there you will go also." Meade's orders were posted on May 3: "Have confidence in your officers and each other. Keep your ranks on the march and on the battlefield, and let each man earnestly implore God's blessings, and endeavor by his thoughts and actions to render himself worthy of the favor he seeks. Either clear consciences [or] strong arms. Actuated by a high sense of duty, fighting to preserve the government and the institutions handed down to us by our forefathers—if true to ourselves—victory, under God's blessings, must and will attend our efforts." The problem of the availability of ammunition for the troops was met by a Meade's statement directing that "every effort be made to economize the ammunition, and the ammunition of the killed and wounded be collected and distributed to the men. Use the bayonet where possible." With this inspiring guidance the 1864 Spring campaign began. It would be a time of continuous fighting or marching, through a country with four main rivers, numerous smaller streams, and dense woods—a time of building defenses and bridges. Sergeant Thomas O'Keefe from the 82nd New York was mustered in as the second lieutenant, Company K; his brother John had enlisted as a private in Company G the preceding December. Corporal Sack was promoted to sergeant in Company E.

The Federal strategy would be to get around Lee's right, east flank, cut him off from Richmond while keeping Union lines to Washington open, and defeat him. Meade's major challenge would be to get past the Wilderness, where Lee had whipped Hooker the year before. Monday, May 4, found the Garibaldians still at Stevensburg. Frank's consolidated brigade was now un-

167

der the division command of twenty-nine-year-old Brigadier General Francis Channing Barlow, in Hancock's II Corps. At about 10:00 P.M. the regiment broke camp in the chilly damp air. The Garibaldians silently marched toward the Rapidan River, preceding the supply train of four thousand wagons. By the next day at noon, they had crossed the river at Ely Ford. Tragically, Private William Wilson drowned in the crossing. David Bogart and Alexander McDevitt deserted. At 2:00 P.M., Birney's division led II Corps but was still some distance behind Hancock. Directly behind Birney were Brigadier Generals Gershom Mott's, John Gibbon's, and Barlow's divisions, with Frank's brigade and the Garibaldi Guard assigned to cover the baggage train in the rear. Fighting began early in the day and grew as battles raged all day. It was not until 6:00 P.M. that Barlow's division, the last in line of march, came up to the main battle area. Frank's brigade with the Garibaldians was stationed at the junction of the Brock road and the road leading to the Catharpin Furnaces, fresh troops holding the left of Hancock's line. They occupied the high ground covering the Fredericksburg and Orange Court House Railroad, supporting the artillery batteries' forty-two guns. Sometime near 5:00 P.M. General Hays was killed in action as his men held their ground. He had sent word to Hancock for reinforcements. Hancock sent an aide to tell him he would have a fresh brigade in twenty minutes. By 6:00 P.M. the rest of Barlow's division pressed the right of Confederate General A. P. Hill's III Corps. At dark the firing died down to the skirmish line. Weary and wounded soldiers laid down among the dead. Captain Trippe, Company E, was wounded in the day's action. The Battle of the Wilderness was under way.

On May 6, at 5:00 A.M., the Union attacks resumed and Lee's right flank gave way. Lee was saved by the timely arrival from Gordonsville of Longstreet's corps, which attacked directly and stalled the Union advance. Lee organized an assault on the Union left. Hancock learned of Longstreet's arrival and reinforcement of A. P. Hill. Hancock had split his corps into commands under Birney on his right and Gibbon on his left because his line was too long for effective personal leadership in the dense woods. He ordered Gibbon to send Barlow's division against the Confederate right flank, but only Frank's brigade with the Garibaldians went forward, since the Federal command erroneously expected a Confederate counterattack upon the Union's left rear and wasted time holding back the rest of the division to meet it. Frank's brigade and the Garibaldians went into battle by passing through the lines of Colonel McAllister's brigade of Mott's division. McAllister reported afterward that "Colonel Frank of General Barlow's division came with a few troops, and said that he wished to pass through my line to the front. I told him that I had skirmishers out and that I was advancing with the line of battle and did not wish them to go, that I had orders to advance when this line advanced, and halt when it halted. He (Frank) replied that he had orders 'to find the enemy wherever he could find him and whip him.' Saying this he spurred his horse, faced his men to the left, and moved around my left flank, and advanced in my front, and soon engaged the enemy. But a very little firing took place until some of his men came back running."

That "little firing" hit the Garibaldians very hard, for at the outset of the engagement Colonel Funk, Lieutenant Colonel Hughes, and five company officers were wounded, as were many enlisted men. Companies C and I took the most casualties. The wounded in Company I included First Lieutenant Valentine, Sergeant A. Baker, and Corporal Vial. Among other wounded were Corporal Olivry, for the second time, and Privates Carboni, Delacosta, Petroli, and Delapores, who died of his wounds four days later. Private James Nicholson, Company E, would be wounded twice during battle in the Wilderness and die in August. Private Garbarini was captured in action and would die in Andersonville prison. Captain Haight and First Lieutenant Rogers of Company H were captured in action. Private Dooley of Company I was captured in action and would die at Andersonville prison of disease in the next month. Jacob Ganser of Company C was captured (he would return on December 10 in a prisoner exchange). Every company had someone wounded or killed in its ranks.[1] Gilfillan was released from arrest and restored to duty. McAllister would report that "in a few minutes a verbal message came for me to relieve [Frank]. This I declined to do, as my orders were to advance with this line. A few minutes more and all his troops came running back. I had my men stop them, and refused to let them through. Colonel Frank said to me, 'I want to get ammunition.' I asked him, 'There?' He replied, 'Away back in the rear.' I informed him that mules loaded with ammunition had just come up on my right and if he would detail a few men I would send them with a sergeant and get the ammunition, which could be had in a few minutes. At this moment the pickets became engaged and I opened up my ranks and let Colonel Frank's Command through, as I supposed, to get ammunition. This is the last I saw of him or his command."[2] Interestingly, the Guard's Captain David A. Allen (Company G) simply wrote in his report on the Garibaldian action, "On the morning of the 6th of May engaged the enemy, but were forced to fall back to original position."

Sometime during this action a delegation of officers from the third brigade reported to Barlow and requested that he relieve Frank because he was drunk and unfit to exercise command. They recommended that a junior officer be placed in command of the brigade and offered to waive their rank if this were done. Barlow considered the request but declined to act immediately, telling the officers that they would have to get along as best they could for the present. Later in the day Colonel Hiram L. Brown, who commanded the 145th Pennsylvania in Brooke's brigade, was placed in command of the third brigade. Frank was relieved and placed under arrest.[3]

The Armies of the Potomac and of Northern Virginia had fought each other to a draw as of May 7. Failing to defeat Lee at the Wilderness, Grant ordered Meade to continue southeast and south toward Richmond, still trying to turn Lee's flank and cut him off. Lee moved rapidly to entrench his army around the important road junction at New Spotsylvania Court House, and he was there when the Union forces arrived. From May 8 through 12, Grant would order frontal attacks all along the line but be unable to dislodge Lee. Captain Allen reported, "The regiment marched from [the] Wilderness to Po River, where on the morning of the 10th May, our skirmishers engaged the enemy and about noon brought in a general engagement, when after holding our position one hour, [we] were forced to fall back. The regiment was sent in to support a battery. The loss in this days action was 1 commissioned officer missing ...." Captain John Funk, Company K, and First Sergeant Silas Spratt and Corporal Hoffman, Company B, were wounded and captured in action. First Sergeant Muller, Company C, Lieutenant McGarry, Company E, Captain Haight, Company H, and Ferdinand Maggi, Company I, were wounded during the action at Po River. Barlow's division, with the Garibaldians, had actually turned Lee's left, west flank, but Union generals failed to recognize their great chance to flush Lee out of position and defeat him piecemeal. Barlow was pulled back. Allen wrote about the Guard, "Marched from the Po River on the 11th of May to Spotsylvania..." There was no real fighting that day; together with the rest of II Corps, the Guard moved to the center of the Union line, to prepare for a frontal attack against the Confederate center, a strongly held, sharp bend in Lee's line that the Federals called "the salient" and the Confederates called "the Mule Shoe."

One of the original officers of the Guard, who left the regiment after the mutiny against D'Utassy in 1861, was James Clay Rice. Like other patriots who first joined the Guard but could not stand D'Utassy, he left and joined another unit. He was commissioned as colonel of the 44th New York in September 1861. He served excellently and was promoted to brigadier general and command of the fifth division in the old I Corps. In Meade's corps consolidation, he had assumed command of the 2nd brigade of the 4th division of V Corps. Now, in the Union advance against Lee, he was mortally wounded at Laurel Hill, near Spotsylvania Court House. Charles C. Coffin related that "General Rice, commanding a brigade in the Fifth Corps, was wounded, and borne to the rear. The surgeon laid down his knife after removing the shattered limb, and stood beside him to soothe with tender words in the last dread hour which was coming on apace....His eyes were closing...his pain was intense. 'Turn me over,' said he, faintly. 'Which way?' 'Let me die with my face to the enemy!'"[4]

Now the Guard faced the salient. On May 12 at 4:35 A.M., the entire II Corps attacked with fixed bayonets straight at the enemy entrenchments. After moving into position in the dark, in a steady rain with heavy fog, Barlow's and Birney's massed divisions led the assault out of the forest, across the ravine in front, past the skirmish line, and through the Confederate picket line, sweeping it away. The heavy Union formations seized the second line of Confederate works, together with Confederate Generals Edward Johnson and

James C. Rice
Former first lieutenant, Company H, 39th New York Volunteer Infantry in his uniform
as a lieutenant colonel of the 44th New York Infantry Volunteers.

Division of Military and Naval Affairs,
New York State Adjutant General Office,
Albany, New York

George H. Steuart. Three thousand men of Ewell's corps, eighteen guns, and
twenty-two standards were captured,[5] before a slashing counterattack by
Confederate Brigadier General John B. Gordon's division threw the bunched-
up Union troops back to the first line of captured trenches. Fighting then
raged all day as the Confederates tried to restore their original line of defense
and the Federals tried to retake the fortifications they briefly held. The result
was a vicious deadlock, but Lee managed to build a new line across the base
of the salient. After midnight, his troops in the salient fell back behind the new
line, and his army was saved. Allen reported, "Early on the morning of the
12th assisted in the charge of the 2nd Corps, the regiment having participated
in the entire engagement of the day, and have to report the loss of 1 line officer
killed, 2nd lieutenant Thomas O'Keefe." Allen did not report the deaths of
Henry Junker of Company G or of Charles Gramms and Frederick Schenk,
both of Company K, or the mortal wounds of Ezekial B. Benton, Company H,
and Henry Gravellius, Company I. Thirteen enlisted men were wounded in
action but would recover, two were captured (one would die in prison; George
Nichols escaped and returned to Company K), and one was missing. Second
Lieutenant Ballou, unassigned up to this time, was mustered as the second
lieutenant of Company K to replace O'Keefe. Captain Gilfillan of Company I
was wounded leading his men. First Lieutenant Rich of Company K was
wounded, and Captain L. Magnus was discharged. May 13 was relatively
quiet, but Francisco Navarreto, Company C, Jacob Derelin, Company E, and
David Wright, Company K, were wounded in skirmishes.

From May 14 through 17, the opposing armies around Spotsylvania
constantly improved their positions and continually skirmished, sniped at,
and shelled each other, although there were no actual attacks of any size. At
4:00 A.M. on Wednesday, May 18, II Corps attacked again into the area of
the salient. Union troops took two lines of rifle-pits, but an impassable abatis prevented any farther advance. After a six-hour struggle, Grant halted the
attack, ending the last Union attempt to defeat Lee at Spotsylvania. Captain
Allen reported that the Guard "participated in the engagement May 18, 1864.
One field officer and 2 line officers wounded." Major Charles C. Baker,
First Lieutenant Tremper, and Second Lieutenant George Dell were the
wounded officers. Tremper and Dell belonged to Company A; Harvey
Baldwin, 7th Artillery, was commissioned a first lieutenant and took com-
mand of the company. First Sergeant McCarron of Company H and Second
Lieutenant Ballou of Company K were also wounded in the action. Surgeon
Charles S. Hoyt was promoted to head surgeon of the Garibaldi Guards, and
Dr. Freeman Stoddard was commissioned as assistant surgeon to tend wounded
Garibaldians. The Garibaldi Guard's losses from the twelve-day battle of
Spotsylvania totalled one officer, Second Lieutenant O'Keefe of Company K,
and fifteen men killed in action, and one officer, First Lieutenant Rich of
Company F, and nine men fatally wounded in action. Eight officers, including
Captain Gilfillan of Company I, and seventy-four men were wounded in ac-

tion; Gilfillan would remain in a hospital till his discharge for disability on August 12. One officer and twenty-seven men were missing in action.

Grant devised a new plan to attack Lee. On May 20, II Corps swung out to the east and south toward Hanover Junction (today's Doswell), ahead of the rest of the army. If Lee took the bait and came out into the open, the rest of the army would attack to overwhelm him before he could dig in again. If Lee ignored the bait, the march would become another operation to turn his right flank and cut him off from Richmond. Suspicious, Lee began sideslipping south and moved below the North Anna River. By Sunday, May 22, the battle of the North Anna had begun. Union forces probed Lee's position and found it too strong for an assault. Captain Allen reported, "The regiment marched with the Division to the North Anna, a rapid stream with high banks. They crossed to the South side of the North Anna and remained the greater portion of the day in line of battle under fire, but were not engaged. The following morning they recrossed the river and marched toward the Pamunkey [River]." On May 25, storms continued all day. The Guard was involved in some skirmishing, with no losses. While First Lieutenant Valentine, Company I, recovered from his wounds, returned to the ranks, and was transferred to Company E, Second Lieutenant Michael O. McGarry died of his wounds at the hospital at Georgetown.

On May 26, the Garibaldians arrived at the Pamunkey at Hanover Town. Lee fell back above the Chickahominy River, southwest of Hanover Town. Allen reported that "The regiment, the 27th of May, crossed the Pamunkey." Four men were killed in the crossing, four men were wounded and later died, two men were missing in action, and First Lieutenant Henry Shaw, Company I, was discharged. Isaac Proper of the 42nd New York enrolled as a second lieutenant in Company H. On May 29, the Garibaldians "advanced with the Division on Hanover town, and Corporal Diefenbach company A. was captured at Hanover Court House. Then they became engaged in skirmishing with the enemy on the 30th and 31st of May. Major Charles C. Baker was discharged from the wounds he received in action at Spotsylvania Courthouse." Although Allen had been a major in the 47th New York Infantry, Adjutant Hyde was promoted to major after Baker's discharge and took command of the regiment. The consolidated brigade containing the Garibaldi Guard was now led by Brigadier General Levin Crandell.

Both armies kept angling southeast, each one trying to gain a tactical advantage over the other. Grant and Lee faced each other at Totopotomoy Creek. II Corps took a position along the creek's north bank and skirmished with the Confederates, gaining some ground, but found their position too strong to assault. During a bayonet charge that pushed the enemy from its outer line of works, Virgilio Pierotti and Sergeant Antonio Oliva of Company C were wounded in action; Oliva died the next day of his wounds. Tuesday, May 31, found both armies maneuvering like enormous snakes southeast toward the crossroads village of Cold Harbor, while Union reinforcements marched up from the southeast. Meade ordered Major General Philip Henry Sheridan, who had just repulsed Confederate cavalry at Cold Harbor, to hold the village at all costs. The assault commenced about 5:00 P.M. when six Federal divisions advanced north of the Cold Harbor-Gaines Mill road. The Confederates were entrenched, and their counterattack sent the Federals toward the rear. It was one of the bloodiest fights in this campaign. The Garibaldians lost three men killed, twelve men wounded, and three missing in this action.

Grant ordered Hancock's Corps to march that night to the crossroads in order to outflank Lee and have an open road to Richmond. If II Corps, probably the army's most experienced fighters, could make it, Grant would have succeeded. So the Garibaldians marched out that night at 10:00 P.M. toward the vital road junction of Cold Harbor, along the Union left on the road leading to Dispatch Station, farther down the Chickahominy River. Early on the morning of June 1, the Guard led the column when it arrived at Cold Harbor by 6:30 A.M., in "an exhausted condition." The remaining officers were as spent as the men, and with the loss of eight officers the Garibaldi Guard was nearly leaderless. The regiment was deployed in front of the enemy. New shoes were provided for the Garibaldians along the line that day since heavy boots were considered the "cause of sore feet and excuse for straggling. Officers were made responsible to carry this out." Throughout the morning Hancock's soldiers straggled in; even the pack horses found straggling from or ahead of the column were taken in charge by the provost guard.

In their present small companies, no man could leave the ranks without being seen by his company commander, if that officer "exercised proper vigilance." Regiment and company commanders were required to march in the rear of their commands in order to see their men. A man could slip out of ranks for water, unobserved. Men were constantly seen going for water without their guns or with only one canteen. This left them open to be easily picked off, wounded, or captured. On Wednesday, June 1, Meade issued the following order: "The attack ordered for 5 P.M. this day is postponed to 4:30 A.M. to-morrow. Corps Commanders will employ the interim in making examinations of the ground in their fronts, and perfecting their arrangements for the assault." A heavy rain started at three in the afternoon and continued through the night. The next morning at 10:30 A.M., Captain John Funk had been paroled, exchanged, and returned to Company K. That same day, Garibaldians received orders from Headquarters:

> The term of service of Companies A., B., C., & D. of the 39th N.Y. Vols. having expired those companies except re-enlisted men and those who have joined since date of the original organization will proceed to the place of first muster in under Command of the senior officer of the 4 companies to be discharged the service.

The veterans and the recruits of these companies will be assigned to the remaining companies of the regiment by the Regimental Commander.

All men sent home must have their descriptive list.

The 4 companies to be mustered out will accompany the 6th Corps train of wounded to the White House as a guard and the Commanding officer will report for instructions to these headquarters by 12 P.M. today.

The question of retaining the field officers of the Regiment will be decided hereafter.

In case the descriptive lists of the men to be discharged cannot be supplied at the hour designated for the Battalion to report at Corps Headquarters the companies will remain at White House until such can be completed from the records of the Regiment contained in the trains. The order to report as guard to the train of wounded is imperative.

by Command of
Major General Hancock

Like the other units of II Corps that were deployed in front of the Confederates, the Guard watched its number diminish as comrades from the old Garibaldi Guard formed ranks and marched away from the battle line in their new shoes, leaving behind later enlistees who were transferred to other companies. About one hundred fifty Garibaldians in Companies A, B, C, and D under Captain Rassmaessler's command accompanied the wounded to Washington and then went on to New York. They arrived June 10 and were mustered out of service on June 23 and 24. The Guard was considerably reduced. Its principal musician, Anton Rang, was mustered out from the field and staff element. Rassmaessler plus Lieutenants Tremper and Doell, among other individuals, were mustered out from Company A. Captain Baer, Lieutenants Hand and Plumb, and noncommissioned officers Henry Goos and Michael Jacky, the musician, were mustered out from Company B. Veterans mustered out from Company C included Lieutenants Bader and Thomas Addi, Sergeant Castelbecchi, Corporal Olivry, and men like Raffaele Bartoli, Lorenzo Caroglio, Antonio Giusti, Antonio Guzman, Miguel Martinez, Virgilo Pierotti, Rafael Quinones, Luigi Rocca, Guiseppe Sambruetti, and Domenico Venturo. Veterans mustered out from Company D included noncommissioned officers Paglio Georgio Domineco, Francisco Naverreto, Joaquin Nones, Felipe Pis, and Juan Jose Torrens. At the time they were mustered out Olivry and Guzman were in a hospital recuperating from wounds suffered in action, and Gotanis was in a hospital sick. Naverreto was transferred to the Veteran Reserve Corps.

The Garibaldians who remained in the ranks at Cold Harbor after the veterans to be mustered out departed for New York prepared for what would be one of the most horrific attacks of the war. On June 3 at 4:30 A.M., three

Federal corps and part of a fourth, forty thousand men, advanced against the Confederate earthworks. The massed Union soldiers attacked straight into the teeth of point-blank, interlocked gun and cannon fire. Hancock was on the Union left. One of Hancock's aides later wrote that the Confederates "behind the works raised deliberately, resting their guns upon the works," and then commenced the "inexplicable and incredible butchery." "Men fell like autumn leaves." The Confederates reported seeing "men falling on top of men, rear rank pushing forward the first rank, only to be swept away like chaff"; "the spectacle in front of our line was simply sickening. The horrible heaps of dead lay so ghastly, and the wounded were so thickly strewn all over the field." Hancock's divisions suffered heavy losses. One of his aides reported, "Altogether, this has been one of the most disastrous days the Army of the Potomac has ever seen, and the old 2nd Corps has especially suffered." Grant had tried to break Lee's lines at Cold Harbor; instead, he lost ten thousand men in twenty minutes. People celebrated in Richmond, claiming, "He is floundering in the swamps of Chickahominy. He had reached the graveyard of Yankee armies." Northern papers called Grant a butcher who had sacrificed a hundred thousand lives.

Instead of retreating, the Federals dug in where they had been stopped, and the two entrenched armies began a harsh standoff that would last until June 12. On June 4, two Confederates, Corporal Lawrence Fleming and Private John Dreadnaught, both from Ireland, deserted to the Garibaldi Guard. Astonished after seeing wagon after wagon marked for the "39th NYV," they remarked, "You boys got more supplies for your one company than we've got for our whole army." On Monday, June 6, Second Lieutenant Schouten of Company H was wounded and captured in action, along with William Roberts of Company E (Roberts would desert to the enemy months later during action at the Weldon and Petersburg Railroad, be recaptured, and subsequently be released as a prisoner of war on July 5, 1865, upon taking the oath of allegiance to the U.S. at Nashville, Tennessee). Grant requested a truce on June 7 to pick up the wounded and to bury the dead. While on detail under a flag of truce, Second Lieutenant Joseph Wilson, Company F, was wounded and went into the hospital, where he would remain until October 5, 1864, when he was finally discharged. June 8 saw Sergeant Charles Summerfield of Company E desert from his detail at the regimental guardhouse and First Lieutenant Valentine be discharged for wounds and remain in the hospital. On June 10, Second Lieutenant Ballou, Company K, was promoted to first lieutenant, and Chief Surgeon Hoyt was detailed by Headquarters Special Order 441 to be executive officer of the 1st Division, II Corps hospital, where he would stay until January 12, 1865. All this time, Grant planned to make a bold, daring flanking maneuver.

Grant's next move was to take the entire Army of the Potomac across the Chickahominy and the James Rivers toward Petersburg, south of Richmond. If Petersburg could be captured, every railroad but one that supplied

Richmond would be cut, and the city and Lee's army would start to starve. Lee would have to stand siege in Richmond or retire west. The first trick was to withdraw from Cold Harbor without Lee's knowledge, since he was a master at catching and defeating enemy units piecemeal, and the rivers would force the Union corps on the march to split up. The Federals did it, starting on June 12 just after dark. Captain Allen's report afterwards to General Crandell read, "On the night of the (Sunday) 12th of June the regiment with the Division left Cold Harbor and marched to the Chickahominy. June 13, crossed the Chickahominy about noon and proceeded to Aiher's Landing on the James River, crossed on the morning of June 15 and on the night of 15th halted about 3 miles from Petersburg, Va."[6]

Soon, the whole Army of the Potomac was halted. The XVIII Corps' commander, leading the Union attack on Petersburg, got cold feet at the edge of the city and wasted his chance to seize it before the Confederates raced in with defenders. Three subsequent days of abortive Union attacks brought heavy losses and negligible gains. The siege of Petersburg, which would last for nine and a half months and end one week short of Lee's surrender, effectively began on Thursday, June 16. The Federals dug in and began skirmishing. Second Lieutenant Charles Schouten and Jose DelaCosta, both of Company H, were wounded on June 16 and taken to the corps hospital, where Juan joined his two brothers, Johanni and Dominico. The brothers had all enlisted that past February, and Johanni, the eldest, and Dominico were still in the hospital after being wounded in action in the Wilderness and at Po River. After Johanni and Dominico both died of their wounds some days later, Jose disappeared from the hospital and all further record on June 28. Schouten left the hospital and the army in September. Meanwhile, Issac Saithof, Company I, died of his wounds when his left leg was amputated at the corps hospital in Albany, New York. And Doctor Hoyt transferred Charles Williams, an Irishman in Company H who had been wounded in action, from the hospital to the Insane Asylum in Washington, D.C.

After entrenching the Union line east of Petersburg, Grant decided to extend it south and sent II and VI Corps out for that purpose. Confederates checked both corps advances, but both corps still managed to extend the line. Captain Allen's report of June 22 reflected the effort: "the Garibaldians were engaged but were driven back to the breastworks."[7] During that operation three men were killed, one officer and twenty-four men were wounded, and twenty-four men came up missing. Allen reported on June 27 that the Garibaldians skirmished with the enemy while working on fortifications. On Tuesday, June 28, the entire Union army started to move south of James River, and capture the important communication center of Petersburg. The Federals rested throughout the morning of June 29. It was the mid-afternoon when four corps pushed forward their skirmishers. Allen reported, "On the 29th recrossed the river marching all night." That evening at roll call Companies C, D, and K were without an officer. Also on that evening, two Confederate army deserters, Albert Schneider and Corporal James Williams, an Irishman, took the oath of allegiance and were sent to Camp Chase, Ohio, for transfer to a regiment at Fort Snelling, Minnesota, in the Northwest Territory.

On the last day of the month, the Garibaldi Guard found itself in Colonel Clinton MacDougall's brigade of Barlow's division. The Guard reported one officer and ninety-nine men present for duty. The regiment itself was now no bigger than one of its original ten companies. The paymaster requested that the regiment submit a muster roll of the men on duty and of the walking wounded and those in the hospital in order to pay everyone what each person was due. One of the regiment's officers, Cornelius McLean, had been ill since March. He had remained absent for medical treatment and done only one day of duty. For failing to file the necessary Surgeon's Certificate of Disability and to make reports to his regiment as required by War Department regulations, Headquarters brought charges against him, and he was dishonorably discharged on July 7 for absence without leave. James C. Wyckoff was mustered in as second lieutenant in Company G to replace McLean. On July 8, at City Point (today, Hopewell), Grant received the gift of the celebrated dagger borne by General Garibaldi in nearly all his battles. Grant responded in a letter to Charles G. Leleand on July 18:

> I shall cherish the dagger as a souvenir of that distinguished soldier & patriot General Garibaldi, who by his devotion and sacrifices to the cause of liberty in Italy is entitled to the highest respect and admiration of every American.
>
> Be good enough to send it at your convenience, by Express, to Mrs. U. S. Grant, St. Louis, Mo. care of Mr. Chas. Ford, Agt. U.S. Ex. company St. Louis, Mo.
> With the highest personal regard, I am,
> > Very respectfully
> > your obt. svt.
> > U. S. Grant
> > Lt. Gen. U.S.A.[8]

When the Garibaldians crossed the James River on July 14, William Moore of Company F took the opportunity to desert to the enemy. Allen reported, "Here the regiment remained until the 15th of July, when they were marched to the right and placed in reserve in the rear of the 5th Corps."[9] By July 18, the regiment was engaged in skirmishes at Strawberry Plains. The only casualty was Private Stucke of Company G, who was wounded in action. On Wednesday, July 20, the regiment was lying in camp when it received word of Sherman's activities near Atlanta, and a general "Hurrah" rose throughout the entire corps. On the morning of July 23, the brigade fell in and marched down the Weldon and Petersburg Railroad line and stacked arms near the Church road. The brigade then proceeded to tear up the track. Colonel Crandell posted pickets to his front to cover the brigade. At about 4:00 P.M., Crandell received orders to fall in. He withdrew his pickets and marched farther south to Ream's Station. The brigade, led by Captain Marlin, Division Inspector, reached Ream's Station at dusk. At that time there was sharp skirmishing on the right-hand side of the road. The brigade formed in the old works of the VI Corps, ready for any emergency. The next day Crandell received orders to move the brigade beyond Ream's Station and proceed to destroy the railroad, which it did. After destroying about eight hundred yards of the road, the brigade was moved opposite Smart's House (about two miles below Ream's Station) and set to work on the left of the 4th New York Heavy Artillery. About 5:30 P.M. Crandell received orders to withdraw his pickets, move back to Ream's Station, and bivouac for the night. Before reaching the station, he received orders from Brigadier General Nelson Appleton Miles to take charge of the picket line, and was separated from his brigade during the action at Ream's Station.

On July 26, the provost marshal was in camp again, this time seeking Domenico Marsala and Antonio Britooni (also spelled Britoonie), two more deserters from the French ship *Tissiaphone*. He ordered Lieutenant Wyckoff to turn over Marsala, alias Antonio Marichi of Company I, and Britooni, alias Antonio Gotanis of Company H, immediately. The problem was, Marichi had been killed in action in the Wilderness in January, and Britooni had mustered out on June 24. The personnel turbulence over three months of constant battle, the heavy losses, discharges, replacements, and unit realignments as commanders tried to sustain fighting organizations, resulted in a Garibaldi Guard that was now made up of raw recruits and found itself under Colonel Crandell in Gibbon's division, the second division, of II Corps. Now Grant sent II Corps north across the James as part of a feint to draw enemy troops away from Petersburg while IX Corps mined a Confederate artillery position to its front. The plan was to blow a hole through the Petersburg defenses and take the city while most of its defenders were elsewhere. The 48th Pennsylvania, which contained many miners, dug underground shafts beneath the Confederate battery and placed four tons of powder at the end of the shafts. Hancock sent two divisions of II Corps and two divisions of Sheridan's cavalry across to the Union Army of the James, where they established a line from Deep Bottom to the New Market road and made an attack that captured four guns. The feint worked; only three Confederate divisions stayed south of the James. On the night of July 29, II Corps, including the Garibaldians now at Deep Bottom, secretly disengaged and marched back to Petersburg. II Corps marched to the rear of XVIII Corps to support the mine assault. Portions of V and XVIII Corps were brought up to support IX Corps for the attack. Early in the moonlit morning hours of July 30, the Garibaldians were assembled in battle formation, awaiting orders for an attack. At 4:45 A.M. the ground trembled beneath them as if an earthquake were upon them. There was a sudden, terrible explosion, a dense cloud of smoke rose, and a mountain of debris, earth, body parts, timbers, cannon, shot, and shell soared into the air. The Union attack that followed was disastrous, humiliating, and disgraceful, a failure of poor leadership and tactics. II Corps was not engaged, and by 6:00 P.M. it moved back and remained in reserve.

Siege operations continued. In Company G on Monday, August 1, Commissary Sergeant Charles LeMarie was mustered out near Petersburg, and Private Stucke, who had been wounded in action at Strawberry Plains, was promoted to corporal. On August 4, the musicians of the Garibaldi Guard band were told to make ready for a salute that evening, that there was need to celebrate: "Direct every Battery bearing upon the line of the enemy and in each of his lines to fire a salute in honor of Sherman's victory in capturing Atlanta; let it be done tonight as soon as word can be got to the different Commanders. The bands will play the National Air as soon as the Cannonade begins." On Saturday, August 6, Sam Lewis, a Black soldier of Company K, died of disease at the II Corps hospital.

From August 14 to 18, the Guard was engaged in skirmishes at Strawberry Plains. Too ill to go on himself, Barlow reported that his men were used up and went to the hospital. General Miles assumed command of the division. In the four days of skirmishes, George Stucke of Company G was wounded in action, as were three men in Company F. One man was captured in action, and William Moore took the opportunity to desert to the enemy.

On August 21, Hancock was moved to the left of the Union line, with orders to destroy some fifteen miles of the Weldon and Petersburg Railroad to the south and prevent the Confederates from using the line at all for their supply operations. Three days later, he had progressed about three miles south of Ream's Station when he was warned of impending attack by a large enemy force. II Corps quickly retired to some abandoned entrenchments at Ream's Station. The brigade which included the Garibaldians, along with the 7th and the 52nd New York,[10] was placed in the works running parallel to the railroad, on the left of the first brigade, its right resting near the gap in the works through which the railroad passes. There were no works on the railroad between the first and the third brigades. In front of the right and center of the brigade was a belt of timber and underbrush with which the Guard worked to build an abatis. The works on the left of the brigade reached into an open field, there being a ten-yard gap in the works between the left of the third and right of the fourth brigades. At 1:00 P.M. on August 25, snipers shot at the first brigade pickets, who fell back in confusion, over the works. A twenty-five man detail was immediately deployed in front of the works to assess the Confederate approach.

At the same time, Lieutenant Colonel Broady, who commanded the fourth brigade, assumed command of the third brigade, although brigade headquarters received no official notice of the change. He immediately ordered Lieutenant Mitchell, aide-de-camp, third brigade, to deploy the three right-most regiments of the brigade, the 111th, the 125th, and the 126th New York, as skirmishers under the command of Captain Penfield, who was to advance them into the woods as far as possible and connect with the 148th Pennsylvania on the left and the first brigade skirmish line on the right. At 2:00 P.M., Hancock observed that the Confederates were making ready for a massive assault against the position held by the consolidated brigade and the fourth brigade. Heavy artillery fire held the enemy at bay for about fifteen minutes, doing little damage, but it had the effect of demoralizing a part of the command exposed to a reverse fire. Shelling was followed by an assault on Miles' division front: "Just at the time when a few minutes resistance would have served the repulse of the Confederate[s] who were thrown into considerable disorder by the severity of the fire they were subjected to and the obstacles to their advance, a part of the line, the 7th, 52nd, and the 39th gave way in confusion... At the same time a break occurred in the right of the same brigade—the 125th and the 126th N.Y. Regiments. I attribute the bad conduct of some of my troops to their great fatigue, owing to the heavy labor exacted of them, the 7th, 52nd and 39th are largely made up of recruits and Substitutes. The first named regiment in particular is entirely new[,] companies being formed in New [Y]ork and sent down here, some officers being unable to speak English." The ensuing panic not even Hancock could stop, and he retired with heavy losses. The Confederates resumed their supply operations through Ream's Station.

For the Garibaldi Guard, the battle was a disaster. Losses were heavy. Captain Theodore F. Rich was killed in action, Lieutenant Wyckoff of Company G and five men were wounded in action, and Captain James Trippe of Company E and twenty men were captured in action. Sergeant Henry Hammond was captured and later paroled. Sergeant Charles L. Lathrop and Lewis Backler of Company F were among those captured in action who would die of disease at prisoner of war camps. Jacob Behr of Company H, recently released from the hospital after wounds received at Cold Harbor, was captured in action and eventually sent to Salisbury, North Carolina, where he would die of disease in November. Jacob Trick of Company I was also captured and sent to Salisbury, but he turned traitor and joined the 8th Confederate Infantry. The day after the battle, matters continued as usual. On August 26, Sergeant David Bruen of the 12th Kansas enrolled as second lieutenant of Company K. On Sunday, five days later, the Garibaldians, now commanded by Captain Allen, were reassigned as part of the third brigade under Lieutenant Colonel William Wilson. The Garibaldians constituted six companies: E, F, G, H, I, and K.

Discipline became increasingly lax due to the loss of officers. Brigades were commanded by majors, regiments by captains, and companies by corporals. Privates were promoted to lieutenant. Colonel Funk remained on medical furlough, which meant that the military qualifications of several new officers like Pletus Field, Baron W. Briggs, and Philo Tuttle went unquestioned. During the month of September, a new Company D composed of one year recruits was raised at Malone, New York, for the Guard. During the same month, Field, Briggs, and Tuttle enlisted as privates in the 185th New York, on September 3, 5, and 22, respectively. Field transferred to the Guard, but was not assigned to a company. On September 28, both Briggs and Tuttle were transferred to the new Company D, where Briggs was promoted to first lieutenant of that company. By September 30, he had been promoted to captain, and Tuttle was promoted to second lieutenant. Field was commissioned a captain. James Clements, late a sergeant of the 16th New York, was mustered in as a private and then promoted to first sergeant of Company D.

On Monday, October 10, Gilfillan, who had recovered from his wounds, returned to the regiment and was recommissioned as the captain of Company I. Twelve days later, the Garibaldi Guard in the third brigade and the 28th Massachusetts of the first brigade were among Miles' general reserve regiments that initially remained near the front. Private Henry Shaw of Company F got a battlefield promotion to second lieutenant of Company I. On October 29, Second Lieutenant Bruen of Company K, who had come from the 12th Kansas and been in the Guard a little over a month, was killed in the trenches of Fort Sedgwick, one of the emplacements along Grant's Petersburg lines. On the last day of October, a Monday, Colonel MacDougall of II Corps' first division resumed command of the consolidated brigade, which included the Guard. Still commanded by Allen, the Guard now had seven companies. Second Lieutenant Wyckoff recovered from his wounds and was promoted to first lieutenant of Company G. First Lieutenant Rogers, Company H, was paroled and exchanged. Private Edward Kellogg of the 17th Veteran Infantry mustered in as second lieutenant, Company K.

The Garibaldi Guard effectively began its fourth stint in winter quarters with the advent of November. First Sergeant Edelmann of Company K was promoted to second lieutenant in Company E on November 18, a Friday, to replace the late Lieutenant McGarry. Edelmann was wounded in the trenches, and First Sergeant Menzler was transferred from Company I to Company E and later promoted to second lieutenant of both Companies E and D, the regiment was so short of officers. First Lieutenant Rogers and Second Lieutenant Proper were promoted to captain and first lieutenant of Company H, respectively. On November 28, the men in Company D who had to serve out their time were transferred to the 185th New York. On Wednesday, November 30, Colonel Funk returned from his medical leave and resumed command of the Garibaldians. He addressed them as though he had never left:

> It is very probable that the regiment will remain encamped
> here for some time. It is the desire of the Colonel Commanding that
> the Company Officers make every effort to keep the camp in a cleanly
> state; they will pay attention to the cleanliness of the Company Corps
> and see that the food is thoroughly and well cooked.

All Officers will be in attendance when the troops are under arms in the morning. The Company Officers will attend personally and direct the building of Quarters for their men. Captain Gilfillan who is charged with the laying out of the camp, will give the necessary information to the Company Officers as to the mode of building the width of streets, etc. they will also make all haste with a vein of furnishing the camp and resuming the drills and parades. The Commander of companies will immediately see to it that their non commissioned officers have their chevrons and stripes prescribed by regulations.

Officers Commanding companies or who have Commanded companies lately will send into these Headquarters a report immediately, whether they have marked their stores monthly, for camp and garrison and ordinance and ordinance stores for the 5th Quarter.

Also when their companies were last paid and all deficiencies in ordinance and ordinance stores.

Company Sergeants will report every morning at 7:30 A.M. with the Police the guards relieved the previous morning, on the color line and report them to the officer in charge of the guard relieved the previous morning, who will see that the camp is thoroughly policed in and around the officer's quarters, the line covered at least 6 inches when he will report to the Commanding Officer for further orders.

Colonel Augustus Funk.

Although the Army of the Potomac was in winter quarters, Grant was determined to keep pressuring Lee. One goal was to cut the Southside Railroad that ran into Petersburg from the west, by swinging around the city from the south. To strike the railroad, the Federals had to get beyond Hatcher's Run, a creek southwest of the city that anchored the west end of the Confederate defenses. On very short notice on December 9, the Garibaldians made ready to move, packing four days' rations of bread, sugar, coffee, and meat. They broke camp and took position about 6:30 A.M. in their brigade's line of march. They marched southwest on the Vaughan road till they passed the outer line of pickets. Then they were thrown out as flankers on the right of the road and advanced until the left flank reached Hatcher's Run, when it was placed on picket. The Guard was on the far right flank, with the 81st Pennsylvania on its immediate left and the 140th Pennsylvania on its far left. Shots were exchanged across the creek and all along the division line. The Guard remained in place until the next afternoon, when it received orders about 2:00 P.M. to assemble on the right and march back to its former position, which it reached near 7:00 P.M.[11]

After returning to camp, on December 13 Colonel Funk had Lieutenant Rich place Captain Field and Lieutenant Tuttle of Company D under arrest for disobedience of orders and confined them to the limits of the regimental camp.

A week later Field was discharged. Tuttle resigned on grounds of incompetency and was actually given a dishonorable discharge retroactive to the date of his muster in. On December 16, a Friday, the Garibaldians and the rest of their division were assembled at 11:00 A.M. at Fort Wheaton, an emplacement on the Petersburg line, to witness the execution for desertion of Privates Christopher Srik and Charles Connell, Company E, 7th New York, and John Thompson, 5th New York:

> The execution of the sentence of Death, by hanging, pronounce[d] against these 3 soldiers were to take place at 12 noon. These men, substitutes, deserted their colors while the Division lay in front of Petersburg. Having received their pay for services not yet rendered, they attempted to escape the performance of their duty by taking advantage of the orders issued by the Rebel President to incite desertion among the soldiers of the Union Army, expecting the promise of the order would be fulfilled, and they [would be] sent to their homes beyond the reach of the U.S. authority. These men were three out of fifty, who having deserted to take advantage of the promise of the Rebel Government, were sent by the Rebel Secretary of War into Kentucky, and left to take care of themselves, and find their way to their homes as best they could. Being captured by our forces, they will suffer the fitting reward of their treachery, a felon's Death. Let those who contemplate deserting their colors recollect that they are not safe after reaching the enemy's lines, and that the enemy's territory is so completely hemmed in by U.S. troops and ships that the promises of his government to action to their homes all who desert to him, are almost impossible to fulfill.

While the worn-out Army of the Potomac rebuilt itself with new recruits, hard drill, and harsh discipline, fighting persisted elsewhere. Confederate General John Bell Hood eluded Sherman at Atlanta and invaded Tennessee in an effort to cut Sherman's communications. Union Major General George H. Thomas routed Hood's army at Nashville on December 16, in the only time a Confederate force ever fled the field. On December 18, in honor of Thomas' victory, the Army of the Potomac fired a salute of one hundred guns at sunrise, under the direction of its chief of artillery. The next day, First Lieutenant Doerdinger and Second Lieutenant Sutter of Company D were discharged, while Giovanni Nesi was mustered in as second lieutenant of Company F; Second Lieutenant Charles Duncan, 14th Connecticut, was mustered in as second lieutenant of Company H; and John Craig was appointed commissary sergeant. On December 23, the Guard and the 7th New York were again assembled under arms at Fort Wheaton, in readiness to witness at noon the executions of John Lynch, alias John Moore, William Miller, alias John Onaiz of Company F, and George Bradely, alias George W. Bates of Company H, 5th New York. The Garibaldians assembled on the parade ground at 11:00 A.M.

and heard the charges at the same time that they were read to the prisoners. On New Year's Eve day, First Lieutenant Rich, Company F, recovered from his wounds and was promoted to captain, and Corporal Vial, Company E, was promoted to sergeant and then first sergeant. With the close of 1864 and the wholesale replacement of its original members by new recruits, the once exotic Garibaldi Guard became the very commonplace 39th New York Volunteers.

Chapter Eleven

THROUGH TO VICTORY

THE Garibaldi Guard spent Christmas of 1864 and New Year's Day of 1865 in Union trenches outside Petersburg. Life in winter quarters had a familiar routine. On January 3, Second Lieutenant Ferdinand Maggi, who remained hospitalized, failed to appear before a military commission to answer charges against him of absence without leave. He was dismissed from the army, but afterward upon providing evidence regarding his medical condition, received a disability discharge. The next day, Sergeant A. Baker was promoted to second lieutenant to replace Maggi. On Monday, January 9, at Sing Sing, Albert Boehler, who was court-martialed for desertion on June 22, 1864, found his death sentence commuted to a dishonorable discharge, forfeiture of all pay and bounty due, and imprisonment at hard labor for the remainder of the war in the Dry Tortugas, Florida. It must have been old home week to be reunited with his fellow deserters, Williams, Niles, and Hamilton. One day later, the Guard received an order issued in Grant's name: "All embalming Surgeons having been excluded from the lines of the Armies operating against Richmond, the friends and relatives of Officers and Soldiers are hereby notified that hereafter the bodies of Officers and Soldiers who die at General or Base Hospitals, can be embalmed without charge upon making personal application to the Chief Medical Officers of Hospitals. Applications for the embalming of Officers and Soldiers who die at the Division Hospitals at the front or on the field of battle, must be made to the Medical Director of the Corps to Which such Officers and Soldiers belonged." William Schwarz, an undertaker and an unassigned private in the Guard, saw the order and requested a transfer to the division hospital in order to practice his profession. On January 11, Dr. Hoyt, surgeon in charge of the division hospital, discharged Lieutenant Colonel Hughes for disability.

Hughes had been in the hospital since he was wounded in the Wilderness, over eight months earlier. Antonio Fortunes of Company C, who was captured in action at the Rapidan, returned to the ranks on the same day. Fortunes related that he escaped while his Confederate guards were transporting prisoners to Andersonville. Alone, he found his way back to Union lines and the Garibaldians. He returned to New York to be mustered out on February 15. On January 27, John McE. Hyde, adjutant and the first lieutenant of Company E, was promoted to lieutenant colonel.[1] Captain Allen was commissioned as the Guard's acting major. Lieutenant Wyckoff was promoted to adjutant, sharing the position with Charles Ballou.

As February began, the seven companies of the Guard found themselves in the third brigade. On February 10, Adjutant Ballou transferred as a first lieutenant to Company H, and Captain Rogers of that company was discharged for disabilities. February 17 was designated a Prisoner Exchange Day; Corporal Diefenbach was paroled and returned to Company A. Though still greatly bothered from his wounds, Funk returned from medical leave to resume command of the regiment: "The Colonel desires to call the attention of the officers to the incomplete and bad situation the men's quarters are in. Many are without barracks, and the chimneys are too low. The colonel directs that officers pay particular attention to this matter at once. Frequent inspections will be made by the Colonel Commanding, accompanied with the Assistant Surgeon, when Company Officers will be present to explain all delinquencies. Company Officers will be held strictly accountable for the men out of the muster rolls for January and February. There have been many mistakes making out the prisoners muster rolls of this Regiment, such as neglecting to have the time entered when a soldier was last paid, bounty due, etc., Commandants of companies will muster men that are sick in the Division Hospital as present sick."[2]

Excess weapons were not allowed in Funk's command, so on February 22, Major Allen, commanding Company G, turned over four Springfield rifled muskets, with complete accouterments. Lieutenant Proper, Company H, turned over one Springfield rifled musket, two cartridge boxes, two waistbelts, two waistbelt plates, one gun sling, and one cap pouch. Captain Briggs, Company D, turned over two Springfield rifled muskets and full sets of accouterments to Second Lieutenant Giovanni D. Nesi, Company F. On Monday, February 27, First Lieutenant Henry Shaw was relieved from command of Company K and returned to Company I for duty under Captain Gilfillan. Colonel Funk called the attention of company commanders to the practice of gambling, which had occurred in the regiment during the past few days under the apparent sanction of noncommissioned officers. Such gambling was harmful to good order and discipline, and Funk issued a regimental order: "All parties who are caught gambling will be punished, and those winning money or articles will be compelled to return them to the original owners. Non-commissioned officers found participating in or sanctioning his violation of Military regulations, will be Court Martialed and reduced to the ranks." The provost marshal inspected the Guard, to uncover and have turned in all irregular means of transportation and horses used by soldiers. Infantry soldiers were not allowed to use public horses. Officers had to be reminded that horses where issued at two per army wagon, two per ambulance, and four per ordnance wagon and authentic medical wagon.

March marked the start of the tenth month in the trenches before Petersburg. On March 1, the descriptive list pertaining to Private Frank Cosey of Company H, a free Negro born in Boston and by trade a sailor, was sent through the commanding officer to Company A, 117th Regiment, U.S. Colored Troops, Army of the James. Sergeant Jeremiah Bow, an Englishman in Company K, and Corporal George Pease, Company I, were both reduced to the ranks, Bow for remaining in his quarters while the regiment was in line to go in action and Pease for firing his gun after taps. Early the next morning, March 4, they deserted together to the Confederate side; it was Pease's second desertion. On March 14, Gilfillan and Lieutenants Shaw, Company I, and Von Rensselaer, Company E, were arrested for drinking and confined to quarters. The next day, Gilfillan, still suffering from his shoulder wound, asked for and received a medical discharge. Second Lieutenant Baker was promoted to captain to replace him. First Lieutenant Briggs, Company D, was promoted to captain of Company K; George W. Foster, formerly of the 5th Veteran Infantry, was mustered in as first lieutenant of Company G; and First Lieutenant Ballou was promoted to captain of Company H. On March 24, William Brown, a Canadian, was hospitalized for an overdose of a concoction the sutlers were selling, which purported to be highly concentrated essence of ginger. A regimental order resulted that using the concoction, "Is hereby prohibited under Surgeons Orders. It was found the extreme use of this article is the cause of serious injury to the men. The Provost Marshall would inspect the Sutler Department of this Division and direct that further sales be made only on Surgeon's orders. Any violation will be sufficient reason for confiscating all property of the parties so violating." Brown would be discharged from the hospital in Washington on June 10.

By this time, Sheridan had finished devastating the Shenandoah Valley so it could not support the South and was on his way to rejoin Grant. The Army of the Potomac was getting stronger, Union forces elsewhere throughout the Confederacy were winning, and Lee's situation was growing increasingly desperate. On March 25, he made a surprise attack on the north end of the Union's Petersburg line in an effort to cripple Grant's army and escape to fight elsewhere. The Guard was on the picket line in front of works at the Watkins house, in the southwestern area of the Union line, and saw no action in Lee's defeat that day. Instead, the regiment prepared to move out; Grant felt that he needed to go on the offensive before Lee escaped from Petersburg. Colonel Funk reported that on "March, 26th, 2nd Lt. Edelmann being left in camp in charge of the brigade guard started, without permission, [to] join his regiment, and being somewhat intoxicated, passed through our advance lines and has not been heard from since."[3] Actually, Lieutenant Edelman, Company E, was admitted to the division hospital, where Dr. Hoyt became surgeon in charge and set up procedures that led to a smooth, efficient operation. Hoyt would now stay at the hospital until his discharge and muster out of the Guard. On March 28, the Appomattox Campaign began.[4]

The next day, Wednesday morning, at 8:00 A.M. heavy rains commenced. The Garibaldians left camp with their brigade and Veteran Volunteers and crossed Hatcher's Run, where they formed a line of battle at 11:00 A.M. and waited in formation. At 4:00 P.M., they were ordered to advance, and they moved forward through five lines of works without opposition. They stopped after dark and bivouacked for the night. March 30 at daybreak found the regiment at Sutherland Station. The Garibaldians anticipated a Confederate charge and continued the advance west in line of battle, again without opposition, until they reached Quaker Road. They constructed a line of breastworks a short distance beyond the road, and bivouac was ordered for the night. They were behind the new works that evening. That day Captain Trippe was paroled and discharged (later he accepted a commission as lieutenant colonel in the 21st U.S. Colored Troops); First Lieutenant Wright Banks of the 28th New York enrolled as first lieutenant of Company K, and Private Ira Slawson of the 120th New York was commissioned as a second lieutenant of the same company. On March 31, the Guard wheeled north and occupied a line of breastworks on Boydton Plank Road, thrown up by V Corps at White Oak Ridge. At 10:00 A.M. the brigade advanced to attack the enemy. Corporal Franklin Lutes of the 111th New York, on line beside the Guard, recalled, "When the order came to fix bayonets and charge, I was left guide of my regiment. Upon jumping from behind our breastworks we were met by an awful volley from the enemy, who understood our move and determined to drive us back to our fortifications. Many fell before this storm of lead, by the remainder pushed on."[5] After moving in line of battle for nearly a mile, the Garibaldians struck the Confederate skirmish line. The brigade wheeled left to attack the Confederate flank. As the Guard was on the extreme right, the men were deployed as skirmishers. Colonel Funk was wounded again by a shot in the hip early during the engagement. Lieutenant Colonel Hyde resumed command of the regiment. Robert Thompson of Company I and Hyronimus Van Wessem were killed, and First Sergeant Smith was captured in action at Eseliaror Hill. The brigade advanced over Hyde's line; he withdrew the regiment and rejoined the brigade. Then the division line was straightened and breastworks were thrown up.

Just before daylight on Saturday, April 1, the Guard moved to the rear and occupied the original line of works on Boydton Plank Road; afterward, the Garibaldians threw up a new line a short distance ahead. In the afternoon, they advanced to the line erected the previous day and lay there, ready to repel an attack, while other regiments demonstrated against different parts of the

Confederate lines. On April 2 at 1:00 A.M., the Guard moved rapidly to its left flank and halted at 4:00 A.M., somewhere near Dinwiddie Court House. At 6:00 A.M. it returned and formed in line of battle before the enemy works, ready to attack. The Confederates were observed withdrawing in confusion, having been outflanked by the 2nd Brigade. Soon after the withdrawal was confirmed, the Guard advanced at the double-quick to occupy the enemy works. The Guard's colors were the third to occupy the site. As the Garibaldians entered the earthworks about 9:00 A.M., the Confederates fired a parting shot which crashed into the woods. It struck and killed Sergeant Charles Walzer of Company I and wounded three others, including Corporal Michael Cain of Company G, who subsequently died of his wound in Douglas Hospital. The Garibaldians found a large number of Confederate wounded and some hiding themselves, who surrendered to the Garibaldians. A soldier from the 125th New York wrote home, "As soon as the rebels were seen to rise behind their works our Brigade was again formed in line, passed over our works, moved over the ground on which we had lately fought, and gained the enemy's works, capturing a battle flag, two pieces of artillery and 600 prisoners, the remainder of the rebels making their escape. The works were a rude affair indeed, but in such good position as to challenge a front assault from ten times the number holding them, much more from a single brigade of tire[d] and worn out troops."[6]

The advance continued until the Confederates were encountered in entrenchments along the Southside Railroad. The 3rd Brigade was ordered to charge the works and although the men were very exhausted from loss of sleep the previous night and the rapid marching they had done, they advanced gallantly through a piece of woods and across an open field, exposed to fire from two artillery batteries and from the Confederates in the breastworks. The Garibaldians, on the brigade's extreme left, succeeded in reaching the crest of a hill, and if a few shots could have been fired in support from a Union artillery battery, they could have entered the enemy works. But, at this time the brigade's right flank fell back, and the Garibaldians were so far ahead that they were in danger of being cut off, so they also fell back. The Confederates counterattacked, and the exhausted brigade scattered through the swamps and tangled underbrush behind it in its retreat. One officer and two men who could not keep up on the retreat were captured at this point. The brigade's battle line was re-formed at a woodline, and a skirmish line thrown out on the left and front. Captain Briggs and Second Lieutenants Charles Menzler and Allen M. Baker succeeded in reestablishing their line with great difficulty, due to their men's exhaustion. They threw up a rude line of works. Shortly afterwards the brigade charged the Confederates once again, but failed to break the enemy line. Most of the Garibaldians were on the skirmish line, and the few men that Hyde commanded could do very little, although the regiment's colors were as far forward as any in the brigade. About 3:00 P.M. another charge was ordered upon the Confederate left flank, and this time artillery fire supported the brigade. It broke the line this time and captured the Southside Railroad. The Garibaldians advanced beyond the railroad to complete the establishment of a new, forward skirmish line. Afterward they rejoined their brigade and bivouacked for the night.

While Miles' division, with the Garibaldians, seized the railroad, the rest of II Corps and other corps had attacked and overpowered the Confederate Petersburg defenses from the west. Lee held out until dark and then evacuated Petersburg and Richmond, retreating south and west. The Union pursuit to intercept Lee began on April 3. The Garibaldians marched west without opposition until 9:00 P.M. and bivouacked for the night. The next day, they moved forward three miles, but at 6:00 P.M. they were ordered back to meet trains and repair roads; they worked until 10:00 P.M. and bivouacked. Corporal Mills, Company I, deserted on the march. The next morning at 5:00 A.M., they resumed the march and met the division at 9:00 P.M. at Jetersville, and then bivouacked. On April 6, they were ordered to move forward about one mile to Sailor's Creek, where the Federals caught up with Lee's rear guard. The Garibaldians fought all day and helped to capture a wagon train and a battery of artillery, as II Corps captured most of the enemy wagons. Farther south along the creek, VI Corps and Union cavalry trapped eight thousand Confederates; all of Ewell's corps and almost half of Lieutenant General Richard Herron Anderson's corps. At the end of the day, the Garibaldians crossed Monkey Run and bivouacked for the night.

Lee continued withdrawing, west toward Farmville where his soldiers got some much-needed rations and north across the adjacent Appomattox River. At 6:00 A.M. on April 7, the Garibaldians were ordered to move forward to High Bridge, a railroad bridge over the Appomattox east of Farmville. The Guard helped thwart Confederates trying to burn the bridge and pursued them across the river to within half a mile of Farmville. Lee formed a line of battle north of the town to save his remaining wagons, and held II Corps at bay. The Guard erected works under heavy artillery fire and bivouacked for the night. Grant sent Lee a note asking him to surrender. Early the next morning, Grant discovered that Lee had abandoned his position. "Great Expectations," wrote a soldier of Company G. The Guard immediately started west in pursuit and marched without opposition until 6:00 P.M., when it bivouacked.

Cut off from withdrawing south, Lee pushed west. But while he successfully eluded II Corps, Union cavalry with infantry close behind flanked him on the south and blocked his line of march at Appomattox Court House. When he arrived there on the evening of April 8, Lee discovered that the cavalry had captured his rations trains from the west. There would be no more food. On April 9, Palm Sunday, Lee tried to break out one more time. At dawn, attacking Confederates drove back the Union cavalry—and discovered that V Corps and the entire Army of the James, two more corps, were advancing behind the cavalry. Meanwhile, II and VI Corps came up from the east. At 6:00 A.M., the Guard marched forward about three miles and halted, awaiting events. Lee asked for an armistice. At 4:00 P.M. the surrender was announced. The war was over. Grant sent twenty-five thousand rations to the Army of Northern Virginia. Dr. Wolf was detailed to tend to wounded Confederates.

On April 12, President Lincoln promoted Luigi Palma Di Cesnola to brigadier general and offered him the position of American consul at Cyprus, a strategically important spot in the eastern Mediterranean. He accepted and received his United States citizenship. That same day in England, Giuseppe Mazzini received news that the American Civil War was over. He sent a dispatch to the American consulate describing the worth of the Union's triumph to his cause: "You have done more for us in four years than fifty years of teaching, preaching and writing from all your European brothers have been able to..." The Garibaldians were soon marching east toward Burkesville, southeast of Farmville, and the railroad there. Grant's plan was to link up his and Sherman's forces to defeat the last Confederates in the field. Their leader, General Joseph Eggleston Johnston, sought an armistice on April 13 and surrendered the next day.

That evening, April 14, Lincoln was assassinated. Along with General Di Cesnola and the Italian consul, the one hundred twenty veterans of the original Garibaldi Guard then in Washington marched in Lincoln's funeral procession there. The Italian Consul General in New York invited five hundred Italians to the ceremony at Cooper Institute in memory of "Abramo" Lincoln. The editor of *L'Eco d'Italia*, Secchi de Casali, one of the invited guests, wrote that Lincoln was an "eminent statesman, from the people and educated in the school of free labor, whose administration had proved a great representative of the people. Lincoln was a high example of honesty who lived in a corrupt age and whose patriotism was pure. Lincoln was modest, friendly, gentle and generous in his life. Lincoln merits veneration for his emancipation of the African Race." As a sign of their admiration for the champion of freedom, the people of Rome sent a stone from the wall of Servius Tullius, the ancient king who built the first stone wall around Rome's seven great hills of Rome and reformed the Roman army to facilitate enrollment in it by the many foreigners who were attracted to the Roman Empire (parts of the wall still stand; the stone is in the Lincoln Memorial at Springfield, Illinois).

While Lincoln's body began its circuitous funeral journey home to Springfield, army life went on. A regimental order issued on April 24 stated, "Hereafter applications for passes to visit Washington must be presented in person to the Regimental Commander, after having [been approved] by the Company Commander. Applicants must report with side arms, and unless clean in every respect will be disapproved." On April 29, Assistant Surgeon William Goodwin was discharged. Lieutenant Rensselaer was transferred from Company E to D. Major Baker was discharged for disabilities. The regiment's members who had not completed the terms of their enlistments were transferred to the 185th

New York to serve out the rest of their enlistments. On Tuesday, May 2, Captain Rich, still suffering from his wounds, was discharged, and the Guard left camp near Chester, Virginia, for the march back to Washington. A soldier in Company I recorded the Guard's final march in the regimental book this way:

May 5th, 1865: Camp in woods illuminated; Preparations to enter Richmond.
6th: Entered Richmond.
7th: In march.
8th: In march.
9th: In march.
10th: Entered Fredericksburg.
11th: On march.
12th: On march.
13th: Arrived in sight of Washington. Camp at Upton's Hill;
14th: In Camp.
16th: Changed camp near Alexandria. Quartermaster Sergeant George Smith deserted at camp. Prisoner exchange Louis Dungstadter returned to ranks.
16th through 19th: On the march.
19th: Reached Alexandria and remained in Camp. The war consid ered over, virtually affordable.
20th: Changed Camp.
21st: Captain John W. Funk was discharged.
Tuesday, May 23rd: GRAND REVIEW.

Dungstadter, who returned to the ranks, had been captured six months earlier. During the march, First Sergeant Clements, Company D, was commissioned a second lieutenant. Lieutenant Colonel Hyde and Second Lieutenant Edelmann, Company E, were discharged for disabilities. Lieutenant Shaw of Company I was discharged four days after the grand review. Then, personnel changes continued unabated from June 1 through 22. Von Rensselaer was mustered out with Company D on June 7. Second Lieutenant Kellogg of Company K was discharged and reenlisted in the 10th New York Infantry. Second Lieutenant Duncan of Company H was discharged, and Sergeant Stucke of Company G was commissioned as a second lieutenant to replace him. Adjutant Wyckoff was discharged and First Lieutenant Wright Banks of Company K was promoted to adjutant to replace him. Corporal Giovanni Yelitz of Company C, First Lieutenant Rensselaer of Company G, and Second Lieutenant Menzler of the new Company D were mustered out near Alexandria with their companies. Those ex-Confederate soldiers, Corporal James Williams and Albert Schneider, were mustered out; Williams at Fort Snelling, Minnesota, and Schneider at Elmira, New York. Asa Knappen, formerly of the 10th New York Cavalry, was commissioned assistant surgeon in the Garibaldi

Guard. Sergeant Major Sack of Company E was promoted to second lieutenant.

On Saturday, July 1, in a ceremony at Alexandria, Colonel Funk and one hundred sixty men and officers left in the ranks of the Garibaldi Guard were honorably discharged and mustered out. Transportation was provided to New York, where the regiment was disbanded. The one hundred seventy officers and noncommissioned officers authorized in an infantry regiment had shrunk to Colonel Funk; Major Allen (promoted to lieutenant colonel); Adjutant Banks (also first lieutenant of Company K); Surgeon Charles S. Hoyt; Quartermaster Leibnitz (also first lieutenant of Company D); Quartermaster Sergeant John O'Keefe; Second Lieutenant Sack of Company E; Captain E. Rich and Second Lieutenant Nesi of Company F; First Lieutenant George Foster and Second Lieutenant Lee of Company G; Captain Ballou (breveted lieutenant colonel of the 140th New York), First Lieutenant Proper, and Sergeant Zeman of Company H; Captain Allen Baker of Company I; and Captain Briggs of Company K.

Major General George Stoneman captured the turncoat, Jacob Trick of Company I, at Nashville and released him on July 6 after he took the oath of allegiance to the United States; Trick was mustered out August 4, in New York City. With the end of the war, Charles Williams and the other deserters imprisoned in the Dry Tortugas were sent to New York for dishonorable discharge. Recuperating Garibaldians who were still in the hospital, including Felix De La Baume, Petro Delapores, Philip Delgardo, and Augustus Erhardt, were mustered out from their hospital beds. David Champion of Company G was the last Garibaldian discharged; on January 13, 1866, he was released from Sing Sing Prison, on the same day General Di Cesnola left for his duties in Cyprus.

Chapter Twelve

After the Battle

The surviving Garibaldians dispersed to the four winds. Adventures throughout the world awaited them. The American West had to be explored, settled
and tamed, the industrial revolution was ahead, and unresolved conflicts in
Europe were yet to be settled. The question of national union still roiled Italy,
where the 39th New York Volunteer Infantry Regiment's spirit had been born
years earlier. The year after the American Civil War ended, General Garibaldi
and his Garibaldinis joined the fray to liberate two Italian territories, Venice and
Rome, from Austria's autocratic clutches and unify them with their democratic cousins. At the outset of the Austro-Prussian War, the Italians allied
themselves with the Prussians against the Austrians. Once again the foe was
Austria and a pope. From April 8 through August 9, General Garibaldi and the
Garibaldini were involved in the Battles of Monte Asello, Caffaro, Ampella
Fortress, and Bezzecca in an effort to unify all of Italy. On October 12, 1866,
the end of the war brought the annexation of Venice. Four years later, on July
19, France declared war on Prussia, and the sixty-three-year-old Garibaldi
offered his sword to the French Republic. Garibaldi was given command of
the Army of the Vosages, for his final active campaigns. When Napoleon III
withdrew the French occupation forces in Rome from the city for service at
his front, an Italian army occupied Rome and the surrounding papal territory.
Resistance was effectively nothing, and Italy formally annexed Rome on October 2, 1870.

Garibaldi retired to his island home on Caprera and watched his beloved
country become the antithesis of all his ideals. He saw northern Italy take over
political and economical control of the country as southern Italy was relegated
to near-colonial status, and the new government move toward making the

country a colonial power in Africa, where it could rule regions just like the Austrians and French once ruled Italian regions. He watched the military draft hundreds of thousands of young men into military service to accomplish Italy's imperial aims. As modern Italy imposed tax after oppressive tax to pay for its military and colonial expeditions, Garibaldi watched the largest mass migration in modern times occur as impoverished, starving Italians sought better lives in the Americas. Aging, he remained on Caprera and died on June 2, 1882. The old general had asked to be cremated and have his ashes spread across the waters of his island home. Instead, the Italian government entombed the great patriot's body, laying a great granite stone on his grave as a monument. According to a Sicilian legend,[1] soon afterward a storm beat upon the little isle. Lightning struck the stone monument and cracked it in two, giving the general the final word.

Men who had responded to the leadership of Guiseppe Garibaldi or the power of his example often went on in their public service. Colonel Allesandro Repetti returned to Italy after testifying at Colonel D'Utassy's court-martial and helped General Fogliardi write his book on the American Civil War. Repetti retired from military service in Italy and died in Genoa in 1887. Hugo Hilderbrandt was appointed by President Grant in 1869 to become the American Consul on the Island of Crete, with Candia as his headquarters. Hilderbrandt married the daughter of the Austrian consul and remained at Crete until 1874, when the consulate was closed at his request. He died on April 7, 1896, at the age of sixty-four, at the home in Brooklyn, New York, of his friend and fellow Hungarian, General Robert Avery.[2] Colonel Augustus Funk remained in the army, in Washington at the adjutant general's office, and wrote an article entitled "Abraham Lincoln, a Character Study" for the Prairie Club of Des Moines, Iowa.[3] Funk died of a heart attack at the age of forty-two on October 18, 1883. Lieutenant Colonel John McEwan Hyde was belatedly breveted to brigadier general in 1872 for gallant and meritorious service. He worked for the Northern Pacific Railroad and took part in the expedition to survey the territory in Wyoming, Arizona, Nevada, Idaho, and California from 1874 through 1883; did recruiting service in New York from 1883 through 1885; took part in the 1878 campaign to drive the Bannocks onto an Indian reservation; was involved in Arizona in the Chimehueva troubles in 1880 and in the Cibicu troubles in 1881; and was the adjutant of the 8th Infantry until 1886 and its quartermaster in 1889. Hyde was the regiment's purchasing commissary in Boston during the Spanish-American War and was sent to Manila in October 1899. Then he went to Nagasaki, Japan, where he set up a depot and joined the expeditionary force that went to Peking to contain the Boxer Rebellion. Transferred to Manila in September 1901 and assigned to duty as chief quartermaster, Department of Visayas, at Iolio, Panay, until September 1902, he went to Portland, Oregon, in January 1903. The chief quartermaster of the Department of California in May 1903, he became the chief quartermaster of the Department of Dakota in August 1903. He was a member of the General

Kearney Association, Loyal Legion. Hyde died at his home in Brooklyn, Massachusetts, on October 25, 1916, at the age of seventy-five.[4]

Hospital steward Herman Bendell had gone on after leaving the Garibaldi Guard in 1861 to continue his medical studies at Albany Medical College and then return to the army first as an assistant surgeon with the 6th New York Artillery and second as the surgeon with the 86th New York Heavy Artillery. He remained in the army after the war, and 1871 saw him become the Superintendent of Indian Affairs for the Arizona Territory. Second Lieutenant Cornelius McLean also became a career army man. He was commissioned a lieutenant colonel on Governor Stoneman's staff in California on January 30, 1883. He had been dishonorably discharged from the Garibaldi Guard in July 1864 for medical absence without leave and for failure to make a proper report. That aside, his service record was unblemished, and he was reinstated by an act of Congress on July 18, 1892. McLean lived at Mount Vernon, where he was a member of the Old Guard, Loyal Legion and the Alexander Hamilton Post of the Grand Old Army. He died at Aiken, South Carolina, on February 18, 1908.

Captain John Gilfillan married Sarah Shippe in February 1867, and they had their only son in 1872. They lived in a small house in Corona, Queens, New York, where he received a medical pension. He never recovered from his shoulder wound at Spotsylvania and was unable to work in his trade as a painter or to do any manual labor. His arm became progressively weaker, and by 1889 he was unable to use it at all. He died on June 15, 1890.

Anton d'Utassy married Laura Wood. Their son, George, named after the colonel, was born November 5, 1870. This George Utassy went on to graduate from Harvard, marry, have two children, and be a successful publisher. His creations included *Cosmopolitan Magazine*, *Hearst's Magazine*, *Harper's Bazaar*, *Good Housekeeping*, *Nash's Magazine* (London), and the *Illustrated Daily News*, afterward the New York *Daily Mirror*, which he published until 1930. First Lieutenant Cornelius Grinnell, the son of Moses Grinnell, an associate of D'Utassy, and the Guard's first adjutant, returned home to New York. On Wednesday, August 11, 1869, he was accompanied home by two associates, James G. Bennett Jr. and Shepperd Homans. Bennett left the two men alone on the second floor. Grinnell went to his window and opened it to step onto the balcony, where he somehow lost his balance and fell to the ground. He was instantly killed. An inquest determined that it was an accidental death.[5]

Francesco Carboni of the Italian company moved to Santa Clara, California, after the war and became a farmer. He married Mary Ferrari in 1870. Their son Aloysius was born in 1875 and baptized by Father Joseph Bixio, the brother of Garibaldi's Italian General Nino Bixio. Francesco Carboni died on September 10, 1889. Giuseppe Raggio settled in Chicago and founded the Societa Italiana Di Unione Fratellaza on May 8, 1866, with one hundred five members; the society's co-founders were A. Quecolli and G. Riboni, veterans of the 38th Illinois Volunteer Infantry Regiment. Lieutenant Edward B. Sturges wrote the *Druggists Legal Directory* in 1870. Charles B. Norton, who died in 1891, wrote one book about the 1876 American Centennial and another entitled *American Inventions*. George Bennett, who served in the Hungarian company, worked as a printer and then founded the *Williamsburg Times* in New York. Later he sold the newspaper and went into the cemetery business; he died in January 1885. Lieutenant Wright Banks served on the political scene. He never held elected office but was appointed as an officer of the deputy register and as a sheriff's clerk. He lived in White Plains, New York, and died on April 30, 1884. Lieutenant Raphael Frizone and his wife settled in Columbus, Ohio, and had one child, a son named Louis. After the war, Frizone continued to suffer from injuries incurred in an accident in 1865 and went on disability pension in July 1890. He died at the age of fifty-seven on July 2, 1895, the day a ceremony at Gettysburg would dedicate a monument to the Garibaldi Guard and its heroic action there, thirty-two years earlier.

George Frederick D'Utassy made a tremendous comeback. After his release from Sing Sing Prison, he returned to New York desperate for employment. He called on Frau Franciska Klein, the lady who sewed the flags for the Garibaldi Guard. When she would not see him, he only left his card for her. Then, from 1865 through 1867 he ran a portrait gallery located on the corner of Broadway and 23rd Street. After that, he was an importer until 1878.[6] His next move was to Cincinnati, Ohio, where he became a prominent, well-known, and much respected insurance agent. During the autumn of 1890, he was promoted to manager of the Baltimore, Maryland, office of the Phoenix Fire Company of Hartford, Connecticut. With his wife, Bertha, and their son, Leo, he moved to the Bristol Hotel in Baltimore. Tragically, within a few months, Leo died.

By 1892 D'Utassy was sixty-five years old. He frequently traveled from Baltimore to Wilmington, Delaware, where he stayed at the Willis Hotel several times within a six-month period. The afternoon of April 29, 1892, he arrived at the hotel, registered, said he had no room preference, was given room 18 on the third floor, and went to supper with his associates, J. A. Fuld and Samuel Fellheimer. He was in a jovial spirit when he subsequently went out to visit Mr. Spry, his local agent and an oculist, but he returned in a melancholy mood. Soon after he retired, he returned to the office manager and asked if he could have room 17, the room next door to 18. The glass in the transom of 18 was broken out, but other than that the rooms were exactly alike. His wish was granted; before going upstairs again, he exhibited and commented on a photograph of his son, his only child who died. After going to room 17, he returned and requested that the bed linen be changed. Two women were sent to change the bedclothes; while they were doing it, D'Utassy returned to the bedroom. During his absence the bed, which he had pulled out to near the center of the room, had been pushed back to its customary corner, and when he saw it there he told them to move it back to the center, claiming he desired it where he could lie on it and see to read by the gaslight. He hung his clothing at various places around the room and his umbrella upon the gas fixture. Before the women left he produced the photograph of his dead son, and after gazing at it a few seconds he began to weep. The women questioned him about the boy, but his grief was so deep he could not reply. He retired at 10:00 P.M.

It was customary to allow guests to sleep as long as they desired, so not until one o'clock on Saturday afternoon, April 30, did a servant go to D'Utassy's room to find out if it was in order. She found the door locked from the inside; while the lower window blinds were open, the transom window was tightly closed. She at once notified J. Wirt Willis, the proprietor's son, who took a couple of men and forced the door open. They found the room filled with gas and D'Utassy unconscious in his bed. He was removed to another room. Dr. John P. Wales was summoned to examine D'Utassy and diagnosed him as suffering from congestion of the brain, caused by inhaling the gas. During the afternoon D'Utassy was removed to Delaware Hospital. D'Utassy's wife and C. W. Jackson, his clerk, were telegrammed to inform them of D'Utassy's condition. They arrived the next day and were at the hospital when a friend, Mr. Robinson, arrived from Baltimore and visited the Hotel Willis. There Robinson gave a statement to the *Sunday Morning Star* that he "believed the general was accidentally overcome by the gas. The general had written to Mrs. D'Utassy and himself that he would return to Baltimore last evening. The object of the general's visit here was to consult an oculist." After a short stay at the hotel, Robinson returned to the hospital, where he remained with Mrs. D'Utassy. She hoped to move her husband back to Baltimore. D'Utassy did not recover consciousness by the late evening, and his case was regarded as extremely critical. There was no hope of recovery. His brother Carl arrived from Philadelphia to be with him. Physicians constantly attended to him. D'Utassy never regained consciousness and remained comatose for over forty-eight hours. His wife and his brother were at his side when the end came at 3:05 A.M., May 2.

On May 4, the coroner, Mr. Sparks, held an inquest upon the remains. Doctor Wales testified as to his actions, as did James Willis, the hotel's proprietor, and J. A. Fuld, Samuel Fellheimer, and John Fay testified as to their actions at the locked door. Detective Hawkins testified as to his findings in the room. Charles Jackson and D. H. Truxworth of Baltimore testified as to D'Utassy's good character. Hawkins doubted considerably whether D'Utassy inhaled the gas accidentally, observing that the stopcock of the gas jet had to be physically turned on for gas to be emitted. The jury resolved "that General George F. D'Utassy came to his death on May 2d, 1892, in Wilmington, from concussion of the brain caused by asphyxiation and from the evidence we believe it to be an accident." An undertaker took immediate charge of D'Utassy's remains and shipped them to Germantown, Pennsylvania, for burial at noon. His obituary claimed that he was a breveted brigadier general.[7]

George E. Waring, Jr., in later life. He wrote an essay on his experience with the Garibaldi Guard. He worked in the New York Sanitary Commission, circa 1892.

Library of Congress

Major George Waring, Jr. returned to his job as a civil engineer with the Streets and Sanitation Department in New York City. During the Centennial Exhibition of 1876, he was a judge in the Engineering Group, and had charge of the examination of the drainage works of Holland and of sanitary engineering works generally. During the World's Fair he was a judge engaged in the examination of sanitary appliances.[8] His article on the Garibaldi Guard, recounting nearly four months' service as major of the regiment, appeared in 1893 in *Liber Scriptorium*, a book published by The Authors Club in New York. He also wrote *Whip and Spur*, based on his service with Fremont. On October 29, 1898, he became the Commissioner of Streets and Sanitation in New York City. After the war with Spain, "The United States Evacuation Commission for Cuba arrived in Havana on September 10, [1898] and Col. George E. Waring, a prominent expert in sanitary work was assigned to the task of reforming the condition of that city, but he contracted the yellow fever while in the discharge of his duty and died of the congestion at New York City."[9]

James Clement, the English sailor who joined the Garibaldians in 1864, traveled to the Klondike in a search for gold and wrote a book entitled *The Klondyke*. Later he was employed by B. R. Baumgardt & Company; he died in 1897. Giovanni Samsa, who was one of the first men to enlist in 1861 and was promoted through the ranks to second lieutenant in the Italian company, went west and settled in Reno Nevada, where he was a member of the local post of the Grand Old Army; he died on October 1, 1900. Ignazio Allegretti, another former lieutenant in the Italian company, went into the prosperous refrigeration business. He died in Chicago on March 10, 1903, survived by his wife, Josephine Fontana Allegretti, and two sons. Killian Von Rensselaer became a lawyer and a politician on New York's local scene and a member of the Loyal Legion. He lived for a time in Baltimore and wrote "The Van Rensselaer Manor" in 1879; he died in New York on November 29, 1905. Charles Edward Zerdahelyi, the Hungarian pianist, played at concerts and gave piano lessons in Boston. Later, he moved to Philadelphia and married the daughter of a prominent farmer in the vicinity. He taught music at Sacred Heart Convent for twenty years. He died at his home in Germantown on August 16, 1906, leaving his widow and a son.[10]

Doctor Charles S. Hoyt returned to his home in Pottersville, New York, and resumed the practice of medicine. During his career he wrote *The Disturbed and Violent Insane in County Asylums and Poor Houses*, published in 1884, and *Report on Immigration*, published in 1893. He died at the end of 1906.[11] Edward Kellogg, another former officer, became a diplomat in the foreign service and died in Geneva, Switzerland, on August 8, 1908.[12] Andrew Fontana, who had been a wealthy nobleman and a soldier in Garibaldi's Sicilian campaign as well as a lieutenant in the Italian company of the Garibaldi Guard, was reduced in his seventies to supporting himself by selling little plaster casts of classical statuary. He had worked at Gans Brothers Umbrella Manufacturers, and on January 1 he went to the office at 467 Broadway to stop in and wish them a Happy New Year, when he had a seizure and died instantly. It was determined that he died of malnutrition. Carl D'Utassy died in Philadelphia on February 15, 1911.[13] Emanuel Lederer was a newspaper man and worked at the *Augustine Daily*. He was also an actor and a manager in the U.S. and in Germany. He died in 1917 and was survived by two sons, one of which was Dr. W. I. Lederer.[14]

July 1, 1888, marked the twenty-fifth anniversary of the Battle of Gettysburg. At the Trostle Farm, a site was dedicated to honor the actions there on July 2, 1863, by the 39th Infantry Battalion (Regiment), the "Garibaldi Guards."[15] Then on July 2, 1895, at Gettysburg, a monument was unveiled and dedicated to the memory of the Garibaldi Guard: the stone marker reads, "On This Spot, July 2d 1863, the 39th N.Y. Infantry recaptured the guns and equipment of Battery I., 5th U.S. Artillery." Henry Dietrich gave the dedication speech in German:

> Comrades! To us, who have fought that fight our hearts could not be higher, but we also return with melancholy and deep emotion as we all think back on that eventful time, a bloody century of brother fighting brother.
>
> At that time we were young, strong, in the abundance of youth, shouting; we were all defiant and fearless, and impudent to the enemy. And, now, today as veterans, fair of cheek and bleached white of head, the grip of nature that marks age comes closer with clear rein. We all stand in agreement with the Palm branch of Peace in hand, on the same ground.
>
> Our truce here characterizes this beauty. On this [occasion] all of us have a right to be proud and for all of us [this is] a time to be able to point to ourselves without self praise and without too much guilt...
>
> Comrades! I speak here to heighten the battles, not depict, but reflect on that given hour the lesson that forever became unchangeable for you in front of your eyes.

The fury of war swung her fiery, blazing torch, and before the sun went down, many young lives had found heroes' deaths. Tramp the ground and bend the flower on the fields on which we stand. The fields store the only decoration people favor. Comrades still...

Today disturb not the slaughtered rest,
and our comrades that have fallen,
covered for a long time now by the green grass.
Store them after today, the aged youth!
To those wounded the fortune not to fail,
to see on them the result of that test,
on them so courageous...
To them the wounded the joy not to fail,
will pale.

This proud monument [which] has been established by the government in appreciation for our taking those guns will pale. However, your names will be honored and remembered so long as one veteran of the 39th Regiment lives to keep their memory.

Look across to the monument. It is the history book of our regiment and is devoted to their memory. It will stand the test of time defiant and illuminate the name of the regiment to the later generations.

We the few survivors, now in rows and ranks stand together and the danger of war courageous, ourselves bind equally the chain of war comradeship for time eternal, and so let it be ourselves then in view of this monument as well as in the future, vow you loyal comradeship, until the last of us to be Mustered in the Army recalls us all.[16]

The monument was a fitting tribute to the Garibaldi Guard, and to all the Garibaldians who came together for many reasons and stayed together for one reason, to save the democratic union. Like the country it volunteered to fight for, the Garibaldi Guard became American as it soldiered through four pivotal years in the maturation of its parent country. It mustered in speaking many tongues, and it mustered out speaking American English. Like its fellow volunteer regiments, it had its share of sunshine patriots and its share of winter warriors. The regiment survived despite villains who robbed it. Unsung heroes gave it their last full measure, and veterans survived who were proud that they had served in its ranks. In the end, the Garibaldi Guard did its duty and helped preserve its country. No one can ask more; the 39th New York Volunteer Infantry earned its place in line of battle.

THE ORIGINAL 39TH NEW YORK VOLUNTEER INFANTRY REGIMENT, THE GARIBALDI GUARD

The officers, noncommissioned officers, and selected privates who would be promoted in the ranks, May 1861:

The Regimental Field & Staff (Headquarters) Element

Colonel Frederick George D'Utassy
Lieutenant Colonel Alexander Repetti
Major Luigi Tinelli
Major George E. Waring Jr.
Surgeon Leopold Zander, M.D.
Surgeon Adolphus Majer, M.D.
Assistant Surgeon Forester Swift, M.D.
Chaplain Theodore Krueger
Adjutant (Lieutenant) Cornelius Grinnell
Quartermaster (Lieutenant) Charles B. Norton
Sergeant Major A. T. Hildebrandt
Quartermaster Sergeant Eugene Subit
Quartermaster Sergeant Ellis D. Lazelle
Quartermaster Sergeant W. P. Molo
Commissary Sergeant Alex Biscaccianti
Hospital Steward Herman Bendell

The Line Companies

1ST COMPANY, OR COMPANY A (ITALIAN)

Captain Caesar Osnaghi
First Lieutenant Antonio dal Molin
First Lieutenant Andrew Fontana
Second Ensign Ignazio Allegretti
First Sergeant Cesare Cavrotti
Sergeant Annibal Ferrari
Sergeant Angelo Gori
Sergeant Giovanni Ferralasco
Sergeant Raffael Frixione
Sergeant Edward Boas
Corporal Pietro Mancini
Corporal Antonio Mazzini
Corporal Luigi Roux
Corporal Giuseppe Verdier

Corporal Enries Destafani
Corporal Giovanni Godini
Corporal Giacomo Antonali

And seventy-one enlisted men.

Promoted in the ranks:
Raffael Castelvecchio
Ferdinando Maggi
Silvio Ronzone
Giovanni Samsa
Antonio Oliva
Giuseppe Griffa

2ND COMPANY, OR COMPANY B (SWISS)

Captain Joseph De Schmidt
First Lieutenant Giovanni Marco Colani
Second Lieutenant Alfred Muller
First Sergeant Ludwig Seippel
Sergeant Emil Joerin
Sergeant Jacob Hafeli
Sergeant Carl Sutter
Sergeant Alphonse Pasquet
Corporal Mathias Monnet

Corporal Andreas Moser
Corporal Jacob Cordet
Corporal Wilhelm Ertinger
Corporal Heinrich Dietrich
Corporal Carl Menzel
Corporal Gottlieb Andreas
Corporal Gottlieb Jehele

And seventy-eight enlisted men.

3RD COMPANY, OR COMPANY C (GERMAN)

Captain Charles Schwarz
First Lieutenant Anthony (Anton) Weekey
Second Lieutenant Joseph Aigner
First Sergeant Charles Hoffman
Sergeant Richard Marshall
Sergeant Franz Haug
Sergeant Julius Hintze
Sergeant Edward Boas
Corporal Edmund Doerfer
Corporal Carl Franz
Corporal George Dill

Corporal George Hoell
Corporal Sebastian Dreher
Corporal Julius Boehing
Corporal Friedrich Dress

And eighty-seven enlisted men.

Promoted in the ranks:
Bernhard Duesburg
Augustus Rumpf

4TH COMPANY, OR COMPANY D (SPANISH AND PORTUGUESE)

Captain Joseph Torrens
First Lieutenant Jose Romero
Second Lieutenant Carlos Dela Mesa
First Sergeant Francisco Lugue
Sergeant Alexander Roy
Sergeant Eduardo Woodbury
Sergeant Jose Maria Moreno
Sergeant Ricardo Dominguos
Corporal Jose Melo Freitas
Corporal Francisco Vallestero
Corporal Aljandro Calvo

Corporal Juan Argumosa
Corporal Eulogio Nato
Corporal Juan Madrid
Corporal Francesco Gutienes
Corporal Antonio Dominquez

And sixty-five enlisted men.

Promoted in the ranks:
Albert Jordan

5TH COMPANY, OR COMPANY E (GERMAN)

Captain John Siegel
First Lieutenant William Robitsek
Second Lieutenant John F. Bauer
First Sergeant Charles Zimmermann
Sergeant Anton Ochada
Sergeant Henry Lindner
Sergeant Gustav Fost
Sergeant Gustav Wiener
Corporal Philip Hughes
Corporal Philip Washeim
Corporal Gustav Kaufman
Corporal Jacob Surer

Corporal John Erben
Corporal Jacob Seip
Corporal Rudolph Schwicardi
Corporal Albert Mehl

And eighty-seven enlisted men.

Promoted in the ranks:
Magnus Bader
Adolph Bauer
Albert Hoffman

6TH COMPANY, OR COMPANY F (GERMAN)

Captain Charles Wiegand
First Lieutenant Conrad Von Schondorf
Second Lieutenant Emil Hollinde
Sergeant Major Fried'rich Stehm
Sergeant Louis Riege
Sergeant Anson Seul
Sergeant Franz Weinberger
Sergeant Bernhard Franz
Corporal William Formansky
Corporal Heinrich Peters
Corporal Charles Galluba

Corporal Theodore Miller
Corporal Jacob Glasin
Corporal Leo(nard) Do(e)rndinger
Corporal Carle Niebuhr
Corporal Otto Rassmaessler

And eighty-four enlisted men.

Promoted in the ranks:
Adolphus Wagner

7TH COMPANY, OR COMPANY G (HUNGARIAN, SLAV, AND PRUSSIAN)

Captain Franz Takats
First Lieutenant John B. Juenger
Second Lieutenant Louis Tenner
First Sergeant Joseph Birlbauer
Sergeant Max Lieser
Sergeant Johann Peter
Sergeant Herrman Muller
Sergeant Joseph Wachter
Corporal Louis Schweikt
Corporal Louis Riedel
Corporal Wilhelm Utzl

Corporal Gustav Diefenbach
Corporal Albert Schulze
Corporal Paul Haedler
Corporal Bernhard Pollak
Corporal John May (Sutler)

And seventy-one enlisted men.

Promoted in the ranks:
Carl Menzel
Ferdinand Muller

8TH COMPANY, OR COMPANY H (GERMAN)

Captain A. Otto Bernstein
First Lieutenant Bernhard Baer
Second Lieutenant John Kaufman
First Sergeant C. Theodore Pausch
Second Sergeant Joseph Zeir
3rd Sergeant Theodore Linder
4th Sergeant Franz Herrmann
5th Sergeant Herrmann Bornkessel
Corporal Adolph Lingner

Corporal Friedrich Hildebrand
Corporal Friedrich Thatewald
Corporal Herrmann Theune
Corporal Heinrich Dahms
Corporal Franz Wilhelmi
Corporal Carl Krebs
Corporal Wilhelm Zimmermann

And eighty-one enlisted men.

9TH COMPANY, OR COMPANY I (GERMAN)

Captain A. H. Von Unwerth
First Lieutenant James C. Rice
Second Lieutenant George Brey
Sergeant Major Carl Ruelberg
Sergeant Christian Enke
Sergeant Otto Peter
Sergeant August Ruckersfield
Sergeant Jean Ziegler
Corporal George Bonin

Corporal Jean Wiedmayer
Corporal Jean Dessauer
Corporal George Glassenapp
Corporal Jean Ziegler
Corporal Heinrich Scheidemann
Corporal Leopold Sachs
Corporal Gustav Raefle

And eighty-nine enlisted men.

10TH COMPANY, OR COMPANY K (FRENCH AND FRENCH CANADIAN)

Captain Louis Tassillier
First Lieutenant Vikor Chandone
Second Lieutenant Anthony Dumazer
First Sergeant Germain Sayve
Second Sergeant Victor Leseine
Third Sergeant Joseph Aubrey
Fourth Sergeant Jean Beaudoir
Fifth Sergeant J. Marie Olivry
Corporal Desire Jacheresse
Corporal Henry Bartholomie

Corporal Louis Beaufits
Corporal Emile David
Corporal Louis Grimiaux
Corporal Baptiste Joseph Leriche
Corporal Louis LaCroix
Corporal Charles Hahn

And ninety-seven enlisted men.

HONOR ROLL OF THE 39TH NEW YORK VOLUNTEER INFANTRY REGIMENT, THE GARIBALDI GUARD

LEGEND:

=	Officer rank
*	Deserted
+	Killed or died
#	Something of added interest--e.g., ex-Garibaldini, member of the German Revolution of 1848
Andrv	Andersonville, Georgia prisoner of war camp
Slsbry	Salisbury, North Carolina prisoner of war camp
Thdr Cstl	Thunder Castle prisoner of war camp in Richmond, Virginia
aka	Also known as
CIA/PAR	Captured in action and paroled
CIA/POW	Captured in action and imprisoned (prisoner of war)
CO?	Unassigned
DOD	Died of disease
DOW	Died of wound
KIA	Killed in action
NR	No Record
SIH	Sick in the hospital at the time of muster
VRC	Unfit for duty, transferred to the Veteran Reserve Corps
WIA	Wounded in action

EXAMPLE:
(1)   (2)   (3)   (4)
+ CRUESIUS, FREDERICK—28; WIA/Recovered, CIA/POW Andrv/DOD

(1) The soldier died (+)
(2) His name: Last, First, any Initial
(3) His age
(4) In this section and instance, the soldier's wartime fate: he was wounded in ac
tion (WIA), recovered, and then later captured in action and imprisoned in
the Andersonville prisoner of war camp (CIA/POW Andrv), where he died
of disease (DOD). This section might include aliases, other military unit
affiliations, or the like.

Bull Run: July 21, 1861

Two men killed in action or died of wounds.

Cross Keys: June 8, 1862

+CANON, JOSEPH—32; WIA/DOW 6/11/1862
+CORDET, JACOB—45; WIA/DOW 6/9/1862
+HOCHHEIMER, KARL—24; KIA
+=JORDAN, ALBERT—31; WIA/DOW 6/15/1862
+KRABELL, HEINRICH—24; WIA/DOW 6/15/1862
+=LESIENE, VICTOR—37; KIA
+MEHL, ALBERT—27; KIA
+MOUSTON, AUGUSTE—19; WIA/CIA/PAR/DOW 7/19/1862
+STEPHAN, JOHN—25; WIA/DOW 6/12/1862
+WEIL, JOSEPH—25; WIA/DOW 7/19/1862
+SCHWARZ, CARL—19; DOD 6/?/1862
+SCHEFFNER, CHARLES—27; DOD 6/21/1862
+NAFFLE, XAVER—30; DOD 6/23/1862

Harpers Ferry

The Garibaldian casualties at Harpers Ferry, September 12 to 15 were 6 men
killed in action.

Gettysburg: July 1, 1863

+SCHAEFER, GEORGE—23; WIA/DOW 7/24/1863

Gettysburg: July 2, 1863

+BONI, PAOLO—24; WIA/DOW 10/9/1863
+BONIN, GEORGE—32; KIA
+DOENECKE, WILHELM—28; WIA/DOD 7/6/1864
+GESSMANN, FRIEDRICH—25; KIA
+HEINZEN, FREDRICK—33; KIA
+HOCKNER, HEINRICH—23; KIA
+JUNGUNST, JOHN—30; WIA/DOW 7/6/1863
+KAMMERER, CLEMENS—28; KIA
+KAUTH, GOTTLIEB—24; KIA
+KERN, THOMAS—18; KIA
+MARLOTT, WILLIAM—27; WIA/DOW 7/8/1863
+MULLER, EMIL—27; KIA
+=PAUSCH, CARL THEODORE—28; KIA
+REINHOLD, PETER—32; WIA/DOW 7/29/1863
+SCHWITZER, CONRAD—20; KIA
+VAN, JOSEPH—26; KIA
+WERNER, MICHAEL—21; KIA
+WITTS, BERNHARD—42; KIA

Gettysburg: July 3, 1863

+HEIMBUCHER, IGNATZ—35; KIA
+METZLER, LOUIS—19; WIA/DOW 7/26/1863
+SCHULZ, PETER—26; KIA
+=WAGNER, ADOLPHUS—20; WIA/DOW 8/25/1863
+WURSCH, JOSEPH II—28; WIA/DOW 7/4/1863

Bristoe Station: October 14, 1863

+STEPHAN, JACOB JOHN—age?; CIA/DOD 2/3/1865 Charleston, S.C.

Mine Run Campaign: November 30, 1863

+KLAIBER, CARL—30; CIA/Died 3/11/1864 Thdr Cstl, Richmond
+MONTAG, GEORGE—29; CIA/Died 7/8/1864 Andrv
+SMAKA, JOHN—22; CIA/DOD 9/23/1864 Andrv

Mine Run Campaign: December 1, 1863

+STUZMAN, PHILIP—25; CIA/Died 8/17/1864 Andrv
+ROTH, LUDWIG—35; CIA DOD 8/9/1864 Andrv
+ZEINER, AUGUST—23; CIA/NR 10/11/1864 Andrv

Mine Run Campaign: December 2, 1863

+KEHRIG, CASPAR—37; CIA/Died 8/1/1864 Andrv
+MESSING, FRANZ—39; CIA/Died 9/16/1864 Andrv
+NILSON, BERNHARD—25; CIA/Died 6/27/1864 Andrv
+ROMANY, CHRISTIAN—26; CIA/DOD 2/19/1864 Richmond
+SCHNEIDER, CHARLES—35; CIA/DOD 8/11/1864 Andrv
+SINGER, ANDRE—21; WIA/CIA/DOD 9/29/1864 Andrv
+STADER, CHARLES—21; CIA/DOD 8/2/1864 Andrv

Morton's Ford: February 6, 1864

+BARRY, HONORE—33; KIA
+BREHMER, EDWARD—27; WIA/DOW 6/1/1864
+ENGEL, WILHELM—21; CIA/DOD 8/18/1864 Andrv
+FRIEE, CARL—22; Baden; CIA/DOD 8/24/1864 Andrv
+McCORMACK, PETER—27; CIA/DOD 5/28/1864 Andrv
+REED, WILLIAM I.—29; WIA/DOW 3/1/1864
+SCHNELL, CARL—21; CIA/DOD 10/5/1864 Charleston, S.C.
+THIERBACH, OTTO—35; CIA/Died 8/17/1864 Andrv

Morton's Ford: February 7, 1864

+FISCHER, LORENZ—24; CIA/DOD 10/14/1864 Andrv
+GAISER, CARL—21; CIA/DOD 9/5/1864 Andrv
+HAAG, CHRISTIAN—27; CIA/DOD Andrv
+KOLBATZ, WILLIAM—38; CIA/Died 8/29/1864 Andrv
+McCORMACK, PETER—27; CIA/DOD Andrv
+MARK, JACOB—age?; CIA/Died 10/13/1864 Andrv

Rapidan River: March 13, 1864

+BACON, BAPTISTE—41; CIA/DOD 10/9/1864 Thdr Cstl, Richmond

The Wilderness: May 5, 1864

+GRAVELIUS, HENRY—21; WIA/DOW 7/12/1864 Washington, D.C.
+McFADDEN, JAMES—42; WIA/CIA/DOD 7/26/1864 Andrv
+UNTERGRUBER, MARTIN—27; WIA/CIA/Died 9/22/1864 Danville, Va.
+WEGNER, CARL—33; CIA/DOD 6/16/1864 Andrv

The Wilderness: May 6, 1864

+ALGOT, GUSTAF—20; CIA/DOD 5/28/1864 Richmond
+ANDERSON, PETER—22; KIA
+BAUMANN, HENRY—27; CIA/DOD 9/11/1864 Andrv

+BURNS, THOMAS H.—32; WIA/DOW 6/14/1864
+CARROLL, JOHN—30; WIA/Died 7/25/1864
+CUDEHEY, MICHAEL—20; KIA
+CUMMING, JOHN—19; CIA/DOD No Date Andrv
+DELACOSTA, DOMINICO—19; WIA/DOW No Date
+DOOLEY, PATRICK—19; CIA/DOD 6/?/1864 Andrv
+EDLER, FREDERICK—28; WIA/DOD 11/15/1864 Andrv
+EMMONS, CONRAD I.—age?; KIA/Wilderness
+FERGUSON, MICHAEL—19; CIA/DOD 9/1/1864 Andrv
+FRACKIN, JOSEPH—34; CIA/DOD 9/24/1864 Andrv
+FROSCHKENECHT, JACOB—24; WIA/DOW 5/22/1864
+GARBARINI, VINCENZO—27; CIA/DOD 9/7/1864 Andrv
+GOLDSMITH, JULIUS—24; WIA/DOW 5/22/1864
+HERMAN, KARL—21; WIA/DOW 7/1/1864
+HETZEL, JOHN—27; KIA
+HILL, TREVOR—21; KIA
+HITCHCOCK, HENRY A.—28; WIA/DOW 5/8/1864
+HOLSTEIN, GUSTAVUS—26; KIA
+HOOK, WILLIAM S.—25; KIA
+HOWARD, WILLIAM—32; CIA/DOD 7/31/64 Andrv
+JONES, THOMAS—22; KIA
+LEE, DANIEL—21; KIA
+LEWIS, AUGUSTUS—23; WIA/DOD 5/13/1864
+LINGART, JOHN W.—31; KIA
+LOMBARD, BERNARD—41; KIA
+MARICHI, ANTONIO—35; KIA
+MILLER, JACOB—38; CIA/DOD 8/13/1864 Andrv
+MORRIS, HENRY C.—18; WIA/DOW 5/18/1864
+OERTLE, ULRICH—31; WIA/DOW 5/7/1864
+PRAHM, JOHN—21; KIA
+RICE, THOMAS—21; CIA/DOD 7/30/1864 Andrv
+RODH, WILLIAM—23; WIA/DOW 5/?/1864
+RYAN, JAMES M.—27; CIA/DOD 8/18/1864 Andrv
+SCHWIEGER, ALOIS—27; CIA/DOD 10/9/1864 Andrv
+SIEBERT, ANDREAS—29; CIA/DOD 1/16/1865 Slsbry

Spotsylvania at Po River: May 10, 1864

+ANDERSON, SVEN JOHAN—24; CIA/DOD 9/16/1864 Andrv
+DELACOSTA, JOHANN— 21; WIA/DOW 6/28/1864
+FESSLER, FRITZ—23; WIA/DOD 10/5/1864
+GILMORE, EDWARD—20; KIA
+HEINE, LOUIS—28; WIA/DOW 5/23/1864
+HULGINSKY, ERNST—21; KIA

+KERR, THOMAS—22; KIA
+LINZEMIRE, FRANK—19; KIA
+=McGARRY, MICHAEL O.—30; WIA/DOW 5/25/1864
+MEINHARDT, CHARLES—28; CIA/Died 10/27/1864 Andrv
+MILLER, JOHN—38; KIA
+MOORE, JOHN—28; CIA/Died 9/10/1864 Andrv
+MURRY, PATRICK—36; KIA
+OSBORNE, EDMUND—21; WIA/DOD 1/20/1865
+PRENDERGAST, JOHN—age?; KIA
+REILLY, JOHN—21; CIA/DOD 8/21/1864 Andrv
+THOMPSON, JAMES—44; CIA/Died 9/23/1864 Andrv

Spotsylvania at Laurel Hill: May 10, 1864

+DEGAN, ADELBERT—26; WIA/DOW 6/16/1864
+MEINHARDT, CHARLES—28; CIA/Died 10/27/1864 Andrv

Spotsylvania at Salient: May 12, 1864

+BENTON, EZEKIAL B.—22; WIA/DOW 5/31/1864
+GRAMMS, CHARLES—21; KIA
ı GRAWDLLIUO, HDNRV ꞓ1, WIA/DOW 7/1ꞓ/10ꞓ1
+JUNKER, HENRY—30; KIA
+=O'KEEFE, THOMAS L.—age?; KIA
+SCHENK, FREDERICK—34; KIA
+UNTERGRUBER, MARTIN—27; CIA/Died 9/22/1864 Danville, Va.

Spotsylvania Court or Landron House: May 18, 1864

+CRUESIUS, FREDERICK—28; WIA/DOD 9/10/1864 Andrv
+ECKERT, ANTON—22; KIA
+HEMILRICK, JOHN—26; CIA/DOD 1/15/1865 Andrv
+LEONARD, JAMES—19; KIA
+LINNE, AUGUST—42; CIA/Died 7/19/1864 Andrv
+MEYER, HEINRICH—34; CIA/Died 9/9/1864
+PAGE, MICHAEL—38; WIA/DOW 5/28/1864

Pamunkey River: May 30, 1864

+RAUK, JOHANN H.—31; KIA

Totopotomoy River: May 30, 1864

+FLECK, HEINRICH—24; KIA
+KAUFMAN, ALBERT—24; WIA/DOW 12/18/1864

+MEYERDERICH, JOHN—37; WIA/DOW 6/18/1864
+NICHOLSON, JAMES—22; WIA/DOW 8/15/1864

Totopotomoy River: May 31, 1864

+MOORE, DAVID—25; CIA/DOD 9/4/1864 Andrv
+OLIVA, ANTONIO—18; WIA/DOW 6/1/1864
+STEWART, ALEXANDER—35; KIA

Hanover Town: May 31, 1864

+MARTIN, WILLIAM—19; KIA

Gaines Mills: June 2, 1864

+LANGENBACHER, JOSEPH—22; CIA/Died ? Andrv

Cold Harbor: June 8, 1864

+EHRHARD, ALEXANDER—22; KIA 6/8/1864

Before Petersburg: June 14, 1864

+REED, WILLIAM—31; KIA

Before Petersburg: June 15, 1864

+BRAIN, PHILIP—39; KIA

Before Petersburg: June 16, 1864

+WEBER, JULIUS—30; KIA

Before Petersburg: June 17, 1864

+CARPENTER, WILLIAM H.—age?; WIA/DOD 1/25/1865
+DOUGHERTY, MICHAEL—23; WIA/CIA/DOW 6/20/1864 Andrv
+SAITHOF, ISAAC—19; WIA/DOW 9/27/1864

Before Petersburg: June 21, 1864

+CHAPPELL, ALPHONZO—19; CIA/DOD 8/16/1864 Andrv
LOUNSBURG, CALVIN—18; CIA; NR

North Anna: June 22, 1864

+BROWN, HENRY—44; WIA/CIA/DOD 3/23/1865 Richmond

+LEHMAN, AUGUST—43; CIA/DOD 8/22/1864 Andrv
+O'NEIL, JOHN—19; CIA/DOD 10/24/1864
+PERRY, ALFRED—35; CIA/Died 10/9/1864 Andrv
+PLEIN, MATHIAS—21; CIA/DOD 1/?/1865 Andrv

Weldon Railroad: June 22, 1864

+BELL, JOHN—22; England; CIA/DOD 9/16/1864 Andrv
+BERGENFELD, LUDWIG—19; CIA/DOD 4/1/1865 Andrv
+BROWN, HENRY—44; WIA/CIA/DOD 3/23/1865 Andrv
+LETTMAN, AUGUST—43; CIA/DOD 8/22/1864 Andrv
+O'NEIL, JOHN—19; CIA/DOD 10/24/1864 Andrv
+PERRY, ALFRED—35; CIA/Died 8/22/1864 Andrv
+PLEIN, MATHIAS—21; CIA/DOD 1/?/1865 Andrv
+REIMBACK, CHRISTIAN—22; CIA/DOD 8/29/1864
+SCHEU, FREDERICK—25; KIA
+WHITNEY, JOHN—34; CIA/DOD 8/31/1864 Andrv

Weldon Railroad: June 23, 1864

+THOMPSON, JOHN—22; CIA/DOD 8/25/1864 Andrv

Weldon Railroad: June 27, 1864

+BOVIER, JOHN F.—33; CIA/DOD 8/9/1864 Andrv

Deep Bottom: August 20, 1864

+BROWER, JOHN—33; CIA/DOD 8/9/1864 Andrv
+SIEBERT, JOHN—26; CIA/DOD 10/28/1864 Slsbry

Reams Station: August 25, 1864

+BEHR, JACOB—23; CIA/DOD 11/24/1864 Slsbry
+DITTMAR, JOHN H.—38; CIA/DOD 9/18/1864 Andrv
+LATHROP, CHARLES—21; CIA/DOD 1/6/1865 Slsbry
+PARKER, JOHN—27; WIA/DOW 9/3/1864
+=RICH, THEODORE F.—19; KIA
+STEINHAL, BALDES—30; CIA/DOD 10/18/1864 Slsbry

Fort Sedgwick: October 27, 1864

+=BRUEN, DAVID—29; KIA Sniper
+PUTNEY, JOSIAH W.—19; WIA

White Oak Ridge: March 31, 1865

+DREW, FRANCIS G.—41; KIA 3/31/1865 City Point, Va.
+LAIN, ALFRED B.—42; WIA 3/31/1865 Petersburg, DOW 5/18/1865
+THOMPSON, ROBERT I.—23; KIA 3/31/1865 White Oak Ridge
+VAN WESSEM, JEROME—34; KIA 3/31/1865 Petersburg

Farmville, Va.: April 2, 1865

+CAIN, MICHAEL—25; WIA/DOW 4/19/1865
+WALZER, CHARLES—33; KIA

CAPTURED IN ACTION—NO DATE AND DIED IN PRISON

+ALTENBORND, EDWARD—19; DOD 9/1/64 Andrv
+ANTLER,—age?; DOD Andrv
+BARNUM, H.—age?; DOD 9/10/1864 Andrv
+BROWN, CHARLES—21; DOD 11/10/1864 Andrv
+HARRICK, LEWIS CHARLES—25; DOD Date? Andrv
+HAYES, JAMES—28; DOD 10/14/1864 Andrv
+HESKELL, ALBERT—20; DOD 10/12/1864 Andrv
+MARTIN, JAMES—26; Died 12/3/1864 Andrv
+McDONALD, JAMES—24; DOD 12/18/1864 Richmond
+MURRAY, ALEXANDER—21; DOD 9/16/1864 Andrv
+ROBINSON, HENRY—35; DOD 10/16/1864 Andrv
+SCHWARTZ, MICHAEL—39; DOD Slsbry
+THURM, JEAN—29; 8/20/1864; Died ? Andrv
+WALSH, JOHN—31; 6/1/1864; DOD 9/8/1864 Andrv
+WALZ, PHILIPP—30; CIA 2/16/1864; NR
+ZENZ, JOSEPH E.—30; DOD 2/16/1865 Slsbry

DEATH BY DISEASE OR ACCIDENT: 1861

+DEVERBOIS, EMIL—age?; Died 5/23/1861 First Casualty
+BUHLER, JOSEPH—20; Drowned 6/22/1861
+SCHWEIKT, LOUIS—19; DOD 6/25/1861
+VIGIL, AUGUSTIN—21; DOD 7/8/1861
+FRANZ, ALBERT—25; DOD 8/8/1861
+MATHIES, DANIEL—26; Died 10/5/1861
+SCHREIBER, FRANCIS—46; DOD 11/17/1861
+GOTZ, HEINRICH—23; DOD 11/17/1861
+HELLER, PETER—24; DOD 12/3/1861

DEATH BY DISEASE OR ACCIDENT: 1862

+MOLENS, JUAN—23; WIA/DOW 7/15/1862 at Regimental Hospital
+WURDMAN, BERNARD—28; DOD 7/30/1862
+SCHMID, JAKOB—38; DOD 8/5/1862
+DEEG, ANDREAS—30; DOD 10/19/1862

DEATH BY DISEASE OR ACCIDENT: 1863

+OLIVER, MIGUEL—23; Murdered 3/8/1863

DEATH BY DISEASE OR ACCIDENT: 1864

+McGROW, PATRICK—21; Died 1/15/1864 Heart Disease
+ALLEN, BENJAMIN—30; DOD 1/19/1864
+GARDINERS, FRANCIS E.—20; DOD 1/24/1864
+GOMEZ, EMANUEL—20; DOD 1/24/1864
+ETHERIDGE, GEORGE B.—age?; DOD 3/2/1864
+WILSON, WILLIAM—age?; Drowned 5/2/1864
+HYDE, DENNIS—37; DOD 6/1/1864
+WEBER, GOTTLIEB—28; WIA ?, DOW 6/7/1864
+HARRISON, JOHN—19; DOD 7/24/1864
+NEILL, JOHN—22; DOD 7/29/1864
+MALONEY, RICHARD—29; DOD 8/8/1864
+KALL, PETER—20; Died 8/18/1864
+CENT, JOHN—28; DOD 8/27/1864
+BRANDENBERGER, HENRY—20; DOD 8/31/1864
+PETERMAN, MAURICE—20; DOD 9/5/1864
+LEWIS, SAM—23; DOD 9/6/1864
+KEENAN, BERNARD—40; DOD 9/8/1864
+GOTZ, FIDAL—21; DOD 9/20/1864
+McDONALD, DANIEL—26; DOD 9/30/1864
+DUBOIS, JOSEPH—20; DOD 10/15/1864
+BACKLER, LEWIS—35; DOD 10/30/1864
+MYERS, JOSEPH—41; DOD 11/5/1864
+CARL, FREDERICK—37; DOD 11/20/1864
+ROSE, ALBERT P.—31; DOD 11/27/1864
+DELOPONA, JOHN—age?; DOD 12/14/1864

DEATH BY DISEASE OR ACCIDENT: 1865

+BECK, CHARLES—21; DOD 1/3/1865
+MOORE, JAMES—38; DOD 1/16/1865
+CRAMLIN, AUGUST—40; DOD 2/1/1865

+HAMILTON, HENRY T.—38; DOD 2/5/1865
+THOMSON, SLYVESTER—43; DOD 2/15/1865
+HURST, ALEXANDER—20; DOD 3/12/1865
+RANDALS, FRANK B.—age?; DOD 4/3/1865
+BARRETT, WILLIAM—18; DOD 6/11/1865

WOUNDED IN ACTION

Bull Run: July 21, 1861

Five men wounded in action.

Cross Keys: June 8, 1862

EBELING, WILLIAM—18; Mustered
GORDINI, GIOVANNI—23; NR
HENNOUT, NICHOL—34; WIA/CIA/PAR, Disability
KALLENBACH, GOTTLIEB—20; Mustered
MENZEL, CARL—21; Disability
OLIVER, MIGUEL—age?; WIA
PICCIONI, GIOVANNI—24; VRC
SAMANIEGE, JOSE—27; Mustered
WEBER, BERNHARD—20; Disability

Harpers Ferry

The Garibaldian casualties at Harpers Ferry, September 12 to 15 were 15 men wounded in action.

Gettysburg: July 1, 1863

DROCKE, EDWARD—22; Deserted from Hospital in N.Y.
KOHNLEIN, GEORG—34; VRC
LORIN, JEREMIE—29; VRC
TIETJEN, HEINRICH—40; Discharged

Gettysburg: July 2, 1863

BIERA, JOAQUIN—27; VRC
DOEGE, AUGUST—28; VRC
FOSTER, BERNHARDT—24; Mustered
FREPON, EMIL—age?; Mustered from Hospital
GEIB, PETER—32; Mustered
GUZMAN, ANTONIO—30; Recovered
HERANDEZ, JUAN—23; Recovered

HINZ, ERNST—23; VRC
JUNCO, ENRIQUS—22; VRC
JUNG, ADAM—25; VRC
KOCH, AUGUST—19; Mustered
KULLMER, GEORGE—19; VRC
MAYER, CARL—25; Recovered
MULLER, FRANZ—18; VRC
OLIVRY, JUAN MARIE—29; Recovered
OTTO, THEODOR—31; VRC
RANTSA, CARL—22; Recovered
RUFNER, JOHANN A.—19; Mustered
SCHANER, FRIEDRICH CHRISTIAN—29; Disability
SCHAUM, PHILIP—19; VRC
SCHUTZ, FRANZ—19; VRC
UNVERZAGT, WILLIAM—22
VALDES, JOSE—25; Discharged

Gettysburg: July 3, 1863

ARCHINAL, LOUIS—23; Disability
BARDO, GIUSEPPE—28; CIA/PAR, Mustered
BERNHARD, ADAM—29; VRC
BRITSCHE, JOHN—26; VRC
=HILDERBRAND, HUGO—36; Discharged
HOLZINGER, AUGUST—26; VRC
REIMLING, FRANZ—33; VRC
RENKHARD, ALBERT—23; Mustered
ROTHWEILER, AUGUST—31; VRC
RUCKERT, CARL—24; Disability
STRADTMANN, HEINRICH—24; Mustered

Bristoe Station: October 14, 1863

ANDREAS, GOTTLIEB—40; Disability
BRIOT, CHARLES—24; Disability
CASTELVECCHIO, RAFFAELE—22; Mustered
COBO, JOSE—22; Mustered
LOWENTHAL, BERNHART—24; CIA/PAR
MARK, JOHN—age?; Mustered

Mine Run Campaign: November 30, 1863

Morton's Ford: February 6, 1864

Officially recorded 17 wounded.

ARNZ, JULIUS—19; Mustered
=DOERNDINGER, LEO—19; Mustered
EBERHARD, GEORGE—23; Mustered
KOBER, FRED (H.) A.—36; VRC
LA FLEUR, ALEXANDER—31; WIA/CIA/PAR, Disability
MILLER, JOHN—27; Mustered
MUNZ, SIMON—21; Recovered
TALLONT, JOHN—31; Recovered
WOELFEL, GEORG—25; Recovered

Rapidan River: March 13, 1864

The Wilderness: May 5, 1864

SCHEEPSMA, ANTON—21; NR
TRIPPE, JAMES—23; CIA at Reams Station, Paroled, Discharged

The Wilderness: May 6, 1864

ANWANDER, JOHANN—24; NR
ARMSTRONG, JAMES—20
=BAKER, ALLEN M.—30; Mustered
BECKER, JACOB—23; Mustered
BELRINGER, FREDERIC—age?; SIH
BETTING, WILLIAM—age?; NR
BISCHOFF, GUSTAV—28; Mustered
BRAYMAN, JOSEPH—21; Disability
BREITING, CARL—23
BROWN, PHILIP—39; SIH
CAIN, MICHAEL—25; Recovered
CARBONI, FRANCESCO—25; Mustered
CONNER, JOHN—28; Discharged
DANNER, FRANK—age?; NR
DEITZ, JOHN A.—37; Recovered
DELAPORES, PETRO—28; Disability
DENIER, EMIL—22; Disability
DENNIS, HENRY—19; CIA/PAR, Mustered
DEUSCHEL, JACOB—28; Mustered
DOMINECO, PAGLIO GEORGE—39; SIH
DONNELLY, PETER—22; VRC

FARBER, GEORGE—28
FASTNACHT, JOHANN—44; Mustered
FELDENZ, JACOB—36; SIH
FRANK, GUSTAV—21; SIH
FRELL, CHARLES—21; Deserted
=FUNK, AUGUSTUS—22; Recovered
GANSER, JACOB—28; CIA/PAR, Mustered
GELB, JOHN—21; Mustered
GERSTENBURG, HENRY—18; NR
GOLDBACH, BERNHARD—29; Deserted
GSELL, FERDINAND—34; WIA/CIA, NR
GUZMAN, ANTONIO—30; WIA, 2nd Time Mustered
=HAIGHT, CHARLES C.—22; Disability
HARTLEY, WILLIAM—19; Mustered
HAUSON, JOHN—38; Disability
HERANDEZ, JUAN—23; Mustered
HOFFMAN, MOSES—33; Disability
HOLT, HERMAN—21; Mustered
HOLTHUSEN, GUSTAV—21; Mustered
HORNIA, CELESTINO—21; Recovered
HUFSCHMIED, FREDERICK—20; Mustered
=HUGHES, JAMES G.—age?; Discharged
JIMEREZ, JUAN J.—25; NR
JONES, JOHN—19; Mustered
KELLER, ANDREW—20; Deserted from Hospital, Washington, D.C.
KING, CONRAD—20; Disability
KOHLER, FRANZ—32; Mustered
LAMMERS, JOHN—19; Recovered
LEONARD, JOSEPH—31; Disability
LEOPOLD, AUGUST—24; Disability
LUPRU, HIPPOLITE—34; NR
MAI, HENRICH—19; Mustered
MAIER, ALBERT—19; Mustered
MARSHALL, ISAIAH—22; NR
MAYER, CARL—25; WIA, 2nd Time Mustered
MAYER, JOHANN MARTIN—42; Mustered
McELROY, GEORGE—37; Disability
McGEE, JOHN—40; NR
MEIER, FREDERICH—21; Mustered
MERGEL, LOUIS—20; Mustered
MILLS, GEORGE E.—age?; Deserted on the March
MOODIE, GEORGE—21; Disability
MUELLER, WILLIAM—26; Mustered
NICHOLSON, JAMES—22; Recovered, WIA 2nd May 30, 1864/DOW

NUTMAN, ALBERT—38; Disability
OLIVRY, JUAN MARIE—29; WIA, 2nd Time Mustered
PEIFFER, JACOB—23; CIA/PAR, NR
PENATE, MIGUEL—23; SIH
PETROLI, PIETRIO—25; NR
PETTREE, JOHN—23; Disability
QUINLEY, THOMAS—21; Mustered
RANTSA, CARL—22; WIA, 2nd Time May 20, Mustered
RIEBKE, HERMANN—age?; Mustered
RODGERS, THOMAS—21; NR
ROLY, LEON—32; CIA, NR
ROOS, MATTHUES—25; Deserted from Hospital, Washington, D.C.
SANTES, OSEE—20; Mustered
SCHMIDT, CHARLES—28; VCR
SCHNOR, FREDRICH—21; Mustered
SEIP, HEINRICH—21; Mustered
SERVIE, JOSEPH—26; NR
SESSLER, FRANZ—27; Mustered
SMITH, JOHN—22; SIH
SMITH, GEORGE P.—23; CIA/PAR, Mustered
STONES, MICHAEL—26; Mustered
TALLONT, JOHN—31; WIA, 2nd Time Mustered
THOMPSON, JOHN—25; SIH
VAIL, FELIX—33; Mustered
=VALENTINE, JOHN E.—29; Disability
VAN NESS, IRA W.—18; Mustered
VAN TASSAL, ABSOLEM—35; Deserted from Hospital, Washington, D.C.
VAN WESSEM, JEROME—34; Recovered
VENTLAND, PETERSON J.—27; SIH
WOELFEL, GEORG—25; WIA, 2nd Time Mustered
ZOBAL, EDWARD—21; Recovered

Spotsylvania: May 9, 1864

KELLY, THOMAS J.—19; Disability

Spotsylvania at Po River: May 10, 1864

ALLEN, THOMAS—19; Mustered
CLAUSSON, CHARLES H.—35; SIH
COSEY, FRANK—18; Transferred to Signal Corps
CUNNINGHAM, ANDREW—43; Disability
+ECKERT, ANTON—22; Returned to Ranks While Still Wounded, KIA
FISHER, JOHN—34; SIH, Deserted from Hospital, Washington, D.C.

HOFFMAN, ALBERT—34; WIA/CIA/PAR, Mustered
HOMAN, CHARLES—22; Disability
JACOBSON, SIMON—46; VRC
JANSEN, JOHN H.—21; Mustered
KERR, WILLIAM M.—40; Mustered
LEE, CHARLES—22; Deserted
=MAGGI, FERDINANDO—32; Discharged
=MULLER, FERDINAND—22; Mustered
MUMPHIR, ANTON—21; Mustered
NOLAN, WILLIAM N.—20; CIA/PAR, Mustered
PETERS, JOHN—38; Mustered
RUGGS, JOHN—23; Deserted from Hospital, Washington, D.C.
SCHABAHA, CHARLES—29; Mustered
SCHMIDT, LOUIS—26; Mustered
SCHOENING, FREDRICH—22; SIH
SCHULTZ, HENRY—30; Deserted from Hospital, Washington, D.C.
SCHWISCKART, NICOLAUS—42; VRC
SMITH, LEVI S.—age?; Mustered
SPRATT, SILAS C.—29; WIA/CIA; Paroled
THROM, WENDELIN—21; WIA/CIA, NR
TORCK, JOHN H.—23; Mustered
ULSIMER, JOSEPH—22; CIA/PAR, Mustered
WALLACE, JOHN—19; Disability
WEST, PETER—21; SIH
WICKS, SAMUEL—33; SIH

Spotsylvania at Laurel Hill: May 10, 1864

JACOBSON, SIMON—46; VRC
JANSEN, JOHN H.—21; Mustered
PETERS, JOHN—38; Mustered
SCHOENING, FREDERICK—22; SIH
SPRATT, SILAS CYRUS—29; CIA/PAR

Spotsylvania at Salient: May 12, 1864

BERGEN, GASTANE—26; Disability
BRADLEY, RALPH—21; VRC
CHAPMAN, JOSEPH—age?; NR
FADDEN, JAMES M.—age?; NR
GILFILLAN, JOHN M.—26; Recovered
LAVOIE, JOSEPH—26; NR
MECKEL, AUGUST—23; Mustered
MOYLAND, THOMAS—age?; VRC

NELSON, CHRISTIAN—28; Mustered
NEWTON, ANDREW—28; Mustered
=RICH, ERSKINE—19; Mustered
SCOTT, OLIVER—22; SIH
SHIELDS, JAMES—26; Mustered
WARD, JAMES—21; Mustered

Spotsylvania at Salient: May 13, 1864

DERELIN, JACOB—age?; NR
NAVARRETO, FRANCISCO—27; Mustered
WRIGHT, DAVID—29; SIH

Spotsylvania at Salient: May 16, 1864

KROEBER, ALFRED—22; Mustered
PRIMROSE, ALEXANDER—44; Mustered

Spotsylvania at Salient: May 17, 1864

HERRMAN, HENRY—20; Discharged
PFANNSCHMIDT, CONRAD—26

Spotsylvania Court or Landron House: May 18, 1864

=BAKER, CHARLES C.—26; Mustered
=BALLOU, CHARLES—19; Mustered
BOW, JEREMIAH—26; Recovered
BRINCKMAN, ADOLPH—32; VRC
CARROLL, PETER—20; Mustered
+CRUESIUS, FREDERICK—28; Recovered, CIA, Andrv DOD
=DELL, GEORGE—36; Mustered
DONAHUE, JAMES—35; VRC
FAUSER, GOTTLIEB—33; Mustered
FILLMORE, JAMES—26; Disability
GULLY, WILLIAM—24; Discharged
=McCARRON, HUGH—29; Mustered
PRATT, JOHN F.—41; VRC
SAMUELSON, SAMUEL—37; Mustered
SCHAAK, JOHN—33; Mustered
SYLVESTER, JAMES—24; Disability
=TREMPER, ROBERT—24; Mustered

North Anna: May 22, 1864

BROWN, HENRY—21; Deserted from Hospital, N.Y. Harbor, 6/30/1864

Pamunkey River: May 30, 1864

Totopotomoy River: May 30, 1864

BANKHOSS, E.—age?; WIA, NR
BAUHOF, ALBERT—19; Mustered
RAPHAEL, SAMUEL—19; Mustered
SEIFERT, ALBERT—21; Disability

Totopotomoy River: May 31, 1864

FLETCHER, RALPH—21; SIH
HAYES, JOHN—34; Recovered
PIEROTTI, VIRGILO—25; Mustered
WARRELL, SAMUEL—23; Disability

Hanover Town: May 31, 1864

Gaines Mills: June 2, 1864

UNVERZAGT, WILLIAM—22; Mustered

Cold Harbor: June 3, 1864

McCAUL, JOHN—20
TAUBENSPECK, EDWARD—21; Mustered

Cold Harbor: June 7, 1864

BETTR, JACOB—23; Recovered
CATTON, BERNARD—32; Mustered
=WILSON, JOSEPH JR.—19; Disability

Before Petersburg: June 14–16, 1864

CARR, THOMAS—30; SIH
CUSKER, MICHAEL—21; Mustered
DELACOSTA, JOSE—age?; WIA, NR
FULLER, WILLIAM—28; Mustered from Hospital
GREGOR, AUGUST—35; Deserted from Hospital
HENDERSON, JOHN—30; NR
JAVELLE, ALFRED—20; VRC

KELLY, THOMAS—18; Deserted on Furlough
MEYER, EDWARD—19; Mustered
MOONEY, JAMES—32; Disability
=SCHOUTEN, CHARLES A.—20; WIA, Discharged
SULLIVAN, PATRICK—26; Disability
TATTEN, JOSEPH—21; Disability
WAGNER, JOSEPH—36; Mustered
WILLIAMS, CHARLES—26; Discharged from Insane Asylum
WILSON, WILLIAM—43; SIH

Before Petersburg: June 17, 1864

EGERLY, LEONARD—27
EMRICK, LOUIS—21; SIH
GOLLE, LUDWIG—21
HAYES, JOHN—34; WIA, 2nd Time Mustered
HUNZINGER, ADOLPH—21; Mustered
LINDEN, JAMES—22; Mustered
RIMBULD, BERNARD—age?; SIH
SMITH, JOHN—19; Mustered
WAGNER, MARTIN—22; Mustered

Before Petersburg: June 21, 1864

WHITE, JOHN—29; Mustered

Weldon Railroad: June 22, 1864

BEHAUS, FREDERICK—19; Disability
CONNELLY, PETER—22; Mustered
KALVOSKY, JOHN—29; Disability
KUTZELMANN, LORENZ—21; Mustered
LEOPOLD, FREDERICK—21; SIH
LESTER, JOHN—19; Disability
SIEVERS, HERMANN—24; Mustered

Weldon Railroad: June 23, 1864

Weldon Railroad: June 27, 1864

Near Petersburg: July 27, 1864

McNARY, JOHN—30; Recovered

Strawberry Plain: August 14, 1864

CARROLL, MARTIN—21; Mustered
FAIRCHILD, BENJAMIN—26; Mustered
=STUCKE, GEORGE—23; Mustered
WELSH, JOHN—34; Discharged

Deep Bottom: August 20, 1864

HORNIA, CELESTINO—21; WIA 2nd Time, Deserted from Hospital

Reams Station: August 25, 1864

FREDERICKS, WILLIAM—19; Mustered
MULLER, URBAN—23; Mustered
MURPHY, PATRICK—21; Mustered
=WYCKOFF, JAMES G. S.—age?; Discharged

Fort Sedgwick: October 27, 1864

LAMMERS, JOHN—19; WIA 2nd Time, Disability

White Oak Ridge: March 31, 1865

EISERHARDT, HUGO—26; Discharged
McCOY, JOHN—25; NR
SCHUTZ, NICHOLAUS—20; Mustered

Farmville, Va.: April 2, 1865

DELGARDO, PHILIP—21; Mustered from Hospital
DURAND, PIERRE—29; Mustered from Hospital
EMHARDT, ALBERT—17; Mustered from Hospital
MUNZ, SIMON—21; WIA 2nd Time, Mustered from Hospital

Farmville, Va.: April 7, 1865

HIRLINGER, WILLIAM L.—30; Mustered

WOUNDED—NO DATE

DEAN, STEPHAN—26; Deserted 3/22/1865
=EDELMAN, LOUIS—31; Disability
=RIEGE, LOUIS—33; Discharged
SOUTHINE, MANUEL—22; SIH
STAHL, CHARLES—22; Mustered
STORYZERK, WENZEL—25

CAPTURED IN ACTION—DIED IN CONFEDERATE PRISONS:

+ALTENBORND, EDWARD—19; Died of Scurvy 9/1/1864 Andrv
+ANDERSON, SVEN JOHAN—24; Died of Gangrene 9/16/1864 Andrv
+ANTLER, F.—age?; Died of Scurvy 12/1/1864 Andrv
+BARNUM, H.—age?; Died of Scurvy 9/10/1864 Andrv
+BAUMANN, HENRY—27; Died of Scurvy 9/11/1864 Andrv
+BELL, JOHN—22; Died of Diarrhea 9/16/1864 Andrv
+BERGENFELD, LUDWIG—19; Died 4/1/1865 Andrv
+BROWER, JOHN—33; Died of Diarrhea 8/9/1864 Andrv
+BROWN, CHARLES—21; Died of Scurvy 11/10/1864 Andrv
+BROWN, CHARLES—40; Died Date Unknown Andrv
+BROWN, HENRY—44; Died of Scurvy 3/23/1865 Andrv
+CARBORIUS, W.—age?; Died of Diarrhea 9/8/1864
+CHAPPELL, ALPHONZO—19; Died of Enteritis 8/16/1864 Andrv
+CRUESIUS, FREDERICK—28; Died of Typhus 9/10/1864 Andrv
+CUMMING, JOHN—19; Died Date Unknown Andrv
+DITTMAR, JOHN H.—38; Died 9/18/1864 Andrv
+DOOLEY, PATRICK—19; Died 6/?/1864 Andrv
+ENGEL, WILHELM—21; Died of Scurvy 8/18/1864 Andrv
+FERGUSON, MICHAEL—19; Died of Diarrhea 9/1/1864 Andrv
+FISCHER, LORENZ—24; Died of Scurvy 10/14/1864 Andrv
+FRACKIN, JOSEPH—34; Died of Scurvy 9/24/1864 Andrv
+FRIEE, CARL—22; Died of Scurvy 8/24/1864 Andrv
+GAISER, CARL—21; Died of Diarrhea 9/5/1864 Andrv
+GARBARINI, VINCENZO—27; Died 9/7/1864 Andrv
+HAAG, CHRISTIAN—27; Died Date Unknown Andrv
+HARRICK, LEWIS CHARLES—25; Died Date Unknown Andrv
+HAYES, JAMES—28; CIA No Date; Died of Scurvy 10/14/1864 Andrv
+HEMILRICK, JOHN—26; Died 1/15/1865 Andrv
+HERRICK, CHARLES—age?; Died of Scurvy 8/1/1864 Andrv
+HESKELL, ALBERT—20; CIA No Date; Died of Diarrhea 10/12/1864 Andrv
+HOWARD, WILLIAM—32; Died of Diarrhea 7/31/1864 Andrv
+KEHRIG, CASPAR—37; Died 8/1/1864 Andrv
+KLAIBER, CARL—30; Died 3/11/1864 Thdr Cstl, Richmond
+KOLBATZ, WILLIAM—38; Died of Diarrhea 8/29/1864 Andrv
+LANGENBACHER, JOSEPH—22; Died of Fever Typhus 6/8/1864 Andrv
+LATHROP, CHARLES—21; Died 1/6/1865 Slsbry
+LAUGIN, A.—age?; Died of Diarrhea 9/30/1864 Andrv
+LEHMAN, AUGUST—43; Died of Diarrhea 8/22/1864 Andrv
+LINNE, AUGUST—42; Died 7/19/1864 Andrv
+MARK, JACOB—age?; Died of Diarrhea 10/13/1864 Andrv
+MARTIN, JAMES—26; No Date; Died of Diarrhea 12/3/1864 Andrv
+McCORMACK, PETER—27; Died of Diarrhea 5/28/1864 Andrv

+McDONALD, JAMES—24; Died 12/18/1864 Richmond, Va.

+McFADDEN, JAMES—42; Died of Dysentery 7/26/1864 Andrv

+MEEK, CHRISTOPHER—21; Died of Diarrhea 7/30/1864 Andrv

+MEINHARDT, CHARLES—28; Died of Scurvy 10/27/1864 Andrv

+MESSING, FRANZ—39; Died 9/16/1864 Andrv

+MEYER, HEINRICH—34; CIA/Died after 9/9/1864 Andrv

+MILLER, JACOB—38; Died 8/13/1864 Andrv

+MONTAG, GEORGE—29; Died of Scurvy 7/8/1864 Andrv

+MOORE, DAVID—25; Died 9/4/1864 Andrv

+MOORE, JOHN—28; Died of Dysentery 9/10/1864 Andrv

+MURRAY, ALEXANDER—21; CIA No Date; Died of Scurvy 9/16/1864 Andrv

+NILSON, BERNHARD—25; Died of Diarrhea 6/27/1864 Andrv

+O'NEIL, JOHN—19; Died of Scurvy 10/24/1864 Andrv

+PERRY, ALFRED—35; Died of Scurvy 10/9/1864 Andrv

+PLEIN, MATHIAS—21; Died 1/?/1865 Andrv

+POSSER, PAUL—23; Died of Scurvy 10/5/1864 Andrv

+REILLY, JOHN—21; Died of Diarrhea 8/21/1864 Andrv

+REIMBACK, CHRISTIAN—22; Died 8/29/1864 Andrv

+RICE, THOMAS—21; Died of Diarrhea 7/30/1864 Andrv

+ROBINSON, HENRY—35; Died of Diarrhea 10/16/1864 Andrv

+ROMANY, CHRISTIAN—26; CIA; Died 2/19/1864 Richmond

+ROTH, LUDWIG—35; Died of Scurvy 8/9/1864 Andrv

+RYAN, JAMES M.—27; Died of Diarrhea 8/18/1864 Andrv

+SCHNEIDER, CHARLES—35; Died 8/11/1864 Andrv

+SCHNELL, CARL—21; Died 10/5/1864 Charleston, S.C.

+SCHWARTZ, MICHAEL—39; CIA No Date; Died 10/30/1864 Slsbry

+SCHWIEGER, ALOIS—27; Died of Scurvy 10/9/1864 Andrv

+SIEBERT, ANDREAS—26; Died 1/16/1865 Slsbry

+SIEBERT, JOHN—26; Died 10/28/1864 Slsbry

+SINGER, ANDRE—21; Died 9/29/1864 Andrv

+SMAKA, JOHN—22; Died of Diarrhea 9/23/1864 Andrv

+STADER, CHARLES—21; Died of Scurvy 8/2/1864 Andrv

+STEINHAL, BALDES—30; Died 10/18/1864 Slsbry

+STEPHAN, JACOB—age?; Died 2/3/1865 Charleston, S.C.

+STUZMAN, PHILIP—25; Died of Disease 8/17/1864 Andrv

+THIERBACH, OTTO—35; Died of Typhus 8/17/1864 Andrv

+THOMPSON, JAMES—44; Died 9/23/1864 Andrv

+THOMPSON, JOHN—22; Died of Diarrhea 8/25/1864 Andrv

+THURM, JEAN—29; CIA 8/20/1864; Died ? Andrv

+UNTERGRUBER, MARTIN—27; Died 9/22/1864 Danville, Va.

+WALSH, JOHN—31; Died of Diarrhea 9/8/1864 Andrv

+WEGNER, CARL—33; Died of Diarrhea 6/16/1864 Andrv

+WHITNEY, JOHN—34; Died of Diarrhea 8/31/1864 Andrv

+ZEINER, AUGUST—23; Died 10/11/1864 Andrv
+ZENZ, JOSEPH E.—30; Died 2/16/1865 Slsbry

CAPTURED IN ACTION—SENT TO CONFEDERATE PRISONS

NO RECORD:

BERNARD, FREDERICK—20; CIA 5/10/1864; NR
BERRY, A.—age?; CIA 6/22/1864; NR
BOGART, DAVID—38; CIA 5/6/1864; NR
CELESTE, GEOFFREY—19; CIA 8/25/1864; NR
COURIER, ANDREW—21; CIA 5/10/1864; NR
GUERSKEY, JOHN—32; CIA 2/6/1864; NR
HEINER, HERRMANN—28; CIA 5/10/1864; NR
KELLER, GEORGE—40; CIA 5/22/1864; NR
LOUNSBURY, CALVIN—18; CIA 6/21/1864; NR
McDEVITT, ALEXANDER—age?; CIA 5/6/1864; NR
MOFFAT, WILLIAM—20; CIA 6/21/1864; NR
NELSON, CHARLES—28; CIA 5/6/1864; NR
ROLY, LEON—32; CIA 5/6/1864; NR
SCHRIEBER, MORITZ—31; CIA 5/6/1864; NR
SCHMITZ, WILH—27; CIA 5/10/1864; NR
SMITH, THOMAS—20; CIA 5/10/1864; NR
THROM, WENDELIN—21; CIA 5/10/1864; NR
WALZ, PHILIPP—30; CIA 2/16/1864; NR
WHITE, MILTON—32; CIA 8/25/1864; NR
WILCOX, HENRY—21; CIA 2/6/1864; NR
WILSON, THOMAS—27; CIA 5/6/1864; NR

MUSTER ROLL OF THE 39TH NEW YORK VOLUNTEER INFANTRY REGIMENT, THE GARIBALDI GUARD

The Garibaldi Guard's muster rolls list a total of 2,282 men and officers. The official number of dead reported was 278 officers and men: 107 men and 8 officers killed or dead of wounds in action, 2 dead of accidents in camp, 1 dead of murder, and 158 men and 1 officer dead of disease. The regiment's international origins and yesteryear's record-keeping, imprecise by today's standards, were a challenge to overcome, but to the best of the author's knowledge, this is the regiment's complete muster roll. Identifiable errors found in cross references were corrected. The names of cities, counties, and states of origin were copied exactly as they appeared in the original muster rolls. Writing that became, or was, illegible is identified by ellipsis (...). When no place of origin was given, the soldier was listed according to the ethnic company in which he first enlisted in May 1861.

Company A, the 1st or Italian company, originally led by Captain Caesar Osnaghi.
Company B, the 2nd or Swiss company, originally led by Captain Joseph De Schmidt.
Company C, the 3rd or German company, originally led by Captain Charles Schwarz.
Company D, the 4th or Spanish company, originally led by Captain Joseph Torrens.
Company E, the 5th or German company, originally led by Captain John Siegel.
Company F, the 6th or German company, originally led by Captain Charles Wiegand.
Company G, the 7th or Hungarian company, originally led by Captain Franz Takacs (Takats).
Company H, the 8th or German company, originally led by Captain A. Otto Bernstein.
Company I, the 9th or German company, originally led by Captain A. H. Von Unwerth.
Company K, the 10th or French company, originally led by Captain Louis Tassillier.

LEGEND:

=	Officer rank
*	Deserted
+	Killed or died
#	Something of added interest--e.g., ex-Garibaldini, member of the German Revolution of 1848
Andrv	Andersonville, Georgia prisoner of war camp
Slsbry	Salisbury, North Carolina prisoner of war camp
Thdr Cstl	Thunder Castle prisoner of war camp in Richmond, Virginia
aka	Also Known As
CIA/PAR	Captured in action and paroled
CIA/POW	Captured in action and imprisoned (prisoner of war)
CO?	Unassigned
DOD	Died of disease
DOW	Died of wound
KIA	Killed in action
NR	No Record
REV	Revolution
SIH	Sick in the hospital at the time of muster
VRC	Unfit for duty, transferred to the Veteran Reserve Corps
WIA	Wounded in action

EXAMPLE:

(1)   (2)   (3)   (4)   (5)   (6)

+   **CRUESIUS, Frederick**—28; Baden, Germany; Baker; WIA/Recovered, CIA/POW Andrv/DOD

(1) The soldier was killed or died (+)
(2) His name: Last, First, any Initial
(3) His age
(4) His birthplace; nothing is stated ·if only the state, province, or country of origin was given.
(5) His peacetime occupation
(6) In this section and instance, the soldier's wartime fate: he was wounded in action (WIA), recovered, and then later captured in action and imprisoned in the Andersonville prisoner of war camp (CIA/POW Andrv), where he died of disease (DOD). This section might include aliases, other military unit affiliations, or the like.

Alsace Lorraine

DIETRICH, AUGUST—21; Reineim; Gilder; Mustered out
JACKY, MICHAEL—29; Muhlhausen; Musician; Mustered out
MUMPHIR, ANTON—21; Alace, France; Laborer; WIA, Mustered out
+SCHAEFER, GEORGE—23; Biesch; Shoemaker

Argentina

SAMANIEGE, JOSE—27; Buenos Aries; Sailor; Mustered out

Armenia

SPIER, FREDERICK—24; Posiaria; Cigarmaker; WIA/VRC

Austria

GSELL, FERDINAND—34; Bregenz; Goldsmith; aka GERSELL, WIA/CIA, NR
    after Wilderness 5/6/1864
SESSLER, FRANZ—27; Soldier; aka FRANCES ZESSLER; WIA, Mustered out
SIETZ, FRANK—19; Sailor; aka SEITZ, Mustered out

Bavaria

ACKERMANN, GEORGE—30; Willendorf; Cooper; VRC
BECKER, JACOB—23; Stutte; Painter; WIA, Mustered out
BERNARD, FREDRICK—20; Bamberg; Locksmith-Bootmaker-Teacher; CIA, NR
BLUM, GEORGE—24; Duezenbach; Locksmith; Mustered out
BOLENDER, PHILIP—19; Shoemaker; Von Unwerth German Co., Mustered out
BURGER, FRIEDRICH—24; Boldzinger; Clerk; CIA/PAR Mustered out
CORRELL, FREDERICK—31; Boldzinger; Clerk; Mustered out
*DAMM, CHARLES—20; Rumback; Swiss Co.; Cigarmaker
+DEGAN, ADELBERT—26; Tailor; aka DAGAN; WIA/DOW
+DUBOIS, JOSEPH—20; Clerk; DOD
EISENAUER, CHARLES—37; Nuremberg; Shoemaker; Mustered out
ELL, FREDERICK—29; Furth; Brewer; Mustered out
ELLBRICK, FREDERICK—29; Asselheim; Locksmith; Mustered out
*ERB, LUDWIG—22; Wernarz; Carpenter
+FISCHER, JOHN—25; Kathosburg; Farmer
+FISCHER, LORENZ—24; Nuremberg; Shoemaker; CIA/POW Andrv
FREMCHEN, JACOB—24; Milbrach; Engineer; aka FROENCHEN, Mustered out
GEIB, PETER—32; Roissthal; Tailor; Siegel Co.; WIA, Mustered out
GELB, JOHN—21; Durheim; Carver; Wiegand German Co., WIA, Mustered out
*GOLDBACH, BERNHARD—29; Peddler; WIA
+HAAG, CHRISTIAN—27; Tinbach; Tailor; CIA/POW Andrv

HAMAUG, HENRY J.—24; Kaiserslautern; Miller; NR
+HEIMBUCHER, IGNATZ—35; Boskbrun; Baker; aka HUMBUCKER
HIPP, HEINRICH—24; Kaiserslautern; Miller; Mustered out
HOFFMAN, ALBERT—34; Wurzburg; Porter; Siegel German Co., WIA/CIA
JUNG, ADAM—25; Hitchenhausen; Tinsmith; Bernstein German Co., aka JOUNG, WIA/VRC
KISSMANN, ADOLPH—28; Hamburg; Baker; Von Unwerth German Co., VRC
KOHNLEIN, GEORG—34; Leap...; Shoemaker; Bernstein German Co., WIA/VRC
KRAUSE, JOSEPH—27; Nurtingen; Tailor; Von Unwerth German Co., Mustered out
KULLMER, GEORGE—19; Brockenheim; Baker; aka KOLMER
LAUTENBACH, NICOLAUS—24; Bruckenau; Carpenter; Unwerth Co., Transferred to 13th Artillery, Rejoined Garibaldi Guard, Mustered out
*LEUTZ, GABRIEL—27; Nuremburg; Machinist; Schwarz Co., aka LEITZ & LUTZ
MOLTER, JOHN—24; Innsbruch; Varnisher; CIA/PAR, Mustered out
NOBINGER, JOSEPH—25; Binswangen; Shoemaker; Siegel Co., Mustered out
PLATZ, MICHAEL—32; Maykamer; Varnisher; Schwarz German Co., VRC
POSSER, PAUL—23; Wurzburg; Varnisher; Wiegand German Co.
+SCHNEIDER, CHARLES—35; Donnsiedes; Shoemaker; Schwarz Co., CIA/POW Andrv
+STADER, CHARLES—21; Numberg; Clerk; Schwarz Co., CIA/DOD Andrv
THORM, WENDELIN—21; Tailor; aka THROM, THRUMM & TROMM, CIA, NR after Wilderness 5/6/1864
ULSIMER, JOSEPH—23; Gchsonford; Tailor; WIA/CIA
+WEBER, JULIUS—30; Turner
WECHSLER, JOHN—29; Pappenheim; Brewer; Bernstein German Co., aka WECHLER, Mustered out
+WERNER, MICHAEL—21; Innsbruch; Cabinetmaker; Bernstein Co.
WOELFEL, GEORG—25; Bayreuth; Miller; Wiegand German Co., aka WOLFEL, WIA, Mustered out
ZANG, ALEXANDER—33; Aschaffenburg; VRC
ZWITZLER, VALENTINE—40; Zeisram; Mason; Disability

Belgium

BEAUDOIR, JEAN—38; aka JOHN BAUDOIN, NR
FREPON, EMIL—age?; Brussels; Clerk; aka FRAIPONT, WIA/SIH
GERLACHER, ANTON—42; aka GORLACHER; Disability
*HAMMEL, FRANK—22; Seaman; SIH
ROLAND, CHARLES—28; Blacksmith; SIH
SAALMANN, JOHANN—36; Luxembourg, Belgium; Fireman; aka JOHN SAHLMANN & JOHN SALMAN, VRC

SCHEEPSMA, ANTON—21; Anivers; Sailor; WIA, NR after Wilderness 5/5/1864
SIENEMUS, HIERN—23; Muhlenrade, Luxembourg; Sailor; Wiegand Co., aka
SENEMUS & SINEMUS, Mustered out
+THURM, JEAN—29; Luxembourg, Belgium; Cigarmaker; French Co., CIA/POW
Andrv

Bohemia

HORACK, WILLIAM—32; Slovak; Disability
KLOSTER, FREDERICK—35; Siegel Co., Disability
KLOSTER, FREDERICK—32; Italian Co., NR
POPP, GEORGE—26; Slavic; Von Unwerth German Co., transferred to 15th Artillery
REZROTH, GEORGE—30; Koningratz; Smith; aka REXROTH, Mustered out
RIEDEL, LOUIS—32; Bohemia-Czech; WIA/SIH
=RIEGE, LOUIS—33; Bohemia-Czech; Wiegand German Co., WIA, Discharged
RUDOLPH, JACOB—25; Bohemia-Czech; Bernstein German Co., Disability
RUDOLPH, JOHN B. & H.—22; Bohemia-Czech; Wiegand German Co., Discharged
STORYZERK, WENZEL—25; Bohemia-Czech; aka STUBBYUKE, STUBBEJOKE,
WIA
WEISE, CARL JACOB—27; Bohemia-Czech; aka CHARLES WEISS, SIH/NR
ZEMAN, JOSEPH—23; Bohemia-Czech; Wagoner; aka ZEHMAN, Mustered out

Baden

#BAUER, JOHN—33; Mannheim, Baden, Germany; Insane; Exile 1848 REV,
Mustered out
BOEHLER, ALBERT—25; Baden, Germany; Laborer; Dishonorably Discharged
BRADLEY, RALPH—21; Sailor; WIA/VRC
+CRUESIUS, FREDERICK—28; Baden, Germany; Baker; WIA, Recovered CIA/
POW Andrv/DOD
+ECKERT, ANTON—22; Bruckneau; Brewer; aka ERHARDT, WIA, Returned to
Ranks While Still Wounded, KIA 5/18/64
*FREY, CARL—25; Tecrach; Farmer; Schwarz German Co.; aka FRIEE
+FRIEE, CARL—22; CIA/POW Andrv
+GAISER, Carl—21; Rastede; Cabinetmaker; Wiegand Co.; aka CHARLES
GUSER, CIA/POW Andrv
GEHRHART, GEORGE—19; Baden, Germany; Musician; Mustered out
*HARTMAN, JOHN—35; Aber...; Musician
HERR, ADOLPH—23; Emmedongon; Clerk; aka HEER, Mustered out
JENTER, WILLIAM—32; Starbach; Baker; Mustered out
+KAMMERER, CLEMENS—28; Thiengen; Cabinetmaker; Siegel Co.
+KALL, PETER—20; Baden, Germany; Laborer; DOD
KOHLER, FRANZ—32; Rip...; Laborer; WIA, Mustered out
KUTTRUFF, JACOB—20; Dillingen; Clerk; Bernstein German Co., aka KUTRUPP,
Mustered out

+LANGENBACHER, JOSEPH—22; Lasbach; Farmer; aka ALLENBERGER & LONGENBACKER, CIA/POW Andrv

LEIBOLD, CHARLES—22; Mannheim; Musician-Cavalryman; NR

MAJER, ALBERT—19; Baker; aka MAIER; WIA/SIH

MAYER, WILHELM—30; Goringen; Tailor; Von Unwerth German Co., Mustered out

OHLENGER, JOHN—38; Reisgner; Shoemaker; Mustered out

QUATLAENDER, JOHN—19; Baden; Cabinetmaker; Wiegand German Co., Mustered out

REIMLING, FRANZ—33; Brusland; Shoemaker; Bernstein German Co., aka REMTING, WIA/VRC

+REINBOLD, PETER—32; Farnholdt; Baker; Siegel Co.

+ROTH, LUDWIG—35; Karlsrauche; Blacksmith; Schwarz German Co. CIA/POW Andrv DOD

ROTHWEILER, AUGUST—31; Bergenhausen; Cabinetmaker; Bernstein German Co., WIA/VRC

SCHMID, HEINRICH—21; Baden, Germany; Seaman; Swiss Co., Disability

SCHMIDT, LOUIS—26; Heidenberg; Clerk; Wiegand German Co., WIA

SCHMITT, HENRY—23; Baden, Germany; aka SMITH, Mustered out

STAHL, CHARLES—22; Auerbach; Tailor; Schwarz German Co., WIA, Mustered out

STANDINGER, JACOB—24; Uttenau; Butcher; Bernstein German Co., Mustered out

+STUZMAN, PHILIP—25; Karls Brucke; Clerk; Swiss Co., CIA/DOD Andrv

+THIERBACH, OTTO—35; Rastadt; Shoemaker; Wiegand German Co., CIA/POW Andrv

WAGNER, JOSEPH—36; Burkall; Clerk; WIA, Mustered out

WALTER, JOHN—29; Heidelberg; Tailor; Bernstein German Co., VRC

+WALZER, CHARLES—33; Baden, Germany; Ironmolder

ZELLER, HENRY—31; Krotzingern; Baker; Siegel Co., Mustered out

ZIEGLER, GEORGE—31; Stebbach; Von Unwerth German Co., aka DANIEL ZIEGELER, Disability

Brandenburg

=#BAUER, ADOLF—30; Bernau; Attorney; Exile 1848 REV; CIA/PAR, Mustered out

Breslingberg

BEHRENDS, OTTO—29; Breslingberg, Germany; Farmer; Bernstein German Co., Mustered out

Canada

BACHELOR, PETER—21; Farmer; Mustered out
+BACKLER, LEWIS—35; New Brunswick; Farmer; aka WILLIAM BACKEN, CIA/PAR/DOD
BEAN, JOSEPH S—21; Farmer; Mustered out
BELDEN, WILLIAM J.—29; Farmer; Mustered out
BLUTEAU, GUILLAUME—22; French Co.; aka BLUTO, SIH
BRACE, ERASKIN H.—28; Farmer; Mustered out
BRITNENY, WILLIAM—24; St. Johns, New Brunswick; Tailor; VRC
BROWN, JOHN—33; New Brunswick; Tailor; Disability
BROWN, WILLIAM—19; Clerk; SIH
BUTLER, PETER—32; Newfoundland; Seaman; Mustered out
DION, LOUIS—28; Clerk; WIA/CIA/PAR
DURYEA, PATRICK—36; Laborer; Mustered out
FLETCHER, RALPH—21; Quebec; Sailor; WIA/SIH
KECK, SAMUEL—26; Laborer; Mustered out
KYLE, HUGH M.—41; Farmer; Mustered out
LABUTE, MITCHELL—23; Chatam; Laborer; Mustered out
LA FLEUR, ALEXANDER—31; Laborer; WIA/CIA/PAR, Disability
+LAIN, ALFRED B.—42; Farmer; WIA/DOW
LORIN, JEREMID 29; St. Martin; Walter; French Co., WIA/VRC
McMAHAN, HARLAND—18; Farmer; Co. F, NR
*MOREAU, CHARLES—20; Painter; French Co.
OSBORNE, ROBERT—23; St. John, Newfoundland; Tinsmith; SIH
SPRATT, SILAS CYRUS—29; Bay of Fundy; Ships Captain; WIA/CIA/PAR
*TUHATE, JOSEPH—18; Toronto; French Co., Reenlisted and Deserted at End of Veteran Furlough
WELCH, JAMES—19; Farmer; Mustered out

Chili

ARELLANO, JOSE—22; Santiago, Chili; Sailor; Mustered out
GONZALEZ, JUAN—27; Cella; Sailor; Spanish Co., Reenlisted and Deserted at End of Veteran Furlough

Cuba

FERNANDEZ, DE SANTIAGO—23; Sailor; Spanish Co., aka JAMES LEE, French Naval Deserter, Discharged 3/25/1864
HERANDEZ, JUAN—23; San Juan Dela Manero; Sailor; aka HERNADER, WIA/SIH
PIS, FELIPE—21; Sanlago; Cigarmaker; Mustered out

Darmstadt

+BONIN, GEORGE—32; Echenbricken; Farmer; Unwerth Co.

=DELL, GEORGE—39; Eichelheim; Weaver; Schwarz German Co., aka DOELL, WIA, Mustered out

DUNGSTADTER, LOUIS—19; Grapernau; Baker; aka LUDWIG TUNGSTELLER, CIA/PAR, Mustered out

HARTLEY, WILLIAM—19; Ardenheim; Carver; Spanish Co., aka HARTLEY, WIA, Mustered out

HESS, ADOLPH—29; Bingm...; Clerk; Von Unwerth German Co., aka HEGS, ADOLPH, Mustered out

HOTTES, WILHELM MICHAEL—25; Simmerw; Brewer; Von Unwerth German Co., Mustered out

KEIL, PETER—21; Averbach; Cigarmaker; Mustered out

KIEHL, JACOB—30; Offenbach; Stonecutter; Wiegand German Co., Mustered out

KOCH, HEINRICH—25; Alsfeld; Shoemaker; Hungarian Co., Mustered out

KROEBER, ALFRED—22; Michelstadt; Confectioner; Wiegand German Co., WIA, Mustered out

KUTZELMANN, LORENZ—21; Steinheim Hesson; Sugarmaker; WIA, Mustered out

LUBRAND, FRANZ—20; Marniz; Baker; Wiegand German Co., aka FRANZ LUBRAND, Mustered out

MAUS, MARTIN—25; Captilahem; Carnert; aka LOUIS MAUS, CIA/PAR, Mustered out

+MEINHARDT, CHARLES—28; Mainz; Baker; Bernstein German Co., CIA/DOD Andrv

MENZEL, CARL—21; Echonbrinke; Farmer; WIA, Disability

NOS, ADAM—31; Baker; Mustered out

PFEIFFER, JOSEPH—22; Tailor; Von Unwerth German Co., CIA/PAR, Mustered out

ROTHAAR, MICHAEL—39; Opwuheim; Cabinetmaker; Bernstein German Co., aka JOHANN, VRC

ROTTHAAR, JOHN—23; Opwheim; Brewer; Bernstein German Co., VRC

SCHAEFER, ERNEST—22; Giessen; Tailor; Wiegand German Co., aka CHARLES SCHAEFER, Mustered out

SCHNEIDER, JOHN—35; Bingard; Farmer; NR

SCHWAMM, JACOB—28; Tankheim; Farmer; Schwarz German Co., Mustered out

SEIFERT, ALBERT—21; Maurz; Baker; WIA, Disability

STELLAMANN, THEODOR—19; Neustadt; Carver; Schwarz German Co., Mustered out

UNVERZAGT, WILLIAM—22; Reidenkopf; Blacksmith; Siegel Co., WIA, Mustered out

WEIHRAUCH, LEONARD—23; Worms; Plumber; Schwarz German Co., aka WEYRAUCH, Mustered out

Denmark

FREDERICKSON, FREDERICK C.—20; Sailor; Mustered out
GOSCH, CARL—34; Rendsburg; Shoemaker; VRC
HAUSEN, CHRISTIAN—21; Friederioria; Merchant; VRC
*NELSON, CHRISTIAN—28; Soldier; WIA
+REIMBACK, CHRISTIAN—22; Blacksmith; aka RHEIMBERG, CIA/POW
  Andrv
THOMPSON, JOHN—25; Copenhagen; Seaman; WIA/SIH

England

ALLEN, JAMES—20; Sailor; 12/1863, Navy
BALONES, WILLIAM—28; Druggist Enlisted 12/1863
+BELL, JOHN—22; Druggist; Enlisted 1/1864; CIA/POW Andrv
=BENNETT, GEORGE—age?; London; Hungarian Co., Dismissed
#BENNETT (2ND), WILLIAM—19; Sailor; 12/1863, CIA/Escaped, Mustered out
*BOW, JEREMIAH—20; Clerk/Plasterer/Sailor; 2/1863
BROWN, RICHARD—23; Clerk; 9/1864, Transferred to U.S. Navy
+BURNS, THOMAS H.—32; Lancaster; Clerk; 12/1863, aka THOMAS
  WARBURTON BARNES & BROWN
BURNS, WILLIAM—43; Lancaster; Clerk; 1/1864, VRC
BURTON, GEORGE—28; Seaman; 11/1863, Discharged
CALLEND, JAMES—23; Tailor; 11/1863, Mustered out
CLEMENTS, JAMES—22; Sailor; 9/1864, Mustered out
CONNER, JOHN—28; Laborer; 12/1863, Disability
CONNORS, WILLIAM—22; Confectioner; 12/1863, Mustered out
CROSS, HENRY—20; Liverpool; Sailor/Artist; Co. I 1863, Disability
CROWELL, WILLIAM—21; London; Servant; 9/1863, VRC
+ETHERIDGE, GEORGE B.—33; Engineer; 12/1863, CIA/POW Andrv
EVANS, GEORGE—42; Bookkeeper; 2/1864, Disability
*FRELL, CHARLES—21; Liverpool; Seaman; 11/1863, WIA
*HAMILTON, JOHN—27; Laborer; 12/1863
HARPER, THOMAS—19; Farmer; 9/1864, Mustered out
HARRIS, ALFRED E.—24; Cooper; 9/1864, Transferred to 185th Infantry
+HARRISON, JOHN—19; Liverpool; Laborer; CIA/POW Andr
*HOGAN, JAMES—31; Printer; 12/1863, SIH
HOGNER, LOUIS—21; London; Printer; Hungarian Co., NR
+HOOK, WILLIAM S.—25; Kent; Carpenter; 11/1863
+HOWARD, WILLIAM—32; Farmer; 12/1863, CIA/POW Andrv DOD
*HURSTWOOD, DAVID—33; Teamster; 12/1863, aka HERSTWOOD &
  HIRSTWOOD
JONES, WILLIAM—44; Blacksmith; 1/1865, Mustered out
*JONES, WILLIAM B.—28; Druggist; 12/1863

*KNOWLES, JOHN—35; Carpenter; 1/1864
LAMBERT, JOHN V.—21; Basketmaker; 12/1863, SIH
McGRANDLES, SEMRAN—21; Liverpool; Laborer; 11/1864, aka SAMUEL
   McGRANVELLS, VRC
*MOORE, WILLIAM—31; Printer; 12/1863
*NICHOLS, THOMAS—20; London; Warehouseman; 11/1863
*O'CONNER, JOHN—28; Laborer; 12/1863
O'KEEFE, JOHN—20; London; Clerk; 12/1863
+OSBORNE, EDMUND—21; Bristoe; Sailor; 11/1863, aka EDMUND GOULD,
   CIA/POW Andrv
+PERRY, ALFRED—35; Mechanic; 12/1863, CIA/POW Andrv
+REED, WILLIAM—31; Sailor & Boatmaker; 1/1864
+REED, WILLIAM I.—29; Soldier; 12/1863
+ROBINSON, HENRY—35; Sailor; 12/1863, CIA/POW Andrv
SCARFE, JAMES T.—31; Soldier; 12/1863, CIA/PAR
SMITH, GEORGE—43; Machinist; 11/1863, Discharged
SMITH, SAMUEL—22; Clerk; 12/1863, Discharged
TIPPING, WILLIAM—34; London; Seaman; 11/1863, CIA
WALLACE, JOHN—19; London; Sailor; 11/1863, WIA, Disability
WARRELL, SAMUEL—23; Liverpool; Sailor; 12/1863, WIA, Disability
WEST, PETER—21; London; Seaman; 11/1863, WIA, SIH
WILCOX, HENRY—21; Sailor; 12/1863, CIA, NR
WORTHINGTON, EDWARD—24; Suffolk; Mechanic; 9/1864, Mustered out

France

ALSTERS, JEAN—40; French Co., NR
ANTOINE, JOHN—28; Seaman; Co.?, CIA, Mustered out
AUBREY, JOSEPH—40; French Co., Disability
AVENEL, AUGUSTE—32; Co.?, NR
+BACON, BAPTISTE—41; Soldier; CIA/POW Slsbry
BADOYE, BENJAMIN 39; French Co., Disability
*BAISE, BENOIR—23; French Co.
+BARRY, HONORE—33; Rouen; Clerk
BARTHOLOMIE, HENRY—39; French Co., Disability
BEAUFITS, LOUIS—33; French Co., Disability
BEAUMONT, LOUIS—19; French Co., NR
BEERSTRECJER, OSCAR—19; French Co., Disability
BELRINGER, FREDERIC—32; Strasburg; Sailor; French Co., aka FRITZ
   BALSINGER, WIA/SIH
BERVIL, MARTIN—24; Sailor; aka BAERRILLE, Mustered out
*BLOCK, THEODORE—29; Bonneville; Clerk
BLONDEAU, HENRY—18; French Co., NR
BOBIE, LEWIS—35; Tailor; Transferred to Headquarters, D.C.

*BODLET, BAPTISTE—age?; French Co.
BODLET, JEAN—30; French Co.; Dropped from Regiment
*BOELL, JEAN—19; French Co.; Upholsterer; Deserted 8/31/1861
BOLTE, FREDERIC—38 Leud...; Locksmith; Mustered out
BORRER, CHARLES—23; Co.?, NR
BOULAY, DESIRE—34; French Co.; Disability
*BRIGHT, JAQUES—23; French Co., deserted 6/5/1862, CIA/PAR
BRIOT, CHARLES—24; WIA, Disability
BROUSSE, ERNEST—23; French Co., Dropped
BUFFLE, GERVAIS—37; French Co., NR
CAUMONT, EUGENE—23; Paris; Carpenter; Mustered out
*CAUMONT, JULES—19; French Co.
+CANON, JOSEPH—32; French Co.
CELESTE, GEOFFREY—19; Sailor; MIA
CHAPOUX, HENRY—22; Co.?, 1862, NR
#CHOOPHALL, HUGER—23; Cooker; Discharged--French Naval Deserter
COSTE, MARTIN—30; aka COSTER, CIA/PAR, Mustered out
COSTELLO, EMANUEL—50; Haveville; Sailor; CIA/PAR, Mustered out
CROISSANT, CHARLES—27; French Co., Disability
*CUNY, FRANCOIS—24; French Co.
DAHIS, FLORIAN—25; U.S. Soldier/Machinist; Disability
DAUPHINE, PIERRE—34; French Co., Disability
DE LABAUME, FELIX O.—age?; Soldier; MIA, Returned, Disability
DENIER, EMIL—22; Laborer; WIA, Disability
DESOUTER, JEAN—21; French Co., Disability
+#DIVERBOIS, EMIL—age?; French Co., Died 5/23/1861, First Casualty
*DUPONT, ANTON—24; Laborer
DURAND, PIERRE—29; Havre; Sailor; WIA
+FAUCHERON, LOUIS—38; French Co., KIA, 7/1861, Gettysburg
*FAVRE, LUCIAN—26; French Co., Deserted 10/3/1861
#FRANCOIS, PETER—32; Sailor; aka LOUIS MARIE BANIER & PIERRE, Dis-
    charged--French Naval Deserter
FROSSARD, ADOLPHE—22; French Co., SIH/NR
*FERON, SYLVAN—32; French Co., Deserted 7/30/1861
*FRECANT, ANTONE—29; French Co.
GAILLARD, DESIRE—40; Rouen; Mason; aka GUILLARD, VRC
GALLICO, GEORGE—40; French Co., SIH/NR
*GARTE, EMILE—37; French Co., Deserted 8/11/1861
GERARD, CHARLES—29; Versailles; Gardener; VRC
GERARD, JOSEPH—22; French Co., NR
GERARD, NICOLAS—24; French Co., aka GIRARD, Disability
GIRARDIN, EMILE—37; French Co., SIH/NR
*GRANDSIRE, JULES—18; French Co.
GRIMIAUX, LOUIS—32; French Co., NR

GULLY, WILLIAM—24; Wurhausen; Soldier; aka GHULLY, Disability
HAERTLING, GEORGES—26; French Co., Disability
HAUPTMAN, JOSEPH—30; Furkheim; Butcher; French Co., Mustered out
HENNOUT, NICHOL—34; French Co., WIA/CIA/PAR, Disability
HERR, ADOLPHE—23; French Co., Mustered out
*HEYER, ADOLPH PIERRE—24; French Co., Deserted 7/30/1861
*HOFFER, PHILLIPE—19; French Co., Deserted 8/31/1861
HUGLEY, FREDERIC—33; French Co., Disability
*HUOT, CHARLES—28; French Co.
JACHERESSE, DESIRE—22; French Co., aka SACHERESSE or VACHERESSE, NR
#JAQUES, JOHN—38; Soldier; aka JERVE PICAUD, Discharged--French Naval
    Deserter
JAVELLE, ALFRED—20; Gilder; WIA/VRC
+JUNKER, HENRY—30; Upholsterer
*KREMPFF, ANDRE—22; French Co., Deserted 8/31/1861
#*LACROIX, LOUIS—32; French Co., the First Man to Desert, 6/7/1861
#LAMBERT, GUSTAVE HERBULOT—age?; Co. I 1864; aka THEOPOLIUS
    HUGER, Discharged--French Naval Deserter
LANE, DESIRE J.—25; Shoemaker; SIH
*LANOIR, HENRY—37; French Co., Deserted 8/31/1861
LEONARD, JOSEPH—31; Lyons; Blacksmith; WIA, Disability
LEOPOLD, FREDERICK—21; Lyons; Laborer; WIA/SIH
*LEPRON, PAUL—30; Paris; Scriber; French Co.
LERICHE, BAPTISTE JOSEPH—39; French Co., Disability
=+LESIENE, VICTOR—37; French Co., aka LERIENE
+LOMBARD, BERNARD—41; Co. I 1863
#LOT, LOUIS—21; Grauvel; Laborer; aka LEAPOLD FREDERICK LAT & LOUIS
    L'HOTE, Discharged--French Naval Deserter
MANGE, ELIE—37; French Co., NR
*MANNIR, BASILE—21; French Co.; aka MONNIN, Deserted 10/3/1861
MARECHAL, JOSEPH—29; French Co., NR
#MARIE, AUGUST—22; Sailor; aka PAUL ORANGE, ANGEL, & LEOPOLD,
    Discharged--French Naval Deserter
MARTIN, ERNEST—37; French Co., NR
MARTIN, LOUIS—34; Musician; French Co., Disability
MARTIN, PETER—35; Sailor; Disability
MASSOR, LOUIS—41; French Co., NR
#*MESNIL, LOUIS JEAN—54; Besancon; Clerk; French Co., Oldest Man in the
    Regiment
MEZERY, EUGENE—30; French Co., Disability
*MOREAU, CHARLES—20; French Co., Deserted 10/3/1861
MORVAN, ANDRE—32; Bonrgogne; Butcher; SIH
+MOUSTON, AUGUSTE—19; French Co., aka MOUSTOR, WIA/CIA/DOW
MUNSCHE, BAPTISTE—24; French Co., NR

*NONNER, EUGENE—19; French Co., Deserted 7/30/1861
*OLIVIER, LOUIS—40; French Co.
OLIVRY, JUAN MARIE—age?; St. Malo; Sailmaker; French Co., aka ALVRY, WIA twice, Mustered out
ORTLIEB, FRANCOIS—22; Cook; Disability
PARIDAENS, JULES—28; Musician; French Co., NR
PFOTZER, GUILLAUME—36; French Co., aka WILLIAM PFOTZER, Mustered out
#PHILLIPS, JOHN—28; Sailor; aka ALEX BERNARD
PIERSON, JULIEN—34; French Co., Discharged--French Naval Deserter
*POISOT, CHARLES—39; French Co., Deserted 7/30/1861
=PUMAZER, ANTHONY—36; French Co., aka DUMAZER, Discharged
*QUERBACH, NICHOLAS—29; Taneguemines; Confectioner
RAETTER, JOHN—45; French Co., aka ROEDER, Mustered out
RICORD, JOHN B.—43; Laborer; aka RECORD, Disability
ROBERT, ANDRE—34; French Co., Transferred to 52nd Infantry
ROBERTH, JOSEPH—24; Bonneville; Watchmaker, Mustered out
ROBINET, ALEXIS—18; French Co., Disability
ROLY, LEON—32; Blacksmith; WIA/CIA, NR after Wilderness 5/6/1864
#ROSEY, CHARLES S.—41; Soldier; Discharged--French Naval Deserter
#ROUSSEAU, LOUIS—30; aka LEAPOLD FREDERICK L'HOTE & ROSEYROUE
*ROUSSELY, EDOUARD—18; French Co., Deserted 7/30/1861
SAYVD, GERMAIN—51, French Co., Discharged--French Naval Deserter, Not Apprehended
*SCHELLING, WILLIAM—23; French Co., Deserted 3/1862
+SCHWARTZ, MICHAEL—39; Hohenheim; Carpenter; French Co., aka SCHWARZ, CIA/POW Andrv
SCUREAU, FRANCOIS—37; French Co., Disability
SERVIE, JOSEPH—26; Clerk; aka AUGUST SERVIS, WIA, NR after Wilderness 5/6/1864
SPECKMAN, HENRY—33; Paris; Gardener; Disability
=TASSILLIER, LOUIS—39; French Co., Dishonorably Discharged
*THERNOR, FRANCOIS—39; French Co., Deserted 6/11/1861
*TREMBLAY, GUILIAUME—34; French Co., Deserted 7/30/1861
*TUHATE, JOSEPH—18; French Co.
=VIAL, FELIX—33; Paris; aka VAILLE, Mustered out
*VILLAUME, NICOLAS—29; French Co., Deserted 6/11/1861
*VOISIN, PIERRE—40; French Co., Deserted 7/30/1861
WALKIERS, BAPTISTE—38; French Co., Disability
WUSSEMBACH, JULIUS—24; French Co., NR
+ZENZ, JOSEPH E.—30; Quentin; Cabinetmaker; aka ZENTZ

Germany

ACHTER, LEWIS—age?; Wiegand German Co., aka JAMES, NR

=AIGNER, JOSEPH—27; Schwarz German Co., Discharged

BAACKE, ANDREW—18; Cigarmaker; aka BAACHE, Mustered out

BACK, CARL—21; Schwarz German Co., Disability

BACKBORN, FRIEDERICH—29; Schwarz German Co., NR

=BADER, MAGNUS—21; Siegel Co., Disability

BAERKEL, JACOB—31; Bernstein German Co., aka BIRKEL & BOERKEL, Mustered out

BANBEL, HENRY—26; Sailor, NR

BARGEBUHR, ADOLPH—19; Von Unwerth German Co., aka BAGEHOUHR, NR

BARISETTE, WILLIAM—21; Wiegand German Co., aka WILHELM BANSITTE, Discharged

BAUDE, JOSEPH—26; Siegel Co.; NR

BAUER, JOHN—33; Sold Liquors; Siegel Co., aka BAVER, Discharged, Insane

=BAUER, JOHN F.—35; Siegel German Co., Mustered out

BECK, GEORGE—19; Bernstein German Co., NR

BEHAUS, FREDERICK—19; Butcher; aka BEBHAUS, WIA, Disability

+BEHR, JACOB—23; Butcher; CIA/POW Slsbry

BENACK, HEINRICH—23; Wiegand German Co., aka BERMACK, Mustered out

BENNETT, WILLIAM—20; Clerk; WIA/VRC

BERGEN, GASTANE—26; Mechanic; WIA, Disability

BERGMANN, EMIL—25; Schwarz German Co., NR

=BERNSTEIN, A. OTTO—39; Captain; Bernstein German Co., Discharged

BERTRAM, ALBERT—21; Bootmaker; Siegel Co., NR

BEYER, HENRY—39; Laborer; Wiegand German Co., NR

BLAUKENFELT, FRANCIS—20; Soldier; Disability

BLOEM, GUSTAV—27; Von Unwerth German Co., CIA/PAR, Disability

BLUM, GEORGE G.—24; Musician/Tailor; Siegel German Co., Dropped from Roll

BOAS, EDWARD—41; Merchant; Schwarz German Co., Disability

BOCKER, HENRY—24; Siegel German Co., aka DOCKER, NR

BOEHNING, JULIUS—32; Schwarz German Co., aka BONING, Disability

BOHLICH, CARL—27; Wiegand German Co., Disability

#BOINER, JOHN F.—41; Merchant; Tallest Man at 6' 3", NR

BONER, CARL—28; Wiegand German Co., Mustered out

BORNKESSEL, HERRMANN—25; Bernstein German Co., NR

BOTGER, CLAUS—28; Bernstein German Co., aka BOETGER & BOETTCHER, Mustered out

+BOVIER, JOHN F.—33; Merchant; aka BROWER, CIA/DOD Andrv

+BRAIN, PHILIP—39; Darnsburg; Mechanic

BRANDUS, EUGENE—31; Wiegand German Co. 1862, Mustered out

BREITING, CARL—23; Schwarz German Co., aka CHARLES BRETTLING, WIA

=BREY, GEORGE—28; Von Unwerth German Co., aka BRAI, Dismissed

*#BRUDER, JOSEPH—20; Morris; Baker; Deserted at End of Veteran Furlough

BRUNZ, JOHN—28; Schwarz German Co., NR

BUCHOLZ, GUSTAV—23; Schwarz German Co., Disability
BUDDING, JULIUS—21; Von Unwerth German Co., aka BUDDIN, Disability
BUEHSING, ADOLPH—21; Schwarz German Co., Disability
*BUERKLE, ERNST—38; Bernstein German Co., Deserted 7/30/1861
+BUHLER, JOSEPH—20; Bernstein German Co., aka BUCHLER, Drowned
BULIE, RUDOLPH—age?; Wiegand German Co., Disability
BULOW, FREDRICK—25; Baker; Mustered out
BURGMANN, JOHN—42; Merau; Farmer; Disability
BURKHARDT, FRANZ—31; Musician; Siegel Co., aka BURGHARDT, CIA
CARES, HEINRICH—26; Wiegand German Co., Disability
CLAUS, HENRY—25; Von Unwerth German Co., NR
CLAUSSON, CHARLES H.—35; Altona; Sailor; WIA/SIH
+CRAMLIN, AUGUST—40; Tailor; DOD
+DEEG, ANDREAS—30; Bernstein German Co., aka DEOG, DOD
DEETZELY, MATHIAS—33; Bernstein German Co., aka DEOTZEL, NR
*DEITZ, JOHN A.—37; Farmer
=DELL, GEORGE—36; Schwarz German Co., aka DILL, WIA
DENNIS, HENRY—19; Clerk; WIA/CIA/PAR, Mustered out
DHAMS, HEINRICH—32; Bernstein German Co., aka DAHMS, Disability
DICKMANN, FRIEDRICH—27; Schwarz German Co., Disability
DICKS, ELIAS—age?; Von Unwerth German Co., NR
*DIETRICH, FRIEDRICH—26; Von Unwerth German Co.
+DITTMAR, JOHN H.—38; Farmer; CIA/POW Andrv
*DOBBLER, DANIEL—23; Von Unwerth German Co.
DOELGER, PETER—33; Schwarz German Co., aka DELGER, NR
=DOERFER, EDMUND—33; Schwarz German Co., aka DORFER & TOEFER,
    Discharged
*DOLL, MICHAEL—21; Bernstein German Co.
DORNBACH, FERDINAND—31; Von Unwerth German Co., NR
DOEGE, AUGUST—28; Ottenstein, Braunschweiger; Tailor; Berstein Co., aka
    DREGE, WIA/VRC
DREHER, SEBASTIAN—39; Schwarz German Co., Disability
DRESS, FRIEDRICH—27; Schwarz German Co., Mustered out
DRESSEL, JACOB—24; Farmer; MIA
*DROCKE, EDWARD—22; Hamburg; Cooper; WIA
DUESBER, BERNHARD—27; Schwarz German Co., Disability, Honorary
    Lieutenant
EBERHARD, GEORGE—23; Unassigned Clerk, Discharged
=EDELMAN, LOUIS—31; Lacory; Clerk; WIA, Disability
EGERLY, LEONARD—27; Spaden; Milkman; WIA
EGGERS, HENRY—23; Spaden; Milkman; Disability
EICHELE, PETER—26; Musician; Wiegand German Co., Mustered out
*EICKE, CHARLES—27; Wiegand German Co.
*EILS, JOHANN—20; Bernstein German Co.

EIPPERSBACH, WILLIAM—25; Siegel Co., Transferred from 15th Artillery
EISERHARDT, HUGO—26; Clerk; aka ESCENHANDT, WIA, Discharged
ELLENBERGER, CASPAR—21; Band Musician, Co. H, Mustered out
ELLENBERGER, JOHN—44; Band Musician 1861, Mustered out
*ELLRICH, ROBERT—20; Siegel Co.
EMHARDT, ALBERT—17; Laborer; WIA, Mustered out
+EMMONS, CONRAD I.—age?; Farmer
EMRICK, LOUIS—21; Baker; WIA/SIH
=ENCKE, CHRISTIAN—30; Von Unwerth German Co., aka ENKE, Mustered out
ENDLICK, GEORGE—age?; Musician; Spanish Co., aka ENOLLICH, NR
+ENGEL, WILHELM—21; Obereschbach, Darmstadt; Cabinetmaker; CIA/POW
   Andrv
ENGELKE, FREDERICH—28; Von Unwerth German Co., Transferred to 15th
   Artillery
ENNINGER, JOHANN—34; Schwarz German Co., Disability
=ERBEN, JOHN N.—34; Siegel Co., Mustered out
ERHARDT, AUGUSTUS W.—21; Farmer; aka EIHARDT, Mustered out
EVELING, FREDERICK WILLIAM—age?; Wiegand German Co., aka
   EBERLING, MIA
FALK, BALTHASAR—38; Wiegand German Co., Disability
FALK, DEY—32; Hamburg; Butcher; Schwarz German Co., Mustered out
FALKENBURG, HERMANN—24; Von Unwerth German Co., Disability
FANSER GOTTLIEB—33; Schwarz German Co., NR
FARBER, GEORGE—28; Mason; WIA
FARMEN, ISSAC—20; Peddler; CIA/PAR/SIH
FASTNACHT, JOHANN—44; Dettenseen, Siegmaringen; Carver; WIA/SIH
*FAUTH, ALEXANDER—39; Wiegand German Co., aka FAUSH, Deserted
   8/10/1861
FIECKE, HYRONIMUS—23; Von Unwerth German Co., aka FAICKE or FUCKE,
   Disability
FISCHER, FRIEDRICH—27; Siegel Co., NR
FISHER, JACOB—31; Laborer; WIA/SIH
FLIEGER, ANDREAS—28; Wiegand German Co., Disability
FORMANSKY, WILLIAM—30; Wiegand German Co., NR
FOST, GUSTAV—21; Siegel Co., aka JOST, Disability
=FOSTER, GEORGE H.—20; Siegel Co., aka FOERSTER, Transferred from 5th
   Infantry, Mustered out
+FRACKIN, JOSEPH—34; Sailor; aka FRANKEN, CIA/POW Andrv
FRANK, GUSTAV—21; Sailor; WIA/SIH
+FRANZ, ALBERT—25; Wiegand Co.
=FRANZ, BERNHARD—23; Wiegand Co., Dismissed
FRANZEL, AUGUST—age?; Band Musician; aka FAUZEL, Disability
FRICKE, CARLE—22; Ostbeavens, Westphalia; Baker; NR
FRITZ, SCHNEIDER—28; Band Musician; Mustered out

+FROSCHKENECHT, JACOB—24; Laborer; aka FICHNECHT
=GALLUBA, CHARLES—22; Wiegand German Co., Discharged
GEBEL, VALENTIN—22; Von Unwerth German Co., Disability
*GEISER, SALADIN—22; Von Unwerth German Co.
*GELDERMANN, HEINRICH—26; Schwarz Co.
GERMAN, AUGUST—24; Wiegand German Co., NR
GERSTENBURG, HENRY—18; Seaman; aka GUSTENBERG; WIA, NR after
   Wilderness 5/6/1864
*GILSON, ADOLPH—22; Clerk
GLASIUS, JACOB—32; Wiegand German Co., aka GLASIN, NR
GLASSENAPP, GEORGE—19; Von Unwerth German Co., Disability
+GOLDSMITH, JULIUS—24; Clerk; WIA/DOW
GOLLE, LUDWIG—21; Bernstein German Co., WIA
*GOLLEY, JULIUS—20; Bernstein German Co.
GORDIS, HENRY—age?; Siegel German Co., NR
+GOTZ, FIDAL—21; Laborer; DOD
+GOTZ, HEINRICH—23; Schwarz German Co., DOD
GRAGE, HEINRICH—28; Musician; Von Unwerth German Co., Disability
*GRAMER, JOHN—age?; Schwarz German Co., aka KRAMMER
*GRAUMAN, CONRAD—29; Carpenter; aka GAUMANN
+GRAVELIUS, HENRY—21; Driver; WIA/DOW
GRUBBELL, JULIUS—23; Schwarz German Co., Disability
GUENTHER, ROBERT—22; Wiegand German Co., Transferred [to?] 2nd
   Artillery
*GUNTHNER, JEAN—23; Unwerth Co.
HABENIGHT, CHARLES—19; Laborer; Mustered out
HAHL, LEOPOLD—22; Baker; Mustered out
HAMEL, HENRY—33; Hospitler; MIA 6/17/1864 Returned; VRC
HAMIK, EDWARD—32; Blacksmith; aka HENRICKE, Discharged
HAMMER, GEORGE—32; Birthplace?; Siegel Co., VRC
HANEMAN, ADOLPH—39; Siegel Co., Disability
HART, MICHAEL—20; Jeweler; CIA
HARTMANN, CARL—22; Von Unwerth German Co., NR
HAUCH, HERMAN—27; Musician; Schwarz German Co., NR
HAUFMANN, PETER—34; Wiegand German Co., Disability
HAUG, FRANZ—26; Schwarz German Co., Disability
*HAUNNARDT, HERRMANN—21; Bernstein German Co., Deserted 7/15/1862
HAUPT, JACOB—23; Musician; Bernstein German Co., Disability
HAURWAS, JOSEPH—40; Laborer; aka HANAVAR, VRC
HAUSER, CHARLES—37; Laborer; aka HOUSER, VRC
HAUSON, JOHN—38; Carpenter; aka HANSEN, WIA, Disability
*HECKERT, HEINRICH—23; Bernstein Co.
HECKLER, FRANCIS—49; Band Musician 1861, Disability
HEDRICH, DAVID—27; Schwarz German Co., Disability

HEELY, JOSEPH—25; Wiegand German Co., NR

*HEILAND, GEORGE—21; Musician; Schwarz German Co., Deserted 5/11/1862

HEINER, HERRMANN—28; Co. H, aka HOEGNER, BERNARD or HEYNER, CIA, NR

HEINTZ, CARL—21; Wiegand German Co., Transferred [to?] 15th Artillery

+HEINZEN, FREDRICK—33; Tenneborg, Holstein; Farmer; Unwerth Co.

+HEMILRICK, JOHN—26; Waiter; CIA/POW Andrv

HENMANN, PETER—20; Averbach; Potmaker; aka HEAUMANN, CIA/SIH

HENSCHEL, ERNEST F.—26; Von Unwerth German Co., NR

+HERMAN, KARL—21; Sailor; WIA/DOW

HERMANN, FRANZ—27; Bernstein German Co., Transferred [to?] 4th Cavalry

HERTHING, CHRISTIAN—30; Farmer; aka HARTLING, Mustered out

HETZEL, JOHN—18; Baker; VRC

+HETZEL, JOHN—27; Baker

HEYLMANN, WILHELM—26; Von Unwerth German Co., NR

=HILDERRAND, FRIEDRICH—29; Bernstein German Co., Mustered out

HILLERBRAND, MICHAEL—28; Waiter; aka HILDERBRANDT, Disability

*HINECKE, DOMINIC—24; Von Unwerth German Co., Deserted 6/13/1861

HINTZE, JULIUS—38; Schwarz German Co., Disability

HINZ, ERNST—23; Espe, Holstein; Tailor; WIA/VRC

HIRLINGER, WILLIAM L.—30; Mason; WIA, Mustered out

+HOCKNER, HEINRICH—23; Dresden; Cook

HOFF, JOSEPH—41; Laborer; aka HOPP, VRC

*HOFFMAISTER, CLORIAN—age?; Schwarz German Co., Deserted 7/30/1861

HOFFMAN, JOSEPH—29; Band Musician 1861, NR

=HOLLINDE, EMIL—28; Wiegand German Co., Disability

HONIG, CHARLES—28; Siegel Co. & Von Unwerth German Co., aka HONIZ, NR

HONIG, JEAN—26; Siegel German Co., Disability

HORATH, FERDINAND—28; Siegel Co., Disability

HORNLEIN, MARTIN—31; Bernstein German Co., Disability

HUBER, HEINRICH—45; Von Unwerth German Co., NR

HUBUER, REINHOLD—31; Band Musician 1861, Mustered out

HUGHES, PHILIP—27; Siegel Co., NR

HUNGARDNER, MATHEWES—34; Italian Co., aka HEINGARDNER, NR

HUNZINGER, JACOB—44; Spanish Co., Disability

ISERN, FERDINAND—20; Wiegand German Co., NR

JACOBSON, SIMON—46; Sugarmaker; WIA/VRC

JAGER, JOHANN—21; Miller; aka TAGER, VRC

JANKOFSKY, LOUIS—33; Wiegand German Co., Transferred to 2nd Artillery

JANSEN, JOHN H.—21; Seaman; aka JOHNSON & TANSEN, WIA

JULIUS, FREDERICK—36; Shoemaker; Disability

+JUNGUNST, JOHN—30; Siegel Co.

KAISER, PETER—28; Wiegand German Co., Transferred [to?] 15th Artillery

=KAUFMANN, JOHN—29; Bernstein German Co., Discharged
*KAUFMANN, PHILLIPP—21; Bernstein Co.
*KECK, FRED'R—23; Wiegand German Co., Deserted 8/31/1861
KEELER, GEORGE—40; Laborer; aka KELLER, CIA/NR
KEIN, ALOIS—30; Siegel Co., aka KLEIN, Disability
*KELLER, ANDREW—20; Farmer; WIA
KELLNER, ADOLPH—25; Farmer; aka KOLLNER, Discharged
+KERN, THOMAS—18; Schwarz Co.
*KESSNER, JOHN—21; Varnisher; Deserted While on Furlough
KIRCHOFF, HENRY—21; Laborer; VRC
KLASEN, ADAM—26; Von Unwerth German Co., Disability
KLAUS, HENRY—26; Schwarz German Co., Disability
KLEIN, JACOB—32; Von Unwerth German Co., Disability
=KLEINE, LOUIS DR.—28; Von Unwerth German Co., NR
KLINGETHOFER, JOHN—19; Bernstein German Co., aka KLINGETTROFER,
  Disability
KLOTZ, JEAN—25; Von Unwerth German Co., Disability
KLUEPENDORF, KARL—27; Wiegand German Co., Disability
KNECHTLE, ANTON—24; Wiegand German Co., NR
KNOPP, RUDOLPH—32; Schwarz German Co., Discharged
KOBER, FRED (H.) A.—36; Barber; WIA/VRC
KOCH, WILLIAM—25; Siegel Co., Transferred [to?] Division Hospital, NR
KOEBELOWSKY, FELIX—41; Wiegand German Co., aka KORBELOSKY,
  Disability
*KOLB, FRANZ—33; Schwarz Co.
*KORN, PAUL—24; Wiegand German Co., Deserted 6/22/1861
*KRAMER, CARL—22; Von Unwerth German Co., Deserted 6/13/1861
*KRAUSS, LUDA—20; Wiegand Co.
KREBS, CARL—34; Bernstein German Co., Discharged
KREHLICH, CHARLES—30; Wiegand German Co., aka KROEBEL or
  KREHBIEL, CIA/PAR, Mustered out
KUBBLER, FRIEDRICH—26; Von Unwerth German Co., NR
KUESTENMACHER, ADALL—33; Wiegand German Co., Disability
KUFAR, SIMON—35; aka KEEFER, Mustered out
KUFFNER, WILLIAM—24; Siegel Co., aka WILHEIM KIEFNER, Mustered out
*KUNZE, WILLIAM—21; Siegel Co., aka KUNTZE
LAGNER, FRITZ—29; Farmer; VRC
LAMMERS, JOHN—19; Clerk; WIA Twice
LAMMESFELD, KARL—33; Birthplace?; Siegel Co., Mustered out
*LAMPEL, CHRISTIAN—24; Siegel Co.
LANE, NICHOLAS—26; Laborer, Mustered out
LANG, CONRAD—age?; Band Musician 1861, Mustered out
LANG, GEORGE—23; Frankfurt; Cigarmaker; Schwarz German Co., Mustered
  out

LANGE, LOUIS—21; Siegel Co., Discharged

LAUGENBACH, STEPHEN—24; Von Unwerth German Co., CIA/PAR, Mustered out

LAUTERBACHER, Wolfgang—21; Schwarz Co., Transferred to 13th Artillery, Rejoined the Garibaldi Guard, Mustered out

LEHANKAR, LOUIS—36; Schwarz German Co., Mustered out

LEHMAN, FREDERICK—30; Stonecutter; Mustered out

LEHMANN, HEINRICH—26; Schwarz German Co., Disability

LEHNER, JOSEPH—30; Laborer; Disability

LEIFELLS, FRANK—27; Band Musician 1861, Mustered out

LEOPOLD, AUGUST—24; Tailor; WIA, Disability

LIEKEFELD, AUG—29; Wiegand German Co., NR

LINDER, LOUIS—32; Von Unwerth German Co., Disability

=LINDNER, CARL HEINRICH—age?; Siegel Co., aka HENRY LINDER, Resigned

LINDNER, THEODORE—28; Bernstein German Co., Disability

+LINGART, JOHN W.—31; Farmer

*LINGNER, ADOLPH—27; Bernstein Co.

LION, SOMON—22; Von Unwerth German Co., NR

LIPPIEN, HENRY—24; Sailor; VRC

LUCKE, HERMANN—22; Schwarz German Co., NR

LUIGMERE, FRANK—19; Laborer; VRC

*LUNTZ, JOHANN—29; Siegel Co.

LUPRU, HIPPOLITE—34; Cook; WIA, NR after Wilderness 5/6/1864

MAESECKE, ERNST—20; Schwarz German Co., Transferred to 15th Artillery

MANCH, HERMAN—27; Band Musician; Schwarz German Co., aka MAUCH, NR

MARK, CARLOS—30; Siegel Co., aka CHARLES MACK & MOCK, VRC

MARK, JOHN—age?; Siegel German Co., aka JOHN MACK, WIA, Mustered

MARKGRAF, GEORGE—30; Siegel Co., Disability

=MARSHALL, RICHARD—26; Schwarz German Co., aka HARSCHAN, Disability

+MATHIES, DANIEL—26; Von Unwerth German Co., DOD

MAYER, HEINRICH—37; Farmer; Transferred to 15th Artillery

MAYER, JOHANN MARTIN—42; Farmer; WIA/SIH

MAYER, RUDOLPH—26; Von Unwerth German Co., aka MEYER, Disability

MECKEL, AUGUST—23; Katzhutte, Schwaze; Carver; WIA

+MEHL, ALBERT—27; Siegel German Co.

MEINCOFF, CHRISTIAN—age?; Schwarz German Co., NR

MERK, HENRY—28; Siegel German Co., NR

MESSENGER, ADAM—35; Porter; aka MESSINGULL, Mustered out

+MEYERDERICH, JOHN—37; Shoemaker; WIA/DOW

MEYERS, HENRY T.—41; Laborer; aka JOSEPH, Transferred to 185th New York Infantry

+MILLER, JACOB—38; Tailor; POW Andrv

MILLER, JOHN—27; Sailor; WIA, Mustered out
MILLER, THEODORE—25; Wiegand German Co., Disability
+MOORE, JOHN—28; Clerk
MOSSE, WOLFGANG—28; Schwarz German Co., Discharged
MUELLER, FREDOLIN—28; Wiegand German Co., NR
MUELLER, WILLIAM—26; Wiegand German Co., WIA, Mustered out
MUHLFELD, WILLIAM—39; Cigarmaker; Mustered out
MUHLHEIM, JOHANN—28; Bernstein German Co., Disability
MULLEN, JAMES—26; Wiegand German Co., NR
=MULLER, FERDINAND—22; Dresden, Sashesen; Sailor; WIA, Mustered out
MULLER, HENRY—24; Siegel Co., Disability
MULLER, HERMANN 1ST—age?; Siegel Co., Disability
MULLER, JACOB—38; Tailor; NR
*MULLER, JOHANNES—23; Bernstein German Co., Deserted 6/20/1861
MULLER, URBAN—23; Blacksmith; WIA
MUNCHENER, WILLIAM—38; Schwarz German Co., Disability
*MUTH, AUGUST—24; Siegel Co.
+MYERS, JOSEPH—41; Laborer; DOD
NAEGELE, JACOB—21; Schwarz German Co., Disability
*NAGEL, GOTTLIEB—23; Schwarz German Co. & Unwerth Co.
NATGE, AUGUST—27; Wiegand German Co., Disability
*NEANDER, JOSEPH—19; Wertheim, Pucker, French Co., Deserted 5/8/1862
NIEBUHR, CARL—38; Wiegand German Co., Disability
=NISSEN, CAESAR—21; Schwarz German Co., aka LISSEN, Dishonorably
    Discharged
NUTMAN, ALBERT—38; Halberstadt; Shoemaker; WIA, Disability
*OBERDORFER, EDWARD—21; Siegel Co.
OBERST, JACOB—39; Schwarz German Co., Disability
OTT, THOMAS—age?; Schwarz German Co., aka CHARLES OTT, Disability
OVERBECK, HERMANN—32; Von Unwerth German Co., NR
PABST, MICHAEL—23; Von Unwerth German Co., NR
=+PAUSCH, CARL THEODORE—28; Bernstein German Co., aka BAUSCH
PEIFFER, JACOB—23; Wiegand German Co., WIA/CIA, NR after Wilderness
    5/6/1864
PETER, JOHAN—28; Siegel Co., Disability
PETER, OTTO—40; Von Unwerth German Co., Disability
+PETERMAN, MAURICE—20; Sailor; DOD
PETERS, HEINRICH—33; Wiegand German Co., Disability
PETERS, JOHN—38; Farmer; WIA, Mustered out
PETRI, PHILLIPP—27; Von Unwerth German Co., aka PETRIE, Mustered out
PHANMULLER, RUDOLPH—26; Laborer; Mustered out
PISSELL, ADAM—42; Schwarz German Co., Disability
PLANMUTH, JOHN—21; German Co., Mustered out
+PLEIN, MATHIAS—21; Driver; CIA/POW/DOD

*POETENSHLAG, JOSEPH—26; Schwarz German Co., aka ADOLF PROTEN-
SCHLAG

POLTERMANN, FREDERICK—36; Wiegand German Co., Disability

PREUSSER, RICHARD—26; Siegel Co., Disability

QUIRK, ELLIS—32; Farmer; aka QUICK, NR

RAEFLE, GUSTAV—25; Von Unwerth German Co., Mustered out

RAMPKE, HEINRICH—26; Schwarz German Co., Disability

RANTSA, CARL—22; Elkenfoule, Holstein; Sailor; Siegel Co., WIA Twice,
Mustered out

REICHLEN, FRIEDRICH—27; Schwarz German Co., NR

REICHLEN, LOUIS—age?; Schwarz German Co., NR

*REINERS, ERNST—22; Wiegand Co.

REINHARDT, JOHN—19; Farmer; Mustered out

REINISCH, HERMAN—40; Musician; aka RUSSKE, Mustered out

REINLANDER, CHARLES—21; Siegel German Co., Disability

RENK, FREDOLIN—42; Schwarz German Co., Disability

RENNER, CHRISTIAN—40; Teamster; VRC

=RIBBECK, RUDOLPH 40; Siegel German Co., Assistant Surgeon, CIA/PAR,
Dismissed

=RICE, JAMES C.—age?; Von Unwerth German Co., Transferred [to?] 44nd Infantry

RICHTER, CARL—39; Siegel German Co., NR

RIENCKE, JOSEPH—24; Musician; Wiegand German Co., Transferred [to?] 2nd
Artillery

*RITCHER, CARL—39; Siegel German Co.

ROBERT, HENRY—age?; Wagoner; Berstein German Co., Mustered out

*ROBITSEK, WILLIAM—36; Siegel German Co., aka BOBITZCHEK &
ROBISCK

ROCHARD, FRANCIS—40; Siegel German Co., VRC

RODENBURGH, WILLIAM—29; Oysterman; VRC

+RODH, WILLIAM—23; Clerk; WIA/DOW

ROEDER, LOUIS—19; Von Unwerth German Co., aka ROEDER, Mustered out

=ROHN, CASPER—43; Bandleader, Field & Staff 1861; Mustered out

#ROHN, JOHN—14; Band Musician 1861, Youngest Soldier, NR

ROSH, CHRISTOPH—28; Wittorf, Hannover; Farmer; Schwarz German Co.,
Mustered out

=ROSSMAESSLER, OTTO—age?; Wiegand German Co., aka RASSMAESSLER,
Mustered out

ROTH, FRIEDRICH—age?; Schwarz Co.

*ROTH, NICOLAUS—30; Bernstein Co.

*ROTHFUS, CHRISTIAN—20; Schwarz German Co.

ROTTLER, MATHIAS—34; Von Unwerth German Co., Disability

RUCKERSFELD, AUGUST—44; Von Unwerth German Co., Disability

RUCKERT, CARL—24; Schwarz German Co., Disability

*RUGGS, JOHN—23; Seaman; aka RUGER, WIA
RUHLE, GOTTLIEB—26; Laborer; SIH
=RULBERG, CARL—26; Von Unwerth German Co., aka CHARLES RUELBERG, Resigned
=RUMPF, AUGUSTUS—24; Schwarz German Co., aka RUMPH, Mustered out
RUST, EMANUEL—30; Schwarz German Co., NR
SACHS, LEOPOLD—28; Von Unwerth German Co., Disability
=SACK, JOSEPH G.—21; Mepm; Butcher; aka SECK, Mustered out
*SANZ, LEONHARDT—24; Siegel Co., Deserted 8/31/1861
SCHABAHA, CHARLES—29; Butcher; WIA, Mustered out
SCHAFER, JACOB—31; Co. E, Band Musician, aka SCHAEFER, Mustered out
SCHAFER, LEO—24; Von Unwerth German Co., aka FRITZ SCHAFER or SHAFER, NR
SCHEEDER, LEONHARD—24; Von Unwerth German Co., NR
+SCHEFFNER, CHARLES—27; Schwarz German Co., aka SCHAFFNER, DOD
SCHEIDEMANN, HEINRICH—28; Von Unwerth German Co., Disability
SCHENK, BALTH—22; Wiegand German Co., Disability
+SCHENK, FREDERICK—34; Blacksmith
+SCHEU, Frederick—25; Laborer; aka THEODORE
SCHEUERMANN, MICHAEL—27; Von Unwerth German Co., NR
SCHILLING, CARL—43; Polisher; VRC
SCHIPPMANN, GEORGE—18; Sailor; aka SCHIPPERMANN, Mustered out
SCHIROSS, ALBERT—27; Wiegand German Co., aka SHIROP, Disability
SCHMELZKOPF, EDWARD ADOLPH—31; Braunschweyer; Merchant; Mustered out
SCHMIDT, CHARLES—28; Sailor; aka HENRY SMITH, WIA/VCR
SCHMIDT, EDWARD—19; Von Unwerth German Co., NR
*SCHMIDT, FRANK—28; Von Unwerth Co.
SCHMIDT, JOSEPH—22; Bernstein German Co., Wagoner, NR
SCHMIDT, JOSEPH HENRY—33; Siegel Co., Wagoner, NR
#SCHMIDT, LEWIS—52; Von Unwerth German Co., Oldest Man, Disability
SCHMIDT, LOUIS—46; Schwarz German Co., NR
SCHMITT, PETER—25; Brewer; aka SMITH, CIA/PAR/VRC
SCHMITZ, WILH—27; Canemaker; aka WILLIAM SMITH, MIA
SCHNEIDER, ERNEST—20; Baker; Mustered out
*SCHNEIDER, FREDERICK—24; Bernstein German Co., Deserted 8/4/1861
SCHNEIDER, GEORGE—18; Wiegand German Co., NR
SCHNEIDER, JOHN—30; Siegel Co., Mustered out
SCHOCH, CARL—33; Bernstein German Co., aka SCHOOH, Disability
SCHOENING, FREDERICK—22; Sailor; aka CHARLES CHOLLES, WIA/SIH
SCHOLTER, JOHN—26; Siegel Co., aka SCHOLTEN, Disability
=SCHONDORF, CONRAD—35; Wiegand German Co., aka VON SCHONDORF, Discharged
SCHOSSETS, JACOB—41; Wiegand German Co., Disability

SCHREBI, CONRAD—22; Bernstein German Co., NR
SCHREINER, SAMUEL—29; Seaman; Transferred to U.S. Navy
SCHROEDER, ERNEST—19; Sailor; SIH
SCHUBER, HENRY—25; Siegel Co., Mustered out
SCHUBERTH, CARL—19; Schwarz German Co., NR
SCHUENMANN, AUGUST—24; Wiegand German Co., Discharged
*SCHULZ, HEINRICH—38; Wagoner; Wiegand German Co., Deserted 6/3/1862
SCHUMAN, ANDREAS—26; Von Unwerth German Co., Disability
SCHUTZ, FRANZ—19; Schwarz German Co., WIA/VRC
=SCHWARZ, CHARLES—31; Captain of Schwarz German Co. 1861, Discharged
=SCHWICKHARDI, RUDOLPH—24; Siegel Co., aka SHERICARDI, SVICKARDI,
    & SWICKHARDY, Disability
SCHWICKHARDT, NICOLAUS—42; Laborer; aka SCHWISCKART, WIA/VRC
SEDLEWSKI, MARTIN—24; Siegel Co., aka SIEDLEWSKY, Disability
SEHUBER, HENRY—25; Siegel Co., aka FRANCIS SCHEUBER, NR
*SEIB, CARL—19; Von Unwerth German Co., Deserted 6/13/1861
SEIBERT, GEORGE—28; Von Unwerth German Co., aka SIEBERT, NR
SEIGEL, AUGUST—24; Von Unwerth German Co., NR
SEIP, JACOB—35; Siegel Co., Discharged
SEIVERS, HIRMONIOUS HENRY—24; Bremen; Clerk, aka SIEVERS, Mustered
    out
SELLING, CHARLES—22; Siegel Co., aka SEELING, Disability
SETAL, JOHN—18; Sailor; aka SITAL, Mustered out
SEUL, ANTONE—32; Wiegand German Co., aka ANSON, NR
SHAEFER, FRITZ—21; Von Unwerth German Co., aka SCHAFER, NR
SHUTMILLER, IGNATZ—18; Teamster; aka SCHUTMILLER, Disability
+SIEBERT, JOHN—26; Seaman; CIA/POW Slsbry
=SIEGEL, JOHN H.—41; Siegel Co., Discharged
SIEGFRIED, WILLIAM—37; Schwarz German Co., Disability
SIEVERS, FRANK—19; Breman, Breman; Clerk; CIA later WIA, Mustered out
SIEVERS, HERMANN—24; Breman, Breman; Clerk; aka HENRY SIEMERS, CIA/
    PAR/WIA, Mustered out
SIMMERS, HEINRICH—24; Laborer; Bernstein German Co., Mustered out
SIMON, JOHN—20; Shoemaker; aka SEMON, WIA, Mustered out
SMITH, GEORGE—28; Baker; VRC
SMITH, JOHN—22; Laborer; WIA/SIH
SOHL, HENRY—22; Schwarz German Co., Disability
SPAIN, JIM—age?; Wiegand German Co., NR
=SPILLER, OSCAR DR.—28; Siegel Co., Disability
SPORLEADER, LOUIS—34; Siegel Co., NR
STABERG, FRITZ—age?; Schwarz German Co., NR
STADER, GEORGE—25; Schwarz German Co., aka STADLER, Disability
STANBACK, FREDERICK—20; Schwarz; aka STAUBACK, Disability
STARK, JACOB—31; Von Unwerth German Co., NR

STAROST, ADOLPH—34; Bernstein German Co., Disability
STAUBITZ, ROBERT—27; Schwarz German Co., Disability
STEHM, FRIED'R—26; Wiegand German Co., NR
*STEIN, LUDWIG—age?; Bernstein German Co., Deserted 6/5/1862
+STEINHAL, BALDES—30; Baker; aka SEINHILBER, CIA/POW Slsbry
+STEPHAN, JOHN—25; Siegel Co.
STEVENSON, WILLIAM—32; Siegel Co., NR
STOLL, CHRISTIAN—22; Schwarz German Co., Disability
STOOP, FRANCIS—30; Siegel Co., Disability
STRADTMANN, HEINRICH—24; Luberk, Lisbeck; Farmer; Bernstein German Co., Mustered out
STRIEGEL, JOSEPH—41; Band Musician 1861, aka STIEGEL, Mustered out
STROMEYER, HEINRICH—31; Von Unwerth German Co., NR
*SULZER, LEOPOLD—23; Schwarz Co.
SUMYESKY, VALENTIN—29; Schwarz German Co., Disability
SURER, JACOB—28; Siegel Co., Mustered out
TAG, ALBERT—24; Cabinetmaker; Mustered out
*THATEWALD, FREDERICK—age?; Bernstein Co.
THEUNE, HERRMANN—26; Bernstein German Co., Transferred to 73rd Pennsylvania
TORCK, JOHN H.—23; Farmer; aka SYGMAN, WIA, Mustered out
#TRICK, JACOB—20; Laborer; CIA/enlisted In 8th C.S.A. Infantry, Recaptured and Mustered
UHLRIG, SIMON—23; Cigarmaker; Mustered out
UNGEMACH, CHRISTOPH—26; Von Unwerth German Co., NR
UNRUH, ANTON—48; Band Musician 1861, Discharged
+UNTERGRUBER, MARTIN—27; Baker; Unwerth Co., CIA/POW Thdr Cstl
VANDIREN, LOUIS—30; Schwarz German Co., aka VAN DUREN, Mustered out
VOLGER, THEODORE—27; Wiegand German Co., Disability
VOLLMER, HENRY—21; Von Unwerth German Co., Disability
VON LINDEN, LUDWIG—21; Birthplace?; Von Unwerth German Co., Mustered out
=VON UNWERTH, A. H.—45; Captain Von Unwerth German Co., Discharged
#WALSTERS, PETER—age?; Messkirch, Messkirch; Teacher; Exile 1848 REV, NR
*WALTERLING, CHARLES—38; Soldier; aka WATTERBURY
+WALZ, PHILIPP—30; Bartender; aka WEILS, CIA/NR
WANIKE, FRIEDRICH—35; Siegel Co., aka WARNICKEL, Transferred [to?] 15th Artillery
WASHEIM, PHILIPP—26; Siegel Co., Disability
WASMUND, BERNHARD—30; Bernstein German Co., Disability
+WEBER, GOTTLIEB—28; Baker; WIA/DOW
*WEBER, WILLIAM—26; Siegel Co., Deserted 4/30/1862
*WEICHEL, PAULUS—25; Von Unwerth German Co., aka WEIGEL

WEICKEL, CHARLES—34; Sugarmaker; NR
WEINBERGER, FRANZ—33; Wiegand German Co., Mustered out
WENDT, PAUL—21; Sailor; Mustered out
WERNER, FRIEDR—32; Wiegand German Co., Disability
WERNER, FRIEDRICH—22; Von Unwerth German Co., Disability
WIEDEMAYER, JEAN—38; Von Unwerth German Co., Disability
=WIEGAND, CHARLES—33; Captain of Wiegand German Co., aka WEIGARD, Discharged
*WIEGAND, GEORGE—28; Wiegand Co.
WIESE, GUSTAV ADOLPH—age?; Band Musician 1861, aka WEISE, Disability
WILLIAMSON, FRIED'R—29; Siegel Co., NR
WILLING, LOUIS—age?; Siegel Co., aka LEWIS WELLING, CIA/POW Paroled & Mustered out
WINTER, JACOB—22; Wiegand German Co. & Von Unwerth German Co., Disability
*WINTER, PHILIPP—22; Wiegand German Co., CIA/PAR then Deserted 6/15/1862
*WISMER, FREDERICH—29; Siegel Co.
=WOLTERS, ERNST—26; Principal Musician, Siegel Co., aka WALTERS, NR
ZACHARIAS, CONRAD—24; Siegel Co., Disability
=ZANDER, CARL—32; Von Unwerth German Co., Resigned
ZEIR, JOSEPH—43; Bernstein German Co., Disability
ZEISS, REINHARD—20; Schwarz Co., aka ZEIHS, CIA/PAR, Mustered out
*ZENN, JACOB—45; Band Musician 1861, aka ZINCK, Deserted 7/16/1862
ZIEGELMEYER, OTTO—19; Shoemaker; Disability
ZIEGLER, JEAN—36; Musician; Von Unwerth German Co., NR
*ZILCHER, FRANZ—36; Schwarz Co.
=ZIMMERMAN, CHARLES—26; Siegel Co., Resigned
ZIMMERMANN, WILHELM—33; Bernstein German Co., NR
ZIN, JOSEPH—age?; Band Musician 1861, NR
ZINK, ELLIS—32; Co. ? 1863, NR
ZINK, XAPHIR—43; Mahlberg; Exile 1848 REV, Schwarz German Co., NR
*ZOBAL, EDWARD—21; Sailor; aka JOBAL
ZORACK, FERDINAND—30; Siegel German Co., NR
ZORN, MATHIAS—age?; Schwarz German Co., Disability
ZWERGEL, JACOB—31; Siegel Co.; Disability
ZWERGEL, JACOB—26; Siegel Co., aka ZWERKEL & ZWERZEL, VRC

Greece

NICKOLLS, JOHN—26; Seaman; Mustered out

Gotha

+BECK, CHARLES—21; Dambach; Carver; Bernstein German Co., CIA/PAR/DOD

FOSTER, BERNHARDT—24; Newstadt, Saxecoburg; Baker; Siegel Co., WIA, Mustered out

KALLENBACH, GOTTLIEB—20; Allendorf, Saxe-Meininger; Pianomaker; Siegel Co., WIA, Mustered out

RODIGUER, AUGUSTO—19 Johannhauser, Sax Weimer; aka RADICHER, Italian Co., VRC

Grenada

PENATE, MIGUEL—23; Candelevia; Sailor; WIA/SIH

Hanover

ALBERS, PETER—21; Hanover; Farmer; Wiegand German Co., Mustered out

BOTGER, CLAUS—28; Eberhart; Clerk; SIH

DETGE, HENRY—38; Hartburg; Carpenter; aka DIETZEN, Mustered out

+DOENECKE, WILHELM—28; Einbeck; Baker; Bernstein Co.

EBELING, WILLIAM—18; Hanover, Prussian[?]; Barber; WIA, Mustered out

EBERHARD, GEORGE—23; Hanover; Clerk; WIA, Mustered out

FRITZCH, WILLIAM—32; Liebnau; Teacher; Mustered out

HUFSCHMIED, FREDERICK—20; Hamburg, Hescend; Upholsterer; aka HUSSCHMIDT, Friedrich, WIA/SIH

KLEEN, ERNST—20; Bromerswordc; Clerk; Wiegand German Co., Mustered out

KNOPF, HEIN'R—22; Teinsen; Barkeeper; Musician in Wiegand Co., Mustered out

KOCH, HENRY—19; Hanover; Trimmings Maker; Siegel Co., Mustered out

KOPP, HERRMANN—23; Bilshausen; Barkeeper; Von Unwerth German Co., Mustered out

+LINNE, AUGUST—42; Hanover; Carver; aka LUNN, CIA/POW Andrv

MERGEL, LOUIS—20; Mollenfeld; Weaver; Wiegand Co., WIA, Mustered out

MEYER, HEINRICH—34; Hanover; Clerk; Schwarz German Co., CIA/POW Andrv

PFANNSCHMIDT, CONRAD—26; Kirschwereson; Cigarmaker; Siegel Co., WIA

+RAUK, JOHANN H.—31; Hanover; Farmer; aka JOHN H. BAUCK

RIEBKE, HERMANN—age?; Hanover; Seaman; aka RUPKE

SCHEPLER, THEODORE—38; Gotlinger; Sailor; aka SCHEAPLER, WIA Paroled/SIH

*TENT, HEINRICH—25; Hamburg, Hamburg; Carpenter

TIETJEN, HEINRICH—40; Achim; Butcher; WIA, Discharged

VALLACHER, FREDERICK—18; Hanover; Waiter; Mustered out

WILKENS, FRIEDRICK—30; Blekede; Tailor; Mustered out

Hessen Homb

BENDER, WILLIAM—36; Suscheid Lumshed; Clerk; Musician, Schwarz Co., CIA, Mustered out

+FLECK, HEINRICH—24; Cassel Hessen; Barkeeper; Von Unwerth Co.

HENKEL, CONRAD—46; Renershaus; Butcher; Von Unwerth German Co., aka HINKEL, VRC

JACOB, JUSTUS—21; Raushenberg; Baker; Bernstein German Co., NR

REITER, PHILIP—31; Hefslon; Baker; Wiegand German Co., aka REUTER, CIA, Mustered out

Hohenzollern

FASTNACHT, JOHANN—44; Dettenseenn, Siegmarwgen; Carver; WIA, Mustered out

+VAN, JOSEPH—26; Benken; Engineer; Unwerth Co.

WAGNER, JOHN JOSEPH—26; Hohewgollean; Sailor; Siegel Co., WIA

Holland

PATNOOTS, JOHN—age?; Transferred from 27th Infantry, Mustered out

SCHICK, JOSEPH—27; Hechinger, Hohenzoller; Cabinetmaker; Mustered out

*SCHULTZ, HENRY—30; Sailor; aka SCHELTZ, WIA

+VAN WESSEM, JEROME—34; Amsterdam; Decorator

Hungary

AMBERGER, JOSEPH—age?; Hungarian Co., Mustered out

=BACON, CHARLES GRAHAM—20; Hungarian Co. 1862, Dismissed

BARTIS, GEORGE—19; Hungarian Co., aka GEORGE BARDES, Disability

BEIN, CHRISTIAN—36; Hungarian Co., Disability

BERNDT, SIGMUND—20; Hungarian Co., Disability

*BODLET, BAPTISTE—age?; Hungarian Co.

BOHME, HEINRICH—32; Musician; Hungarian Co., Mustered out

BONDY, HENRY—25; Hungarian Co:, Transferred to 2nd Independent Battery

BORNKESSEL, HEINRICH—34; Hungarian Co., aka BRONKESSEL, CIA/PAR, Disability

BRAXMEYER, THOMAS—34; Shoemaker; Hungarian Co., NR

BROGLI, ROBERT—31; Hungarian Co., NR

BROSAMLE, CHRISTIAN—36; Painter; Hungarian Co., NR

*BRUST, EMANUEL—27; Hungarian Co.

BURGER, JOHN—16; Musician; Hungarian Co., Transferred to 45th Infantry

CASSEN, CONSTANT—27; aka CONSTANTZ CASSET, Musician, Hungarian Co., Mustered out

=CHANDORY, VICTOR—38; French Co.; aka CHANDONE, VRC

DEIGERT, FLORIBUSH—25; Hungarian Co., NR
DIEFENBACH, CHARLES—age?; Hungarian Co., NR
DIENER, JOHN—28; Gypsy; Hungarian Co., aka GIOVANDRA DUAR, Disability
DIFLO, LOUIS—28; Hungarian Co., Disability
=*D'UTASSY, ANTHONY—30; Temensai; aka VON UTASSY & UTASSY
=D'UTASSY, CARL—age?; aka VON UTASSY & UTASSY, Mustered out
=D'UTASSY, FREDERICK GEORGE—34; Temensai; aka STRASSER, Dishonorably Discharged
ECKSTEIN, LOUIS—20; Hungarian Co., NR
EGGER, JOHANN—26; Hungarian Co. and Swiss Co., Disability
GAUS, GEORG—30; Hungarian Co., MIA
GILLMAIER, JOSEPH—40; Hungarian Co., aka KILLMAYER, Disability
GRAMLICH, ADAM—28; Hungarian Co., Disability
*GREBE, CONRAD—age?; Hungarian Co.
GROW, GEORGE—20; Hungarian Co., NR
HAEDLER, FRIEDRICH—25; Hungarian Co., Disability
*HEADLER, PAUL—23; Hungarian Co., aka HEDLER, Deserted 6/3/1862
=HEILMANN, WILHELM DR.—25; Hungarian Co., Discharged
+HELLER, PETER—24; Hungarian Co., DOD
=HILDERBRAND, HUGO—36; Siegel Co.; aka KILDERBRANDT,
   HILDERBRANDT, HILLERBRAND, & HILDEBRANDT, WIA, Discharged
HIPPEL, ANTON—35; Hungarian Co., aka HAPPEL/HEPPEL, Mustered out
HIRTREITER, LORENZ—19; Hungarian Co., aka LORENZO HERTRIETER, &
   LOREN HIRTRIETER, NR
JUNGER, JOHN B.—35; Birthplace?; Hungarian Co., aka YUAGER, [JOHN] BAPTIST, & FUNGER, Discharged
*KAPP, AUGUST—23; Hungarian Co., Deserted 5/11/1862
+KEHRIG, CASPAR—37; Birthplace?; Hungarian Co., CIA/POW Andrv
KEINER, MARTIN—44; Hungarian Co., aka JACOB KEUNER, NR
KEM, WILHELM—32; Hungarian Co., Mustered out
KISS, ANTHONY—34; Hungarian Co., Discharged
KLEE, CHARLES—age?; Hungarian Co., NR
KORDES, HEINRICH—36; Hungarian Co., Transferred to 2nd Independent
   Battery
KOULOSY, CAROLY—age?; Hungarian Co., NR
KROLING, AUGUST—age?; Hungarian Co., Disability
KRUEGER, CHARLES—23; Hungarian Co., MIA
KRUGER, PHILIP—24; Hungarian Co., CIA/PAR, Disability
LANSIEDEL, HEINRICH—36; Hungarian Co., CIA, NR
LEFRANIG, CHARLES—36; Hungarian Co., NR
LONZE, CARL—33; Hungarian Co., aka LONGE, Disability
MANDER, JOHN—25; Hungarian Co., aka MUNDER, NR
+MARK, JACOB—age?; Hungarian Co., aka MACK, CIA/POW Andrv
MAY, JOHN—28; Hungarian Co., Mustered out

MILITSCH, STEPHAN—32; Hungarian Co., Disability
MUHRING, WILHELM—32; Hungarian Co., NR
*MULLEN, GUSTAVUS—20; Hungarian Co., Deserted 5/11/1862
MULLER, HERMANN—32; Hungarian Co., NR
*MULLER, LOUIS—35; Hungarian Co.
PETER, JOHAN—25; Hungarian Co., Disability
RATHERS, FRANZ—29; Hungarian Co., aka RATTHARDS, NR
REHN, FERDINAND—20; Hungarian Co., aka GUSTAVE ROEHM, Mustered out
RENK, SEBASTIAN—25; Hungarian Co., Disability
RICHTER, BERTHOLD—23; Hungarian Co., aka GUSTAV, NR
RIEDEL, MAX—20; Birthplace?; Hungarian Co., VRC
=RIEGE, LOUIS—33; Hungarian Co., aka REIGE, WIA, NR
=ROESNBURG, A.—age? Neustaz; Furrier; NR
ROSENBERG, CARL—23; Hungarian Co., NR
*SALZMANN, CARL—26; Birthplace?; Hungarian Co., aka SALTZMANN
=SCHADA, ANTON—25; Siegel Co., aka ANTHONY SCHAA & SCHEADA,
    Dismissed
+SCHREIBER, FRANCIS—46; Band Musician, Hungarian Co., DOD
SCHULZE, ALBERT—28; Hungarian Co., Disability
SCHUTZ, NORBERT—31; Hungarian Co., aka SCHETZ, NORMAL, & SCHITZ,
    NORMAN, Mustered out
SCHWARZ, ANTON—39; Hungarian Co., Disability
+SCHWARZ, CARL—19; Hungarian Co., DOD
+SCHWEIKT, LOUIS—19; Hungarian Co., DOD
SMITH, CARL—29; Hungarian Co., aka SCHMIDT, Disability
SMITH, FRIEDRICH—25; Hungarian Co., aka SCHMIDT, Disability
SPINK, HEINRICH—32; Hungarian Co., NR
*SZABO, JOSEF—44; Hobaly; aka JOSEPH SCABO
=TAKATS, FRANCIS—35; Hungarian Co., aka TACACS, Resigned
=TENNER, LOUIS—29; Hungarian Co., Discharged
THIES, AUGUST HENRY—38; Hungarian Co., Mustered out
TIEDEMAN, MATHS—22; Hungarian Co., NR
ULRICH, GEORG—24; Hungarian Co., NR
UNDERREIDER, WILLIAM—42; Hungarian Co., Transferred to 8th Infantry
UTZL, WILHELM—26; Hungarian Co., NR
VONOKY, LOUIS—age?; Hungarian Co., NR
WACHTER, JOSEPH—32; Hungarian Co., aka WECHTER, Disability
WALL, LORENZ—age?; Hungarian Co., Disability
*WASCHE, WILLIAM—31; Hungarian Co., Deserted 5/11/1862
WEBER, BERNHARD—20; Hungarian Co., WIA, Disability
=+WEEKEY, ANTHONY—28; Attorney; Schwarz Co., aka ANTON WEEKEY &
    VEKEY, DOD
WILACZENSKY, R. CONST—33; Hungarian Co., aka WILAZENSKY &
    CONSTANTINE DE WILACSKY, Disability

*WITTEMBERG, WILHELM—22; Hungarian Co., Deserted 9/9/1862
=ZERDAHELYI, CHARLES—age?; Pianist; NR
ZIRLBAUER, BERTHA—25; Hungarian Co., NR

Ireland

*BARTHOLOMEW, COURTNEY—26; Boiler Maker
BAXTER JR., DAVID—32; Sandy; Mustered out
BLACKWELL, RICHIE—35; Laborer; Mustered out
BURKE, MICHAEL—30; Laborer; Mustered out
BURKE, PATRICK—age?; Spanish Co., Mustered out
BURROWS, WILLIAM—17; Lime...; CIA/PAR/SIH
CAHILL, MARTIN—21; Laborer; Mustered out
+CAIN, MICHAEL—25; Bricklayer; WIA Twice/DOW
CARR, THOMAS—30; Teacher; WIA/SIH
+CARROLL, JOHN—30; Laborer; WIA, Died on Furlough
CARROLL, MARTIN—21; Kings County; WIA, Mustered out
CARROLL, PETER—20; Laborer; WIA, Mustered out
CASHIN, WILLIAM W.—age?; Laborer; Mustered out
CASSIDY, PATRICK—27; Caney; Laborer; Mustered out
CATTON, BERNARD—32; Tailor; WIA, Mustered out
CLEARY, JAMES—21; Tipperary; Machinist; VRC
CLEARY, JAMES—34; Machinist; VRC
COLEMAN, DENNIS—38; Laborer; VRC
COLLINS, THOMAS—19; Limerick; Hospitler; SIH
*COLLINS, WILLIAM B.—38; Clerk; Deserted at End of Furlough
CONKLIN, JOHN—19; Farmer; Mustered out
CONNELLY, PETER—22; Laborer; WIA, Mustered out
CONNOR, JAMES J.—25; Waiter; Co.?, NR
COURTNEY, BARTOLD—26; Bricklayer; Co.?, NR
CROWLEY, FRANCIS—21; Laborer
+CUDEHEY, MICHAEL—20; Clerk
+CUMMING, JOHN—19; Farmer; CIA/POW Andrv
CUNNINGHAM, ANDREW—43; Laborer; WIA, Disability
CUNNINGHAM, PATRICK—37; Mason; VRC
CUSKER, MICHAEL—21; Laborer; WIA, Mustered out
DAY, WILLIAM—22; Kerry; Laborer; NR
*DELANEY, JOHN—20; Edwards; aka FARMER, Transferred to Navy
DOLAN, JOHN—25; Laborer; CIA/PAR, Mustered out
DONAHUE, JAMES—35; Laborer; WIA/CIA/PAR/VRC
DONNELLY, PETER—22; Laborer; WIA/VRC
DOODY, JAMES—20; Limerick; Decorator; Mustered out
+DOOLEY, PATRICK—19, Laborer; CIA/POW Andrv
+DOUGHERTY, MICHAEL—23; Cartman; WIA/DOW

DOYLE, DENNIS—19; Farmer; Mustered out
DOYLE, PATRICK—39; Farmer; NR
DREDNOT, JOHN—29; Hatter; aka DREADNAUGHT, Mustered out
DUFFY, JOHN J.—24; Monaghan; Clerk; Mustered out
DWYER, JAMES—28; Sailor; Transferred to Navy
FARRELL, RICHARD MICHAEL—21; Seaman; Mustered out
+FERGUSON, MICHAEL—19; Seaman; CIA/POW Andrv
FITZGERALD, PATRICK—21; Laborer; MIA/NR
FLEMING, GEORGE—27; Dublin; Boatman; Mustered out
FLEMING, THOMAS—25; Laborer; Mustered out
FLEMING, WILLIAM—26; Printer; Disability
*FOLEY, JOHN—28; Laborer
FORBES, JAMES—21; Laborer; Mustered out
FORBES, JOHN A.—age?; Laborer; Mustered out
FOX, DENNIS—32; Baker; Mustered out
*GAYNOR, WILLIAM—24; Sailor; aka GAINER
GILLIGAN, PATRICK—23; Laborer; Mustered out
GLEASON, PETER—34; Farmer; Disability
GOOLDEN, PATRICK—28; Cork; Laborer; CIA/PAR, Mustered out
GORMAN, THOMAS—28; Laborer; Mustered out
GRAHAM, JOSEPH—35; Mason; Mustered out
GRAHAM, MICHAEL—20; Mongrail; Sailor; Mustered out
GRIFFIN, JAMES—34; Claier; Sailor; VRC
GRIFFIN, MICHAEL—44; Farmer; SIH
*GROGAN, DANIEL—27; Blacksmith
HENDERSON, JOHN—30; Butcher; WIA, NR after Petersburg 6/1864
+HILL, TREVOR—21; Seaman
HOWARD, STEPHEN D.—43; Laborer; Disability
HURST, JOHN—18; Farmer; Mustered out
+HYDE, DENNIS—37; Farmer; DOD
JOHNSON, ROBERT—22; Laborer; Mustered out
JONES, PETER—23; Dublin; Sailor; Mustered out
+JONES, THOMAS—22; Laborer
+KEENAN, BERNARD—40; Lonford; Laborer; DOD
KELLY, JAMES—44; Laborer; Mustered out
*KELLY, JOHN—40; Laborer; WIA
*KELLY, THOMAS—28; Laborer; WIA
KENNY, PATRICK—18; Peddler; VRC
+KERR, THOMAS—22; Belfast; Bookmaker
LANEY, THOMAS—21; Sailor; MIA/NR
LAVOIE, JOSEPH—26; Laborer; WIA, NR after Spotsylvania at Salient 5/12/1864
LAWLER, JAMES—18; Laborer; Mustered out
*LEE, CHARLES—22; Dublin; Laborer; WIA
+LEE, DANIEL—21; Cork; Laborer

=LEE, PETER—32; Carpenter
+LEONARD, JAMES—19; Laborer.
*LYONS, JOHN—21; Seaman/Teamster; SIH
+MALONEY, RICHARD—29; Limerick; Farmer; DOD
+MARTIN, JAMES—26; Laborer; CIA/POW Andrv
MARTIN, JOHN—30; Laborer; Disability
MARTIN, JOHN—35; Laborer; Disability
+MARTIN, WILLIAM—19; Laborer
MATHERS, WILLIAM—35; Meath; Musician; Mustered out
=McCARRON, HUGH—29; Sailor; aka McCANNON, WIA
McCOLLOUGH, WILLIAM J.—43; Farmer; Mustered out
+McCORMACK, PETER—27; Ironmolder; CIA/POW Andrv
+McDONALD, JAMES—24; Laborer; DOD
McELROY, GEORGE—37; Laborer; WIA, Disability
+McFADDEN, JAMES—42; Laborer; CIA/POW Andrv
McGEE, JOHN—40; Hospitler; WIA, NR after Wilderness 5/6/1864
McGRAIN, JOHN—31; Soldier; VRC
+McGROW, PATRICK—21; Laborer; Co. F 1863, Died Suddenly of Heart
    Disease
McMANUS, WILLIAM—32; Limerick; Laborer; CIA/PAR, Mustered out
McNARY, JOHN—30; Blacksmith; WIA, NR After Deep Bottom 8/20/1864
MONTIGUE, WILLIAM—22; Soldier; MIA
MOONEY, JAMES—32; Laborer; WIA, Disability
+MOORE, JAMES—38; Printer; CIA/POW Andrv
MORRISON, ANDREW—26; Confectioner; aka MONESON, Mustered out
MOYLAND, THOMAS—age?; Soldier; aka MAYLAND, WIA/VRC
MURPHY, PATRICK—21; Tyrone; Blacksmith; WIA
+MURRY, PATRICK—36; Laborer
MURRY, WALTER—24; Queens County; Sailor; Mustered out
NELIGAN, DENIS—30; Wheelwright; Mustered out
O'BRIEN, DANIEL—25; Limerick; Painter; Mustered out
O'BRIEN, JOHN—30; Laborer; Mustered out
O'BRIEN, PATRICK—28; Laborer; Mustered out
O'CONNELL, BARTHOLOMEW—38; Laborer; Mustered out
O'CONNER, JAMES J.—25; Waiter; Mustered out
=+O'KEEFE, THOMAS L.—27; Co. K 1864
+O'NEIL, JOHN—19; Laborer; CIA/POW Andrv
PRATT, JOHN F.—41; Laborer; WIA/VRC
+PRENDERGAST, JOHN—age?; Servant; aka PENDERGAST
RODGERS, JAMES THOMAS—24; Laborer; NR
SMITH, DAVID—30; Soldier; Mustered out
SMITH, EDWARD—24; Farmer; Transferred to 185th N.Y.V.I.
SMITH, GEORGE 2ND—21; Sailor; Mustered out
SMITH, JOHN—38; Seaman; NR

SMITH, THOMAS—30; Laborer; Mustered out
SNOW, EDWARD—25; Fireman; aka MICHAEL MAY, Transferred to Navy
ST. JOHN, MICHAEL—20; Laborer; CIA/PAR, Mustered out
+STEWART, ALEXANDER—35; Belfast; Merchant
STONES, MICHAEL—26; Bricklayer; WIA, Mustered out
SULIVAN, JOHN—40; Laborer; Disability
SULLIVAN, PATRICK—26; Laborer; WIA, Disability
TALLONT, JOHN—31; Boilermaker; aka FALLANT, WIA, Mustered out
THOMPSON, PATRICK—24; Laborer; Mustered out
TIERNEY, JOHN—42; Laborer; aka THERNEY, VRC
TIMMIN, JOHN—40; Laborer; VRC
WALLACE, JAMES—22; Sailor; Mustered out
WALLACE, JOHN W.—34; Laborer; Transferred to Navy
WARD, JAMES—21; Soldier; WIA, Mustered out
*WELCH, MICHAEL—23; Boatman
WELSH, JOHN—34; Tailor; WIA, Discharged
WILLIAMS, CHARLES—26; Seaman; WIA, Discharged from Insane Asylum
WILLIAMS, JAMES—29; Laborer; Mustered out
WILSON, CHARLES THOMAS—27; Laborer; CIA/NR
WRIGHT, DAVID—29; Laborer; WIA/SIH

Italy

=ADAMOLI, LUIGI—age?; Farmer; Principal Musician, NR
=ALLEGRETTI, IGNAZIO—21; Italian Co.; Transferred to 29th N.Y.V.I.
*ANAGIO, FRANCISCO—29; Italian Co.
ANDRE, JOHN—26; Naples; Student; aka GIOVANNI ANDURS, Mustered out
ANTONALI, GIACOMO—33; Italian Co., Dishonorably discharged
BARDO, GIUSEPPE—28; Italian Co., aka VINCENZIO, WIA/CIA/PAR,
   Mustered out
BARTOLI, RAFFAELE—25; Lucca; Miller; Disability
BENNETT, PIETRO—29; Rag Dealer; Italian Co., NR
BERNABO, GUISEPPE—age?; Italian Co. 1862, aka BARNABO, Disability
=BISCACCIANTI, ALEXANDER CHARLES DI—43; Disability
=BOGGIALI, GIOVANI—age?; Musician; Wiegand German Co., aka BAGGIOLI
   & ROGIALLI, Discharged
BOIX, ANGEL J.—21; Italian Co. 1862; Disability
+BONI, PAOLO—24; WIA/DOW
*BOTTERA, CALCEDONIO—age?; Italian Co.
*BOTTINI, GIOVANNI—29; Italian Co.
BREMORE, JOHN—24; Seaman; Mustered out
BRESCIANI, BARTOLOMEO—32; Italian Co., Disability
BRUSI, MICHELE—35; Italian Co., Disability
CADOZA, PASQUALE—25; Italian Co. 3/7/1864, NR

CAPOTTINI, CARLO—38; Italian Co., Disability
CARBONI, FRANCESCO—25; Genova; Farmer; WIA, Mustered out
CAROGLIO, LORENZO—35; Mont Forreto; Coachman; aka CAROLIO, Mustered out
CAROLI, PAOLO—33; Italian Co., Disability
*CASTELBECCHI, RAPHAEL—29; Germany; Italian Co., Deserted 4/30/1862, Apprehended
CASTELVECCHIO, RAFFAELE—22; Italian Co., WIA, Mustered out
CATONI, LUIGI—29; Co.?, NR
CAVAGNARO, GIOVANNI—24; Italian Co.
CAVROTTI, GUISEPPE—25; Italian Co., Mustered out
CEBBALLE, MAURICE—age?; Italian Co., NR
CEDONI, CESARE—age?; aka SEDONI, Italian Co., Disability
CELLA, ANTONIO—25; Italian Co., Disability
CLERMONT, ALEXANDER—35; Birthplace?; Italian Co., VRC
COFFI, FRANZESCO—24; Co.? 1864, NR
*COLLA, GIOVANNI—27; Italian Co.
COLOMBANI, J. M.—22; Co.?, NR
COLOMBO, LUIGI—34; Italian Co., VRC
*COSTA, GIOVANNI—25; Italian Co.
*COSTA, STEFFANO—22; Italian Co.
CRAIO, JOHN—20; Malta; Liquor Dealer; Italian Co. 1862, Mustered out
*CUTTA, ANTONIO—29; Italian Co.
CUTORMINI, ANTONIO—age?; Seaman; 1864, NR
DAGUANO, ANTONIO—20; Italian Co., CIA/PAR, Mustered out
=DAL MOLIN, ANTONIO—24; Italian Co., aka DEL KOLIN, Disability
DEGRETO, LUIGI—age?; Italian Co., NR
+DELACOSTA, DOMINICO—19; Laborer; Co. C 1864, WIA/DOW
+DELACOSTA, JOHANNI—21; Laborer; Co. C 1864, WIA/DOW
DELACOSTA, JOSE—age?; Laborer; Co. H 1864, WIA, NR after Petersburg 6/1864
DELAPORES, PETRO—28; Laborer; WIA, Disability
#DE LUCCHI, LUIGI—28; Sperzia; Soldier; Italian Co., Veteran of Garibaldi, Disability
*DE MARTINI, AGOSTINO—20; Italian Co.
*DEPICTO, LUIGI—22; Italian Co.
DESTEFAINI, ENRICO—24; Italian Co., Disability
DESTEFANI, EGIDO—22; Italian Co., aka ENRIES, Disability
DOMINECO, PAGLIO GEORGE—39; Sailor; WIA/SIH
*DRAGUTINOVITCH, THOMAS—23; Italian Co., aka TRACONOVITCH, Deserted 9/2/1862
EMIDIO, ANDREOLI—35; Co.? 1862, NR
FENELLI, FRANCESCO—19; Italian Co., Disability
FERRALASCO, GIOVANNI—30; Italian Co., NR

FERRARI, ANNIBAL—30; Italian Co., Disability, Transferred to U.S. Colored Troops
FERRERO, CARL—19; aka FARIA & FARRIER, Mustered out
=FONTANA, ANDREW—24; Soldier; Italian Co., Discharged
FRASCARI, LUIGI—age?; Italian Co., NR
=FRIZONE, RAPHAEL—24; Italian Co., aka FRISSIONE, Dismissed
*FUNAGHI, RAFFAELE—21; Italian Co.
+GARBARINI, VINCENZO—27; Birthplace?; Italian Co., CIA/POW Andrv
GARIBALDI, LUIGI A.—25; Co.? 1863, aka GEORGE, NR
GAZZERA, FRANCOIS—32; Co.? 1862, NR
*GERAZIO, GIUSEPPE—27; Italian Co., aka GERVASIO
=GERRANNA, ROGEALLA—age?; Co.? 1862, Discharged
*GHILONI, CHRISTOFORO—26; Barza; Cigarmaker; aka Christoforo CHILOSI, GILLONI & CHILOSU
GIOACCHINO, GIORGETTI—22; Italian Co., Disability
GIONSON, JIMI—24; Italian Co., NR
GIUSTI, ANTONIO—28; Catania; Molder; Mustered out
*GOETZ, EUGENIO—19; Italian Co.
*GORDINI, GIOVANNI—23; Italian Co., aka GODINI, ANTONIO, WIA after Cross Keys 6/8/62
GORI, ANGELO—32; Italian Co., aka GERRI, ANGIOLO, Disability
GOTANIS, ANTONIO—25; Coal Heaver
GRIFFA, GIUSEPPE—25; Italian Co., SIH
GUIDI, GIUSEPPE—23; Italian Co., Disability
GUISEPPE, BALLA POSTA—40; Co.? 1862, NR
JOHNSON, JAMES—age?; Italian Co., Mustered out
*LA ROSA, VINCENZO—age?; Italian Co.
LATANIO, ANTONIO—age?; Italian Co. 1864, NR
LA VINERE, ANTONIO—30; Soldier; aka LABINERE, Mustered out
*LEVERONI, DARIDE—18; Italian Co.
LUPICINI, GIORGIO—29; Italian Co., Disability
*LURASCHI, FRENCESCO—age?; Italian Co., aka LORUSCHI
*MAGGI, ANTONIO—28; Italian Co.
MAGGI, FERDINANDO—32; Birthplace?; Italian Co., WIA, Discharged
MALCHIODI, ANTONIO—age?; Italian Co., Disability
MANCINI, PIETRO—32; Italian Co., Disability
MARCOS, ANTONIO—22; Italian Co., Disability
+MARICHI, ANTONIO—35; Sailor; aka DOMENICO MARSALA & MARACHI, Co. I, KIA Wilderness 1/12/64
MAURI, ANTONIO—age?; Italian Co., NR
*MAURI, GIOVANNI—23; Italian Co.
MAZRINI, ANTONIO—25; Italian Co., aka MAZZINI, Disability
*MERSINA, VITA—20; Co. I. 1863
MIRANDE, FILIPPO—20; Italian Co., Disability

MIRANDO, GIOVANNI—age?; Italian Co., NR
MONTEGRIFA, AGOSTINO—30; Italian Co., Disability, Became Sutler
*MORINO, PAOLINO—age?; Italian Co.
MUNERATI, GUISEPPE—35; Italian Co., aka MOUNARATTA, Disability
NANETTI, CARLO—27; Italian Co., Discharged
=NESBIE, GIOVANNI D.—18; Co. F 1864, aka DNESI & D'NESI, Mustered out
+OLIVA, ANTONIO—18; Genoa; Farmer; Italian Co., WIA/DOW
=ORNESI, FRANCISCO—36; Italian Co., Dishonorably discharged
=OSNAGHI, CESARE—30; Italian Co., aka OSNAGI, Discharged
PALMER, HENRY—22; Italian Co., Mustered out
#PARISOTTI, NATALE—25; Italian Co., Disability, Veteran of Garibaldi Italian
    Campaigns
*PATALANI, PASQUALE—24; Tuscani; Seaman; Italian Co., Deserted on
    Veteran Furlough
*PAVARINI, ALESSANDRA—25; Italian Co.
PELI, GAETANO—35; Italian Co., Disability
PERANTO, JOSEPH—34; Co.?, NR
PERATTI,—25; Italian Co., Transferred [to?] 15th Artillery
PETROLI, PIETRIO—25; Laborer; WIA, NR after Wilderness 5/6/1864
PFEIFER, GIOVANNI—age?; Italian Co., CIA/PAR, Mustered out
*PICCONI, GIOVANNI—24; Lucca; Moldmaker; Italian Co., WIA, Reenlisted in
    VRC
PIEROTTI, AMEDEE—28; Italian Co., Transferred [to?] 3rd Artillery
PIEROTTI, VIRGILO—25; Lucca; Plasterer; Italian Co., WIA, Mustered out
*RADETZKY, FRANCESCO—29; Italian Co.
*RAGGIO, GUISEPPE—36; Co. E. 1862
*RANICRI, LUIGI—age?; Italian Co., aka RAINIERI
RAPHAEL, HENRY—19; Italian Co., NR
=REPETTI, ALESSANDRO—39; Genoa; aka RAPPETTI & RIPETTI, Resigned
*RIZRI, GIACOMO—30; Geniva; Looking glass maker; Italian Co., aka
    GIOVANNI RIZZI, Deserted at End of Veteran Furlough
*ROBINSON, GIOVANNI—28; Italian Co.
ROCCA, LUIGI—29; Miland; Shoemaker; Mustered out
ROCK, LEWIS—age?; Italian Co., NR
=RONZOME, SILVIO—30; Italian Co.; aka SILVIS RANSONI & RANZONE,
    SILVSYLVIA RONZONI, Discharged
*ROPETTI, GIOVANNI—23; Italian Co.
*RUX, LUIGI—age?; Nice, Savoy; Soldier; aka ROUX
SACCHI, FRANCESCO—age?; Italian Co., Disability
SACHINI, PIETRO STEFARO—30; Italian Co., NR
=SALVIATTI, ERCIOLE—27; Spanish Co., aka SAREATTI & SALVIATTI,
    Dismissed
SAMBRUETTI, GUISEPPE—32; Genova; Fireman; Italian Co., Mustered out
=SAMSA, GIOVANNI—28; Fiume, Dalmatia; Merchant; Italian Co., Disability

*SANTI, ANTONIO—24; Italian Co.
SASCON, MAYER GUISEPPE—35; Italian Co., aka SAXONMEYER, Disability
SASSET, GIACOBA—age?; Italian Co., Disability
*SAULPREY, GIORGIA—age?; Italian Co., aka GEORGE SAUERBREY
#SCOPINI, AMBROGIO—28; Co.? 1862, Veteran of Garibaldi Italian campaigns, NR
SEIDEL, GABRIEL—21; Italian Co. 1862, NR
STENROCK, LUIGI—23; Italian Co., NR
*VALDEMAYER, EDWARDO—30; Italian Co., aka WALDMEYER
VENTURA, ALESSANDRO—age?; Italian Co., Disability
VENTURINO, DOMENICO—27; Birthplace?; Italian Co., Mustered out
=VENUTI, EDWARD—36; Co. H 1861, aka VENENTI & VENNTI, Transferred [to?] 52nd Infantry
=VERDI, CIRO DR.—30; Italian Co., Transferred [to?] 101st New York Infantry
VERDIER, GIUSEPPE—22; Italian Co., NR
VIGO, ANDREA—41; Italian Co., Disability
VINELLI, FRANCESCO—age?; Italian Co., NR
YELITZ, GIOVANNI—age?; Italian Co., aka TELLECK, Mustered out
ZARONI, PIETRO—age?; Italian Co., Disability

Jews

COMPANY B (SWISS)

+HOCHHEIMER, KARL—24
=LEIBNITZ, FERDINAND—21; aka LEITBRUTZ, Mustered out
LOWENTHAL, BERNHART—24; Schwerin, Mecklenburg, Prussia; Clerk; WIA, later CIA/PAR
MAI, HENRICH—19; Freysa, Kurk Hausen; Baker; aka MAY, WIA, Mustered out
MEIER, HERMANN—20; Breman, Germany; Tailor; aka MAYER
WOLF, JACOB—23; NR

COMPANY C (GERMAN)

BLUHM, JACOB—25; NR
#BROD, HERMAN—26; Rzezow, Gaillizien, Russia; Engraver; Shortest Man, Five Feet Tall, Disability
JACKEL, JULIUS—25; Wertheim, Bavaria; Brewer; Disability
LEHMANN, HEINRICH—26; Disability

COMPANY D (SPANISH)

ARNZ, JULIUS—19; Ronsdorf, Prussia; Carpenter; WIA, Mustered out

COMPANY E (GERMAN)

*FREUDENBERG, ALEXANDER—23; Berlin, Prussia; Clerk
KAUFMAN, GUSTAV—30; Disability
+WEIL, JOSEPH—25; WIA/DOW
WIENER, GUSTAV—31; NR

COMPANY F (GERMAN)

BERLINER, SIGISMUND—26; Mustered out
=DOERNDINGER, LEO—19; aka DENDINGER, WIA, Mustered out
ENGEL, HERMAN—36; Disability
GOTTSCHALK, MICHAEL—33; Stoyle, Prussia; Machinist; VRC
JACOBS, CARL—23; New York, New York; Casketmaker; Mustered out
*ROSE, DAVID P.—age?; Birthplace?; Co. F 1864
ROSENTHAL, GUSTAV—36; Mustered out
SIEGMUND, OSCAR—25; Disability
=WOLF, FREDERICK DR.—32; Transferred to U.S. Volunteers[?]
WOLFF, FRIEDRICH—26; St. Petersburg, Russia; Mechanic; Mustered out

COMPANY G (HUNGARIAN)

ALDKANDDR, SAMUDL 21, Also in Company II, NR
BENJAMIN, ELIAS—age?; Disability
COHN, DAVID—18; Halle, Prussia; Peddler; Mustered out
GANSER, JACOB—28; Maison, Prussia; Baker; WIA/CIA/PAR, Mustered out
=LEDERER, EMANUEL M.—24; Pesth, Hungary; Composer; Disability
LIESER, MAX—22; Disability
MAYER, CARL—25; Oberflacht, Wurttemberg; Carriagemaker; aka MEIER &
    MAYER, WIA, Mustered out
=POLLAK, BERNHARD—24; Hungarian Co., aka POLLOCK, Mustered out
ROSENBURG, CARL—23; NR

COMPANY H (GERMAN)

=BAER, BERNHARD—33; Millinery & Shoes; Discharged, Reenlisted, Mustered
    out
BEHRENDS, AUGUST—27; Musician; Transferred to 2nd Artillery
BERNHARD, ADAM—29; Gladbach, Bavaria; Cigarmaker; WIA/VRC
*EHRLICH, HERMANN—31
+HEINE, LOUIS—28; Ritznitz, Saxony; Trapper; aka Louis HAYNE, WIA/DOW
MEIER, FREDERICH—21; Zelle, Hanover; Sailor; aka MAYER & MEYER, WIA,
    Mustered out
*NIEMANN, CARL—24

COMPANY I (GERMAN)

HESS, ADOLPH—29; Bingm..., Darmstadt; Clerk; aka ADOLPH HEGS, Mustered out
LION, SOMON—22; NR
MAYER, WILHELM—30; Goringen, Baden; Tailor; Mustered out
SACHS, LEOPOLD—28; Disability

COMPANY K (FRENCH)

*DAVID, EMILE—28; Deserted 7/30/1861
HAHN, CHARLES—30; CIA/PAR, Disability
HERZOG, LOUIS—38; Mustered out
LEVY, ADOLPHE—20; Hagenau, France; Merchant; Mustered out
MUNZ, SOMON—21; Austria; Schwolkeshu[?]; aka MEUENTZ & MEUNTZ

Koln

BECKER, FRANZ—21; Koln, Prussia; Cook; Mustered out
+MESSING, FRANZ—39; Koln, Prussia; Schwarz German Co., CIA/POW Andrv
+SCHWIEGER, ALOIS—27; Koln, Prussia; Clerk; Schwarz German Co., CIA/POW Andrv
+SINGER, ANDRE—21; Koln, Prussia; Cigarmaker; CIA/POW Andrv

Kurk Hesson

ARCHINAL, LOUIS—23; Wetten; Farmer; Wiegand German Co., WIA, Disability
BRANER, HEINRICH—20; Marsburg; Confectioner; Bernstein Co., aka BRAUER, Mustered out
*FRANZ, CARL—34; Heinau; Goldsmith; Schwarz Co.
GOOS, HENRY—31; Birkenburg; Blacksmith; Siegel Co., aka GOSS, Mustered out
HUFNAGEL, BERNHARD—26; Heinau; Butcher
=MENZLER, CHARLES—20; Freysa; Baker; Swiss Co., aka MENSLER, Mustered out
MULLER, GEORGE—28; Wiskershade; Farmer; Bernstein German Co., Mustered out
OTTMANN, CONST[A]NTINE—20; Ahl; Cabinetmaker; Wiegand Co., aka OTTOMANN, CIA/NR
+SCHULZ, PETER—26; Eschwege; Sailor; aka GEORGE SCHULZ
+SCHWITZER, CONRAD—20; Weibach; Varnisher; Wiegand Co.
SCHOLL, HENRY—22; Loelbach; Upholsterer; Wiegand German Co., CIA/PAR, Mustered out
+SMAKA, JOHN—22; Krebonstein; Boatfitter; aka SCHMACKE, CIA/POW Andrv/DOD

Lichtenau, Prussia

LE MARIE, BERNHARD—23; Clerk; Hungarian Co., Mustered out
LE MARIE, CHARLES—34; Clerk; French Co., Disability
LE MARIE, CHARLES—19; Clerk; Hungarian Co., NR
LERNIER, BERNARD—23; Clerk; NR

Lippe Detweld

+ALTENBORND, EDWARD—19; Blumberg, Lippendartstadt; Clerk; Wiegand Co., aka ALTENBEREN, CIA/POW Andrv
KOWALS, FERDINAND—30; Detwold, Lippe Detwold; Bookbinder; aka KAWATZ & KOWATZ, CIA/PAR, NR

Malta

CRAIG, JOHN—28; Liquor Dealer; aka CRAY, Mustered out

Mecklenburg

BRINCKMAN, ADOLPH—32; Rosxtwick; Clerk; Wiegand German Co., WIA/VRC
KNUGDR, CHARLES—23; Fostock; Tailor; Wiegand German Co., MIA
HINSCH, ALBERT—21; Paln; Farmer; Disability
HINSE, WILHELM—32; Plain; Farmer; Von Unwerth German Co., VRC
+KOLBATZ, WILLIAM—38; New Strelitz; Stonecutter; Wiegand Co., CIA/POW Andrv
+WITTS, BERNHARD—42; Malshow; Barber

Nassau

DEIFENBACH, GUSTAV—25; Bieberich; Gardener; CIA/PAR, Mustered out
GUNTERMANN, LOUIS—38; Westburg; Shoemaker; Bernstein German Co., Mustered out
+METZLER, LOUIS—19; Harborn; Axelmaker; WIA/DOW
SCHAFER, FRIEDRICH—32; Weisbaden; Farmer; Mustered out
SCHANER, FRIEDRICH CHRISTIAN—29; Weisbaden; Farmer; Siegel Co., WIA, Disability

Nicaragua

*FRATUS, JOSEPH—30; Grenada; Sailor

Norway

*BROWN, HENRY—21; Sailor; WIA

+BROWN, HENRY—44; Sailor; WIA/CIA/DOD Richmond, Va.
PETTREE, JOHN—23; Sailor; aka J. PATRICK, J. PATTRIE & JOHN BATTERY, WIA, Disability
SAMUELSON, SAMUEL—37; Sailor; WIA, Mustered out
SCOTT, OLIVER—22; Tailor; WIA/SIH
SMITH, THOMAS—24; Sailor; Mustered out
+THOMPSON, JOHN—22; Sailor; CIA/POW Andrv

Poland

GUERSKEY, JOHN—32; CIA/POW Andrv ?
GUISKI, GIOVANNI—32; Sailor; NR
HOLT, HERMAN—21; Glaiser; WIA
KALVOSKY, JOHN—29; Farmer; aka KOLVOSKEY, WIA, Disability
KLEINMAN, WILLIAM—40; Cashier; Wiegand German Co., NR
+KRABELL, HEINRICH—24; Breslau; Tinsmith; Swiss Co.
KRAMS, AUGUST—20; Selesia; Clerk; Mustered out
=NIEDZIELSKI, THOMAS—41; Fencing instructor; Italian Co., aka
   NEIDZIELSKI, Dismissed, Dismissal Revoked, Mustered out
OTTO, THEODOR—31; Stettin; Tailor; Von Unwerth German Co., WIA/VRC
RICH, GEORGE—23; Posen; Clerk; Von Unwerth German Co., CIA/PAR,
   Mustered out
WELLASCHAFSKI, RUDOLPH—age?; Co.? 1861, NR
YEUTSCH, EDWARD—18; Breslau; Hatter; aka YENTZ, Mustered out
=ZYLA, ANTHONY P.—45; aka TYLA, Transferred to 58th Infantry

Portugal

BIERA, JOAQUIN—27; Operto; Seaman; WIA/VRC
*FREITAS, JOSE MELO—26; Villa Reale; Sailor; Spanish Co., aka MELOFREIRAS
   & MELOFRATAS, Deserted on Veteran Furlough
*JORGE, JOAQUIN—21; Nazre; Sailor; Spanish Co., aka GEORGE, Deserted on
   Veteran Furlough
NONES, JOAQUIN—28; Quimba; Seaman; Spanish Co., Mustered out
*PERIRA, (E)MANUEL IGNACIO—21; Ville Matalda; Steward; Spanish Co.
SAITARIOS, MANUEL—22; Carpenter; NR

Prussia

=BAUER, WILLIAM—26; Tailor; NR
+BERGENFELD, LUDWIG—19; Brewer; aka BERKENFELD, CIA/POW Andrv
BRADLEY, RALPH—21; Prussia, Germany; Sailor; WIA/VRC
BRAUN, CARL—28; Deman; Farmer; Mustered out
+BREHMER, EDWARD—27; Strausland; Farmer; Schwarz German Co., DOD
+BROWN, CHARLES—21; Derman; Farmer; CIA/POW Andrv

BROWN, JOHN—26; Sailor; Mustered out

DEVERAUX, EMIL—23; Clerk; Mustered out

DREYER, AUGUST—24; Conitz; Painter; Berstein Co., aka EDWARD DROYER, Mustered out

EDELMANN, LOUIS—age?; Biekfield; Tailor; NR

+EDLER, FREDERICK—28; Biekfield; Tailor; POW/CIA Andrv DOD

+GRAMMS, CHARLES—21; Prussia, Germany, aka GRANNES, CHARLES

*GREGOR, AUGUST—35; Berlin; Waiter; WIA

GUNTHER, FRIEDRICH—26; Berlin; Tailor; aka GUENTHER, VRC

HAPPE, ARNOLD—27; Berlin; Cabinetmaker; CIA/PAR, Mustered out

HAUNNARMANN, RUDOLPH—23; Goeletz; Tailor; Bernstein Co., aka HAMMARDT, Mustered out

HENKEL, GEORGE—31; Essust; Farmer; Wiegand German Co., Mustered out

HERRMAN, HENRY—20; Baker; WIA, Discharged

*HOFFMANN, CARL—22; Kleinsena; Farmer; Schwarz Co. & Bernstein Co., Deserted 7/20/1861

=HOFFMANN, CHARLES—34; Kleinsena; Farmer

+HOLSTEIN, GUSTAVUS—26; Seaman

+HULGINSKY, ERNST—21; Merchant

JANSEN, CARL—50; Wolgast; Baker; VRC

JOHANNES, FRIEDRICH—36; Rahdeberg; Laborer; Hungarian Co., Mustered out

+KAUFMAN, ALBERT—24; Mechanic; WIA/DOW

*KRIENINGER, EDWARD—40; West Prussia; Laborer; Swiss Co.

+LEHMAN, AUGUST—43; Berlin; Cigarmaker; aka LEAMAN, CIA/POW/Andrv DOD

+MEEK, CHRISTOPHER—21; Carpenter; POW/Andrv/DOD

*MEHREN, HEINRICH—24; Brewer; Wiegand German Co., Deserted 6/24/1862

MEYER, EDWARD—19; Waiter; WIA, Mustered out

+MONTAG, GEORGE—29; Kern; Locksmith; Siegel Co., CIA/POW Andrv

MULLER, FRANZ—18; Sellentsch; Sailor; Bernstein German Co., WIA, VRC

NIESCHAFFER, CARL—42; Dyer; VRC

PRAEDEL, CHARLES—42; Seaman; NR

QUADE, JULIUS—26; Hagen; Clerk; CIA/PAR, Disability

RAPHAEL, SAMUEL—19; Berlin; aka JOSE RAPHAEL, WIA, Mustered out

REINKE, THEODOR—33; Dutch Krowe; Blacksmith; aka REINECKE, CIA/PAR, Mustered out

RENKHARD, ALBERT—23; Krosse; Tailor; aka RENKHARDS & RINGHARDT, WIA, Mustered out

RIEMANN, HERMAN—20; Erfurt; Carver; Wiegand German Co.

RODIGUER, JULIUS—21; Weissenfels; Clerk; NR

SCHAUM, PHILIP—19; Glieberg; Cigarmaker; WIA/VRC

SCHILLING, GUSTAV—43; Halberstadt; Bookbinder; VRC

SCHWARZ, WILLIAM—37; Conitz; Undertaker; Co.?, NR

+**SIEBERT, ANDREAS**—29; Magdeburg; Blacksmith; aka Andrew SEIBERT, CIA/ POW Slsbry

SOMMERS, LOUIS—25; Watzler; Hatter; Schwarz German Co., Mustered out

SPOTH, WILHELM—37; Kenigsberg; Cook; aka SPOHR, Mustered out

TAUBENSPECK, EDWARD—21; Berlin; Clerk; aka FANBENSPECK & FAUBENSPEK, WIA, Mustered out

*****UHLMAN, HENRY**—age?; Co. I, Deserted 12/12/1861

ULLMER, MOSES—21; Sangerfeld; Butcher; aka UHMER & ULMER, SIH

WEBER, NICOLAUS—23; Baker; Schwarz German Co., Mustered out

WEIS, FRANZ DR.—40; Doctor; Mustered out

WILHELMI, FRANZ—36; Bernstein German Co., Discharged

Russia

BROWN, JOHN—41; Kronstadt; Carpenter; CIA/PAR, Mustered out

BROWN, JOHN—38; Kronstadt; Laborer; Disability

CISCO, JOHN—40; Laborer; CIA/PAR, Mustered out

FENERO, CARL—19; Sailor; Co.?, NR

+**WEGNER, CARL**—33; Seaman; aka WAGNER & WAGGONER, CIA/POW Andrv

Saxony

BISCHOFF, GUSTAV—28; Ruhla; Shoemaker; Wiegand Co., aka GUST BRICKOF, WIA, Mustered out

=**EDELMAN, LOUIS**—31; Lacory; Clerk

GLINGHARD, HOHN—25; Ackenburg; Stonecutter; Mustered out

KAESTNER, CARL—18; Eisencah; Carpenter; Wiegand Co., aka KESTNER, Mustered out

SAALBORN, HUGO—34; Camburg; Farmer; Bernstein German Co., aka SAULBORN, Disability

WALTHER, CHRISTIAN—37; Coburg; Cabinetmaker; Schwarz German Co., aka WATTHER, VRC

Schwarzberg

KOCH, AUGUST—19; Sonderhausen; Clerk; Bernstein Co., WIA, Mustered out

Scotland

=**ADDI, THOMAS J.**—33; Agent; Co. C 1864, Transferred from 73rd Infantry, Mustered out

+**ALLEN, BENJAMIN**—30; Glasgow; Carrier; DOD

ALLEN, DAVID A.—37; Glasgow; Laborer; Transferred from 42nd Infantry, Served as Major, Mustered out

BIDHIE, CHARLES—35; Weaver; aka BIDHIL, CIA/VRC

McCAUL, JOHN—20; Boatman; aka McCALL, WIA
McCOLLUM, JAMES C.—28; Shoemaker; aka McCULLUM, Mustered out
+McDONALD, DANIEL—26; Laborer; DOD
MOFFAT, WILLIAM—20; Sailor; CIA/NR
MOODIE, GEORGE—21; Sailor; WIA, Disability
+MOORE, DAVID—25; Cottonspinner; CIA/POW Andrv
PRIMROSE, ALEXANDER—44; Tailor; WIA, Mustered out
#ROBERTS, WILLIAM—21; Sailor; CIA, Joined Confederate Army, Recaptured
   & Released as POW
SHIELDS, JAMES—26; Cottonspinner; WIA, Mustered out
SMITH, THOMAS—20; Boatman; CIA/NR
SMITH, WILLIAM—29; Edinborough; Sailor; WIA/VRC
+THOMPSON, JAMES—44; Farmer; CIA/POW Andrv

Spain

ALEXANDRE, D. JUAN T.—29; aka JOHN ALEXANDER, Co.?, NR
ALFONSO, FRANCISCO—23; Spanish Co., aka JOAE ALFONZIO, VRC
ALFONSO, MANUEL—32; Spanish Co., Disability
AMARO, MANUEL—25; Spanish Co., Discharged
*ARGUMOSA, JUAN—21; Spanish Co., Deserted 7/10/1861
AUGUSTI, ANTONIO—35; Spanish Co., Disability
BANOS, COMAS—26; Spanish Co., aka THOMAS BANOS, Disability
BARRE, JUAN—20; Spanish Co., aka JOAQUIN BARRO, CIA/PAR, NR
BORES, MARTIN—age?; Spanish Co., Mustered out
BORGES, VINCENTI—25; Spanish Co., Disability
=BURMAZOR, SYLVIS—age?; Spanish Co., Discharged
CABALLOS, MANUEIS—21; Discharged
CASTIELLO, FRANCISCO—26; Spanish Co., Disability
=CASTILLO, JUAN RUIZE Y.—28; aka CARTILLIER, Discharged
CAZENAVE, HENRY—19; Spanish Co., Disability
COBO, JOSE—22; St. Andrea; Sailor; Spanish Co., WIA, Mustered out
COCU, SEBASTIEN—28; Co.? 1862, aka COCA, NR
COFFI, FRANZESCO—24; Co.? 1864, NR
CONCIGHERO, EMANUEL—38; Co.? 1863; aka CORRCELIO, NR
DE LA HAY, FERDINAND—25; Co.? 1863, aka DELA FERDINAND HAUS, NR
=DE LA MESA, CARLOS A.—32; Spanish Co., VRC
DELGARDO, PHILIP—21; Waiter; WIA, Mustered out
DE LOS SANTOS, MANUEL—25; Spanish Co., aka SANTES, Mustered out
*DEMPSEY, JAMES—18; Spanish Co., Deserted 8/4/1861
DIAZ, ANTONIO—age?; Spanish Co., NR
*DOMINGUEZ, ANTONIO—21; Spanish Co., Deserted 11/18/61
*DOMINGUOS, RICARDO—22; Spanish Co., aka DOMINQUEZ, Deserted
   11/18/61

ESTABAN, FELIX—35; Spanish Co., aka FELIZ, ESTEBEU, NR
FERNANDEZ, ANTONIO—29; Spanish Co., Disability
FERREGUS, RAMON—25; Spanish Co., aka ROMAN FERUGER, NR
*FERRIS, CARLOS—33; Spanish Co., Deserted 8/10/1861
FEYT, JOSE—30; Italian Co., aka FEITH, FYTH & TEYL, Disability
FORTUNES, ANTONIO—30; Spanish Co., CIA, Escaped
GARCIA, ANTONIO—23; Spanish Co., NR
GATES, WILLIAM—23; Spanish Co., Disability
+GOMEZ, EMANUEL—20; Clerk; DOD (Acute Bronchitis)
GOMEZ, JANITO—25; Spanish Co., NR
*GONZALEZ, JUAN—27; Cella, Chilli; Sailor; Spanish Co.
GUELPA, FRANCISCO—24; Co.? 1862, NR
*GUETIERVEZ, MANUEL—28; Spanish Co., aka GUTIERREZ
GUTIENES, FRANCISCO—27; Spanish Co., aka GUTIERREZ, NR
*GUTTIENEZ, ANTONIO—20; Spanish Co., aka GUTIERREZ, Deserted 11/18/61
GUZMAN, ANTONIO—30; Birthplace?; Spanish Co., WIA, Mustered out
HOGNER, JUAN—23; Spanish Co., NR
HORER, MANEWELL—21; Sailor; MIA
*HORNIA, CELESTINO—21; Avidio; Photographist; WIA Twice, Deserted from
    Hospital
HYPLOITE, LORENZ—age?; Spanish Co., Disability
*JACOMA, MANUEL—33; Spanish Co., Deserted 9/5/1862
JIMEREZ, JUAN J.—25; Co. E 1864, WIA, NR after Wilderness 5/6/1864
JOSE, FRANCISCO—23; Spanish Co., NR
JUNCO, ENRIQUS—22; Birthplace?; Spanish Co., WIA/VRC
KORRELL, JOHN—23; Spanish Co., Musician, Mustered out
*KOSTER, DANIEL—31; Spanish Co.
+LEWIS, AUGUSTUS—23; Cook; WIA/DOW
LEWSON, JOSEPH—17; Spanish Co., Mustered out
LIONERD, JORGE—21; Spanish Co., NR
LOARTE, JUAN—25; Spanish Co., aka LOARSE, NR
LOPEZ, ANTONIO—30; Italian Co., Discharged
=LUGUE, FRANCISCO—30; Spanish Co., aka LAQUE, Discharged
*MADRID, JUAN—26; Spanish Co., Deserted 7/8/1861
*MANNING, THOMAS—19; Spanish Co., Deserted 8/4/1861
+MARLOTT, WILLIAM—27; Birthplace?; Spanish Co., aka MAC COTT &
    McCORT
MARTINEZ, MIGUEL—25; Malaga; Sailor; Spanish Co., Mustered out
MARTINEZ, RADRIGUEZ Y JUAN—21; Co.? 1862, NR
*MAYO, ANTONIO SILVA—20; Spanish Co., Deserted 7/22/1861
METANTEN, LEON—35; Spanish Co., NR
METO, FERNANDO—22; Spanish Co., NR
MINDER, BAPTIST—43; Spanish Co., Disability
+MOLENS, JUAN—23; Spanish Co., WIA/DOW

*NATO, EULOGIO—22; Spanish Co., aka NETO, Deserted 11/24/1861
NAVARRETO, FRANCISCO—27; Birthplace?; Spanish Co., WIA
#+OLIVER, MIGUEL—23; Spanish Co., Murdered
*PASOS, ANDRES FERNANDEZ—19; Spanish Co., aka PAROS, Deserted 8/11/1861
PEREZ, ELIA—28; Birthplace?; Italian Co., Discharged
PIRO, CRISTOBAL—22; Spanish Co., Disability
*PORRAS, JOSE FLORAS—25; Malaga; Sailor; Spanish Co., aka FLORES PERES
QUINONES, RAFAEL—20; Estudies; Clerk; Spanish Co., aka GUINONES &
     JUINONES, Mustered out
*RIVERIRO, MANUAL—28; Spanish Co.
*RODRIGUEZ, JUAN—age?; Co. C 1862, aka JOSE, Deserted 7/5/1862
=ROMERO, JOSE G.—34; Spanish Co., Discharged
ROSI, FRANCIS—33; Painter; Mustered out
ROY, ALEXANDER—34; Spanish Co., Disability
SANCHES, PETER—24; Soldier; CIA/PAR
SANTES, OSEE—20; Blacksmith; WIA
SAUREZ, FERNAND—29; Baker; Co. E 1864, NR
SOUTHINE, MANUEL—22; Co. K 1864; WIA/SIH, aka LARTRUCIO &
     SARDUNIO
*SOUZA, EUGENIO MARY—45; Spanish Co.
SRICK, VINCENT—31; Spanish Co., NR
SUAREZ, CELESTINO—23; Spanish Co., NR
SUAVIS, FERNANDO—33; Baker, Mustered out
*TOMSON, JOHN—18; Spanish Co., Deserted 8/4/1861
TONEN, JOSE—21; Spanish Co., NR
TORRENS, JOSEPH—40; Transferred to "Enfants Perdus"
TORRENS, JOSE JUAN—26; Bayma; Merchant; aka TANNER, Mustered out
*TURRA, PEDRO—22; Spanish Co.
VALDES, JOSE—25; Spanish Co., WIA, Discharged
VALDIS, ANTONIO—23; Neandella; Mason; CIA/PAR, Mustered out
*VALLE, MARTIN—36; Catalonia; Mason
VALLESTERO, FRANCISCO—31; Spanish Co., aka VALLESTEN/BALLESTRA,
     NR
VARELA, ALEJANDRO—23; Spanish Co., Disability
+VIGIL, AUGUSTIN—21; Spanish Co., DOD
=WOODBURY, EDUARDO—21; Spanish Co., Discharged
YAMANIEGO, JOSE—32; Co. C 1864, NR

Sweden

+ALGOT, GUSTAF—20; Sailor; aka AUGUSTUS ALKUS & OLKUT, CIA/POW
     Thdr Cstl
+ANDERSON, PETER—22; Sailor
+ANDERSON, SVEN JOHAN—24; Shoemaker; CIA/POW Andrv

HOLSTEIN, AUGUST—20; Lavende; Seaman; Mustered out
+NEILL, JOHN—22; Farmer; DOD
NELSON, CHARLES—24; Sailor; CIA/NR
NELSON, FREEMAN—26; Farmer; Discharged
+NILSON, BERNHARD—25; Guttenberg; Carpenter; CIA/POW Andrv

Switzerland

ALTHEER, JOHANN—40; Butcher; Swiss Co., Disability
ANDREAS, GOTLIEB—40; Arau; Plasterer; Swiss Co., WIA, Disability
BACKESS, MAURICE—36; aka MORISE BAKESS, Swiss Co., NR
BEIGER, GEORGE—37; Painter; Swiss Co., Disability
BEISWINGER, CARL—23; aka WILLIAM, Swiss Co., Disability
BINDSCHADLER, JOHANN—20; Swiss Co., Disability
BOSCH, JOHANN—26; Swiss Co., Discharged
+BRANDENBERGER, HENRY—20; Clerk; DOD
BRITSCHE, JOHN—26; Scheffhausen; Farmer; Siegel Co., WIA/VRC
BULACHER, FRANZ—45; Swiss Co., NR
CATUFF, LOUIS—38; Swiss Co. 1862, NR
CHAPAUS, JOHN—44; Carver; Disability
CHAPPIUT, PIERRE—31; Swiss Co. 1862, Disability
CHRIST, GEORG—21; Swiss Co., Discharged
=COLANI, GIOVANNI MARCO—38; Swiss Co., aka TOLANI, Discharged
+CORDET, JACOB—45; Swiss Co., WIA/DOW
+CORDET, MARTIN—21; Granbuntten; Butcher; aka CARLEY, Mustered out
CURTHAUSEN, PETER—24; Swiss Co., NR
DAMM, HEINRICH—19; Swiss Co., NR
DANNER, JACOB—24; Avon; Farmer; Disability
DE BEAUMONT, MAURICE—25; Swiss Co., aka BEAUMONT, NR
DELHORME, PIERRE—35; Swiss Co. 1862, NR
=DE SCHMIDT, JOSEPH—age?; Swiss Co., Resigned
=DESSAUER, JOHN—20; Swiss Co., Dismissed
=DIETRICH, HEINRICH—27; Swiss Co., aka HENRY DEITRICK, Discharged
*DIEZ, MICHAEL—31; Swiss Co.
DORMONT, JULIUS—24; Swiss Co. 1862, NR
DORNBIRER, JACOB—27; St. Gallen; Butcher; Bernstein German Co., Mustered
    out
*DUBENDORFER, JACOB—23; Hardt; Carpenter; Swiss Co.
DUVAL, CHARLES—23; Swiss Co., Disability
EBERHARD, WILHELM—28; Swiss Co., Discharged
*ERB, JOHANN—20; Swiss Co.
ERTINGER, WILHELM—42; Swiss Co., Discharged
FICKO, HEINRICH—age?; Swiss Co., Mustered out
FONTANA, ABRAHAM—39; Swiss Co., Transferred to 2nd Artillery

FREY, JOHN—30; Brack; Butcher; MIA
FRIDLI, JACOB—32; Swiss Co., Disability
FURTWENGLER, JOSEPH—25; Rietenschel; Cabinetmaker; Wiegand Co., Mustered out
GEBNER, RUDOLF—23; Swiss Co., Mustered out
GERZ, WILHELM—27; Swiss Co., NR
GIRARD, ROBERT—20; Swiss Co., Transferred to Mountain Department, Union Army
GRELL, JACOB—24; Swiss Co., Transferred to 15th Artillery
GUTKNECHT, HEINRICH—25; Swiss Co.
HAFELI, JACOB—26; Swiss Co., Mustered out
*HERTNER, PIERRE—24; Bazil; Confectioner; French Co., aka PETER HOETNER
HINNEN, GOTTLIEB—24; Swiss Co., Disability
HOFFMAN, JOSEPH—23; Musician; Swiss Co., NR
HOLZINGER, AUGUST—26; Swiss Co., aka HEMSINGER, ADOLPH, WIA/VRC
HUBER, RUDOLPHE—28; Zurich; Clerk; French Co., Mustered out
HUNZINGER, ADOLPH—21; Aogara; Baker; WIA, Mustered out
ISLER, GUSTAV—19; Swiss Co., Disability
JEHLE, GOTTLIEB—42; Swiss Co., aka TELE, Disability
=JOERIN, EMIL—23; Swiss Co., aka TOERIN & TORIN, Mustered out
+JORDAN, ALBERT—21; Swiss Co.
+KASLE, ALOIS—23; Swiss Co., DOD
KELLER, JOHANN—25; Swiss Co., Mustered out
KEMPF, HEINRICH—26; Swiss Co., Disability
KIMBEL, MARTIN—26; Swiss Co., NR
KING, CONRAD—20; Clerk; WIA, Disability
KINGLE, JOSEPH—38; Baker; Wiegand German Co., VRC
KINGLE, JOSEPH—38; Baker; Wiegand German Co., VRC
KLEIN, LOUIS—28; Swiss Co., NR
*KLEPFER, FRIDRICH—27; Swiss Co.
KNOTTER, CARL—40; Swiss Co., Disability
KUCHLER, JOSEPH—23; Baker; Swiss Co., Disability
LA FOR, GABRIEL—25; Swiss Co., NR
=LEIBNITZ, FERDINAND—21; Swiss Co., aka LEITBRUTZ, Mustered out
LUDIN, JOHANN—39; Swiss Co., Disability
*MATHYAS, JACOB—22; Swiss Co., aka MATTHIAS, Deserted 9/26/1861
MAURER, PETER—36; Swiss Co., Transferred to 2nd Artillery
*METZEN, JEAN B.—32; Swiss Co.
MONNET, MATHIAS—35; Swiss Co., Disability
MOSER, ANDREAS—22; Swiss Co., NR
=MULLER, ALFRED—32; Swiss Co., Discharged
+MULLER, EMIL—27; Swiss Co.
MULLER, FRIEDRICH—30; Swiss Co., NR

+NAFFLE, XAVER—30; Swiss Co., aka HAVER NAPFLE, DOD

+OERTLE, ULRICH—31; Laborer; aka ARTLE & ORTLE, WIA/CIA/POW
Andrv DOD

OEST, HENRY—age?; Swiss Co., NR

=PASQUET, ALPHONSE—25; Swiss Co., aka ALFRED, Discharged

PIERSON, JULIUS—34; Swiss Co., NR

PUNTER, ROBERT—21; Swiss Co., NR

=RANG, ANTON—32; Swiss Co., Principal Musician, aka PRANG, RANKE &
RAUKE, Mustered out

RAYMANN, JOHANN—27; Swiss Co., Disability

REVIERE, ALEXANDRE—38; Swiss Co., aka RIVIERE, NR

ROEBER, CARL—19; Swiss Co., Mustered out

+ROMANY, CHRISTIAN—26; Bern; Lawyer; CIA/POW Thdr Cstl

ROSEHARDT, FRANCOIS—39; Geneva; Carpenter; NR

ROTTMANN, CARL—23; Swiss Co., NR

RULBERG, CARL—26; Swiss Co., Discharged

SCHAUB, JOHANN—45; Swiss Co., Discharged

SCHEEMANN, GOTTFRIED—35; Swiss Co., aka SHEEMAN, WIA/NR

SCHERPICH, WILHELM—25; Swiss Co., Disability

SCHEUTZLER, HEINRICH—19; Swiss Co., aka SCHNETZLER, Transferred to
15th Artillery

SCHLEICHER, KASPAR—23; Swiss Co., NR

+SCHMID, JAKOB—38; Swiss Co., DOD

SCHOEN, JOHANN—23; Swiss Co., Disability

SCHOULER, CHARLES—37; Swiss Co., 1862, NR

SCHWARZENBACH, ALBERT—24; Kufsnach; Bookbinder; Swiss Co., aka
SMALLBARGER, CIA/POW Andrv?

*SEIB, CARL—19; Swiss Co., aka SCIB

SEIPPEL, KARL LUDWIG—32; Swiss Co., aka Carl SCIPPEL, Disability

SHEKEL, AUGUST—23; Swiss Co., NR

SIEBERT, OSKAR—25; Swiss Co., Disability

*SPEK, GOTTLIEB—17; Swiss Co.

STAUBLE, JOSEPH—28; Lutz; Farmer; Swiss Co., CIA/PAR/NR

=STEIGER, EMIL DR.—23; Swiss Co., Discharged

STEINER, PETER—30; Oheried; Farmer; Swiss Co., NR

+STEPHAN, JACOB JOHN—age?; Birthplace?; Swiss Co., DOD

STREHL, CARL AUGUSTUS—40; Swiss Co., Disability

=SUTTER, CARL—27; Wuppenau; Cabinetmaker; Swiss Co., aka CHARLES
SULTER, CIA/PAR, Discharged

TUCHSCHMIED, TUL—26; St. Weir; Tailor; SIH

ULMER, HEINRICH JOHN—31; Swiss Co., Transferred to 15th Artillery

VONLINDEN, LUDWIG—21; Swiss Co., aka LOUIS VON LINDEN, Mustered
out

=+WAGNER, ADOLPHUS—20; Adgara; Baker

WALTHER, GEORG—26; Swiss Co., Transferred to 2nd Artillery

WEBER, LUDWIG—28; LUTZ; Tailor; Swiss Co., Mustered out

WEINMANN, EDWARD—25; Zurich; Printer; Wiegand German Co., aka VEINMAN, CIA

WERNDLI, HENRY—32; Waran; Barber; aka WENDLE, Mustered out

WERNER, SIMON—28; Swiss Co., Disability

+WURDMAN, BERNARD—28; Swiss Co., aka WERDMAN, DOD

WURSCH, JOHANN I—31; Emmetten; Laborer; Swiss Co., VRC

WURSCH, JOHANN II—33; Swiss Co., Disability

WURSCH, JOSEPH I—24; Swiss Co., NR

+WURSCH, JOSEPH II—28; Emmetten; Laborer; WIA/DOW

WURSCH, LUDWIG—27; Swiss Co., Disability

ZANDER, LEOPOLD—41; Swiss Co., Disability

ZEHUDER, LUDWIG—28; Swiss Co., NR

+ZEINER, AUGUST—23; Emmetten; Laborer; Hungarian Co., CIA/POW Andrv, NR

ZIEGLER, JOHANN—22; Swiss Co., NR

ZIMMERMAN, CASPER—21; Farmer; VRC

ZOBRIST, JOHN—41; Rupperswue; Haberdasher; Swiss Co., Mustered out

ZOPFI, ANDREAS—32; Birthplace?; Swiss Co., Mustered out

ZULINDEN, EUSEBIUS—35; Bottwieson; Haberdasher; Swiss Co., Mustered out

Wurttemberg

ANWANDER, JOHANN—24; Bibach, Wurtenbach; Sailor; Berstein German Co., aka JOHN ANIVANDER, WIA, NR after Wilderness 5/5/1864

BAUHOF, ALBERT—19; Baker; WIA, Mustered out

*BAUMANN, JOHN—38; Goreburg; Shoemaker

BERGHEIMER, GOTTLIEB—34; Beckenheim; Shoemaker; Disability

*BETTING, SIMON—28; Farmer; Deserted from Hospital

+CARL, FREDERICK—37; Obrendorf; Farmer

DEUSCHEL, JACOB—28; Wellingen; Farmer; Schwarz German Co., WIA, Mustered out

ENGELHARDT, LOUIS—23; Stutgardt; Baker; Siegel German Co., Mustered out

FAUSER, GOTTLIEB—33; Fuerbach; Farmer; WIA, Mustered out

+FESSLER, FRITZ—23; aka FOSSLER

+GESSMANN, FRIEDRICH—25; Lauffen; Tailor; Von Unwerth German Co., aka GELSMANN

GRAF, JOHANN—25; Volmaningson; Tailor; Bernstein German Co., NR

GROAT, ANTHONY—45; Wurstenbach; Farmer; Disability

HUGLEY, FREDERIC—32; Heidheim; Carpenter; French Co., Disability

HOMAN, CHARLES—22; Evangon; Farmer; aka Herman, WIA, Disability

*HORN, PETER—33; Heidenheim; Carpenter

JORDAN, JACOB—34; Gropvillard; Tailor; Schwarz German Co., Mustered out
+KAUTH, GOTTLIEB—24; Emmenhausen; Shoemaker
+KLAIBER, CARL—30; Thalheim; Tinsmith
*MACK, THOMAS J.—27; Sangert; Farmer; Spanish Co., Deserted 8/4/1861,
    Caught & Brought Back to his Company
MULLER, WILHELM—30; Schweisburg; Pianomaker; Bernstein German Co.,
    Disability
RAAB, HENRY—31; Cesslinger; Jeweler; Siegel German Co., Disability
RAU, JOHANN—23; Wildbad; Jeweler; Bernstein German Co., aka RACH,
    Disability
ROLL, GEORGE—43; Laborer; Disability
*ROOS, MATTHUES—25; aka MATHEW ROSS, WIA
SCHAEFER, JEAN—30; Regonzingan; Gunsmith; Von Unwerth German Co.,
    Mustered out
SCHICKLER, GEORGE—26; Albach, Wurstenburg; Farmer; Siegel German Co.,
    Mustered out
SCHMIDT, LOUIS—33; Ottenes...; Farmer; aka LUDWIG SCHMITT, NR
+SCHNELL, CARL—21; Ben...; Butcher; CIA/POW Andrv
SCHONBEIN, CHAS.—21; Ellwanger; Varnisher; CIA/SIH
SCHUMACHER, ALBERT—21; Tubingen; Baker; Schwarz German Co.
SCHUMACHER, CHRISTIAN—27; Grafenhausen; Clerk; Von Unwerth German
    Co., aka CHRISTOPHER SCHUMACHER, Mustered out
SCHWEILSER, ADOLPH—30; Leonburg; Tinsmith; Disability
TRAUB, JACOB—40; Esbengen; Coppersmith; Mustered out
WAGER, AUGUST—23; Fried...; Painter; Siegel German Co., aka WAGNER, VRC
WERNER, CARL—20; Riedlinger; Carpenter; Swiss Co., Disability

United States

CALIFORNIA

MORENO, JOSE MARIA—age?; Spanish Co., aka MORENS, NR

CONNECTICUT

+BENTON, EZEKIAL B.—22; Hartford; Laborer; aka EDWARD BENTON, WIA/
    DOW
BIXBY, WILLIAM—24; Lynn; Sailor; Mustered out
FREDERICKS, WILLIAM—19; West Milford; Laborer; WIA, Mustered out
=HOYT, CHARLES DR.—41; Ridgefield, Fairfield County; Surgeon, 1864,
    Transferred from 125th Infantry, Mustered out
LEACH, ROYAL DR.—43; Litchfield; Physician; aka FELIX, Mustered out
ROMINE, JAMES A.—21; West Milford; Farmer; aka ROMAINE, Discharged

DAVIS, PETER—36; Savannah; Laborer; Mustered out

BRADY, HENRY E.—24; Laborer; Mustered out

=BAKER, ALLEN M.—30; Bangor; Teamster; aka BACKER, WIA, Mustered out
INGRAHAM, GEORGE—22; Portland; Sailor; Transferred to Navy
*McINTYRE, GEORGE—28; Seaman; aka MAC INTYRE

SMITH, LEVI S.—33; Baltimore; Shoemaker; WIA, Mustered out

ALDRICH, DANIEL—34; Clarbough; Farmer; Mustered out
BOSSONG, ALBERT—20; Chester Factory; Baker; Bernstein German Co., Mustered out
COSEY, FRANK—18; Boston; Colored Man [African-American]; Sailor; WIA, Transferred to U.S. Signal Corps
GRIFFIN, JOHN B.—19; Cigarmaker; Transferred to 2nd Cavalry
HATHAWAY, BENJAMIN F.—41; New Bedfor[d]; Sailor; Disability
HAYES, JAMES—19; Boston; Farmer; Disability
JONES, JOHN—19; Pittsfield; Laborer; WIA, Mustered out
LATHROP, WILLIAM A.—36; Springfield; Bricklayer
OFREE, NICHOLAS—22; Pookeepsi; Laborer; CIA/PAR, Mustered out
+PARKER, JOHN—27; Teamster; WIA/DOW
PARKER, THOMAS—41; Seaman; Mustered out
SCHIEL, VALENTINE—20; Boston; Trunkmaker; aka SHIELDS, Mustered out
SMYTHERMAN, JOHN—19; Boston; Stonecutter; Transferred to 2nd Cavalry
WOOD, MARCUS—21; Springfield; Bookkeeper; aka THEODORE A.
    GAMMAGE, GRAMMAGE & MAMMAGE, Absent from Detail at Muster

BRAYMAN, JOSEPH—21; Sailor; WIA, Disability

ABER, JOHN—19; Laborer; Mustered out
*BOGART, DAVID—38; Mason
BRANNAN, WILLIAM—18; Hudson; Laborer; aka BRENNAN, VRC
+CARPENTER, WILLIAM H.—age?; Jersey City; Farmer; DOD

CASEY, EDWARD—18; Calton; Farmer; Discharged
*COMBS, WILLIAM—39; Farmer
COURIER, ANDREW—21; Brewer; CIA/NR
*DEAN, STEPHAN—26; Farmer; WIA
+SAITHOF, ISAAC—19; Patterson; Laborer; WIA/DOW
*TITUS, THOMAS—18; Patterson; Laborer

NEW YORK (STATE)

ALLEN, THOMAS—19; Pokispie; Seaman; WIA, Mustered out
ARMSTRONG, JAMES—20; Laborer; WIA
BALLARD, BENJAMIN—40; Onodaga; Shoemaker; aka BULLARD & BALLAD, Transferred to 185th New York Infantry, Mustered out
=BANKS, WRIGHT—35; Mount Plesants; Co. K 1865, Transferred from 38th Infantry, Mustered out
+BARRETT, WILLIAM—18; Farmer; DOD
BASTIAN, WILLIAM—16; Lawrence; Farmer; Mustered out
BIDDLEBORROUGH, JOSEPH R.—18; Pitcher; aka BURDLEBOUGH, Transferred to 185th Infantry
BIRLBAUER, JOSEPH—34; Pitcher; Farmer; Disability
BOUGHTON, JOSEPH—23; Delaware; Fireman; Transferred from 72nd Infantry, Mustered out
BROOKS, WILLIAM W.—26; Farmer; Mustered out
+BROWN, CHARLES—40; Melrose; Machinist; CIA/POW Andrv
CADY, CHARLES W.—25; Mahin County; Blacksmith; Mustered out
CARRICK, WILLIAM W.—29; Bookbinder; aka McCARRICK, VRC
CASHIN, WILLIAM—29; Colton; Farmer; Mustered out
CAVANAH, ROBERT—19; Clerk; VRC
+CENT, JOHN—28; Sullivan County; Laborer; aka KENT, DOD
CHAMPION, DAVID—20; Oganburg; Shoemaker; Discharged
CHENY, JESSE A.—16; Farmer; Mustered out
DIXON, THOMAS—19; Albany; Cabinetmaker; Mustered out
+DREW, FRANCIS G.—41; Chatanavgay...; Carpenter
DUKE, HENRY CLAY—23; Printer; Mustered out
*EARLL, WILLIAM H.—40; Printer
EASTMAN, SAMUEL E.—18; Oswegathie; Schoolteacher; Mustered out
EICHENBERG, JOHN WILLIAM—20; Boatman; Transferred to 2nd Cavalry
*EVANS, EDWARD B.—33; Elmira; Lumberman
FAIRCHILD, BENJAMIN—26; Fairfield; Hatter; WIA, Mustered out
FALK, GEORGE L.—21; Co.?; Farmer; NR
*FAXTON, THOMAS M.—21; Rondout; Field Operator
FEENEY, JOHN—age?; Laborer; VRC
FIELD, GEORGE C.—17; Rushfort; Mustered out
FILLMORE, JAMES—26; Meir; Seaman; WIA, Disability

FITHIAN, JAMES JOHN—21; Laborer; Disability
FRY, CHARLES E.—18; Perth; Farmer; Mustered out
=FUNK, AUGUSTUS—22; Fla.; Colonel 1863, Transferred from 38th New York
    Infantry, WIA twice, Mustered out
=FUNK, JOHN—24; Co. G. 1863; CIA/PAR, Discharged
GIBSON, JOHN E.—20; Butcher; Mustered out
=GILFILLAN, JOHN M.—26; Painter; 1862, Disability
+GILMORE, EDWARD—20; Rochester; Clerk
*GOULD, WILLIAM—22; Tailor
GRAY, FRANCIS L.—32; Fort Crovington; Farmer; Mustered out
GRAY, JAMES—23; Sullivan; Butcher; Mustered out
HAMLIN, SAMUEL W.—25; St. Lawrence; Farmer; Discharged
HARRINGTON, RICHARD A.—20; Pitcher; Mechanic; Transferred to 185th New
    York Infantry
HASLETT, JOSEPH—25; Machinist; MIA/NR
HAWKINS, RICHARD—21; Essex County; Mustered out
HAYES, CHARLES P.—18; Cininatta; Farmer; Transferred to 185th New York
    Infantry
HEATH, WILLIAM—19; Madria; Sailor; Mustered out
HOFFMAN, MOSES—33; Cooper; WIA, Disability
HOLMES, WILLIAM—21; St. Lawrence; Carman; VRC
-HYDE, JOHN McEWAN—22; Co. E 1863, aka HOYDE, Transferred from 38th
    New York Infantry, Disability
HYDE, JOSEPH—42; Washington County; Machinist/Safemaker; NR
JOSLIN, JOHN—40; Levoy; Farmer; Mustered out
JUSTICE, HIRAM W.—18; Kisetown; Farmer; Transferred to 185th New York
    Infantry
LACOY, FEDERICK—48; Ontar...; Seaman; Disability
+LATHROP, CHARLES—21; Fishkills; CIA/POW Slsbry, DOD 1/26/1865
LAWRENCE, DAVID—37; Madeira; Farmer; Mustered out
LAWRENCE, JAMES M.—27; Maderia; Farmer; Mustered out
*LEE, JOHN—21; Painter
LINDEN, JAMES—22; Laborer; WIA, Mustered out
LOCKWOOD, JAMES R.—40; Madeira; Farmer; Musician, Mustered out
LOUNSBURY, CALVIN—18; Westchester; Farmer; CIA/NR
MACKY, HENRY—21; Postdam; Farmer; Mustered out
MACKY, JAMES—28; Folsdarn; Farmer; Mustered out
*MATTIEE, GEORGE—35; Seaman; aka MATHISE, MATHEN, MATHEU,
    MATHIZE, & MATHISE
McCARTY, JOHN—19; Brooklyn; Packer; VRC
McCOY, JOHN—25; Canaghaine; Farmer; WIA, NR after Deep Bottom 8/20/1864
*McDEVITT, ALEXANDER—21; Machinist
*McGRADY, JAMES—19; Laborer & Musician
McKNIGHT, JOHN—43; Laborer; Mustered out

MEYER, HENRY—38; Folsum; Farmer; Mustered out
MEYERS, ALLAN, B. L.—30; Madaria; Farmer; Mustered out
MILLER, JOHN—18; Osenage...; Farmer; CIA/PAR, Mustered out
*MILLS, GEORGE E.—age?; Long Island; Tinsmith; aka WELLS, WIA
+MORRIS, HENRY C.—18; Brooklyn; Clerk; WIA/DOW
NEWTON, ANDREW—28; Albany; Boatman; WIA, Mustered out
NICHOLS, GEORGE—24; Bookbinder; CIA & Escaped, Discharged
*NILES, CHARLES—21; Laborer; aka MILES
NOLAN, WILLIAM N.; 20; Rueblen County; Laborer; aka KNOWLDEN, WIA/
    CIA/PAR, Mustered out
PACKARD, JONAS F.—age?; Paishville; Farmer; Mustered out
+PAGE, MICHAEL—38; Cook
PAUL, ORIENTAL—20; Farmer; VRC
POST, JOHN W.—24; Transferred to 185th New York Infantry
QUINLEY, THOMAS—21; Laborer; aka QUINLAND, WIA, Mustered out
+REILLY, JOHN—21; Buffalo; Shoemaker; CIA/POW Andrv
REYNOLDS, JOSEPH—22; Coldsprings; Farmer; Disability
+RICE, THOMAS—21; Butcher; CIA/POW Andrv
*RILEY, PHILIP—22; Albany; Painter
ROBINSON, GEORGE—19; Kingston; Laborer; VRC
+ROSE, ALBERT P.—31; Canlor; Farmer; DOD
ROSS, WILLIAM—21; Osighei; Cooper; Mustered out
SACKETT, WILLIAM—21; Parishville; Farmer; Mustered out
SELLICK, OSCAR P.—18; Parishville; Farmer; Mustered out
SERGEANTS, LEWIS H.—29; New Berlin; Farmer; aka SARGENT, Transferred
    to 185th New York Infantry
SHAW, HORACE—33; St. Ann; Farmer; Mustered out
SMITH, GARRETT C.—19; Smithville; Farmer; Transferred to 185th New York
    Infantry
*SMITH, GEORGE 1ST—34; Brooklyn; Painter
SMITH, GEORGE P.—23; Rockland; Laborer; WIA/CIA/PAR, Mustered out
SOULES, GEORGE—43; Obselk; Farmer; Transferred to 185th New York Infantry
STINER, DANIEL—40; Livingston Shore; Cooper; VRC
STREETER, BENJAMIN—31; Stockholen; Farmer; Mustered out
SULIVAN, ANDREW O.—28; Shoemaker; Mustered out
SULLIVAN, DANIEL—24; Seaman; Mustered out
*SUMMERS, JAMES—26; West Chester; Tailor
SWEET, THOMAS H.—18; Morovia; Farmer; Transferred to 185th New York
    Infantry
TAYLOR, JOHN—21; Farmer; aka JOHN BECKET, VRC
THOMAS, WILLIAM R.—33; Wadington; Farmer; Mustered out
THOMPSON, WILLIAM—31; Farmer; NR
THOMPSON, WILLIAM—20; Farmer; Mustered out
+THOMSON, SYLVESTER—43; Florence; Painter; CIA/POW Andrv

TIPPING, JAMES—19; Laborer; CIA/PAR, Mustered out
VAN NESS, IRA W.—18; Hormanville; Farmer; WIA, Mustered out
=VAN RENSSELAER, KILLIAM—19; Co. I 1864; aka WILLIAM VON RENSALAER, Mustered out
*VAN TASSAL, ABSOLEM—35; Tarrytown; Seaman; WIA
WALLACE, ISAAC C.—32; Farmer; Mustered out
=WARING, GEORGE E. JR.—28; Westchester County; Field & Staff 1861; Transferred to Fremont's Cavalry
WEAVER, GEORGE M.—26; Pitcher; Carpenter; Transferred to 185th New York Infantry
WEINGARD, ABRAM—29; Walton; Mechanic; Mustered out
WHITE, JOHN—29; Sailor; WIA, Mustered out
*WHITMORE, JOHN—43; Seaman
+WHITNEY, JOHN—34; Lockporte; Carpenter; CIA/POW Andrv
*WILLIAMS, CHARLES—24; Orange; Fireman; Dishonorably Discharged
WILLIAMS, JOHN—28; Sailor; VRC
WILSON, WILLIAM—26; Sailor; Transferred to Navy
+WILSON, WILLIAM—26; Soldier; Drowned

LISBON, NEW YORK

CALLEND, JAMES—23; Farmer; Mustered out
CHAMBERS, GEORGE M.—22; Farmer; Mustered out
FORBES, THOMAS O.—18; Laborer; Mustered out
GETTY, ROYAL Q.—18; aka ROYAL Q. GELLY
GIBBONS, WILLIAM H.—37; Farmer; Mustered out
GRAHAM, JOHN—20; Laborer; Mustered out
GREGORY, STEPHAN H.—32; Mechanic; Mustered out
HANNAH, JAMES N.—20; Laborer; NR
HITSMAN, WILLIAM—19; Farmer; Mustered out
+HURST, ALEXANDER—20; Farmer; DOD
LAWRENCE, AMON—20; Farmer; Mustered out
LAWRENCE LEONARD—25; Farmer; Mustered out
McCOLLOUGH, JAMES—22; Blacksmith; Mustered out
MEYERS, JONATHAN G.—22; Farmer & Musician; Mustered out
MIDDLEMANS, GEORGE—22; Farmer; Mustered out
PURVEE, WALTER—18; Farmer; Mustered out
+PUTNEY, JOSIAH W.—19; Farmer; KIA
+RANDALS, FRANK B.—21; Farmer; DOD
ROBINSON, ROBERT D.—22; Farmer; Mustered out
SMITH, DANIEL—23; Cooper; Mustered out
SPRAWLES, DAVID—34; Farmer; Mustered out
+THOMPSON, ROBERT I.—23; Laborer; KIA
WALWORTH, ORIN—18; Farmer; CIA/PAR, Mustered out

*CORTILER, THOMAS—20; Teamster; aka COSTELLO
DENTON, HIRAM H.—23; Farmer; Mustered out
DONOHOUE, THOMAS—19; Shoemaker; CIA/NR
+GARDINERS, FRANCIS E.—20; Laborer; DOD
GRAHN, WILLIAM—29; Machinist; Siegel German Co., Mustered out
HAYES, JOHN—34; Printer; WIA, Mustered out
*KELLY, THOMAS—18; Foundry Worker
KELLY, THOMAS J.—19; Clerk; WIA, Disability
KERR, WILLIAM M.—40; Merchant; WIA/SIH
MARSHALL, ISAIAH—22; Boatman; WIA, NR after Wilderness 5/6/1864
=McLEAN, CORNELIUS—28; Laborer; Dishonorably Discharged
+MILLER, JOHN—38; Teamster
MOSHIER, LEWIS—18; Farmer; Disability
MULLER, JOHN—age?; Teamster; NR
+MURRAY, ALEXANDER—21; Carman; CIA/POW Andrv
NEUNHOFER, HENRY—27; Soldier; Transferred from 10th Infantry, Discharged
+NICHOLSON, JAMES—22; Soldier; Transferred from 30th Infantry, WIA twice, DOW
O'CONNELL, JOHN—21; Farmer; Disability
+PRAHM, JOHN—21; Printer; KIA (minie ball)
PRATT, ISSAC—19; Seaman; NR
*ROONEY, JAMES—19; Laborer; Co. I, SIH
ROONEY, JAMES—19; Laborer; Co. A, SIH/NR
RUFNER, JOHANN A.—19; Cigarmaker; Bernstein German Co., WIA, Mustered out
+RYAN, JAMES M.—age?; Framemaker; CIA/POW Andrv
*SPEAR, ABRAHAM—21; Carpenter
=STUCKE, GEORGE—23; Milkman; WIA, Mustered out
WACHTER, FREDERICK—19; Cigarmaker; Mustered out
WARREN, HARRY—20; Silkmaker; Mustered out

OHIO

*GILMOUR, JOHN—22; Mechanic; aka GILMORE

PENNSYLVANIA

BROADHEAD, SAMUEL F.—38; Luzerene; Lumberman; Transferred [to?] 185th Infantry
HAGAN, JOHN—18; Philadelphia; Mustered out
HAWKINS, JAMES SAMUEL—19; Philadelphia; VRC
MURRAY, SAMUEL—18; Philadelphia; Boatfitter; CIA/PAR, Mustered out
*PEASE, GEORGE—29; Boatman; aka PEESE & PEASE, Deserted on Furlough

SCOTIN, JOHN—19; Porter; NR
*SPRAGUE, FRANKLIN—21; Montgommery; Laborer; aka SPRAGE, SIH
SYLVESTER, JAMES—24; Eastern; Carpenter; WIA, Disability
WHITE, MILTON—32; Philadelphia; Seaman; CIA/NR
WILSON, WILLIAM—43; Doningville; Sailor; WIA/SIH

RHODE ISLAND

+CHAPPELL, ALPHONZO—19; Providence; Seaman; CIA/POW Andrv
HAMMOND, HENRY B.—31; Newport; Engineer; aka HANNEL, CIA/PAR

VERMONT

FULLER, WILLIAM—28; Westlow; Farmer; WIA/SIH
FULSAM, RODNEY C.—38; Weston; aka FOLSAM, Mustered out
+HAMILTON, HENRY T.—38; Albage; Cooper; DOD
+HITCHCOCK, HENRY A.—28; Clerk; WIA/DOW
READ, ALANSON—40; Plainfield; Cooper; Mustered out
*WALTER, HORACE—28; Philadelphia; Clerk
WHITE, WILLIAM—29; Undershire; Laborer; SIH
WICKS, SAMUEL—33; Walson; Farmer; aka WEEKS, WIA/SIH

VIRGINIA

+LEWIS, SAM—23; Culp[e]per; Colored [African-American]; aka SAM LOUIS, DOD

The remainder of the men are those on whom no background information was found or who were unassigned and had no further record:

ALLEN, JAMES—43; Co. G 1864, MIA
=BAKER, CHARLES C.—26; Major of Regiment; WIA, Mustered out
=BALDWIN, HARVEY A.—age?; Co.?, Transferred from 7th Artillery
=BALLOU, CHARLES—19; aka BALLEAU; Co. K 1864, WIA, Mustered out
BANKHOSS, E.—age?; Co. K 1864, WIA, NR after Totopotomoy River 5/30/1864
+BAUMANN, HENRY—27; Cigarmaker; Co. H 1863, CIA/POW Andrv
=BENDELL, HERMAN—28; Field and Staff, Resigned, September 1, 1861
BERRELL, MARTIN—24; Cooper; Co.? 1864, NR
BERRY, A.—age?; Saloonkeeper; Co. G 1864, MIA
BETTING, WILLIAM—age?; Co. A 1864, WIA, NR after Wilderness 5/6/1864
BLAKE, ANDREW—19; Co.? 1864, NR
BODELLE, CHARLES—28; Co.? 1862, NR
BODELLE, VICTOR—34; Co.? 1862, NR
*BOGART, DAVID A.—38; Carman; Co. K 1863
BORRER, CHARLES—23; Co.? 1862, NR
BOSQUET, CHARLES–30; Co.? 1862, NR

BOUKE, CORNELIUS—17; Co.? 1862, NR
=BRIGGS, BARON—27; Co. K 1864, Mustered out
BROEMMELL, WILLIAM—29; Co.? 1864, NR
BROOKS, GEORGE H.—age?; Birthplace?; Co. K 1864, Transferred from 83rd
    Infantry
BROWN, ANDREW—19; Co.? 1864, NR
BROWN, PHILIP—39; Co. E 1864, WIA/SIH
BROWNE, JOHN—33; Co. F 1863, VRC
=+BRUEN, DAVID—39; Co. K 1864, aka BRAIN
BURCHARZ, EDWARD—23; Co.? 1862, NR
BURI, GEORGE—22; Co.? 1862, NR
BURWIG, JULIUS—21; Co.? 1864, NR
BUSH, JOHN—32; Co.? 1864, NR
CAILLET, GEORGE F.—age?; Co.? 1863, NR
CALLAGHAN, GEORGE—41; Porter; Co.? 1863, NR
CARESCENCIA, PETER—age?; Co. B, NR
=CHAPIN, JOSEPH B.—age?; Unassigned; aka CHOPPEN, Muster declined
CHAPMAN, JOSEPH—age?; Co. F 1864, WIA, NR after Spotsylvania at Salient
    5/12/1864
COAKLEY, JOHN—20; Co.? 1864, NR
COLEMAN, WILLIAM—22; Co.? 1863, NR
COLLBERT, BARNY—19; Co. A 1864, aka BERNARD COLLVERT, NR
COLLUMS, HENRY—26; Co.? 1863, NR
=COOPER, WILLIAM S.—age?; Co. K 1864, Not Mustered out
CORNELL, ALEXANDER C.—40; Co.? 1863, aka CONNELL, NR
CORTE, CARLO—22; Co.? 1862, NR
COUTURE, THOMAS—28; Co.? 1862, NR
*CROWLEY, JAMES—age?; Co. I 1863, NR
*CURLEY, PATRICK—25; Co. I 1864, NR
DANNER, FRANK—age?; Co. A 1864, WIA, NR after Wilderness 5/6/1864
DAVE, LOUIS—24; Co.? 1862, NR
DAVIS, HENRY J.—age?; Co. G, Transferred from 50th Engineers, NR
=DAY, EBENEZAR DR.—35; Field & Staff 1863, Transferred to 78th Infantry
DAY, WILLIAM—22; Co. E 1863, NR
DE BIRAGUE, FREDERIC—41; Co.? 1862, NR
DE CHAMBERD, ALFONSO—23; Co.? 1862, NR
DE CHEPPE, HENRY—39; Co.? 1862, NR
DELOPONA, JOHN—age?; Co. H 1864, Enlistment Date Unknown
DERLIN, WILLIAM—19; Co.? 1863, NR
#+DEVERBOIS, EMIL—age?; Co.?, First Man to Die (Gunshot Wound in Camp)
=DINGEE, ORVILLE—age?; Co.? 1864, aka DUNGEE, Transferred from 48th
    Infantry; Not Mustered out
DOREN, PONIFACIUS—32; Co.? 1864, NR
DORHAN, ALFRED—21; Co.? 1864, NR

DOUGHEY, JAMES—30; Co.? 1864, NR
DUFFY, JAMES—30; Co.? 1864, NR
DUFFY, JOHN J.—24; Co. E 1863, Mustered out
=DUNCAN, CHARLES—29; Co. H 1864, Transferred from 14th Connecticut
Infantry, Discharged
DUNN, JOHN—21; Co.? 1863, NR
DURAND, ALEXANDRE—31; Co.? 1862, NR
DURHAM, ALFRED—21; Co.? 1864, NR
EBNER, AUGUST—23; Co.? 1863, NR
EDELMAN, LOUIS—20; Co. K 1864, NR
+EHRHARD, ALEXANDER—22; Co. K 1864, aka ALEXANDER ERHARDT, NR
EICHHOLZER, FRANCIS—40; Co.? 1864, NR
ENGLIS, NEIL—19; Co.? 1864, NR
FADDEN, JAMES M.—age?; Co. F 1864, WIA, NR after Salient at Spotsylvania,
5/12/1864
FAIRCHILD, WILLIAM—27; Co.? 1863, NR
FANHOULTE, CHARLES—24; Co.? 1864, NR
FARNUM, WILLIAM—39; Co.? 1863, NR
FELDENZ, JACOB—36; Co. E 1864, aka FIELDING & DERELIN, WIA/SIH
FENOT, LOUIS—30; Co.? 1862, NR
FERDINAND, JOOOPII 22; Co.? 1864, NR
=FIELD, PLETUS A.—39; Co. D 1864, Discharged
*FISHER, JOHN—34; Co. K 1863, WIA/SIH
FIUET, FRANCIS—35; Co.? 1863, NR
#FLEMING, LAWRENCE T.—25; Co. G 1863, Confederate Deserter
*FOLEY, PATRICK—28; Co.? 1864, NR
*FOLK, GEORGE L.—21; Co. H 1863, CIA/PAR then Deserted
*FREEMAN, BAILEY DAYTON—28; Co. H 1863, aka BARTON FREEMAN, NR
FREO, NICHOLAS O.—22; Co.? 1863, NR
FURMAN, ISAAC—20; Co.? 1864, NR
=GALLERBAD, CHARLES—age?; Co.? 1862, Discharged
GAVELLE, ALFRED—20; Co.? 1863, NR
GIBBON, THOMAS—21; Co.? 1863, aka GRIBBON, NR
GILBERT, LEWIS E.—16; Co.? 1864, NR
GILLAN, JOHN—25; Co.? 1864, NR
GLENN, WILLIAM—32; Co.? 1863, NR
=GOODWIN, WILLIAM W.—38; Assistant Surgeon, 1864, Transferred from 2nd
Artillery, Discharged
GRANGER, AUGUSTE—22; Co.? 1862, NR
=GRINNELL, CORNELIUS—36; Field & Staff 1861, Muster In Revoked
GUSTAR, FRANK—21; Co.? 1864, NR
=GYSIN, SAMUEL—age?; Assistant Surgeon 1864, Muster In Revoked
HAGERTY, FRANCIS—23; Co.? 1863, NR
HAGERTY, JOHN—25; Co. H 1864, MIA Returned, SIH

=HAIGHT, CHARLES C.—22; Co. H 1863, WIA, Disability

*HAND, GEORGE CHARLES—19; Co. I 1863, aka HAN, CHARLES, NR

=HAND, THOMAS M.—28; Co. B 1864, Transferred from 40th Infantry, aka McHAND, Mustered out

HANOND, JOHN—24; Co.? 1863, NR

+HARRICK, LEWIS CHARLES—25; Co. C 1864, NR

HAYER, ALBERT—18; Co. D 1864, NR

+HAYES, JAMES—28; Co. E 1863, CIA/POW Andrv

+HESKELL, ALBERT—20; Co. B 1864, aka HASKELL, CIA/POW Andrv

HEUER, HERMANN—26; Co.? 1864, NR

=HIBBARD, ANDREW—age?; Co. F 1863, Muster In Revoked

HIESCHAFFER, CARL—42; Co.? 1863, NR

HOELSTREM, AUGUST—22; Co.? 1863, NR

HOFFMAN, JOHN—25; Co.? 1863, NR

HOFMEISTER, FRANZ—26; Co.? 1863, NR

HOLTHUSEN, GUSTAV—21; Co. H 1863, aka HOETHUSEN, WIA, Mustered out

HOPKINS, GEORGE—20; Co. H 1863, NR

=HUGHES, JAMES G.—31; Lieutenant Colonel 1864, Disability

HYETT, CHRISTOPHER—40; Co.? 1864, NR

INSTE, STEFANO—23; Co.? 1862, NR

IVES, JACOB—45; Co. G 1863, Transferred from 13th Infantry, SIH

JOHANNOT, AUGUST—38; Co. B 1862, NR

JOHNSON, ELIJAH—38; Co.? 1863, NR

*JONES, JAMES—age?; Co. H 1863, NR

JOSEPH, JOHN—28; Co.? 1864, NR

KAISTED, JASPER—16; Co.? 1864, NR

KELLER, WILLIAM—28; Co.? 1864, NR

=KELLOGG, EDWARD G.—26; Co. K 1864, Transferred from 17th Infantry

KEYSER, JOSEPH—21; Co. B 1864, aka KAISER, CIA/PAR, Furlough, NR

KINNEY, JAMES—44; Co.? 1863, NR

=KITTLE, JACOB S.—19; Co. C 1862, Discharged

KLAPTER, HEINRICH H.—age?; Co.? 1862, NR

KLEIN, CARL—21; Co.? 1862, NR

=KNAPPEN, ASA P.—age?; Assistant Surgeon 1865, Discharged

KOCH, CHRISTIAN—44; Co.? 1862, NR

KRANLEIN, AUGUST—40; Co.? 1864, NR

=KRUGER, THEODORE—34; Chaplain Field & Staff 1861, Resigned

LAGER, JOSEPH—29; Co.? 1863, NR

LA GRANGE, LEON—31; Co.? 1862, NR

LATIN, WILLIAM—17; Co.? 1864, NR

=LASELL, ELLIS D.—28; Field & Staff 1861, aka LAZZELLE, Discharged

LEBERT, VICTOR—28; Co.? 1862, NR

LEGER, AUGUST—31; Co.? 1862, NR

LEHMANN, JOSEPH—38; Co. E 1863, NR
LEIB, ANDREAS—27; Co.? 1862, NR
LEROY, EUGENE—32; Co.? 1862, NR
LESCORNEZ, LOUIS—35; Co. B 1862, NR
LESTER, JOHN—19; Co. F 1864, WIA, Disability
=LEUT, JAMES W.—age?; Co.? 1864, NR
=LE VISEUR, LOUIS—37; Co. H 1862, aka LOUIS DE VISCAR, Disability
LINDIN, JOHN—age?; Co. D 1862, Transferred [to?] 14th Cavalry
+LINZEMIRE, FRANK—19; Co. I 1863, NR
=MAGNUS, LEONARD—35; Co. K 1863, Discharged
MAGUIGNAZ, JOSEPH—28; Co.? 1862, NR
MAHONEY, HENRY—24; Co.? 1864, NR
=MAJER, ADOLPHUS DR.—40; Surgeon Field & Staff 1861, Transferred [to?]
    4th Cavalry
MANSFIELD, SILAS W.—18; Co.? 1864, NR
*MARIN, CHARLES—25; Co. H 1863, aka MORIN, NR
MARTIN, SIMON—34; Co.? 1862, NR
McCARTHY, JAMES—18; Co.? 1864, NR
McCOMBS, JOHN—23; Co. G 1864, SIH
*McFARLAND, ALEXANDER—age?; Co. F 1864, Mustered out
=+McGARRY, MICHAEL O.—30; Co. F 1864, NR
*MEHEN, WILLIAM—27; Co. G 1863, NR
MENK, HANS PETER—23; Co.? 1863, NR
MERTZ, FRANZ—28; Co.? 1862, NR
MESINO, WEDO—19; Co.? 1864, NR
MEYER, IGNATZ—40; Co.? 1863, NR
MICHAN, LEOPOLD—31; Co.? 1862, NR
*MILLER, GEORGE—age?; Co A; No Description, Apprehended in Pittsburgh,
    Assigned to Company K, Date Unknown
MILLER, JOHN—27; Co. H 1863, WIA, Mustered out
MOHLER, CHARLES—30; Co.? 1862, NR
MOLO, W. P.—age?; Quartermaster Sergeant 5/31/1861; NR
MOMPER, ANTHONY—21; Co.? 1863, NR
MONDRICH, JOHN—20; Co.? 1864, NR
MONIA, JOHN H.—age?; Co.? 1864, Discharged
MOORE, SOLON S.—31; Co. D 1864, SIH
MORA, BAPTISTE—28; Co.? 1864, NR
MOREL, PETER—35; Co.? 1862, NR
MOREN, MICHAEL—16; Co.? 1864, NR
MORTEN, JAMES—26; Co.? 1863, NR
#*MOWRY, GEORGE L.—age?; Awaiting Trial, NR
*MULLER, JOSEF—21; Co. K 1862, NR
MYERS, JAMES—36; Unassigned 1864, NR
NAY, JAMES—19; Co.? 1863, NR

NOLAN, JOHN D.—24; Co.? 1864, WIA/CIA/PAR, Mustered out
*NOONEN, JOHN—age?; Co. E 1862, NR
NORMAN, LYMAN—20; Co.? 1863, NR
=NORTON, CHARLES B.—age?; Field & Staff 1861, Transferred to 50th
Engineers
NOVER, MONIWELL—21; Co.? 1864, NR
OLEIN, MATHIAS—21; Co.? 1864, NR
OLIVER, ALOIS—26; Co.? 1862, NR
O'TOOLE, JAMES—age?; Co. I, Transferred from 29th Infantry, SIH
PAGLIO, GION DOMINICO—39; Co. I 1864, NR
PANTO, CHARLES—35; Co.? 1862, NR
PENN, JOSEPH—41; Co. K 1863, SIH
PICOT, AMEDEE—28; Co.? 1862, NR
=PLUMB, GEORGE—24; Co. B 1863, Mustered out
=PROPER, ISAAC—23; Co. H 1864, Mustered out
QUEHL, WAHRENFEST—28; Co.? 1864, NR
RACE, LORENZO—36; Co.? 1864, NR
REGAN, JAMES—22; Co. E 1864, NR
=RICH, ERSKINE—19; Co. F 1864, WIA, Mustered out
=+RICH, THEODORE F.—19; Co. F 1863, NR
RIDHIE, CHARLES—35; Co.? 1863, NR
RIMBULD, BERNARD—age?; Co. K 1864, No Description, WIA/SIH
=ROBERSON, JOHN W.—age?; Co.? 1864, Dismissed
ROCHAND, FRANCIS—40; Co. E 1862, VRC
ROGERS, JOHN—21; Co.? 1863, NR
=ROGERS, PHILIP CLAYTON—age?; Co. H 1863, aka RODGERS, Disability
ROURKE, CORNELIUS—age?; Musician; Co. A 1864, Mustered out
RUELLAND, VINCENT—23; Co.? 1864, NR
RUGA, SILVESTER—24; Co.? 1862, NR
*RUGS, JOHN—25; Co. H 1863, NR
SANTO, JOHN S.—36; Co.? 1863, NR
SATURNIN, MAURICE—31; Co.? 1862, NR
SCHILL, JOSEPH—25; Co. E 1862, Disability
SCHLEICHER, ANTON—age?; Quartermaster Field & Staff 1861, NR
SCHMIDT, JACOB—36; Co.? 1863, VRC
SCHMIDT, JOHAN—30; Co.? 1862, NR
SCHMITZ, CARL—21; Co.? 1863, aka SMITH, NR
SCHNEFF, JOHN—27; Co.? 1863, NR
*SCHNEIDER, ALBERT—25; Co. I 1863, No Descriptive List Ever Received
SCHOLS, JOSEPH—30; Co.? 1862, NR
=SCHOUTEN, CHARLES A.—20; Co. H, aka SCENETEN, SCANEON or
SCOUTING, WIA, Discharged
SCHREIBER, MORITZ JOSEPH—31; Co. I 1864, CIA/NR
SCHRODER, WILHELM—27; Co. G 1862, Disability

=SEAMAN, JOSEPH—age?; Co.? 1865, aka LEAMAN, NR

SEGALE, JOHN—25; Co.? 1864, NR

SHAUGHNESY, JAMES—19; Co.? 1863, NR

=SHAW, HENRY—29; Co. F 1862, Discharged

SHAW, JAMES R.—34; Co.? 1864, NR

=SHRIBER, ROBERT C.—age?; Co. D 1862, aka SCHREIBER, Muster In
    Revoked

SHUTZENBERG, FERDINAND—age?; Co. F 1864, aka SCHURTSENBERG,
    Transferred from 29th Infantry, SIH

SIEMONETT, HENRY—28; Co.? 1862, NR

=SLAWSON, IRA M.—age?; Co.? 1865, NR

SMITH, GEORGE—32; Co.? 1863, NR

SMITH, GEORGE H.—22; Co.? 1863, Discharged

SMITH, JAMES—23; Co.? 1863, NR

STARK, CHRISTIAN—age?; Co. F 1862, NR

STARK, ROBERT—29; Co.? 1862, NR

STEIN, MARTIN—32; Co.? 1862, NR

=STODDARD, FREEMAN—age?; Assistant Surgeon 1864, NR

STOLLBERG, WILLIAM—21; Co.? 1862, NR

=STURGES, EDWARD—18; Co. K 1863, Transferred [to?] 20th Massachusetts

=SUBIT, EUGENE—34; Quartermaster 1861, also SOUBIT & LUBIT, Dismissed

*SUMMERFIELD, CHARLES—25; Sergeant; Co. E, NR

=SWIFT, FOSTER DR.—age?; 2nd Surgeon Field & Staff 1861, Transferred [to?]
    8th Militia

TATTEN, JOSEPH—21; Co. E 1863, aka FATTEN, WIA, Disability

THALBERG, HEINRICH F.—32; Co. E 1864, aka VAN THALBERG, NR

TORIOS, VICTOR—25; Co.? 1862, aka JORIOS & TORIOS, NR

=TREMPER, ROBERT—24; Co. K 1863, aka TRIMPER, WIA, Mustered out

=TRIPPE, JAMES M.—23; Co. E 1864, CIA/PAR, Transferred to 21st U.S.
    Colored Troops

=TUTTLE, PHILO J.—43; Co. D 1864, Dishonorably Discharged

=VALENTINE, JOHN E.—29; Co. I 1864, WIA, Disability

VALLETTE, ALPHONSE—21; Co.? 1862, NR

VANHOUTTE, CHARLES—24; Co.? 1864, NR

VENTLAND, PETERSON J.—27; Co. I 1864, aka VETLAND & VETTEAN, WIA/
    SIH

*VEYANKS, JOSEPH—age?; Co. H 1863, aka VAILLANCOURT & GEORGE
    VALANCOURT, NR

VINCOTT, FELIX—age?; Co.? 1862, NR

VIQUAKO, JOSEPH—25; Co.? 1863, NR

VOEBEL, HENRY—26; Co. E 1864, aka VAUBEL, Mustered out

VOLLACHER, FREDERIC—18; Co.? 1863, NR

VONISKE, LOUIS—age?; Unassigned; Transferred from 4th Cavalry; aka VOUIKE
    LOUIS

VON WALD, JOSEPH—28; Co.? 1862, NR
WADE, THOMAS—22; Co. G 1863, CIA/PAR, Mustered out
WAGNER, MARTIN—22; Co. G 1864, WIA, Mustered out
+WALSH, JOHN—31; Co. H 1864, aka WELSH, CIA/POW Andrv
WANDELL, JOHN B.—35; Co. H 1863, aka WENDELL, VRC
WARBUTRON, EDWARD—34; Co.? 1863, NR
WARD, CHRISTOPHER—28; Co.? 1864, NR
WEECHEL, CHARLES—34; N/R Co. I 1864, CIA
WEIDO, MESINO—19; Co.? 1864, NR
WHITE, SYLVANUS T. F.—25; Co.? 1863, NR
=WHITLOCK, DANIEL D.—age?; Co. I 1864, NR
WILLIAMS, WILLIAM—22; Co. H 1863, CIA/Escaped
=WILM, OTTO—37; Co. I 1862, Disability
=WILSON, JOSEPH JR.—19; Co. F 1864, WIA, Disability
WINFIELD, ANDREW—18; Musician; Co. A 1864, aka WINFIELD ANDREWS,
    VRC
WOODMAN, CHARLES—22; Co.? 1863, NR
=WYCKOFF, JAMES G. S.—22; Co. G 1863, WIA, Discharged
YENTZ, JOHN—18; Co.? 1864, NR
YOUNG, ALEXANDER G.—25; Co.? 1864, NR
ZINDLER, CHARLES—age?; Co. F, NR

Endnotes

Chapter One

1. Meyer Howard Abrams, gen. ed., *The Norton Anthology of English Literature*, vol. 2, 3rd ed. (New York: W. W. Norton & Company, Inc., 1974), p. 369. Byron would die in 1824 while training an expeditionary force that he financed to help in the Greek war for independence from the Turks.

2. Young Europe was a precursor to President Woodrow Wilson's League of Nations, according to E. E. Y. Hales, *Mazzini and the Secret Societies* (New York: P. J. Kenedy & Sons) Library of Congress Card Catalog #56-9830, pp. 13 & 202.

3. Mazzini adopted this code from Claude Henri de Rouvroy Saint-Simonian, as expressed in *Doctrine de Saint-Simon* (Paris, 1788).

4. Garibaldi's exploits in South America were recorded by his friend Giovan Cuneo in *La Battaglia di San Antonio del Salto* (N.p.: Carmicia Rossa, 1932).

5. *New York Herald*, 28 March 1848.

6. *New York Evening Post*, 22 March 1848.

7. Frederick George D'Utassy File, Public Archives, vol. 91, no. 5 (Call No. MG 100), Hallifax, Nova Scotia.

8. General Avezzana, an experienced old veteran, had participated in the Spanish Revolution of 1821 and in the Mexican War of Independence of 1824. Mexican General Santa Anna made him a colonel and governor of two provinces. Eventually, the two became foes and the Italian had to escape to New York. He traveled back to Italy to participate in the liberation struggle.

9. George Macaulay Trevelyan, *Garibaldi and the Thousand* (London: Longmans, Green & Co., 1909), p. 14.

10. George MacAulay Trevelyan, *Garibaldi and the Thousand* (New York: Longmans, Green and Co., 1909), p. 14.

11. George E. Waring, Jr., *The Garibaldi Guard* (The First Book of the Author's Club, Liber Scriptorium 1893), p. 568. Published by the Author's Club, New York, N.Y.

297

12. Trevelyan, *Garibaldi and the Thousand*, p. 23.

13. Ibid., pp. 21–22.

14. Justin McCarthy, *Portraits of the Sixties* (New York: Harper & Brothers, 1903), p. 224, and Michael St. John Packe, *Orsini* (Boston: Little, Brown & Co., 1957), p. 141.

15. Trevelyan, *Garibaldi and the Thousand*, p. 29.

16. *Ballou's Pictorial* (Boston), X, No. 5 (2 February 1856), p. 1.

17. Trevelyan, *Garibaldi and the Thousand*, pp. 69–70. Note: Piscane's expedition against the Bourbons was related to Garibaldi's successful expedition three years later, exactly as John Brown's raid on Harpers Ferry was related to the American Civil War. Like Brown, Piscane exacerbated the feud, made compromise impossible, and so helped to bring on the final struggle. Like Brown, he committed some acts that were criminal and some that were sublime, and above all else, he knew how to die.

18. Ibid., pp. 71–74.

19. Martin Windrow, *The French Foreign Legion* (New York: Hippochene, 1976), p. 17; Douglas Porch, "The French Foreign Legion: A Complete History of the Legendary Fighting Force." (New York: Harper Collins Publishers, 1991), pp. 346–347.

20. Irving Werstein, *Kearny, the Magnificent* (New York: John Day Co., 1962), pp. 143–148.

21. Edward A. Richards, *Encyclopedia International*, vol. 15, p. 326. American National Red Cross Office of Publications, 1965.

22. Mark M. Boatner III, *The Civil War Dictionary* (New York: David McKay Co., Inc., 1959), p. 449.

23. T. Okey, "With Garibaldi in 1860," *Cornhill Magazine*, (September 1929), p. 372. Induction papers received by Edward Charles Bowra were typical of those received by members of the British Legion in the Italian army:
    di professisone: Gentleman; enrolled at Caserta on 14 October 1860, in the Southern Army, Division 15, of Victor Emmanuel King of Italy; served under Colonel John Peard in the Brigata di Volontari Brittancici. His age was given as 18 years, stature 5 feet 10 inches, hair brown, high forehead, eyes blue, fresh-colored, sight good. His papers certify that he took part in the action of the 19th before Capua, was also at the passage of the Volturno, was recommended for his behavior on the 19th, and was slightly wounded while on an official expedition in the mountains. He was promoted to second-lieutenant and acting secretary to the officer commanding at Salerno, 7 December 1860. His coolness under fire evoked particular notice.

24. E. C. M. Bowra, "With Garibaldi in 1860," *Cornhill Magazine*, (September 1929), pp. 370–371.

25. Bowra, p. 372.

26. *New York Times*, 8 October 1860.

27. Bowra, p. 371.

28. Frances M. Peard, "Garibaldi's Englishman," *Cornhill Magazine*, (August 1903), p. 274.

29. Charles L. Dufour, *Gentle Tiger* (Baton Rouge: Louisiana State University Press, 1957), pp. 113–115.

30. Bowra, p. 373.

31. Donaldson Jordan, Ph.D. and Edwin Pratt, *Europe and the American Civil War* (New York: Houghton Mifflin Co., 1931), p. 4.

32. Dr. Robert J. Loeffler, *Bandwagon*, March–April 1973, Circus World Museum, Baraboo, Wisconsin. In existence from the winter of 1852 to 1854, Franconi's circus featured an equestrian corps of mounted men and women in costume of all colors, riding elephants, camels, ponies, stags, reindeer, and ostriches.

Chapter Two

1. Excerpt from Ella Lonn, "Foreigners in the Confederacy, 1940," *Louisiana State University Press, New Orleans Bee*, 20 January 1861.
2. Records in the archives of the American Embassy, Rome. Gazzetta Officale, May 17, 1861, Romaine Dilliva—American Charge D'Affaires.
3. Boatner, p. 274.
4. List of the Garibaldini provided by the Garibaldi/Meuci Museum, Staten Island, New York from the 1000 Red Shirts photo album.
5. Adjutant General's Report on the New York State Volunteers 1861–1865, the muster roll of the Independent Light Infantry Regiment (Enfants Perdus).
6. Boatner, p. 40.
7. Ibid.
8. Edmund Vasuary, *Lincoln Hungarian Heroes* (Washington, D.C.: Hungarian Reformed Federation of America, 1939), and Eugene Pivany, *Hungarians in the American Civil War* (Cleveland, Ohio: self-published, 1913).
9. Waring, p. 569.
10. Excerpt from Ella Lonn, "Foreigners in the Union Army and Navy," 1951, *Criminial-Zeilig* [German/American journal; Louisiana State University Press], 26 April 1861.
11. *New York Herald*, 10 April 1861, and *New York Herald*, 30 April 1861.
12. Luigi Tinelli, another of the political exiles, immigrated to New York in the 1830's and earned a living as a lawyer, politician, and silk manufacturer. He attained a prominent position in political circles when in 1041 he was appointed as the American Consulate General at Oporto, Portugal, remaining there until he returned to New York in 1852. During the 1856 Presidential campaign he supported Brigadier General John C. Fremont as a candidate and wrote a book entitled *Fremont, Buchanan and Fillmore: The Parties Called to Order.*
13. *New York Herald*, 27 April 1861.
14. *New York Daily Tribune*, 28 April 1861.
15. *I'Eco d'Italia*, 27 April 1861.
16. *New York Herald*, 27 April 1861.
17. "Garibaldi Guard," *New York Herald*, 29 April 1861.
18. Waring, p. 569.
19. *New York Daily Tribune*, 29 May 1861.
20. Glen Tucker, *Hancock The Superb* (Bobbs-Merrill, 1960).
21. Mustered in, to date from 28 May 1861. Pfisterer's File 2188–2213, Registrar Serial No. 23, 1–313.
22. *New York Herald*, 25 May 1861.
23. Waring, p. 569.
24. *New York Herald*, 10 May 1861.
25. Waring, pp. 570–571.
26. Waring, p. 570.
27. Margaret Leech, *Reveille in Washington 1860–1865* (New York: Harper & Brothers, 1941), p. 85.
28. Carl Schurz, Personal letters and manuscripts relating to the Frederick George D'Utassy court-martial, 1861–1863, Schurz Collection, Wisconsin State Archives, Madison, Wisconsin.

29. "Movements of Troops in New York: Departure of the Garibaldi Guard," *New York Herald*, 29 May 1861.
30. *New York Herald*, 22 May 1861, and *New York Herald*, 23 May 1861.
31. *New York Herald*, 28 May 1861.
32. Howard Marraro, *Lincoln's Italian Volunteers* (New York: Columbia University, 1943), pp. 62–63.
33. Waring, pp. 570–571.
34. Louis Blenker was a native of Hesse-Darmstadt and a revolutionary leader in the Palatinate and Baden. Blenker was an old soldier of fortune who had fought in Greece and in the German revolution of 1848, where he was a leading member of the movement. He too had come to America in 1849 as an exile and become a New York City business man. In 1861 he organized the 8th New York Volunteer Infantry; on August 9, he was named brigadier general. If his past was rather dubious, he was a magnificently martial figure as he rode through Washington in his red-lined cape. Major Waring, critical of Blenker, claimed that the Garibaldi Guard did not see much of him, implying Blenker neglected them.
35. Tucker, p. 127.
36. Quoted source "Reveille in Washington," *The Washington Star,* pp. 69, 85.
37. Waring, p. 572.
38. Anthony P. Zyla, Report to Frederick George D'Utassy, 26 March 1862, D'Utassy Papers, Manuscript Department, New York Historical Society, New York, N.Y., and Catherine C. Catalfamo, *The Thorny Rose* (Ann Arbor, Mich.: University Microfilms International, 1989).
39. General court-martial convened at Centreville, Va., 31 March 1863, General Orders No. 38, Casey's Division, Washington, D.C., General Orders No. 246, 1863, both regarding the Antonali court-martial.
40. Waring, p. 572.
41. *New York Herald*, 31 May 1861.
42. Captain Franz Takats [Takacs], Letter to Frederick George D'Utassy, 31 May 1861, D'Utassy Papers, New York Historical Society.
43. Francis Scala served as bandmaster of the Marine Band which played at the reception given for the famous Hungarian patriot Lajos Kossuth in 1851. Scala played at the presidential inaugurals of James K. Polk, Millard Fillmore, James Buchanan, and Abraham Lincoln. A. C. Clark, *Records of the Columbia Historical Society of Washington, D.C.,* vols. 35–36 (1935) (Washington, D.C.: Columbia Historical Society, 1935), pp. 222–234.
44. Leech, p. 71.
45. Luigi De Lucchi's photo and name are listed as such in a composite book made up by Garibaldi's staff to commemorate the invasion of Sicily. De Lucchi was six feet tall, with a dark complexion, black eyes, and black hair. His qualifications were well received when he enrolled in May of 1861 in the 1st Company of the Garibaldi Guards.
46. Luigi De Lucchi, Original File of Records on Pension, File No. SO 576-196 (Civil War), Military Service Records, National Archives, Washington, D.C.
47. Nelson Gay, "Lincoln's Offer of a Command to Garibaldi: Light on a Disputed Point of History," *The Century Magazine*, LXXV (November 1907), pp. 63–74.
48. *New York Herald*, 13 June 1861.
49. Louis W. Tinelli, Original Files of Records on Pension, File No. SC33-647, Military Service Records, National Archives. During the war Tinelli recruited the Hancock Guards,

which later were consolidated with the McClellan Rifles. Tinelli's two sons joined the Union as officers. At 18, Francis Tinelli enlisted as a private in his father's regiment, but was discharged to accept a commission as a lieutenant in the 13th Heavy Artillery, and Joseph J. Tinelli was acting Master in the Navy. In May of 1863, Louis Tinelli contracted malaria; he was discharged for disability on May 31 in New Orleans.

50. Waring, p. 569.
51. Alessandro Repetti, Letter regarding officers' protest to Frederick George D'Utassy, no date given but probably on par with Tassillier's protest. D'Utassy Papers, New York Historical Society.
52. Alessandro Repetti, Letter requesting money and passes to Frederick George D'Utassy, undated: Near the time when they were used to help the engineers in building fortifications. D'Utassy Papers, New York Historical Society.
53. Gay, pp. 63–74.
54. Waring, p. 573.
55. Gay, pp. 63–74.
56. Leech, p. 88.
57. William Russell, quote in "Reveille in Washington," *London Times*, p. 89.
58. Louis Tassillier et al., Petition to Frederick George D'Utassy, 6 July 1861, D'Utassy Papers, New York Historical Society.
59. *New York Times*, 3 July 1861.
60. Waring, p. 572, and D'Utassy File, Public Archives, Halifax, Nova Scotia.
61. The Long Bridge was, "for land travel, the main link of communication" between Washington, D.C. and Alexandria and the principal routes south. It spanned the Potomac River from the foot of Fourteenth Street on the Washington side to a point on the Virginia side below the modern-day Pentagon. The bridge was one mile long; two-thirds of it was "solid causeway," and the other third rested on piles. It had two draw sections, one near each end. Its wooden sections and both draws were completely rebuilt in 1861 so the bridge could handle army traffic. See Benjamin Franklin Cooling III and Walton H. Owen II, *Mr. Lincoln's Forts: A Guide to the Civil War Defenses of Washington* (Shippensburg, PA: White Mane Publishing Company, 1988), p. 26.
62. Charles Carleton Coffin, *The Boys of '61* (Boston: Estes and Lauriat, 1881), pp. 11–13.
63. Leech, p. 93.

Chapter Three

1. Colonels Dixon S. Miles, Report on the Bull Run Campaign, 21 July 1861, and Louis Blenker, Report on the Bull Run Campaign, 4 August 1861, both in *War of the Rebellion: A Compilation of the Official Records of the Union and Confederate Armies [OR-Armies]*, 70 vols. in 128 bks., ed. Robert N. Scott et al., ser. I, vol. 12, (Washington, D.C.: U.S. Congress, 1881–1901), pp. 426–428, and Waring, pp. 573–575; Miles Report, pp. 425–426; Blenker Report, pp. 427–428.
2. Gay, pp. 63–74.
3. Boatner, p. 671.
4. Alessandro Repetti, Letter requesting men to Frederick George D'Utassy, no date, D'Utassy Papers, New York Historical Society.
5. Lieutenant Frederick E. Prime, U.S. Engineers, Report on Four Mile Run, Virginia, 1 August 1861, in *OR-Armies*, ser. I, vol. 12, p. 9.
6. D'Utassy File, Public Archives, Halifax, Nova Scotia.

7. Casey's Division, Hq., Washington, D.C., Special Orders No. 159, 1863, regarding charge
    3, specification 8 of the Frederick George D'Utassy court-martial, p. 3, and an account
    about the court-martial in the Washington, D.C. *Daily Chronicle*, 17 April 1863.
8. Waring, p. 575.
9. Boatner, p. 274.
10. Regimental records of the 39th New York Volunteer Infantry Regiment, Garibaldi Guards,
    U.S. National Archives, including Orders from December 1862 through July 1865.
11. Special Orders No. 159, charge 3, specification 18, p. 8, and the Washington, D.C. *Daily
    Chronicle*.
12. General Orders No. 159, D'Utassy court-martial, changes/specifications p. 4.
13. Captain Cesare Osnaghi, Letter to Frederick George D'Utassy, 12 August 1861, D'Utassy
    Papers, New York Historical Society, and Personal Letters and Manuscripts relating to
    the incident of the challenge to a duel between D'Utassy and Osnaghi, Schurz Collec-
    tion.
14. Gay, pp. 63–74.
15. Ibid.
16. Osnaghi, Military Service Board, File No. C.A.C., Regimental Records of the 39th New
    York Volunteer Infantry Regiment, the Garibaldi Guards, U.S. National Archives.
17. Personal letters and manuscripts relating to the Frederick George D'Utassy court-mar-
    tial, 1861–1863, Schurz Collection.
18. Headquarters, Army of the Potomac, Washington, D.C., 30 August 1861, Special Orders
    No. 10, item 5 (Tassillier court-martial).
19. Frank Machon, *Poles in America* (Stevens Point, Wis.: Worzalla Publishing, 1978), p.
    240 (n. 339).
20. Gay, pp. 63–74.
21. Ibid.
22. Howard Marraro, *Lincoln's Offer of a Command to Garibaldi* (*New York History* Maga-
    zine), New York, N.Y., 1943.
23. Special Orders No. 159, charge 3, specification 9, p. 3.
24. Special Orders No. 159, charge 2, specifications 1 and 2, p. 1.
25. This writer's research has not borne out any "Sepoys, Turcos, Chinese, Esquimaux, Zeph-
    yrs, or men from Algiers" who served with the Garibaldians, though several African-
    Americans served and later transferred to the colored troops, and a regimental order men-
    tions using the black soldiers among the Spanish company to perform some tasks. Luigi
    Palma De Cesnola never served with the Garibaldians and was at this time in fact a
    cavalry officer in the 4th New York Cavalry; he would eventually receive the Medal of
    Honor for his actions at Aldie, Virginia.
26. Adjutant General's Report on the New York State Volunteers 1861–1865, the muster roll
    of the Independent Light Infantry Regiment (Enfants Perdus). N.Y. State Legislative
    Assembly, Leg. 481.2–3, Microfiche 9 of 10, 10 of 10, pp. 773–961.
27. Special Orders No. 159, charge 3, specification 10, p. 4.
28. Special Orders No. 159, charge 3, specification 13, pp. 4–5.
29. Special Orders No. 159, charge 3, specification 14, p. 6.

Chapter Four

1. Personal Letters and manuscripts relating to the Frederick George D'Utassy court-mar-
    tial, 1861–1863, Schurz Collection.

2. *Abend Zeitung*, Thursday, 23 January 1862.
3. *Courrier des Estats-Unis*, Friday, 6 June 1862.
4. Personal Letters and manuscripts relating to the Frederick George D'Utassy court-martial, 1861–1863, Schurz Collection.
5. Tucker, p. 127.
6. Boatner, pp. 314–315.
7. Casey's Division, Washington, D.C., 31 March 1863, General Orders No. 38, court-martial of Private G. Antonali.
8. Brigadier General John C. Fremont, Reports from Virginia collected in *OR-Armies*, ser. I, vol. 12,: at Luray, 8 June 1862, pp. 17–21; at Port Republic, 9 June 1862, pp. 654–655; at Harrisonburg, 10 June 1862, pp. 655–656; and at Mount Jackson, 12 June 1862, pp. 656–657.
9. Charles L. Dufour, "Gentle Tiger," Louisiana State University, 1957.
10. They got the nickname from the custom of wearing bucks' tails in their hats to signify their marksmanship.
11. Carlo Romang, a Swiss officer who served with Garibaldi, observed that a Garibaldian "bayonet attack was more decisive than the four or five hours of gunfire. "La Guarda Garibaldi," *L'Eco d'Italia*, 3 July 1862, p. 1.
12. Headquarters Blenker's Division, Camp near Mt. Jackson, Va., 14 June 1862, Special Orders No. 60, regarding the Ornesi court-martial.
13. Waring, p. 575.
14. Author's note: Time/Life Books (*The Civil War*, 28 vols.,Alexandria, Va., 1987) charged that Alessandro Repetti resigned "in disgrace for having pointed a gun at a gravely wounded man." Having found no reference whatsoever to this incident in any of the official records, newspapers, military journals, or regimental histories, I believe the charge to be contrary to Repetti's personality, totally without evidence.
15. Alessandro Repetti, Letter of resignation to Major General Edwin Sumner, 31 March 1862, D'Utassy Papers, New York Historical Society, and Catalfamo, p. 184.
16. Vasuary, p. 85.
17. Personal Letters and manuscripts relating to the Frederick George D'Utassy court-martial, 1861–1863, Schurz Collection.

Chapter Five

This was assembled from testimonies of and about members of the Garibaldi Guard. Perhaps this should be entitled The Maryland Campaign and the Garibaldi Guards' involvement. 2 September 1862, was the movement of the troops to H.F.

1. Volume 12, part 2, Maryland Campaign.
   D'Utassy and 39th N.Y. mentioned in Reports pp. 527, 533, 536–539, 542–544.
   Return of casualties, p. 549.
   Report of Brigadier General D. Tyler, 23 September 1862, p. 552.
   Report of Lieutenant Charles Graham Bason 39th N.Y., 23 September 1862, pp. 552–553.
   Hilderbrandt's testimony, p. 554.
   D'Utassy and Bacon mentioned as witnesses, p. 555.
   D'Utassy mentioned in testimony, p. 558.
   39th mentioned in testimony, p. 570.
   D'Utassy questioning witness, p. 575.

Garibaldi Guards and D'Utassy mentioned in testimony, pp. 580–586.
D'Utassy's testimony, pp. 595–600.
Hilderbrandt's testimony, pp. 601–605.
D'Utassy mentioned, pp. 622–623.
D'Utassy questioning a witness, p. 628.
D'Utassy mentioned, p. 629.
39th or D'Utassy mentioned in testimony, pp. 645–646 and 658.
Bacon questioned by D'Utassy, pp. 664–669.
D'Utassy mentioned, pp. 682–683.
D'Utassy questioning witness, pp. 686–687.
39th or D'Utassy mentioned, pp. 695, 700, 706–707, 713 and 727.
Hilderbrandt and Garibaldi Guards mentioned, p. 778.
Hilderbrandt's testimony, pp. 783–784.
D'Utassy testimony, pp. 786–787.
Garibaldi Guards mentioned in testimony, p. 795.
2. General Orders No. 38 and No. 246, Antonali court-martial.
3. *New York Times*, 18 September 1862, and Catalfamo, pp. 298–299.

Chapter Six

1. Comments concerning sutlers at Camp Douglas, Chicago, Illinois, 20 July 1863, *OR-Armies*, ser. II, vol. 3, 549–550.
2. Special Orders No. 159, charge 1, specification 1, p. 1.
3. A. T. Andreas, *History of Chicago from the Earliest Periods to the Present Time* (Chicago: New York Arno Press, Reprint 1975; 1884–1886), pp. 301–303.
4. Camp Douglas, *Chicago Tribune*, 6 October 1862.
5. Special Orders No. 159, charge 3, specification 4, p. 2.
6. Personal letters and manuscripts relating to the Frederick George D'Utassy court-martial, 1861–1863, Schurz Collection.
7. Andreas, p. 304.
8. Gay, pp. 63–74.
9. Affairs at C. B., *Chicago Tribune*, 20 November 1862.
10. Special Orders No. 159, charge 3, specification 5, p. 3.
11. Major General Franz Sigel, Report at Fairfax Court House, Va., 12 November 1862, *OR-Armies*, ser. I, vol. 21, 846–847.
12. Arabella S. Wilson, *Disaster, Struggle and Triumph, The Regimental History of the 125th New York State Volunteers*, pp. 129–133.
13. 30 July 1863, General Orders No. 249, Court-martial of Lieutenant Caesar Nissen, pp. 7–10.
14. Special Orders No. 159, charge 3, specification 12, p. 4.
15. Wyndham was badly wounded at Brandy Station; when he recovered, he returned to service with the Italian army.
16. Colonel Frederick George D'Utassy, Report at Union Mills [Maryland], 30 December 1862, *OR-Armies*, ser. I, vol. 21, 716.
17. D'Utassy, p. 717.

Chapter Seven

1. Gustave Lidenmueller, "An Invitation to the First Fancy Ball," n.d., Schurz Collection.
2. Fleming, George Thorton and Gilbert Adams Hays, *Life and Letters of Alexander Hays* (Pittsburgh: Self-Published, 1919), p. 293.
3. Fleming, p. 313.
4. Fleming, p. 304.
5. Fleming, p. 339.
6. Tucker, p. 127.
7. Fleming, pp. 339–341: Lieutenant Shields' recollection of Colonel D'Utassy's dinner for General Hays.
8. Fleming, pp. 340–341.
9. Fleming, pp. 315–316.
10. Fleming, p. 313.
11. Special Orders No. 159, charge 1, specification 2, p. 1, and Personal letters and manuscripts relating to the Frederick George D'Utassy court-martial, 1861–1863, Schurz Collection.
12. Fleming, pp. 316–317.
13. General Orders No. 38 & No. 246, Antonali court-martial.
14. Personal letters and manuscripts relating to Chaplain Anthony P. Zyla, 1861–1863, Schurz Collection.
15. Personal letters and manuscripts relating to the Frederick George D'Utassy court-martial, 1861-1863, Schurz Collection.
16. Fleming, p. 323 (footnote).
17. Fleming, p. 336.
18. Wilson, p. 138.
19. Wilson, p. 139.
20. Opinion on the United States vs. Antonali, Lieutenant E. Walter West, aide-de-camp to Major General Casey, Washington, 16 April 1863.
21. Wilson, p. 141.
22. Ibid.
23. Wilson, p. 138.
24. On 9 November 1863, Anthony P. Zyla was mustered in as chaplain of the 58th New York, the "Polish Legion." The regiment was described on 7 March 1863, in the *Narod Polski* as being "made up of Germans, French, Poles, Danes, Italians, Hungarians and Russians... Built around a hard core of freedom fighters...its commanding officer was a Pole, Colonel Waldimir B. Kryzanowski." Zyla died of disease on 5 April 1865.
25. Early in the Civil War, the Federal government adopted the policy of confiscating slaves as contraband of war, since the South argued that slaves were property and put them to work on all kinds of military projects. Union officials quickly saw that using blacks could free soldiers from logistical chores for field duties, and by early 1862 the army used blacks for many military support activities. Joseph T. Glatthaar, *Forged in Battle: The Civil War Alliance of Black Soldiers and White Officers* (New York: The Free Press, 1990), pp. 4–6.

Chapter Eight

1. Wilson, p. 177.

2. New York Monuments Commission, *Final Report on the Battlefield of Gettysburg*, vol. I (New York Monuments Commission, 1900), 281-282.

3. Wilson, p. 103.

4. New York Monuments Commission, p. 284.

5. Wilson, p. 177.

6. John Purifer, *Confederate Veteran Magazine*, (January 1926), vol. xxiv, no. 1, p. 19, "With Splendid Valor Shown at Gettysburg, July 2, 1863".

7. W. F. Beyer and O. F. Keydel, *Deeds of Valor: How America's Heroes Won the Medal of Honor* (Detroit: The Perrien-Keydel Co., 1900), pp. 241–242.

8. Beyer and Keydel, p. 242.

9. New York Monuments Commission, p. 284.

10. Charles Carleton Coffin, *The Boys of '61* (Boston: Estes and Lauriat, 1881), p. 295.

11. Coffin, pp. 295–296.

12. *Confederate Veteran Magazine*, vol. xxiv, no. 9, pp. 410–411; vol. xxxi, no. 1, p. 259; vol. xxxiv, no. 1, p. 19. Museum of the Confederacy, 1201 E. Clay Street, Richmond, Va. 23219. Flag of the 11th Mississippi Infantry captured by Sergeant Maggi, July 3, 1863, I.D. Number WD #39. Coffin, p. 297.

13. Major Hugo Hilderbrandt, Report at Bristoe Station [Virginia], 22 October 1863, *OR-Armies*, ser. I, vol. 29, book 1, pt. 1, 301.

14. Colonel Clinton MacDougall, Report at 111th Headquarters, Camp at Mitchell's Ford, Va., 17 October 1863, *OR-Armies*, ser. I, vol. 27, pt. 1, 302.

15. Wilson, p. 213.

16. MacDougall, p. 302.

17. Ella Lonn, *Foreigners in the Union Army and Navy* (Baton Rouge: Louisiana State University Press, 1951).

18. New York Monuments Commission, p. 285.

19. Lieutenant General Richard S. Ewell, C.S.A., Report to General Robert E. Lee regarding a Garibaldian deserter, 17 April 1864, *OR-Armies*, ser. I, vol. 51, pt. 2, 864.

Chapter Nine

1. Captain John M. Gilliffan, File WC 299-908, Military Service Records, U.S. National Archives.

2. Lieutenant Colonel James G. Hughes, Report on Morton's Ford, 2 February 1864, *OR-Armies*, ser. I, vol. 33, pt. 2, 134–135.

3. Brigadier General Alexander Hays, Report on Morton's Ford, 13 March 1864, *OR-Armies*, ser. I, vol. 33, pt. 2, 127.

4. Brigadier General Joshua Owen, Report on Morton's Ford, 9 February 1864, *OR-Armies*, vol. 33, pt. 2, 134.

5. Raffael Frixione succeeded in clearing his name and reenlisted in the 2nd Pennsylvania Cavalry, Company G, on 2 February 1865. When he went to water his horse in Richmond early one day in April, it lost its footing and fell in the water on top of him. The fall injured his full left side, and he was excused from duty for about two weeks, which caused him to be absent from Dismounted Camp. He was discharged soon after, but suffered medical complications for the remainder of his life.

6. Robert G. Scott, *Fallen Leaves: The Civil War Letters of Major Henry Livermore Abbott* (Kent, Ohio: Kent State University Press, 1991), p. 237.

7. Headquarters 3rd Division, 6 March 1864, Special Orders No. 65 (trial of deserters).
8. Ibid.
9. Second Lieutenant Cornelius McLean, Military Service Records, U.S. National Archives, File No. SC 15057, 7 May 1906.
10. Tucker, p. 178.
11. New York Monuments Commission, p. 285.
12. Ewell, p. 864.

Chapter Ten

1. New York Monuments Commission, p. 286, and Captain David A. Allen, Reports [about the 39th New York Volunteer Infantry Regiment in action] on Po River, Spotsylvania, North Anna [River], Hanovertown and Cold Harbor, *OR-Armies*, ser. I, vol. 36, pt. 1, 400–401.
2. Colonel Robert McAllister, Report on HQ 3rd Brigade, 2nd Army, 11 August 1864, *OR-Armies*, ser. I, vol. 36, pt. 1, 488–489.
3. William D. Matter, *If it Takes All Summer* (Chapel Hill: University of North Carolina Press, 1988), pp. 188–189.
4. Coffin, p. 325.
5. Coffin, pp. 325–326.
6. Allen, Report on Chickahominy [River], no date, *OR-Armies*, ser. I, vol. 40, pt. 1, 346–347.
7. Allen, p. 347.
8. John Y. Simon, *The Papers of Ulysses S. Grant*, vol. II (Carbondale. Southern Illinois University Press, 1967), pp. 278–279.
9. Allen, p. 347.
10. Major General Harrick, Report on Ream's Station, 12 September 1864, *OR-Armies*, ser. 1, vol. 42, pt. 1, 227, and Brigadier General Nelson Miles, Report on the Richmond Campaign, 30 August 1864, *OR-Armies*, ser. 1, vol. 42, pt. 1, 253–254.
11. Colonel William Wilson, Report on Hatcher's Run, 10 December 1864, *OR-Armies*, ser. I, vol. 42, pt. 1, 274.

Chapter Eleven

1. John McEwen Hyde has been confused with Captain Joseph Hyde, then forty-five years of age, who is mentioned in the regimental history of the 125th New York Regiment. (Joseph H. was a first lieutenant, Company H, 125th, who rose in the ranks after Colonel Crandell resigned.) That regiment's historian claimed that it was their Hyde who became the lieutenant colonel of the Garibaldians, but this was not the case. Joseph Hyde had an interesting career, which included service as inspector general on the staffs of Generals Alexander Hays, Joshua Owen, and Clinton McDougal.
2. Garibaldi Guard regimental books: Circular Special Orders No. 158, 28 January 1865, of Major Hyde.
3. Colonel Augustus Funk, Report at 27 March 1865, *OR-Armies*, ser. II, vol. 4, pt. 1, 203–205.
4. Major John McEwen Hyde, Report on the Appomattox Campaign, 10 April 1865, *OR-Armies*, ser. I, vol. 46, pt. 1, 734–735, 738–740, and Brigadier General Clinton McDougall,

Report on the Appomattox Campaign, 15 April 1865, *OR-Armies*, ser. I, vol. 46, pt. 1, 734–735, 738–740.
5. Beyer and Keydel, p. 507.
6. Arabella S. Wilson, p. 281.

Chapter Twelve

1. Jessie White Mario, *Garibaldi ei suoi tempi*, (Supplement 1884 and 1904), p. 461, and author's collection of oral histories. According to the account of Anthony F. Cardinale, taken 6 January 1970, "The Lightning Legend arose as a result of the protestations of Garibaldi's Sicilian volunteers against the oppressive politics exerted against them by the Northern Italian controlled government."
2. *New York Times*, 8 April 1896.
3. *New York Times*, 23 October 1883, and *New York Times*, 26 October 1883.
4. *New York Times*, 26 October 1916.
5. *New York Times*, 12 August 1869.
6. Catalfamo, pp. 386–387.
7. *Every Evening* (Wilmington, Del.), 2 May 1892, p. 3, and 4 May 1892, p. 3, plus *Sunday Morning Star* (Wilmington, Del.), 1 May 1892, pp. 1, 3.
8. George E. Waring, Jr., File LC-USZ62-68298, Library of Congress, Washington, D.C.
9. John Gilmary Shea, *The Cross and the Flag*, (The Catholic Historical League of America 1900, War With Spain section), pp. 25 (n. 2), 29, and *New York Times*, 30 October 1898.
10. Vasuary, p. 88, and Pivany, p. 34.
11. Arabella S. Wilson, pp. 361–362.
12. *New York Times*, 10 September 1908.
13. Vasuary, p. 84, and Pivany, p. 13.
14. Funk and Wagnall's, *New Standard Encyclopedia*, 1944 Edition, vol. 7 (New York: Unicorn Press, 1931), p. 17.
15. New York Monuments Commission, *Final Report on the Battlefield of Gettysburg*, vol. 1 (Albany, New York: J. B. Lyon Co., Printers, 1900), pp. 276–286.
16. Ibid.

Bibliography

Official Records

Robert N. Scott et al., ed. *War of the Rebellion: A Compilation of the Official Records of the Union and Confederate Armies*. 70 vols. in 128 bks. Washington, D.C.: U.S. Congress, 1881–1901. Usually abbreviated *Official Records, Armies* or *OR-Armies*. Heareafter *OR-Armies*.

Reports of Officers

Allen, David A. Captain, Union. Report on Po River, Spotsylvania, North Anna [River], Hanovertown, and Cold Harbor. 5 August 1864. *OR-Armies*, ser. I, vol. 36, pt. 1, 400–401.

———. Report on Chickahominy [River]. 5 August 1864. *OR-Armies*, ser. I, vol. 40, pt. 1, 346–347.

Blenker, Louis. Colonel, Union. Report on the Bull Run Campaign. 4 August 1861. *OR-Armies*, ser. I, vol. 12, pt. 1, pp. 315, 335, 425, 426, 427, 428.

Bull, James. Colonel, Union. Report at HQ 3rd Brig, 3rd Division, 2d Army Corps—Camp near Frederick, Md., 8 July 1863. *OR-Armies*, ser. I, vol. 27, pt. 1, 472.

Coons, John. Colonel, Union. Report near Gettysburg. 5 July 1863. *OR-Armies*, ser. I, vol. 27, pt. 1, 458.

Davis, Thomas. Captain, Union. Report at Fairfax Court House. 17 July 1861. *OR-Armies*, ser. I, vol. 51, pt. 1, 18.

Dow, Edwin. First lieutenant, Union. 6th Maine Battery. *OR-Armies*, ser. I, vol. 27, pt. 1, 898.

D'Utassy, Frederick George. Colonel, Union. Report at Union Mills [Maryland]. 30 December 1862. *OR-Armies*, vol. 21, 716–718.

Ewell, Richard S. Lieutenant general, Confederacy. Report to General Robert E. Lee regarding a Garibaldian [39th NY Volunteers] deserter. 17 April 1864. *OR-Armies*, ser. I, vol. 51, pt. 2, 864.

Fremont, John C. Brigadier general, Union. Report at Luray [Virginia]. 8 June 1862. *OR-Armies*, ser. I, vol. 12, pt. 1, pp. 17–21.

———. Report at Port Republic [Virginia]. 9 June 1862. *OR-Armies*, ser. I, vol. 12, pt. 1, 654–655.

———. Report at Harrisonburg [Virginia]. 10 June 1862. *OR-Armies*, ser. I, vol. 12, pt. 1, 655–656.

———. Report at Mount Jackson [Virginia]. 12 June 1862. *OR-Armies*, ser. I, vol. 12, pt. 1, 657.

Funk, Augustus. Colonel, Union. Report at HQ 3rd Brig., 1st Div., 2nd Army Corps 27 March 1865. *OR-Armies*, ser. I, vol. 46, pt. 1, 203.

Hancock, Winfred S. Major General, Union. Report on Reams's Station. 12 September 1864. *OR-Armies*, ser. I, vol. 42, pt. 1, 227.

Hays, Alexander. Brigadier general, Union. Report on Morton's Ford. 13 March 1864. *OR-Armies*, ser. I, vol. 33, pt. 2, 127.

Hilderbrandt, Hugo. Major, Union. Report at Bristoe Station. 22 October 1863. *OR-Armies*, ser. I, vol. 27, pt. 1, 301.

Hughes, James G. Lieutenant Colonel, Union. Report on Morton's Ford. 9 February 1864. *OR-Armies*, ser. I, vol. 33, pt. 1, 134–135.

Hyde, John McEwen. Major, Union. Report on the Appomattox Campaign. 10 April 1865. *OR-Armies*, ser. I, vol. 46, pt. 1, 734–735 & 738–740.

MacDougal, Clinton. Colonel, Union. Report at Hq III Reg., New York Infantry, Camp Mitchell, Ford, Va. 17 October 1863. *OR-Armies*, ser. I, vol. 27, pt. 1, 302.

———. Report at Mitchell's Ford. November 30, 1863. *OR-Armies*, ser. I, vol. 29, pt. 1, 670, 680.

MacDougall, C. D. Brigadier General, III N.Y.V. Infantry, Union. Report on the Appomattox Campaign. 15 April 1865. *OR-Armies*, ser. I, vol. 46, pt. 1, 734, 735.

Martin, A. P. Captain, Union. 3rd Mass. Battery. Camp near Warrenton, Va., 31 July 1863. *OR-Armies*, ser. I, vol. 27, pt. 1, 659–600.

McAllister, Robert. Colonel, Union. Report on Po River Operations, Spotsylvania, North Anna [River], Hanovertown, and Cold Harbor. 3–13 May 1864. *OR-Armies*, ser. I, vol. 36, pt. 1, 488–492.

Miles, Dixon S. Colonel, Union. Report on the Bull Run Campaign. 21 July 1861. *OR-Armies*, ser. I, vol. 12.

Miles, Nelson Colonel, Union. 2nd Infantry, Commanding 5th Division. Report on the Richmond Campaign. 30 August 1864. *OR-Armies*, ser. I, vol. 42, pt. 1, 253–254.

———. Report on garrison duty at Fort Emery. 7 April 1865. *OR-Armies*, ser. I, vol. 46, pt. 1, 80.

Owen, Joshua. Brigadier general, Union. Report of Demonstration on Rapidan. 9 February 1864. *OR-Armies*, ser. I, vol. 33, pt. 1, 132–134.

Prime, Frederick E. Lieutenant, U.S. Engineers. Report at Four Mile Run, Virginia. 1 August 1861. *OR-Armies*, ser. I, vol. 2, pp. 334–335.

Seeley, Aron. Captain, Union. Report did not mention where. ——— 1863 *OR-Armies*, ser. I, vol. 27, pt. 1, 475–476.

Sigel, Franz. Major general, Union. Report at Fairfax Court House, Va. 11 December 1862. *OR-Armies*, ser. I, vol. 21, 846–847.

Sykes, George. Major general, U.S. Army. Report at HQ 5th Army Corps, Camp Warrenton, Va. 31 July 1863. *OR-Armies*, ser. I, vol. 27, pt. 1, 594.

Von Schack, George. Colonel, Union. Report on garrison duty at Fort Emery. 5 February 1865. *OR-Armies*, ser. I, vol. 46, pt. 1, 202.

Wilson, William. Colonel, Union. Report on Hatcher's Run. 10 December 1864. *OR-Armies*, ser. I, vol. 42, pt. 1, 274.

Woodall, Daniel. Major, Union. 39th N.Y. No date. *OR-Armies*, ser. I, vol. 27, pt. 3, 797.

Tyler, Daniel. Brigadier general, Union. HQ Camp Douglas. Comments concerning prisoners at Camp Douglas, Chicago, Illinois. 23 October 1862. *OR-Armies*, ser. II, vol. 4, 152.

Union Commissary. General of Prisoners. Comments concerning prisoners at Camp Douglas, Chicago, Illinois. 7 July 1862. *OR-Armies*, ser. II, vol. 8, 986.

Hoffman, William. Lieutenant colonel, 8th Infantry, Commissary General of Prisoners, Union. Comments concerning sutlers at Camp Douglas, Chicago, Illinois. 17 May 1862. *OR-Armies*, ser. II, vol. 3, 549–550.

Series I, Volume 5.

Series I, Volume 25.

Series I, Volume 28.

Series I, Volume 29.

Report of the Adjutant General of the State of New York 1861, 1862, 1863, 1864, 1865.

Adjutant General, New York. Muster roll of the Independent Light Infantry Regiment (Enfants Perdus). In Adjutant General's Report on the New York State Volunteers 1861–1865. Microfiche

39th New York Volunteer Infantry Regiment. Regimental records. ID No. Fee 166. Microfilm. U.S. National Archives, Washington, D.C.

Orders from December 1862 through July 1865, Regimental Records of the 39th New York Volunteer Infantry Regiment.

Special Orders No. 10, item 5, Headquarters, Army of the Potomac, Washington, D.C., 30 August 1861.

Special Orders No. 60, 1862. The Ornesi court-martial. 13 June 1862. Mount Jackson, Va., Blenker's Division HQ.

Special Orders No. 65, 6 March 1864. Trial of deserters. Charles Williams.

Special Orders No. 139, item 13, 1862. Repetti's resignation.

Special Orders No. 159, 1863. Washington, D.C.

Special Orders No. 209, 5 August 1864, vol. 36, pt. 1, pp. 488–489.

General Orders No. 246, 30 July 1863, pp. 7–10. Court-martial of Lieut. Nissen. EN6/13

General Orders No. 38 & No. 246, 1863. The court-martial of Private G. Antonali.

General Orders No. 159, pt. 1, charge 1, specification 1.

Adjutant General of the State of New York, 1863.

Maryland Campaign, Series I, vol. 19, pt. 1.

Return of casualties, p. 549.

Report of Brig. Gen. D. Tyler; HQ Annapolis, Md. 23 September 1862, p. 552.

Report of Lt. Chas. Bacon, 39th NYV; HQ Annapolis, Md. 23 September 1862, pp. 552–553.

Hilderbrandt testimony mentions D'Utassy and Bacon; HQ Annapolis, Md. 23 September 23, 1862, pp. 554–555.

D'Utassy mentioned in testimony of Col. William Maulsby, 1st Maryland Reg. Potomac Home Brigade; Washington, D.C., p. 558.

39th mentioned in testimony of Major S. M. Hewitt, 32nd Ohio Infantry, 4 October 4, 1862, Washington, D.C., p. 570.

D'Utassy questioning Hewitt, 4 October 1862, p. 575.

39th and D'Utassy mentioned in testimony of L. Henry M. Binney; Washington, D.C. 7 October 1862, pp. 580–586.

D'Utassy testimony, Washington, D.C., 7 October 1862, pp. 595–600.

Hilderbrandt testimony, Washington, D.C., 8 October 1862.

D'Utassy mentioned in testimony of Lt. Col. S. W. Downey, 3rd Reg. Potomac Home Brigade; Washington, D.C. 9 October 1862, pp. 622–623.

D'Utassy questioning Col. Simeon Sammon, 115th N.Y.V.; Washington, D.C. 9 October 1862, p. 628.

39th mentioned in testimony of Lt. John L. Willmon, Aide-De-Camp General Miles; Washington, D.C. 10 October 1862, pp. 645–646, 658.

Bacon questioned by D'Utassy, Washington, D.C. 10 October 1862, pp. 664–669.

D'Utassy mentioned in testimony of Col. Jesse Segoine, 111th N.Y.V.; Washington, D.C. October 10, 1862, pp. 682–683.

D'Utassy questioning witness Capt. John Philips, 2nd Reg., III Light Artillery; Washington, D.C. 10 October 1862.

39th mentioned in testimony of Capt. Eugene McGrath, 5th Artillery, N.Y.V., Washington, D.C., 14 October 1862, pp. 695, 700.

39th mentioned in testimony of Capt. C. J. Brown, 1st Maryland Reg., Potomac Home Brig.; Washington, D.C., 15 October 1862, p. 713.

39th mentioned in testimony of Major Charles Russell, 1st Md. Cavalry; Washington, D.C., 16 October 1862, p. 727.

39th mentioned in the report of Commissioners John Joliffe and Sanders W. Johnston, Washington, D.C., 27 October 1862, p. 778.
39th mentioned in the report of Major General D. Hunter, Washington, D.C. 3 November 1862.

Evacuation of Winchester: Series I, vol. 12, pt. 2.

Hilderbrandt testimony, Washington, D.C. 18 October 1862, pp. 783–784.
D'Utassy testimony, Washington, D.C., 18 October 1862, pp. 786–787.

Books, Magazines, and Collections

Abrams, Meyer Howard, gen. ed. *The Norton Anthology of English Literature.* Vol. 2, 3rd ed. New York: W. W. Norton & Company, Inc., 1974.
Allegretti, Ignacio. Military service record. In *Military Service Records: A Select Catalog of National Archives Microfilm Publications.* National Archives and Records Administration. Washington, D.C.: Government Printing Office, 1985.
American National Red Cross Office of Publications, 1965.
Andreas, A. T. *History of Chicago from the Earliest Periods to the Present Time.* Chicago. Self-published, 1884–1886.
Beyer, W. F. and O. F. Keyde. *Deeds of Valor: How America's Heroes Won the Medal of Honor.* Detroit: The Perrien-Keydel Co., 1900.
Boatner, Mark M. III. *The Civil War Dictionary.* New York: David McKay Co., Inc., 1959.
Bowra, E. C. M. "With Garibaldi in 1860." *Cornhill Magazine.* London, England: 50 Albemarle Street, W1, September 1929.
Catalfamo, Catherine C. *The Thorny Rose.* Ann Arbor, Mich.: University Microfilms International, 1989.
Clark, A. C. *Records of the Columbia Historical Society of Washington, D.C.* Vols. 35–36 (1935). Washington, D.C.: Columbia Historical Society, 1935–1936.
Coffin, Charles Carleton. *The Boys of '61.* Boston: Estes and Lauriat, 1881.
———. *Four Years of Fighting.* Boston: Hurst and Co., 1866.
Cooling, Benjamin Franklin III and Walton H. Owen II. *Mr. Lincoln's Forts: A Guide to the Civil War Defenses of Washington.* Shippensburg, Pa.: White Mane Publishing Company, 1988.
Cuneo, Giovan B. *La Bataglia di San Antonio de Salto.* Genova: Camicia Rossa, 1932.
De Lucchi, Luigi. Military service record. In *Military Service Records: A Select Catalog of National Archives Microfilm Publications.* #50-576-196 C.W. National Archives and Records Administration. Washington, D.C: Government Printing Office, 1985.
Dufour, Charles L. *Gentle Tiger.* Baton Rouge: Louisiana State University Press, 1957.

Dupuy, R. Ernest and Trevor N. Dupuy. *The Harper Encyclopedia of Military History: From 3500 B.C. to the Present.* 4th ed. New York: Harper Collins Publishers, 1993.

D'Utassy, Carl. Military service record. In *Military Service Records: A Select Catalog of National Archives Microfilm Publications.* National Archives and Records Administration. Washington, D.C.: Government Printing Office, 1985.

D'Utassy, Frederick George. Military service record. In *Military Service Records: A Select Catalog of National Archives Microfilm Publications.* National Archives and Records Administration. Washington, D.C.: Government Printing Office, 1985.

————. Frederick George D'Utassy Papers. Manuscript Department, New York Historical Society, New York City, N.Y.

————. Frederick George D'Utassy File. Vol. 91, no. 5, call no. MG 100. Public Archives, Halifax, Nova Scotia.

Dyer, Frederick H. *A Compendium of the War of the Rebellion.* Dayton, Ohio: Morningside Publications, 1959.

Fleming, George Thorton and Gilbert Adams Hays. *Life and Letters of Alexander Hays.* Pittsburgh, Pa., self-published, 1919.

Freeman, Douglas Southall. *Lee's Lieutenants: A Study in Command.* New York: Charles Scribner's Sons, 1946.

Frixione, Raffael. Military service record. In *Military Service Records: A Select Catalog of National Archives Microfilm Publications.* National Archives and Records Administration. Washington, D.C.: Government Printing Office, 1985.

Funk and Wagnall's. *New Standard Encyclopedia.* Vol. VII. New York: Unicorn Press, 1931.

Garibaldi, Giuseppe. Letter to Abraham Lincoln. 6 August 1863. Library of Congress.

Garibaldi, Giuseppe [Peppino]. *A Toast to Rebellion.* Garden City, N.Y.: Garden City Publishing, 1937.

Gay, Nelson. "Lincoln's Offer of a Command to Garibaldi: Light on a Disputed Point of History." *The Century Magazine,* LXXV (November 1907), pp. 63–74.

Gillifan, John M. Military service record. In *Military Service Records: A Select Catalog of National Archives Microfilm Publications.* National Archives and Records Administration. Washington, D.C.: Government Printing Office, 1985.

Glatthaar, Joseph T. *Forged in Battle: The Civil War Alliance of Black Soldiers and White Officers.* New York: The Free Press, 1990.

Hales, E. E. Y. *Mazzini and the Secret Societies.* New York: P. J. Kenedy & Sons, no year given.

Hooker, S. O. Letter to his sister. Chicago Historical Society.

Jordan, Donaldson and Edwin Pratt. *Europe and the American Civil War.* New York: Houghton Mifflin Co., 1931.

Leech, Margaret. *Reveille in Washington 1860-1865.* New York: Harper & Brothers, 1941.

Loeffler, Dr. Robert James. "The History of Madison Square Garden." *Bandwagon*, March–April 1973, vol. 17, no. 2, pp. 4–12.

Lonn, Ella. *Foreigners in the Union Army and Navy*. Baton Rouge: Louisiana State University Press, 1951.

Machon, Frank. *Poles in America*. Stevens Point, Wis.: Worzalla Publishing, 1978.

Mario, Alberto. *The Red Shirt*. London: 1865.

Mario, Jessie White. *The Life of Giuseppe Mazzini*. Milan: 1896.

———. *Agostino Bertani ei suoi tempi*. Florence: 1888.

———. *Garibaldi ei suoi tempi*. Milan: 1884.

Marraro, Howard. *Lincoln's Italian Volunteers*. From New York, New York History: Columbia University. 24 January 1943, pp. 56–67.

Nelson, Gay. *Lincoln's Offer of a Command to Garibaldi*. New York: *Century* magazine, 1907.

Matter, William D. *If It Takes All Summer*. Chapel Hill: University of North Carolina Press, 1988.

McCarthy, Justin. *Portraits of the Sixties*. New York: Harper & Brothers, 1903.

McElroy, John. *This Was Andersonville*. New York: Fairfax Press, 1957.

McLean, Cornelius. Military service record. In *Military Service Records: A Select Catalog of National Archives Microfilm Publications*. National Archives and Records Administration. Washington, D.C.: Government Printing Office, 1985.

Meier, Heinz K. "The United States and Switzerland in the 19th Century." Hague, Netherlands: Mouton Co., 1963.

Nelson, T. Letter to his sister. Chicago Historical Society, Chicago, Illinois.

New York Monuments Commission. *Final Report on the Battlefield of Gettysburg*. Vol. I. New York: State of New York Printing Office, 1900.

Okey, T. "With Garibaldi in 1860." *Cornhill Magazine*, (January 1930), pp. 94–95.

Osnaghi, Cesare. Letter to Frederick George D'Utassy. 12 August 1861. Frederick George D'Utassy Papers, Manuscript Department, New York Historical Society, New York, N.Y.

Osnaghi, Cesare. Military service record. In *Military Service Records: A Select Catalog of National Archives Microfilm Publications*. National Archives and Records Administration. Washington, D.C.: Government Printing Office, 1985.

Packe, Michale St. John. *Orsini*. Boston: Little, Brown & Co., 1957.

Peard, Frances M. "Garibaldi's Englishman." *Cornhill Magazine* (August 1903), p. 274.

Pfisterer, Frederick. *Statistical Record of the Armies of the United States*. New York: Charles Scribner's Sons, 1883.

———. *New York in the War of the Rebellion, 1861–1865*. 3rd ed. Albany, N.Y.: J. B. Lyon Company, 1912.

———. File 2188–2213, Registrar Serial No. 23, 1–313.

Pierce, Bessie Louise. "The History of Chicago." Chicago: University of Chicago, 1937. Vol. 2, pp. 246–302.

Pivany, Eugene. *Hungarians in the American Civil War.* Cleveland, Ohio: Self-published, 1913.

Porch, Douglas. "The French Foreign Legion." New York: Harper Collins, 1991.

Quiggle, J. W. Letter to Giuseppe Garibaldi. July 1861.

Repetti, Allessandro. Letter regarding officers' protest to Frederick George D'Utassy. Frederick George D'Utassy Papers, New York Historical Society.

———. Letter requesting money and passes to Frederick George D'Utassy. No date. Frederick George D'Utassy Papers, New York Historical Society.

———. Letter requesting men to Frederick George D'Utassy. No date. Frederick George D'Utassy Papers, New York Historical Society.

———. Letter of resignation to Major General Edwin Sumner. 31 March 1862. Frederick George D'Utassy Papers, New York Historical Society.

39th N.Y. Infantry. Military service record. In *Military Service Records: A Select Catalog of National Archives Microfilm Publications.* National Archives and Records Administration. Washington, D.C.: Government Printing Office, 1985.

Saint-Simon, Claude Henri de Rouvroy. *Doctrine de Saint-Simon.* Paris, 1829.

Samsa, Giovanni. Military service record. In *Military Service Records: A Select Catalog of National Archives Microfilm Publications.* National Archives and Records Administration. Washington, D.C.: Government Printing Office, 1985.

Schiavo, Giovanni. *Four Centuries of Italian American History.* New York: Vigo Press, 1958.

———. *The Italians in America Before the Civil War.* New York: Vigo Press, 1934.

Schurz, Carl. Personal letters and manuscripts. 1861–1863, relating to the court-martial of Frederick George D'Utassy. Carl Schurz Collection, Wisconsin State Archives, Madison.

Schwarz, Charles. Letter to Lieutenant R. C. Perry. Regarding Zyla's request for transfer, 1863, Wisconsin State Archives, State University Press.

Scott, Robert G. *Fallen Leaves: The Civil War Letters of Major Henry Livermore Abbott.* 1991.

Shea, John Gilmary. "The Cross and the Flag." The Catholic Historical League of America 1900, War With Spain Section, pp. 25, 29.

Sideman, Belle Becker and Lilian Friedman. *Europe Looks at the Civil War.* New York: Orion Press, 1960.

Simon, John Y. *The Papers of Ulysses S. Grant.* Vol II. Carbondale: Southern Illinois University Press, 1967.

Military Order of the Loyal Legion of the United States. Record of Cornelius McLean, State of New York, 2 May 1906.

Sommers, Richard. *Richmond Redeemed: The Siege of Petersburg.* Garden City, N.Y.: Doubleday and Company, Inc., 1981.

Takats [Takacs], Franz. Letter to Frederick George D'Utassy. 31 May 1861. Frederick George D'Utassy Papers, New York Historical Society.

Tassillier, Louis et al. Petition to Frederick George D'Utassy. 6 July 1861. Frederick George D'Utassy Papers, New York Historical Society.

Time/Life Books. *The Civil War*. 28 vols. Alexandria, Va.: Time/Life Books, Inc., 1987.

Tinelli, Louis W. Military service record. In *Military Service Records: A Select Catalog of National Archives Microfilm Publications*. File SC 33-647 C.W. National Archives and Records Administration. Washington, D.C.: Government Printing Office, 1985.

Trevelyan, George Macaulay. *Garibaldi and the Thousand*. New York: Longmans, Green and Co., 1909.

———. *Garibaldi's Defence of the Roman Republic 1848–1849*. London: Longmans, Green & Co., 1910.

Tucker, Glen. *Hancock the Superb*. New York: The Bobbs-Merrill Company, Inc., 1960.

Vasuary, Edmund. *Lincoln's Hungarian Heroes*. Washington, D.C.: Self-published, 1939.

Virgilio, Varzea. *Garibaldi in America*. Rio de Janeiro, Brazil, 1902.

Waring, George E. Jr. *The Garibaldi Guard*. The First Book of the Authors Club, "Liber Scriptorum." New York, 1893.

———. File LC-USZ02-00202. Library of Congress, Washington, D.C.

Werstein, Irving. *Kearny, the Magnificent*. New York: John Day Co., 1962.

Wilson, Arabella S. *Disaster, Struggle, Triumph: The Regimental History of the 125th New York State Volunteers*. Albany, N.Y.: Argus, Co., 1870.

Windrow, Martin. *The French Foreign Legion*. New York: Hippocrene Books, 1973.

Winthrop, Theodore. "Washington as a Camp." *Atlantic Monthly* (July 1861).

Wolf, Simon. "The American Jew as Patriot, Soldier, and Citizen." Irvington, 1895; The American Jewish Archives, Cincinnati, Ohio.

Zyla, Anthony P. Report to Frederick George D'Utassy. 26 March 1862. Frederick George D'Utassy Papers, Manuscript Department, New York Historical Society, New York, N.Y.

———. Letter to Lieutenant Colonel Charles Schwarz. 1863. Wisconsin State Archives, Madison, Wisconsin.

Newspapers

Abend Zeitung [German language journal]. 23 January 1862.

Ballou's Pictorial. Boston. Magazine, Boston, Mass., vol. x, no. 5. (2 February 1856), front page.

Chicago Tribune. 6 October 1862.

———. 20 November 1862.

Courrier des Estats-Unis. 6 June 1862.

Criminial-Zeilig [German/American journal]. 26 April 1861.

Daily Chronicle. Washington, D.C. 17 April 1863. EN3/7, 3/11

Every Evening. Wilmington, Delaware. 2 May 1892, p. 3. EN12/7

————. 4 May 1892, p. 3.

Harper's Weekly. 8 June 1861.

L'Eco d'Italia. 27 April 1861.

————. 18 October 1862.

————. 25 October 1862.

————. 3 July 1862.

The London Times. Report on the Union Army. William Russell. July 1861.

Morning News. Wilmington, Delaware. 1 May 1892.

New Orleans Bee. 19 and 20 January 1861.

The New York Daily News. 16 May 1861.

————. 29 May 1861.

The New York Evening Express. 23 May 1861.

————. 29 May 1861.

New York Evening Post. 22 March 1848.

New York Herald. 28 March 1848.

————. 29 March 1861.

————. 10 April 1861.

————. 30 April 1861. Repetti joins the Cosmopolitan Group.

————. 27 April 1861. "Organ grinder" remark.

————. 29 April 1861. Italian Legions join Garibaldi Guard.

————. 10 May 1861. Vets of Italian War.

————. 22 May 1861. Death of Diverbois. Flag presented.

————. 23 May 1861. Ellsworth mentioned by D'Utassy.

————. 25 May 1861. Preparation to leave for Washington.

————. 28 May 1861. Arrive in Washington.

————. 29 May 1861. Status of married men.

————. 31 May 1861. In front of Lincoln.

————. 13 June 1861. Tinelli resigns.

The New York Times. 8 October 1860.

————. 26 May 1861. Preparation to leave N.Y.

————. 3 July 1861.

————. 28 March 1862.

————. 18 September 1862. Harpers Ferry and movement to Chicago.

————. 23 March 1863.

————. 16 April 1863. References to D'Utassy's court-martial.

————. 12 August 1869. C. Grinnell's obituary.

————. 23 October 1883. A. Funk's obituary.

————. 26 October 1883. A. Funk's obituary.

————. 8 April 1896. Hilderbrandt's obituary.

————. 30 October 1898. Waring's obituary.

————. 10 September 1908. McLean obituary.

————. 26 October 1916. McEwan Hyde's obituary.

The New York Tribune. 29 April 1861. Various companies joining G. G.

————. 29 May 1861. Arrival in Washington.

Sunday Morning Star. Wilmington, Delaware. 1 May 1892, pp. 1, 3.

The Washington Star. Quoted from "Reveille in Washington," p. 85. [praised D'Utassy as "theatrical commander of Garibaldi Guards"]

Canzio MS. Ciampoli, 71 Risorgimento., anno i. 3–4, pp. 683–684.

1/9	Giovanni Schiavo "Four Centuries of Italian American History," p. 316.
2/4	Garibaldi/Merci Library.
2/34	Columbia Historical Society, vol. 35–36, pp. 222–234.
2/45	*Century* Magazine "Lincoln offers a command to G. G."
3/12	General Orders #159. D'Utassy court-martial.
3/25	My comment as to the ethnic make-up.
4/10	Boatner's Civil War Dictionary.
4/14	The charge of Repetti pointing a gun at a soldier is unfounded, as proven by this author's research.
6/13	Court-martial of Lt. Nissen, General Orders #249, 30 July 1863.
6/15	Series 1, vol. 27, pt. 1, p. 302. Col. McDougal, III N.Y., 17 October 1863.
11/1	125th New York N.Y.S.V., pp. 261–262.
11/3	Colonel Funk's regimental books, February.

Index

A

Abbott, Henry L. (Maj., 20th Mass.), 158
Abercrombie, John J. (Gen., U.S.A.), 118, 130
Adams Express, 141
Adamoli, Luigi (Principal Musician, 39th N.Y.), 69
Addi, Thomas (Lieut., Co. C, 39th N.Y.), 164, 175
Aigner, Joseph (Lieut., Co. C, 39th N.Y.), 44
Albany, N.Y., 110, 131, 177
Alexandria, Va., 47, 75, 78, 150
Allegretti, Ignazio (Lieut., Co. A, 39th N.Y.), 44, 62, 64, 66, 128, 200
Allen, Benjamin (Sgt., Co. G, 39th N.Y.), 155
Allen, David A. (Capt., Co. G, 39th N.Y.), 150, 169, 170, 172, 173, 177, 181, 187, 194
Amaro, Manuel (Pvt., 39th N.Y.), 150
Anderson, Richard H. (Gen., C.S.A.), 191
Andersonville Prison, Ga., 146, 147, 158, 169, 187
Andreas, Gottlieb (Cpl., Co. B, 39th N.Y.), 74, 132–133
Annandale, Va., 55
Annapolis, Md., 101, 103, 104, 105, 106, 107, 165
Antonali, Giacomo (Cpl., Co. A, 39th N.Y.), 69, 122, 123, 124, 127, 141
Arellano, Jose (Pvt., Co. C, 39th N.Y.), 132, 144
Argumosa, Juan (Cpl., Co. D, 39th N.Y.), 41
Ashby, Turner (Gen., C.S.A.), 80
Auburn, Va., 142

B

Bacon, Charles G. (Adj., 39th N.Y.), 62, **63**, 75, 78, 88, 95, 97, 100, 102, 106, 107, 121, 124, 131
Bader, Magnus (Pvt., Co. E, 39th N.Y.), 41, 117, 121, 122, 123, 133, 145, 161, 175
Baer, Bernhard (Lieut., Co. H, 39th N.Y.), 44, 67, 69, 78, 88, 89, 124, 132, 145, 148, 150, 157, 158, 175
Baise, Benoit (39th N.Y.), 121
Baker, Allen M. (Pvt., Co. I, 39th N.Y.), 157, 169, 186, 188, 190, 194
Baker, Charles C. (Maj., 39th N.Y.), 155, 158, 161, 172, 173, 192
Baldwin, Harvey (Lieut., Co. A, 39th N.Y.), 172
Ballou, Charles (Lieut., Co. C, 39th N.Y.), 155, 172, 176, 187, 188, 194
Ball's Ford (Va.), 52
Baltimore and Ohio Railroad, 90
Baltimore, Md., 90, 91, 104, 105, 109
Banks, Wright (Lieut., Co. K, 39th N.Y.), 189, 194, 198
Barksdale, William (Gen., C.S.A.), 136
Barlow, Francis C. (Gen., U.S.A.), 168, 169, 180
  division of: 170, 178
Barras, Samuel (Adj., 32nd Ohio), 94, 95
Barre, Juan (Pvt., Co. E, 39th N.Y.), 147
Bartholomie, Henry (Cpl., Co. K, 39th N.Y.), 64

320

Plumb, George (Lieut., Co. D, 39th N.Y.), 161, 175
Po River (Va.), 170, 177
Pollak, Bernhard (Cpl., Co. G, 39th N.Y.), 73, 82, 84, 89, 131
Pope, John (Gen., U.S.A.), 86, 111
Port Republic, Va., 80
Potomac River, 39, 41, 91, 95, 96, 97, 134
Potts, Benjamin F. (Capt., Ohio Btty.), 91
Prime, Frederick E. (Capt., U.S. Engineers), 55
Proper, Isaac (Lieut., Co. H, 39th N.Y.), 173, 182, 194

Q

Quade, Julius (Pvt., Co. D, 39th N.Y.), 147
Quiggle, J. W. (U.S. Consul, Belgium), 39, 41, 42, 55, 61, 66

R

Raefle, Gustav (Cpl., Co. I, 39th N.Y.), 87, 131
Raggio, Giuseppe (Pvt., Co. C, 39th N.Y.), 78, 197
Rapidan River (Va.), 141, 144, 145, 146, 147, 157, 130, 166, 169
Rappahannock River (Va.), 110, 111, 130, 134, 141, 144
Rassmaessler, Otto (Cpl., Co. F, 39th N.Y.), 100, 142, 145, 153, 154, 155, 161, 175
Regiments
    Connecticut (Infantry)
        14th, 139, 158
    Delaware (Infantry)
        1st, 139, 141, 142
    Indiana (Artillery)
        15th Battery, 94, 96, 103
    Illinois (Artillery)
        2nd, 94
    Illinois (Cavalry)
        8th, 98
        12th, 98
    Illinois (Infantry)
        65th, 96, 97, 103
    Maryland (Cavalry)
        1st, 91
    Maryland (Infantry)
        3rd Potomac Home Brigade, 93
    Massachusetts (Artillery)
        10th Independent Battery, 126
    Massachusetts (Infantry)
        9th, 130
        15th, 165
        20th, 131, 158, 159
        28th, 182

    Michigan (Cavalry)
        1st, 114, 159
    New Jersey (Cavalry)
        1st, 79
    New Jersey (Infantry)
        12th, 139
    New York (Artillery)
        4th Heavy, 179
        6th, 64
        13th, 62
        15th Heavy, 65, 85
    New York (Cavalry)
        2nd, 155
        4th, 56, 79, 81, 114, 152
        8th, 97
        29th, 64
    New York (Engineers)
        50th, 58
    New York (Infantry)
        5th, 139
        7th, 164, 180, 181, 184
        8th Militia, 41
        8th, 49, 51, 52, 55, 58, 72, 82, 84
        12th, 52
        16th, 127
        27th ,162
        29th, 49, 51, 52, 61, 69
        33rd, 162
        38th, 145
        39th (see Garibaldi Guard)
        41st, 82
        44th, 64, 170
        51st, 56
        52nd, 88, 109, 137, 164, 180, 181
        55th, 73
        57th, 164
        61st, 163
        78th, 141
        90th, 39
        100th, 141
        101st, 58
        111th, 96, 97, 99, 100, 103, 117, 118, 126, 130, 134, 139, 140, 143, 158, 164, 180
        115th, 93, 96, 99, 103
        125th New York Infantry, 126, 127, 130, 134, 136, 139, 140, 143, 164, 180, 181
        126th, 93, 94, 96, 99, 104, 107, 111, 126, 130, 134, 135, 139, 140, 143, 153, 164, 180, 181
    Ohio (Infantry)
        16th, 80
        32nd, 91, 93, 94, 95, 97
        60th, 91, 96